ACCA

STUDY TEXT

PAPER F4

Corporate and Business Law
(Global)

BPP Learning Media is an **ACCA Approved Content Provider**. This means we work closely with ACCA to ensure this Study Text contains the information you need to pass your exam.

In this Study Text, which has been reviewed by the **ACCA examination team,** we:

- Highlight the **most important elements** in the syllabus and the **key skills** you need

- **Signpost** how each chapter links to the syllabus and the study guide

- **Provide** lots of **exam focus points** demonstrating what is expected of you in the exam

- **Emphasise** key points in regular **fast forward summaries**

- Test your knowledge in **quick quizzes**

- Examine your understanding in our **practice question bank**

- Reference all the important topics in our **full index**

BPP's **Practice & Revision Kit** also supports this paper.

FOR EXAMS FROM 1 SEPTEMBER 2016 TO 31 AUGUST 2017

First edition 2007
Ninth edition February 2016

ISBN 9781 4727 4421 0
(Previous ISBN 9781 4727 6742 2)

e-ISBN 9781 4727 4663 4

British Library Cataloguing-in-Publication Data

A catalogue record for this book
is available from the British Library

Published by

BPP Learning Media Ltd
BPP House, Aldine Place
London W12 8AA

www.bpp.com/learningmedia

Printed in the United Kingdom by

Polestar Wheatons
Hennock Road
Marsh Barton
Exeter
EX2 8RP

Your learning materials, published by BPP Learning
Media Ltd, are printed on paper obtained from
traceable sustainable sources.

We are grateful to the Association of Chartered Certified
Accountants for permission to reproduce past
examination questions. The suggested solutions in the
practice answer bank have been prepared by BPP
Learning Media Ltd, unless otherwise stated.

A note about copyright

Dear Customer

What does the little © mean and why does it matter?

Your market-leading BPP books, course materials and e-
learning materials do not write and update themselves.
People write them on their own behalf or as employees of
an organisation that invests in this activity. Copyright law
protects their livelihoods. It does so by creating rights
over the use of the content.

Breach of copyright is a form of theft – as well as being a
criminal offence in some jurisdictions, it is potentially a
serious breach of professional ethics.

With current technology, things might seem a bit hazy
but, basically, without the express permission of BPP
Learning Media:

- Photocopying our materials is a breach of
  copyright

- Scanning, ripcasting or conversion of our digital
  materials into different file formats, uploading them
  to facebook or e-mailing them to your friends is a
  breach of copyright

You can, of course, sell your books, in the form in which
you have bought them – once you have finished with
them. (Is this fair to your fellow students? We update for a
reason.) Please note the e-products are sold on a single
user licence basis: we do not supply 'unlock' codes to
people who have bought them secondhand.

And what about outside the UK? BPP Learning Media
strives to make our materials available at prices students
can afford by local printing arrangements, pricing policies
and partnerships which are clearly listed on our website.
A tiny minority ignore this and indulge in criminal activity
by illegally photocopying our material or supporting
organisations that do. If they act illegally and unethically
in one area, can you really trust them?

BPP
LEARNING MEDIA

Contents

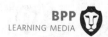

Helping you to pass

BPP Learning Media – ACCA Approved Content Provider

As ACCA's **Approved Content Provider**, BPP Learning Media gives you the **opportunity** to use study materials reviewed by the ACCA examination team. By incorporating the examination team's comments and suggestions regarding the depth and breadth of syllabus coverage, the BPP Learning Media Study Text provides excellent, **ACCA-approved** support for your studies.

The PER alert

Before you can qualify as an ACCA member, you not only have to pass all your exams but also fulfil a three-year **practical experience requirement** (PER). To help you to recognise areas of the syllabus that you might be able to apply in the workplace to achieve different performance objectives, we have introduced the 'PER alert' feature. You will find this feature throughout the Study Text to remind you that what you are **learning to pass** your ACCA exams is **equally useful to the fulfilment of the PER requirement**.

Your achievement of the PER should now be recorded in your online *My Experience* record.

Tackling studying

Studying can be a daunting prospect, particularly when you have lots of other commitments. The **different features** of the Study Text, the **purposes** of which are explained fully on the **Chapter features** page, will help you whilst studying and improve your chances of **exam success**.

Developing exam awareness

Our Study Texts are completely **focused** on helping you pass your exam.

Our advice on **Studying F4** outlines the **content** of the paper, the **necessary skills** you are expected to be able to demonstrate and any **brought-forward knowledge** you are expected to have.

Exam focus points are included within the chapters to highlight when and how specific topics were examined, or how they might be examined in the future.

Using the syllabus and study guide

You can find the syllabus and study guide on pages ix – xvii of this Study Text

Testing what you can do

Testing yourself helps you develop the skills you need to pass the exam and also confirms that you can recall what you have learnt.

We include **Questions** – lots of them – both within chapters and in the **Practice Question Bank**, as well as **Quick Quizzes** at the end of each chapter to test your knowledge of the chapter content.

Chapter features

Each chapter contains a number of helpful features to guide you through each topic.

Topic list

Topic list	Syllabus reference

What you will be studying in this chapter and the relevant section numbers, together with ACCA syllabus references.

Introduction

Puts the chapter content in the context of the syllabus as a whole.

Study Guide

Links the chapter content with ACCA guidance.

Exam Guide

Highlights how examinable the chapter content is likely to be and the ways in which it could be examined.

Knowledge brought forward from earlier studies

What you are assumed to know from previous studies/exams.

FAST FORWARD

Summarises the content of main chapter headings, allowing you to preview and review each section easily.

Examples

Demonstrate how to apply key knowledge and techniques.

Key terms

Definitions of important concepts that can often earn you easy marks in exams.

Exam focus points

When and how specific topics were examined, or how they may be examined in the future.

Formula to learn

Formulae that are not given in the exam but which have to be learnt.

Gives you a useful indication of syllabus areas that closely relate to performance objectives in your Practical Experience Requirement (PER).

 Question

Gives you essential practice of techniques covered in the chapter.

 Case Study

Real-world examples of theories and techniques.

Chapter Roundup

A full list of the Fast Forwards included in the chapter, providing an easy source of review.

Quick Quiz

A quick test of your knowledge of the main topics in the chapter.

Practice Question Bank

Found at the back of the Study Text with more comprehensive chapter questions. Cross-referenced for easy navigation.

Studying F4

This paper examines a basic understanding of legal principles and their application. You may find the material a little different from what you are used to because there are virtually no numbers involved. All students should attempt as many exam standard questions as they can, and those taking a paper based exam should develop a concise style of writing in order to get points across quickly and clearly.

1 What F4 is about

The main aims of the F4 exam are:

- To develop knowledge and skills in the understanding of the general legal framework and of specific legal areas relating to business, but

- To recognise the need to seek further specialist legal advice where necessary

The exam is not designed to turn you into a legal expert. Instead you will be a well-informed professional accountant who appreciates the legal issues of doing business but who recognises the boundaries of your legal knowledge and therefore the point at which professional legal expertise must be sought. The sequence of the syllabus and study guide takes you through the main areas of what you need to know.

Essential elements of legal systems

In this part of the syllabus you are covering areas that underlie all the other areas, namely: what is law and how does it fit into a country's political, economic and legal system. The distinctions between criminal and civil law, and between common law, civil law and sharia law systems, are very important. Most of the paper is concerned with civil law, namely the law that sets out the rights and duties of persons in relation to each other. There are elements of criminal law as well, however, especially in relation to companies, insolvency, insider dealing and international money laundering.

The distinction between public and private international law is also important, affecting as it does the status of the various UN Conventions and Model Laws that are contained in the syllabus. These are intended, at least in part, to address the problem of private international law, namely the conflict of laws.

International business transactions

The central part of this section of the syllabus is concerned with the international sale of goods, covered by the UNCITRAL Convention on the International Sale of Goods. Its detailed provisions cover formation of the contract, the obligations and remedies of the buyer and seller, the right to damages, and rules on matters such as unexpected impediment and the passing of risk.

Transportation and payment of international business transactions

In any sale of goods the seller wants to make sure they get paid, and international trade operates much more effectively if it is properly financed. There is a variety of means of payment, such as letters of credit, credit transfers and bills of exchange. This is an area in which international bodies have been very active, so there is a Convention and a Model Law to be studied.

Formation and constitution of business organisations

The syllabus is very concerned with the various legal forms through which business transactions may be conducted. It is important to distinguish initially between natural persons (human beings) and legal persons (including natural persons, but extending to some forms of partnership and, most significantly, companies). The law of agency underlies a substantial part of our study of business forms, since partners and directors can, and sometimes do, act as agents.

Capital and the financing of companies

Most trading companies are financed by a mix of share capital (provided by their owners) and loan capital (provided by third-party lenders). Share capital may take a variety of forms, with each class of share having different rights within the company. However, the primary responsibility of the shareholder is to

contribute funds to the company in accordance with the terms of the company's constitution and the shares which they own.

The return of these funds to shareholders is restricted, since they are seen as the 'creditors' buffer'; that is, the funds which are available to settle creditors' outstanding debts in preference to amounts due to shareholders. Hence there are detailed laws on 'capital maintenance'. These extend to how far companies may distribute accumulated retained earnings to their shareholders in the form of dividends or buyback of shares.

Loan capital is usually provided by lenders only if they can be assured of its repayment to them. If lenders supply funds in return for debentures in the company, they usually require security for their loan: the debenture is secured by means of a registered charge on particular or general assets of the company, which can (within limitations) be realised so that the loan is repaid.

Management, administration and regulation of companies

As an artificial legal person a company cannot manage itself. This is the role primarily of the company's directors, who owe duties to the company to manage it for the benefit of the company and thereby for the benefit of its owners, the shareholders. There are a great many legal rules which regulate the appointment, remuneration, disqualification, powers and duties of directors. These have grown up largely because of problems that frequently occur. Most of these can be said to arise from conflicts between directors' personal interests and their duties to act in the company's interest. Directors are termed officers of the company, along with the company secretary. Many companies also have to have an auditor.

Directors come into immediate contact with shareholders via company meetings, and the resolutions that are passed at these meetings. There are, therefore, a plethora of legal rules on meetings and resolutions, designed to ensure that the company is taking decisions properly and in accordance with the legitimate interests of shareholders as a body.

Insolvency law

Not everything goes according to plan and frequently companies will encounter financial or other difficulties, or will even reach crisis point and find themselves insolvent. At this point all parties – shareholders, directors, lenders, customers, suppliers and employees – are in danger of losing out. There are procedures designed to protect struggling companies to give them a 'breathing space' while they resolve their issues. There are also rules for how a company which cannot be saved should be 'wound up', depending on whether or not the company has any funds left.

Corporate fraudulent and criminal behaviour

Finally, the syllabus covers the situations where activities of directors and others have strayed into criminal behaviour. This often arises in the context of companies running out of money, but the law is also concerned with company insiders, with superior knowledge, benefiting from insider dealing, and crime in the form of money laundering.

2 What skills are required?

To pass the F4 exam you will need to bring different professional attributes to bear.

First, you need **technical knowledge**. There is a huge amount of technical content in the syllabus: case law, conventions, codes of practice and legislation. You need to learn this and be able to identify which parts of the knowledge are being called for in a particular question.

Second, you need to be able to **apply knowledge** to the scenarios that are presented in the last five questions on the paper. You are aiming to solve practical problems here.

3 How to improve your chances of passing

- There is no choice in this paper, all questions have to be answered. You must, therefore, study the **entire syllabus**; there are no short-cuts
- The first section of the exam consists of **45 Multiple Choice Questions** (MCQs) worth either one or two marks each. The total marks on offer in this section is 70. These will inevitably cover a wide range of the syllabus
- The second section of the exam consists of **5 Multiple Task Questions** (MTQs) worth six marks each. Each MTQ will be broken down into sub-questions. The total marks on offer in this section is 30. Each MTQ question will be based on a scenario and will require some application of your knowledge
- Practising questions under timed conditions is essential. BPP's **Practice and Revision Kit** contains questions on all areas of the syllabus
- Keep an eye out for **articles**, as the **examination team** will use *Student Accountant* to communicate with students
- Read journals etc to pick up on ways in which real organisations apply the law; think about your own organisation, if that is relevant

4 Brought-forward knowledge

There is no brought-forward knowledge for the F4 Exam.

5 The exam paper

Format of the paper

The exam lasts two hours and is divided into two sections.

Section A consists of 45 MCQs, a mixture of one or two marks each, so a total of 70 marks are available in this section. One-mark MCQs will require you to choose one correct option from three, and two-mark MCQs will require you to choose one correct option from four.

Section B consists of 5 MTQs of 6 marks each, so a total of 30 marks are available in this section. For students sitting the written paper, questions will require a short written answer. For those sitting the computer-based exam, questions will include MCQs and other forms of objective testing such as ticking boxes or selecting two or more correct answers from a list.

All questions are compulsory.

The exam will cover as much of the syllabus as possible.

Syllabus and Study Guide

The F4 syllabus and study guide can be found below.

Syllabus

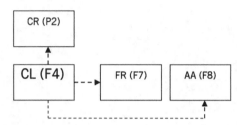

AIM

To develop knowledge and skills in the understanding of the general legal framework within which international business takes place, and of specific legal areas relating to business, recognising the need to seek further specialist legal advice where necessary.

MAIN CAPABILITIES

On successful completion of this paper candidates should be able to:

A   Identify the essential elements of different legal systems including the main sources of law, the relationship between the different branches of a state's constitution, and the need for international legal regulation, and explain the roles of international organisations in the promotion and regulation of international trade, and the role of international arbitration as an alternative to court adjudication

B   Recognise and apply the appropriate legal rules applicable under the United Nations Convention on Contracts for the International Sale of Goods, and explain the various ways in which international business transactions can be funded

C   Recognise different types of international business forms

D   Distinguish between the alternative forms and constitutions of business organisations

E   Recognise and compare types of capital and the financing of companies

F   Describe and explain how companies are managed, administered and regulated

G   Recognise the legal implications relating to insolvency law

H   Demonstrate an understanding of corporate fraudulent and criminal behaviour

RELATIONAL DIAGRAM OF MAIN CAPABILITIES

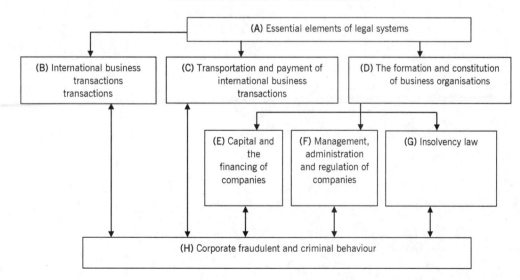

RATIONALE

Corporate and Business Law Global is divided into eight areas. The syllabus starts with an introduction to different legal systems, different types of law and those organisations which endeavour to promote internationally applicable laws. It also introduces arbitration as an alternative to court adjudication. It then leads into an examination of the substantive law as stated in UN Convention on Contracts for the International Sale of Goods, which relates to the formation, content and discharge of international contracts for the sale of goods.

The syllabus then covers a range of specific legal areas relating to various aspects of international business of most concern to finance professionals. These are the law relating to the financing of international transactions, and the various legal forms through which international business transactions may be conducted. Particular attention is focused on the law relating to companies. Aspects examined include the formation and constitution of companies, the financing of companies and types of capital, and the day–to-day management, the administration and regulation of companies and legal aspects of insolvency law.

The final section links back to all the previous areas. This section deals with corporate fraudulent and criminal behaviour.

BPP
LEARNING MEDIA

DETAILED SYLLABUS

A   Essential elements of legal systems

1.   Business, political and legal systems

2.   International trade, international legal regulation and conflict of laws

3.   Alternative dispute resolution mechanisms

B   International business transactions

1.   Introduction to the UN Convention on Contracts for the International Sale of Goods and ICC Incoterms

2.   Obligations of the seller and buyer, and provisions common to both

C   Transportation and payment of international business transactions

1.   Transportation documents and means of payment

D   The formation and constitution of business organisations

1.   Agency law

2.   Partnerships

3.   Corporations and legal personality

4.   The formation and constitution of a company

E   Capital and the financing of companies

1.   Share capital

2.   Loan capital

3.   Capital maintenance and dividend law

F   Management, administration and the regulation of companies

1.   Company directors

2.   Other company officers

3.   Company meetings and resolutions

G   Insolvency law

1.   Insolvency and administration

H   Corporate fraudulent and criminal behaviour

1.   Fraudulent and criminal behaviour

APPROACH TO EXAMINING THE SYLLABUS

The syllabus is assessed by a two-hour paper-based examination, and is also offered as a computer-based examination.

The examination consists of:

Section A
- 25 x 2 mark objective test questions   50%
  - 20 x 1 mark objective test questions   20%

Section B
- 5 x 6 mark multi-task questions   <u>30%</u>

<u>100%</u>

All questions are compulsory.

NOTE ON CASE LAW

Candidates should support their answers on the paper-based multi-task questions with analysis referring to cases or examples. There is no need to detail the facts of the case. Remember, it is the point of law that the case establishes that is important, although knowing the facts of cases can be helpful as sometimes questions include scenarios based on well-known cases. Further it is not necessary to quote section numbers of Acts.

Study Guide

A ESSENTIAL ELEMENTS OF LEGAL SYSTEMS

1. Business, political and legal systems

a) Explain the inter-relationship of economic and political and legal systems.[2]

b) Explain the doctrine of the separation of powers and its impact on the legal system.[2]

c) Explain the distinction between criminal and civil law.[1]

d) Outline the operation of the following legal systems:[1]
   i) Common law
   ii) Civil law
   iii) Sharia law.

2. International trade, international legal regulation and conflict of laws

a) Explain the need for international legal regulation in the context of conflict of laws.[1]

b) Explain the function of international treaties, conventions and model codes.[1]

c) Explain the roles of international organisations, such as the UN, the ICC, the WTO, the OECD, UNIDROIT, UNCITRAL and courts in the promotion and regulation of international trade.[1]

3. Alternative dispute resolution mechanisms

a) Explain the operation, and evaluate the distinct merits, of court-based adjudication and alternative dispute resolution mechanisms.[2]

b) Explain the role of the international courts of trade including the International Court of Arbitration.[1]

c) Explain and apply in detail the provisions of the UNCITRAL Model Law on International Commercial Arbitration.[2]

d) Describe the arbitral tribunal. [2]

e) Explain arbitral awards. [2]

B INTERNATIONAL BUSINESS TRANSACTIONS

1. Introduction to the UN Convention on Contracts for the International Sale of Goods and ICC Incoterms

a) Explain the sphere of application and general provisions of the Convention.[1]

b) Explain and be able to apply the rules for creating contractual relations under the Convention.[2]

c) Explain the meaning and effect of the ICC Incoterms.[1]

2. Obligations of the seller and buyer, and provisions common to both

a) Explain and be able to apply the rules relating to the obligations of the seller under the Convention:[2]
   i) delivery of goods and handing over documents
   ii) conformity of the goods and third party claims
   iii) remedies for breach of contract by the seller.

b) Explain and be able to apply the rules relating to the obligations of the buyer under the Convention:[2]
   i) payment of the price
   ii) taking delivery
   iii) remedies for breach of contract by the buyer.

c) Explain and be able to apply the rules relating to the provisions common to both the seller and the buyer under the Convention:[2]
   i) breach of contract and in particular anticipatory breach and instalment contracts
   ii) damages
   iii) interest
   iv) exemptions
   v) effects of avoidance
   vi) preservation of the goods.

d) Explain and be able to apply the rules relating to the passing of risk under the Convention.[2]

C   TRANSPORTATION AND PAYMENT OF INTERNATIONAL BUSINESS TRANSACTIONS

1.   **Transportation documents and means of payment**

a)   Define and explain the operation of bills of lading.[1]

b)   Explain the operation of bank transfers.[1]

c)   Explain and be able to apply the rules of UNCITRAL Model Law on International Credit Transfer.[2]

d)   Explain and be able to apply the rules of the UN Convention on International Bills Of Exchange And International Promissory Notes.[2]

e)   Explain the operation of letters of credit and letters of comfort.[2]

D   FORMATION AND CONSTITUTION OF BUSINESS ORGANISATIONS

1.   **Agency law**

a)   Define the role of the agent and give examples of such relationships paying particular regard to partners and company directors.[2]

b)   Explain the formation of the agency relationship.[2]

c)   Define the authority of the agent.[2]

d)   Explain the potential liability of both principal and agent.[2]

2.   **Partnerships**

a)   Demonstrate a knowledge of the legislation governing the partnership, both unlimited and limited.[1]

b)   Discuss the formation of a partnership.[2]

c)   Explain the authority of partners in relation to partnership activity.[2]

d)   Analyse the liability of various partners for partnership debts.[2]

e)   Explain the termination of a partnership, and partners' subsequent rights and liabilities.[2]

3.   **Corporations and legal personality**

a)   Distinguish between sole traders, partnerships and companies.[1]

b)   Explain the meaning and effect of limited liability.[2]

c)   Analyse different types of companies, especially private and public companies.[1]

d)   Illustrate the effect of separate personality and the veil of incorporation.[2]

e)   Recognise instances where separate personality will be ignored (lifting the veil of incorporation).[2]

4.   **The formation and constitution of a company**

a)   Explain the role and duties of company promoters, and the breach of those duties and remedies available to the company.[2]

b)   Explain the meaning of, and the rules relating to, pre-incorporation contracts.[2]

c)   Describe the procedure for registering companies, both public and private, including the system of streamlined company registration.[1]

d)   Describe the statutory books, records and returns, including the confirmation statement and the register of people with significant control, that companies must keep or make.[1]

e)   Analyse the effect of a company's constitutional documents.[2]

f)   Describe the contents of the model articles of association.[1]

g)   Explain how the articles of association can be changed.[2]

h)   Explain the control over the names that companies may or may not use.[2]

E   CAPITAL AND THE FINANCING OF COMPANIES

1.   Share capital

a)   Examine the different types of capital.[2]

b)   Illustrate the difference between various classes of shares, including treasury shares, the procedure for altering class rights.[2]

c)   Explain allotment of shares, and distinguish between rights issue and bonus issue of shares.[2]

d)   Examine the effect of issuing shares at either a discount, or at a premium.[2]

2.   Loan capital

a)   Define companies' borrowing powers.[1]

b)   Explain the meaning of loan capital and debenture.[2]

c)   Distinguish loan capital from share capital and explain the different rights held by shareholders and debenture holders.[2]

d)   Explain the concept of a company charge and distinguish between fixed and floating charges.[2]

e)   Describe the need, and the procedure for, registering company charges.[2]

3.   Capital maintenance and dividend law

a)   Explain the doctrine of capital maintenance and capital reduction.[2]

b)   Explain the rules governing the distribution of dividends in both private and public companies.[2]

F   MANAGEMENT, ADMINISTRATION AND REGULATION OF COMPANIES

1.   Company directors

a)   Explain the role of directors in the operation of a company, and the different types of directors, such as executive/ non-executive directors or

de jure and *de facto* directors, and shadow directors.[2]

b)   Discuss the ways in which directors are appointed, can lose their office and the disqualification of directors.[2]

c)   Distinguish between the powers of the board of directors, the managing director/chief executive and individual directors to bind their company.[2]

d)   Explain the duties that directors owe to their companies, and the controls imposed by statute over dealings between directors and their companies, including loans.[2]

2.   Other company officers

a)   Discuss the appointment procedure relating to, and the duties and powers of, a company secretary.[2]

b)   Discuss the appointment procedure relating to, and the duties and rights of, a company auditor, and their subsequent removal or resignation.[2]

3.   Company meetings and resolutions

a)   Distinguish between types of meetings: general meetings and annual general meetings.[1]

b)   Distinguish between types of resolutions: ordinary, special and written.[2]

c)   Explain the procedure for calling and conducting company meetings.[2]

G   INSOLVENCY LAW

1   Insolvency and administration

a)   Explain the meaning of, and procedure involved, in voluntary liquidation, including members' and creditors' voluntary liquidation.[2]

b)   Explain the meaning of, the grounds for and the procedure involved, in compulsory liquidation.[2]

c) Explain the order in which company debts will be paid off on liquidation .[2]

d) Explain administration as an alternative to liquidation.[2]

e) Explain the way in which an administrator may be appointed, the effects of such appointment, and the powers and duties of an administrator.[2]

H   CORPORATE FRAUDULENT AND CRIMINAL BEHAVIOUR

1   Fraudulent and criminal behaviour

a) Recognise the nature and legal control over insider dealing .[2]

b) Recognise the nature and legal control over market abuse.[2]

c) Recognise the nature and legal control over money laundering.[2]

d) Recognise the nature and legal control over bribery.[2]

e) Discuss potential criminal activity in the operation, management and liquidation of companies.[2]

f) Recognise the nature and legal control over fraudulent and wrongful trading.[2]

SUMMARY OF CHANGES TO F4 GLO

ACCA periodically reviews its qualification syllabuses so that they fully meet the needs of stakeholders such as employers, students, regulatory and advisory bodies and learning providers.

The main areas that have been clarified in the syllabus (all were implicitly included) are shown in Table 1 below:

Table 1 – Amendments to F4 GLO

Section and subject area	Syllabus content
B2c)i) Obligations of the seller and buyer, and provisions common to both	Breach of contract
F1a) Company directors	Shadow directors
F1d) Company directors	The controls imposed by statute over dealings between directors and their companies, including loans

The areas where additions have been made to the syllabus are shown in Table 2 below:

Section and subject area	Syllabus content
D4c) The formation and constitution of a company	The system of streamlined company registration
D4d) The formation and constitution of a company	The confirmation statement and the register of people with significant control

There have been no deletions from the syllabus.

:

Essential elements
of legal systems

Business, political and legal systems

1

Topic list	Syllabus reference
1 The concept of global law	A1(a)
2 Economic systems	A1(a)
3 Political systems: separation of powers	A1(a), A1(b)
4 Legal systems	A1(a)
5 Criminal law	A1(c)
6 Civil law	A1(c)
7 Common law systems	A1(di)
8 Civil law systems	A1(dii)
9 Sharia law systems	A1(diii)

Introduction

In this chapter we will be looking at the overall **context – economic, political and legal –** in which international law exists. There is no all-encompassing global law as such; instead there are **national legal systems** (of three kinds: **common law, civil law and Sharia law**). These may be contradictory (creating the problem of **conflict of laws**), therefore some **model international laws** have been put together by international organisations, such as the United Nations, to resolve the problem. In these ways the relations between states, and between individuals in different states, are regulated.

The kind of **legal system** used by a country depends on historical and cultural factors, and to some extent on economic and political factors. Whatever the legal system, we will be looking in particular at: **principles of law, sources of law** and **the role of judges**.

Study guide

		Intellectual level
A	**Essential elements of legal systems**	
1	**Business, political and legal systems**	
(a)	Explain the inter-relationship of economic and political and legal systems	2
(b)	Explain the doctrine of the separation of powers and its impact on the legal system	2
(c)	Explain the distinction between criminal and civil law	1
(d)	Outline the operation of the following legal systems: (i) Common law (ii) Civil Law (iii) Sharia law	1

Exam guide

Questions in this area may focus on the differences and features of the different legal systems and types of law. You should also be prepared to identify political systems and their constituent parts.

1 The concept of global law

FAST FORWARD

There are some **model international laws** that regulate the relationship of sovereign states, and their rights and duties with respect to each other. Most law, however, consists of **national laws**, which nevertheless follow certain **common methodologies**.

Exam focus point

Exam questions on the topics in this chapter are most likely to be looking to test your knowledge and understanding of distinctions, and so are unlikely to be scenario-based. You should not rule out the possibility of scenario questions being set, though.

1.1 Model international laws and exemplar national laws

Although 'law' is a global concept, it is **usually organised on national lines**, and there is only a **limited amount of truly international law**. In this Study Text we shall consider some **national laws that have been examples** for other countries developing their legal systems. These may therefore indicate the practice of law in many countries worldwide. We shall also see **model laws that have been developed by international bodies** and which have been adopted by various countries so that nations may interact with one another more easily.

First of all we shall look in general terms at **how nations have ordered their own legal systems**. We shall give examples of a number of nations, but we shall by no means be comprehensive in world terms.

Attention!

If you are studying in a country to which we do not make reference, find out the origins of your nation's legal system, so that you can compare it to the ones we lay out here. Remember that you are not going to be examined on any one nation's legal system; rather, you will be examined on **principles of law that have international significance**.

FAST FORWARD

There are **three key legal systems** or **underlying methodologies of law** operating in the world that have been adopted by different countries for different reasons: common law, civil law and Sharia law.

1.2 Common law

Common law is a system named after a **historic system formulated in England**. The terminology associated with this system can be confusing. You will find that the legal system is named after one distinctive source of law within itself, but that the system comprises several sources of law. Common law systems developed in **England**, but have been **exported to many ex-British Empire and Commonwealth countries**, notably, for our purposes, the **United States of America**.

1.3 Civil law

Civil law systems originated in **continental Europe**, but have similarly been exported through world empires and so are equally prominent in other world areas, for example, **South America**. Civil law systems are much younger than common law ones, although they come from equally old legal heritages. We shall use **France** and **Germany** as examples of these systems. Increasingly in modern times, civil and common law systems share common elements, although historic differences still remain.

1.4 Sharia law

Sharia law is significantly different from both common and civil law systems. It is a legal system **bound up in the religion of Islam**, which makes it **different in both purpose and practice**. It has influence in many Islamic countries worldwide, and has been adopted as a comprehensive legal system in some. We shall look at two countries where such adoption has taken place: **Pakistan** and **Iran**.

1.5 The effects of economics and political systems on legal systems

Business activity takes place within a particular **economic**, **political** and **legal context**, and each of these areas will affect each other to an extent. The economic and political context of each nation is not the same (although many groups of nations are similar) and, therefore, nations' legal systems vary considerably from one another.

The **differences** between the nations, in terms of economics, politics and, most importantly for this syllabus, law, can present **problems** for **international trade**. In this Study Text, we shall explore the difficulties presented and the solutions created by various international bodies, particularly the United Nations.

2 Economic systems

FAST FORWARD

> Economics can be described as the ways in which society decides **what to produce, how to produce it** and **who to produce it for**. There are three basic kinds of economic system – planned, market and mixed economies.

Each **individual** is involved in economics, in 'providing' (by salary or labour) for himself and his family. On a wider scale, **governments** are involved in economics for the whole country. There are various types of economic system that might exist in a country: **planned**, **market** and **mixed**.

2.1 Planned economy

A **planned economy** exists where the decisions and choices about resource allocation are made by the government. Money values are attached to resources and to goods and services, but it is the government that decides what resources should be used, how much should be paid for them, what goods should be made and what their price should be. Although the individual might be allowed to own some personal possessions, most kinds of wealth would not be available for ownership by individuals.

2.2 Market economy

A **market economy** exists where the decisions and choices about resource allocation are left to **market forces of supply and demand**, and the workings of the price mechanism. In the market economy, most wealth is owned by individuals, with a minimum being collectively owned.

2.3 Mixed economy

In a **mixed economy**, decisions and choices are made partly by free market forces of supply and demand, and partly by government decisions. Economic wealth is divided between the private sector and the public sector. In practice, all modern national economies are mixed economies, although with differing proportions of free market and centrally planned decision making from one country to the next.

3 Political systems: separation of powers

Political systems affect legal systems. There may be a **democracy** or a **dictatorship**, which generally influences the **nature of the rule of law** in the nation. In democratic systems there is usually **separation of powers** between the head of state, the executive, the legislature and the judiciary. In dictatorial systems some or all of these powers may be combined so that one person or party has total power.

We have already referred to the role of government in **national economics**. Governments, as we shall see, are also heavily involved in law making. Politics, the process of how nations are governed and by whom, is clearly relevant to how law is developed.

Law making can be a **democratic** process, where law is developed by citizens, or a more **dictatorial** process, where law is developed by a government put in place by another method, for example military coup.

What process is in force in a nation also affects two very important factors: the **rule of law**, and the **separation of powers**.

3.1 The rule of law

How and what laws are made and enforced in a country depends to a large extent on the emphasis that the country's political system places on the nature of the **rule of law**. This is the degree to which individual behaviour is regulated by law.

In **dictatorial** systems there tends to be emphasis on state or government regulation and control of resources. This means individual freedom is heavily subject to the rule of state-made law, and the behaviour of individuals is, to a large extent, dictated by the state by means of law.

In more **democratic** or *laissez-faire* political systems, the emphasis is on the law being a means of sorting problems out where they arise. Provided individuals act within the letter and spirit of the law, they are free to choose for themselves how they regulate their lives and how they relate to other people and groups.

3.2 Separation of powers

The concept of the 'rule of law' is closely bound up with that of **separation of powers**. Most 'consensual' democratic nations in the world have power held in different places, so that no part of the political process holds too much influence. They usually have:

- An elected **legislature**, a body which enacts, amends and repeals laws so that the people's wishes – for freedom, wealth etc – are met. Members of the legislature are elected by the people and represent the areas of the country in which they live. In the UK, Parliament is the legislature and consists of the House of Lords and House of Commons.

- An elected **executive**, or government body, which makes the decisions of what laws should be put into action. A nation's head of state and head of government are the two main roles in the executive. Working for the head of government (often known as the prime minister) are normally a number of ministers of state with responsibility for various government areas such as defence, education, business, finance and foreign relations.

The executive does not make the law, instead it instructs the legislature as to what laws should be made. In the UK, the executive is the political party that can command a majority of the House of Commons. In practice, the decisions of the executive are taken by the prime minister and ministers of state (a group in the UK known as the Cabinet).

- A **judiciary** (which may or may not be elected) that rules on any disputes about laws, whether between the government and the people (**criminal law**) or between individuals (**civil law**). The role of the judiciary is to interpret and apply the laws created by the legislature.

In some nations – such as the US – the **legislature**, the **executive** and the **judiciary** are completely separate. Therefore each is accountable to, and can operate as a 'check and balance' on, the others. In most states, such as the UK, there is a **complex relationship** between the three sets of powers. This means that a balance is struck between control and accountability, on the one hand, and actually 'getting things done' on the other.

In the UK, the **legislature** (Parliament) is said to exercise '**parliamentary sovereignty**. This means it can **make** and **repeal laws**, as well as **overrule** or **modify case law** created by the **judiciary**. However, since the UK joined the European Union (EU), parliamentary sovereignty has been reduced as certain UK laws must comply with EU legislation.

The other separation of powers that is frequently seen is where the person who is **head of the executive** is **not** the same person as the **head of state**. In most European nations, for instance, the two persons are separate. In the UK, the head of state is the monarch, while the head of the executive is the prime minister. In France there is the president and the prime minister. In the US, on the other hand, the president is both head of state and head of the executive.

4 Legal systems

FAST FORWARD

'Legal systems' can be used in **two** senses: to describe the body of laws and mechanisms for their enforcement in a country, and to describe the underlying nature of a country's law.

4.1 What is a legal system?

A legal system in a country embodies both the **laws** of that country and the **mechanisms** the country has in place for regulating and enforcing those laws. Therefore, a legal system incorporates:

- The country's **laws**
- The **legislature**: the law-making body
- The **judiciary**: the body that sits in judgement on disputes about laws
- The **prosecution system**: the system that seeks to ensure the criminal law is enforced and people who break the law are prosecuted
- The **police**: the body which seeks to enforce the law and protect the public
- The **prison** system: the system that ensures people who have broken the criminal law are detained in accordance with their sentence

The term **'legal system'** is also used to describe the **underlying nature of the country's law**.

4.2 What is law?

FAST FORWARD

Law is the enforceable body of rules that govern any society. **Positive law** is the body of law imposed by the state.

Law is a body of rules that enables society to operate. As such, it **does not have to be written down**, but can be simply rules that everyone in the society knows. Given the sheer size of the world, then, **law has not historically been seen in global terms**, but rather in manageable 'societies'.

Both far back in human history and today in some societies, law has been seen in terms of **families and tribes**. More recently in much of the world, it has been seen in terms of **nation states**. Many states have **written constitutions** outlining citizens' basic legal rights, and a body of **national law**, or rules, which governs how the state operates. This is known as **positive law**.

4.3 Types of law

The main distinctions to be made between types of law are between **national** and **international** law, and between **criminal** and **civil** law.

Each nation has a set of laws which regulate how entities within it relate to each other and to the state; this is known as **national law**. This is distinct from **international law**, which reflects the interrelationship of sovereign states, and which attempts to resolve the problem of **conflict of national laws**. Within each state, and increasingly across national boundaries, there is also a distinction between **civil law** and **criminal law**.

4.4 Conflicts of laws

In addition to the existence of positive (state) or national law, individuals and corporations interact with one another globally, and that has led to **conflict of laws**. This occurs in situations where people from different states, with different legal rules, have been in relationship with each other.

While nations have interacted happily with one another over many years, improved **communication systems,** resulting in increased **international trade** and other **relationships**, has prompted moves by various bodies to develop international legal systems and understandings with each other.

Conflict of laws occur when people from different legal jurisdictions trade with each other and their respective legal rules conflict. **International law** is the system of law regulating the interrelationship of sovereign states and their rights and duties with regard to one another.

Certain **international organisations** (such as the **United Nations**), **companies** and sometimes **individuals** (for example, in the area of human rights) may have **rights or duties under international law**. **International law** is the system of law regulating the relations between sovereign states, and the rights and duties they have with regard to each other.

International law deals with matters such as:

- The formation and recognition of states
- Acquisitions of territory
- War
- The law of the sea and of space
- Treaties
- Treatment of aliens
- Human rights
- International crimes and international judicial settlement of disputes

4.5 Sources of international law

Sources of international law are **public** (treaties, custom and general legal principles) and **private** (a nation's own national laws which regulate international dealings).

There are various **sources** of **international** law:

- Conventions and treaties
- International custom
- The general principles of law recognised by civilised nations

For example, the **European Union** is a collection of nations which have agreed between them on some common laws, by signing conventions and treaties. This is **public international law**. You may also come across the term **private international law**, which is the part of a nation's own law that establishes rules for dealing with cases involving a foreign element.

4.6 Types of legal system

As we have already discussed, law is usually organised on national lines. There are **three main ideologies**, or **legal systems**, which underlie state systems of law: common law, **civil law** and **Sharia law** systems. We shall discuss these three key systems later, but first we shall look in more detail at the distinction between two key types of law: the criminal and the civil law.

5 Criminal law

FAST FORWARD

A **crime** is conduct prohibited by the law. It is usually **punished** by the State, which **prosecutes** the case, by means of **fines** or **imprisonment**. There is usually a **heavy burden of proof**.

In a criminal case the State is the prosecutor because it is the community as a whole which suffers as a result of the law being broken. **Persons guilty of crime may be punished by fines payable to the State or by imprisonment**. In some circumstances the court may make a compensation order, by which the criminal must pay some compensation to the victim or their family.

In the UK, the **police** or the **Director of Public Prosecutions** take the initial decision to prosecute, but this is then reviewed by the **Crown Prosecution Service**.

In a criminal trial, the **burden of proof** to convict the **accused** rests with the **prosecution**. The prosecution must meet the **standard of proof**, which means proving its case **beyond reasonable doubt**.

In the UK and parts of the Commonwealth, a **criminal case** might be referred to as *R v Smith*. The prosecution is brought in the name of the Crown (R signifying *Regina,* the Queen). In the US, it might be referred to as *State v Smith.*

As we discussed in the introduction, what is considered a **crime** will vary from state to state. Other differences include the types of punishments delivered to guilty parties, the degree of evidence required to convict someone of an offence, and the extent to which the court may order the guilty criminal to compensate the victim.

In resolving criminal issues, the outcome is usually punishment of the wrongdoer, although a compensation order may be made in some circumstances. Some legal systems based on Sharia or Islamic law (which we will see in detail shortly) contain the concept of **qisas**, or **retribution**. In certain cases these give a legal right to inflict on the wrongdoer the same hurt as he has perpetrated on the victim, or to accept **diyat**, **compensation**, instead.

This provides some **compensation** to the victim of criminal activity, who is not necessarily considered in Western law. In the West, the focus of the law is mainly to punish the wrongdoer; victims might have to undertake a civil law action to receive significant compensation.

6 Civil law

FAST FORWARD

Civil law exists to regulate disputes about the rights and obligations of persons when dealing with each other. The state is not party to a civil case, and there is a lighter burden of proof.

Terminology in civil cases is different from that in criminal cases. The **claimant** sues the **defendant**. A civil case would therefore be referred to as, for example, *Smith v Megacorp plc.* One of the most important areas of civil liability for business, and accountants in particular, is the law of **trade and contract**.

Civil law is a form of **private law**. In civil proceedings, the **standard of proof** means that the claimant must prove their case on the **balance of probability**. The claimant must convince the court that it is more probable than not that their assertions are true.

6.1 Distinction between criminal and civil cases

It is not an act or event which creates the distinction between criminal and civil cases, but the **legal consequences**. A single event might give rise to criminal and civil proceedings.

A broken leg caused to a pedestrian by a drunken driver is a single event which may give rise to:

- A **criminal case** (prosecution by the state for the offence of driving with excess alcohol), and
- A **civil case** (the pedestrian sues for compensation for pain and suffering)

The two sorts of proceedings are usually easily distinguished because three vital factors are different:

- The **courts** where the case is heard
- The **procedures**
- The **terminology**

In criminal cases the **rules of evidence** are usually very strict. For example, a confession will be carefully examined to see if any pressure was brought to bear upon the accused. An admission in a civil case will not usually be subjected to such scrutiny.

Point to note

> We will look at areas of both criminal and civil law in this Study Text. You should be aware that in some legal areas looked at in this Study Text, both types of law might be relevant. For example, as we shall see, in the area of company law, both criminal law (for example, insider dealing, fraudulent trading) and civil law (for example, 'passing-off') will be relevant.

7 Common law systems

Common law systems derive from, and are named after, the **law developed in England** between **1066 AD** and about **1400 AD**.

Although the law was developed in England, it has been exported globally as a result of the British Empire and Commonwealth. It is the basis of the legal system of the United States of America (US). We shall use **England** and the **US** as exemplars of the system.

Attention!

> You should note that England has been part of the United Kingdom (UK) for over three hundred years. Some of England's legal system remains peculiar to itself, but many modern aspects are common to the other nations (Scotland, Northern Ireland and Wales). You will find both England and the UK referred to in this Study Text.

7.1 Principles of common law

FAST FORWARD

> **Common law builds up over time**, added to by the legislature (statutes are presumed to add to, not alter, existing law) and by **judicial precedent**.

In English law, **principles of law** do **not become inoperative** through the **lapse of time**. In other words, law does not become irrelevant and invalid just because it is old. This applies to all sources of the law. Also, **new laws developed by the legislature (parliament) are presumed not to alter**, merely to add to, **the existing law**, unless they specifically state otherwise.

Another important principle of common law is the concept of **judicial precedent**.

A **precedent** is a previous court decision which another court is bound to follow, by deciding a subsequent case in the same way.

The doctrine of **judicial precedent** means that a judge is bound to apply a decision from an earlier case to the facts of the case before him, provided, among other conditions, that there is no material difference between the cases.

7.2 Sources of law in common law systems

There are various **sources of law in England**:

- Common law (from which the legal system derived its name)
- Equity – based on case law
- Statute
- Custom (of little modern significance, so we shall not consider it any more)
- European Union law

European Union law is not a source of law in the US as it has not been a party to the treaties with other European countries that the UK has. The US, however, does have a significant additional source of law, the **American Constitution**. The UK does not have a written constitution.

Common law and equity form what is known as **case law**. Case law is a significant difference between the common law system and the civil law system. We shall consider it in detail later on, in connection with the role of judges.

Attention!

Equitable principles supplement and improve the **common law**. Both are based on **case law** and **statutes** from the national and EU parliament – an additional source of law.

7.2.1 Common law and equity

The earliest element of the legal system to develop was the **common law**, a system incorporating rigid rules applied by royal courts, often with harsh consequences. **Equity** was developed, two or three hundred years later, as a system of law applied by the Lord Chancellor in situations where justice did not appear to be done under common law principles.

Key terms

Common law is the body of legal rules, common to the whole country, which is embodied in judicial decisions.

Equity is a term which applies to a specific set of legal principles which were developed by the Court of Chancery to supplement (but not replace) the common law. It is based on fair dealings between the parties. It added to and improved on the common law by introducing the concept of fairness.

The **interaction** of **equity** and **common law** produced three major changes.

(a) **New rights**. Equity recognised and protected rights for which the common law gave no safeguards.

(b) **Better procedure**. Equity may be more effective than common law in resolving a disputed matter.

(c) **Better remedies**. The standard common law remedy for the successful claimant was the award of damages for his loss. The Chancellor developed remedies not available in other courts. Equity was able to make the following orders.

    (i)   That the defendant must do what he had agreed to do (**specific performance**)

    (ii)   That the defendant must abstain from wrongdoing (**injunction**)

    (iii)   Alteration of a document to reflect the parties' true intentions (**rectification**)

    (iv)   Restoration of the pre-contract status quo (**rescission**)

Where equitable rules **conflict** with common law rules, then **equitable rules** will **prevail**: *Earl of Oxford's case 1615*.

Case law incorporates decisions made by judges under both historic legal systems and the expression 'common law' is often used to describe all case law whatever its historic origin. **A court's decision** is expected to be **consistent with previous decisions** and to provide an opinion which can be used to direct future relationships. This is the basis of the system of **judicial precedent**.

7.2.2 Statute

Key term

> **Statute law** is made by Parliament (or in exercise of law-making powers delegated by parliament, known then as delegated legislation; or, in the civil law system (see later), known as administrative regulations).

Until the UK entered the European Community (now the European Union) in 1973 the UK Parliament was completely **sovereign** – its law-making powers were unfettered, and there was **no written constitution**.

In that respect there was a marked contrast with the position in some other countries, such as the US. Here, there is a written constitution and it is possible to challenge in the courts (as unconstitutional) legislation made by the statutory law-making body.

In recent years, however, UK membership of the **European Union** has restricted the previously unfettered power of parliament. There is an obligation, imposed by the Treaty of Rome, to bring UK law into line with the Treaty itself, and with **directives made by the European Commission or Council**.

On certain subjects the EU may make **regulations** under provisions of the Treaty of Rome. These have direct force of law in EU states, and do not have to be enacted by statute.

The UK tradition is to **draft statutes in comprehensive detail** to attempt to cover all eventualities that the statute is designed to cover.

> PO1 requires you to 'act diligently and honestly, following codes of conduct, giving due regard to, and keeping up to date with, relevant legislation'.
>
> The contents of this Study Text should help you identify legal and regulatory compliance requirements to help achieve this.

7.2.3 Codification in common law systems

From time to time, Parliament will produce a **codifying statute**, which puts common law in an area on a statutory footing. In that respect, codifying statutes are similar to civil law codes, which we shall consider later.

However, **codification is not common** in England, and many areas of law, for example, contract law, still largely derive from common law.

7.2.4 American Constitution

The **American Constitution** is the ultimate source of law in the US. Any statute passed by the American Senate, by the federal government or in individual states, may be challenged by a citizen on the grounds that it is unconstitutional.

Attention!

> The US Constitution sets out the basic rights of US citizens and the systems of government for them. You can access it on the internet, for example, at www.usconstitution.net.

7.3 Role of judges in common law systems

FAST FORWARD

> Judges play two roles in building up **case law** in common law systems – by setting and applying **judicial precedent** and, by **interpreting statutes**, they also perform the important function of **judicial review**.

7.3.1 Judicial precedent in case law

It is generally accepted that **consistency** is an important feature of a good decision-making process. Judges are required to treat similar cases in the same way.

A judge's decision is expected to be **consistent with previous decisions**. It should provide an opinion which the parties, and others, can use to direct their future relationships as it creates law. This is the basis of the system of **judicial precedent**.

Judicial precedent is based on three elements:

- **Reports.** There are comprehensive law reports of earlier decisions.
- **Rules.** There must be rules for extracting a legal principle from a previous set of facts and applying it to current facts.
- **Classification.** Precedents must be classified into those that are **binding** and those which are merely **persuasive**. (Decisions of lower courts are never binding.)

Four **rules** must be considered when examining a precedent before it can be applied to a case:

- A decision must be based on a **proposition of law** before it can be considered as a precedent. It may **not** be a decision on a **question of fact**.
- It must form part of the *ratio decidendi* of the case.
- The **material facts** of each case must be the same.
- The preceding court must have had a **superior (or in some cases, equal) status** to the later court, such that its decisions are binding on the later court.

Key term

> 'The *ratio decidendi* of a case is any rule of law expressly or impliedly treated by the judge as a necessary step in reaching their conclusion, having regard to the line of reasoning adopted by them, or a necessary part of their direction to the jury.'
> (Cross: *Precedent in English Law*)

The English legal system comprises a **hierarchy of courts**. In terms of the status of the courts for precedents, you should be aware that lower courts do not create binding precedents. They are bound by the decisions of higher courts, each of which is bound by the courts higher to itself.

A precedent in a previous case can be avoided by a judge if they '**distinguish on the facts**'. A precedent is only binding if the **material facts** of the later case are the same as the previous case. This is a matter of judicial judgement. Precedents may also be **overruled** by higher courts than the court that set them. This tends to be rare, particularly if the precedent has existed for a long time.

7.3.2 Statutory interpretation in case law

When deciding cases based on statute law, **judges will be required to interpret the statutes that Parliament has enacted**. There are various rules and presumptions associated with the interpretation of statute.

Presumptions of statutory interpretation:

(a) **Statutes do not override existing law** on a subject unless they specifically state that they do so. In other words, statutes are generally seen to **supplement existing case law**.

(b) **A statute does not alter the existing common law**. If a statute is capable of two interpretations, one involving alteration of the common law and the other one not, the latter interpretation is to be preferred.

(c) **If a statute deprives a person of their property**, say by nationalisation, they are to be compensated for its value.

(d) **A statute is not intended to deprive a person of their liberty**. If it does so, clear words must be used. This is relevant in legislation covering, for example, mental health and immigration.

(e) **A statute does not have retrospective effect** to a date earlier than its becoming law.

(f) **A statute does not bind the Crown**. In certain areas, the Crown's potential liability is great and this is, therefore, an extremely important presumption.

(g) **A UK statute has effect only in the UK**. However, a statute does not run counter to international law and should be interpreted so as to give effect to international obligations.

(h) **A statute cannot impose criminal liability** without proof of guilty intention. Many modern statutes rebut this presumption by imposing strict liability, say for dangerous driving under the Road Traffic Act.

(i) A statute does not **repeal** other statutes.

(j) **Any** point on which the statute leaves a **gap or omission** is **outside its scope**.

The courts have also developed a number of **rules of statutory interpretation**.

Rules of statutory interpretation	
Literal rule	Words should be given their plain, ordinary or literal meaning. Normally a word should be interpreted in the same literal sense wherever it appears throughout the statute.
Purposive rule	Under this approach to statutory interpretation, the words of a statute are interpreted not only in their ordinary, literal and grammatical sense, but also with reference to the context and purpose of the legislation, ie what is the legislation trying to achieve? This shows how the court took account of the mischief or legal wrong which the statute was explicitly intended to remedy. In *Gardiner v Sevenoaks RDC 1950,* the purpose of an Act was to provide for the safe storage of film wherever it might be stored on 'premises'. The claimant argued that 'premises' did not include a cave and so the Act had no application to his case. The purpose of the Act was to protect the safety of persons working in all places where film was stored. If film was stored in a cave, the word 'premises' included the cave.
Contextual rule	A word should be interpreted in its context. It is permissible to look at the statute as a whole to discover the meaning of a word in it.
***Eiusdem generis* rule**	Statutes often list a number of specific things and end the list with more general words. In that case the general words are to be limited in their meaning to other things of the same kind (Latin: *eiusdem generis*) as the specific items which precede them.
***Expressio unius est exclusio alterius* rule**	To express one thing is, by implication, to exclude anything else. For example, a statutory rule on 'sheep' does not include goats.
***Noscitur a sociis* rule**	A word draws meaning from the other words around it. If a statute mentioned 'children's books, children's toys and clothes' it would be reasonable to assume that 'clothes' meant children's clothes.
***In pari materia* rule**	If the statute forms part of a series which deals with similar subject matter, the court may look to the interpretation of previous statutes, on the assumption that Parliament intended the same thing.

7.3.3 Judicial review in common law systems

We noted previously that a US citizen has the right to challenge law which appears to be unconstitutional. The role of **determining whether created law conflicts with the Constitution falls to judges**, in the courts, notably the US Supreme Court.

There are two major theories in the US as to how judges should do that. The first is called **originalism**.

Key term | **Originalism** is the theory that the Constitution should be interpreted according to the original intent of its authors.

The alternative theory is sometimes known as **constructivism**.

> **Constructivism** is the theory that the Constitution should be interpreted looking beyond the original intent of its authors.

The originalism theory is based in the idea that if judges try and look **beyond** the **original intent** of the authors of the Constitution, they do not have a solid base on which to make a decision. There is greater chance of a decision being made on the grounds of personal or political preference. However, there are **several problems** with such an approach to interpretation.

For example, the fact that the drafting process was long and involved many different parties - whose intent should the judges look at? In addition, the method does not account for **change over time**, which is necessary in the context of social development.

The **risk** in any interpretation, but particularly in **constructivism**, going beyond the intent of the authors, is that in effect, nothing acts as a check to the court except its own good judgement.

Attention!

> When we look at **corporate law** later in this Study Text, we shall be looking at the system in the UK as an example of other systems adopted around the world. You should bear in mind that this law has been developed in a **common law** system. Hence, although much company law in the UK is **statute** based, and found in the Companies Act 2006, some of it is based in **case law** which has developed over the last 100 and more years.

8 Civil law systems

FAST FORWARD

> Civil law systems seek to ensure **comprehensibility** and **certainty** by means of **codification** by means of **statutes** and **administrative regulations**. In simple terms, so that common law and custom do not apply.

Civil law developed in **continental Europe**, during a period of revolutionary change and state forming. The following section uses the French legal system to illustrate the main features of civil law systems.

8.1 Principles of civil law

Two key principles in civil law are **comprehensibility** and **certainty**. This can be seen in the codes that provide the hallmark of civil law, and the different role allocated to judges in the civil law system compared with the common law systems.

8.2 Codification in civil law

Civil law tradition historically owes much to the **law of the Roman Empire**, and is sometimes given a date of origin as early as 450 BC.

In more recent times, a key period in the development of civil law was the era of **revolution** in western Europe in the late eighteenth and early nineteenth centuries. It was after these revolutions that **emerging nations** decided to **codify their law**, abolishing the mixture of common law and custom remaining from Roman times, and establish a **national law**.

In France, the process of law making can been seen in the period after the French Revolution, in the years following 1789. The French Civil Code, the **Code Napoleon**, published in 1804, is the key example. France now has a large number of such codes of law. The German Civil Code was published in 1896.

Where law is **codified** in civil law systems, it is generally codified so as to provide a comprehensive code of the enacted law in a certain area. Codes of law are a common feature of civil law, although they are not a compulsory feature. While France has the **Code Napoleon** other civil law countries, such as **South Africa**, do not have codified law.

8.3 Sources of civil law

There are various **sources of law in France**:

- Constitution
- EU law
- Statutes
- Administrative regulations
- Custom (of limited importance, so we shall not consider this further)

The key source of law is **statute**, much of which is **codified**. Administrative regulations are also codified. Statute law is usually **drafted** as **general principles** and in **simple language** as far as possible, so as to ensure that the law is accessible. This is in stark contrast to English statutes, which are complex and drafted to cover many eventualities.

8.4 The role of judges in civil law

FAST FORWARD

In civil law systems, **judges simply apply the law** – they do not make law by way of judicial precedent, although they may perform **judicial review** to ensure that statutes etc are in line with the **constitution**.

The role of judges in a civil law system is significantly different in theory from the role of a common law judge. In **France**, there is a **distinct division** between those who **draft the law** and those who **apply the law**, judges being the latter.

There is no such thing in France as judge-made law. Hence, while previous decisions of other judges will be **persuasive** to other judges making decisions, they do not create precedent in the same way as in the common law system.

8.4.1 The Court of Cassation

The top court of appeal in France is the **Court of Cassation**. 'Cassation' comes from the French that means 'to quash'. When the Court of Cassation was originally formed, it was a government department set up to quash any court decisions where the legislators felt that the law has been incorrectly interpreted.

The history of the Court of Cassation is, therefore, not as a court. Originally it was manned not by judges, but by legislators, whose role was to **quash** the original decision and return the case to the court system to be retried.

In practice, the Court became a **court of appeal**, where the people determining that the law had been incorrectly interpreted also set out what the correct interpretation should have been, so that the case was not returned to the judicial system. In time, then, the Court of Cassation has been incorporated into the judicial system.

8.4.2 Statutory interpretation in civil law

There is no general principle in French law on how judges should interpret statute. This is probably due to the historic feeling that judges should not interpret the law but merely apply it to the letter. However, some **general principles** of statutory interpretation have developed.

Statutory interpretation	
'Quand la loi est claire, il faut la suivre'	'Where the meaning of the law is clear, it must be followed.' French judges will not extend or restrict the scope of a statute that is unambiguous.
'Quand elle est obscure, il faut approfondir les dispositions pour en penetrer l'esprit'	'Where the statute is obscure or ambiguous, one should construe it in accordance with the spirit of it', rather than to the letter, in order to determine its legal meaning.
'Si l'en manqué de loi, il faut consulter l'usage ou l'équité'	'If there is a gap in the law, judges must resort to custom and equity.' However despite this, custom is only of limited application in France.

There are also the following alternative methods of **statutory interpretation**:

- **Teleological method**. This is where a judge seeks to identify the social purpose of the legislation and apply it in a manner that achieves it.

- **Historical method**. This is where the judge looks at the intention of the legislator and then tries to envisage what the intention would be if the law was being drafted in modern times. The judge then applies that intention.

8.4.3 Judicial review in civil law

Although in the civil law tradition judges do not have a key role interpreting statute, a system of **judicial review** has grown in certain civil law countries. This role is to comment on whether statute law is in accordance with the country's constitution.

This is the case in **Germany**, where **constitutional courts** have been set up for the purpose. However, the judges in constitutional courts are not the same as in the normal court system. In other words, special judges are created to comment on whether legislation in constitutional.

Exam focus point

Many of the model laws that we shall look at later in this Study Text are drafted in accordance with civil law principles.

9 Sharia law systems

FAST FORWARD

Sharia law is based on the religion of Islam. This means that the law extends into **areas of belief and religious practice** and that the **law is God-given** and so has **wider significance than social order**.

The major difference between Sharia law and other legal systems is that **Sharia law is explicitly based on**, and connected with, **the religion of Islam**. We shall describe Sharia law in general terms, but also use Pakistan and Iran as examples of countries that have adopted Sharia.

Sharia is 'a way to a watering place', in other words, a path to be followed. **Sharia law** is ordained by Allah as guidance for mankind.

9.1 Principle of Sharia law

The main principle of Sharia law is that it is **the divine way** ordained by Allah for man to follow. The law, therefore, is **sourced directly from Allah** and this has a significant impact on how it is interpreted by judges. In true Sharia tradition, judges are clerics, known as Imam.

9.2 Sources of Sharia law

FAST FORWARD

The main sources of **Sharia** law are the **Quran** and the **Sunnah**. The secondary sources of law are the Madhab.

The **key source of law** in Sharia is the **Quran**, which contains various injunctions of a legal nature.

Key term

The **Quran** is Allah's divine revelation to his Prophet, Muhammad.

The Quran was revealed to the **Prophet Muhammad** during the last years of his life, around 619–632 AD. It was written down piecemeal during his lifetime but not fully collated until after his death.

The **Muslim calendar** is different from the Western systems of years BC and AD. However, for the purposes of comparability with common and civil law systems, the AD dates are being used here.

The Quran includes various injunctions of a legal nature, but it does not cover every detail, so **another primary source of law** in Sharia is the **Sunnah**.

The **Sunnah** is 'the beaten track', in other words, what has come to be the acceptable course of conduct. It is derived from the sayings of the Prophet, known as **Ahadith** (known in singular as Hadith).

There are also five **major secondary sources** of law in the Muslim world, known as **Madhab**. These are schools of thought based on **writings and thoughts of major jurists** formed in the years immediately following the death of the Prophet and are named after those jurists:

- The Shia school
- The Hanafi school (Imam Abu Hanifa)
- The Maliki school (Imam Malik)
- The Hanbali school (Imam Ahmad Ibn Hanbal)
- The Shafii school (Imam As-Shafii)

These schools of law are given more prominence in certain parts of the world, so, for example, parts of Iraq and parts of **Iran** follow the Shia school ('Shia Muslims'). The majority of the Muslim world follows the other four schools, which together, are termed Sunni (hence 'Sunni Muslims'). In **Pakistan**, the generally preferred school is Hanafi.

9.2.1 Constitution

Many Muslim countries (such as Iran and Pakistan) have a **written constitution**. The Iranian Constitution upholds the role of Sharia law in Iran, as can be seen from Article 2 of the Constitution.

 Case Study

Iranian Constitution, Article 2

The Islamic Republic is a system based on belief in:

1   The One God (as stated in the phrase 'There is no god except Allah'), His exclusive sovereignty and the right to legislate, and the necessity of submission to His commands

2   Divine revelation and its fundamental role in setting forth the laws

3   The return to God in the Hereafter, and the constructive role of this belief in the course of man's ascent towards God

4   The justice of God in creation and legislation

5   Continuous leadership (imamah) and perpetual guidance, and its fundamental role in ensuring the uninterrupted process of the revolution of Islam

6   The exalted dignity and value of man, and his freedom coupled with responsibility before God; in which equity, justice, political, economic, social, and cultural independence, and national solidarity are secured by recourse to:

- Continuous ijtihad of the fuqaha' possessing necessary qualifications, exercised on the basis of the Qur'an and the Sunnah of the Ma'sumun, upon all of whom be peace

- Sciences and arts and the most advanced results of human experience, together with the effort to advance them further

- Negation of all forms of oppression, both the infliction of and the submission to it, and of dominance, both its imposition and its acceptance

9.3 The role of judges in Sharia law

FAST FORWARD

> In Sharia law, judges may need to **interpret** the law (it cannot be changed). They do this in line with the **Sunnah Ahadith** (sayings of the Prophet) that are varyingly reliable. **Fiqh** is the process of further legal interpretation, using **ijtihad**. Judges may also perform a form of judicial review.

As we have observed, the **religious nature** of Sharia means that in true Sharia tradition, **judges are clerics**, known as Imam. This is the situation in **Iran**, for example. However, in other Muslim states, there are a **mixture of clerical judges and secular judges**.

Judges are required to apply the law to cases brought before them. However, given the **nature and source** of the law, there are **particular considerations** with regard to **interpretation** of the law.

9.3.1 Interpretation of Sharia law

The **Quran cannot be altered**, being the Word of Allah. It may only be **interpreted**. This leads to the problem in Islamic circles of who is **qualified to interpret** the Quran. Muhammad, as Allah's prophet, was qualified to do so.

When clear guidance cannot be obtained from the Quran, the judge may turn to the **Sunnah** to see **how the Quran was interpreted by the Prophet**. The Sunnah is used by Muslim jurists to:

- **Confirm** the law in the Quran
- **Explain** matters mentioned in the Quran in general terms
- **Clarify** verses in the Quran that may seem ambiguous
- **Introduce** a rule where the Quran is silent

The **Ahadith** that comprise the Sunnah were recorded some time after the death of the Prophet and are **classified according to reliability**. Some are **virtually guaranteed**, and are known as **muwatir**. Others are **less certain** and known as **mashtur**. Lastly, where there is **little certainty** as to their authenticity, Ahadith are called **ahad**.

9.3.2 Schools of Sharia law

There is **controversy** in the Muslim world as to **whether matters of legal and religious significance should be interpreted further**, or whether everything is clear and new cases should not bring the need for further development of the law. Those that believe more development is needed have developed a science of understanding and interpreting legal rules, known as fiqh, through the techniques of ijtihad.

The theory that no more interpretation is needed is known as **Taqlid**, which is the process of strict adherence to established doctrine. Orthodox Muslims would adhere to Taqlid, although some would claim there was a need to deal pragmatically with the results of new, Western influences in their countries.

Taqlid was the result of what is known as '**closing the gates of Ijtihad**' which took place during the course of the sixteenth to nineteenth centuries AD.

Key term

> **Ijtihad** are the processes for ascertaining the law. It is the use of intellectual exertion by a jurist to derive an answer to a legal question.

The basis for Ijtihad is a **Hadith** which records that the Prophet approved an Imam who told him that in making a judgement, he would rely first on the Quran, then on the Sunnah, and then he would exert his own judgement.

There are various rules associated with exercising an ijtihad:

- It **must not be exercised on certain matters** (for example, the existence of Allah)
- The judge must be **suitably qualified**, known as a **muhtahid**
- There are various **recognised methods**

In order to **qualify** as a muhtahid a person must be:

- **Well-versed** in the **study** of the **Quran**
- **Well-versed** in the **traditions** of the **Prophet**
- **Understand** the **principle** of **ijma'**
- **Understand** the **conditions** for **qiyas**
- A **good** and **practising Muslim**
- **Just**, **reliable** and **trustworthy**

One reason there is controversy about whether interpretation should still take place is that many people believe that these **qualification criteria** are **too difficult** to meet in modern times, given the time lapse since the death of the Prophet.

Two of the recognised methods for exercising Ijtihad have been mentioned in these **qualification criteria**. The full list of methods is:

- Ijma'
- Qiyas
- Istihsan
- Maslahah mursalah
- 'Urf
- Istishab

The first three are **key methods**. Maslahah mursalah means something very similar to Istihsan. 'Urf is the theory that local custom may be subsumed into the law if it is not contrary to Sharia.

Istishab is a **legal presumption** that the current state of affairs continues until the contrary is proved. Something is permitted until it is shown that it is forbidden.

Key terms

> **Ijma'** is a consensus of opinion. It should be based on consultation between jurists.
> **Qiyas** is analogical deduction. In other words, it is a comparison of two things with a view to evaluating one in the light of the other.

An **example of qiyas** is to say that taking drugs is forbidden, on the basis that the Quran states that alcohol is forbidden, and the effects of taking drugs are similar to the effects of taking alcohol.

Key term

> **Istihsan** is the concept of equity, or of fairness. However, in Sharia, the exercise of equity is clearly only permissible within the bounds of the Sharia as it is integral to the system.

9.3.3 Judicial review in Sharia law

In some Muslim states, the state will issue **statutes**, although these should be based on Sharia law principles. In addition, since wholesale adoption of Sharia by Islamic nations is a fairly recent trend, they may have enacted law from before adoption. The Hudood Ordinances in Pakistan from the 1970s set out, in statute, the Sharia law relating to criminal law.

Pakistan has a **Federal Shariat Court** which has a key role in judicial review. One of its objectives is to determine whether a provision of (statute) law is repugnant to the injunctions of Islam.

Another aspect of the **Federal Shariat Court's** role is to hear appeals under the **Hudood rules**.

9.4 The rule against usury

A rule in Sharia law that has a significant impact on commerce and trade is the rule against usury, known in Sharia as **riba**.

Key term

> **Riba** is the Islamic concept of unlawful gain, usually translated as interest, which is strictly forbidden by the Quran.

In theory, riba, 'unlawful gain' translates to be **qualitative inequality** and is a highly technical area. For our purposes, and **in practice**, it is often seen as a **rule against charging or receiving interest**.

The concept of riba also has a significant impact on the way that Muslims bank, which you should be aware of, although we shall not look at the details of **Muslim banking** in this Study Text.

Chapter Roundup

- There are some **model international laws** that regulate the relationship of sovereign states, and their rights and duties with respect to each other. Most law, however, consists of **national laws**, which nevertheless follow certain **common methodologies**.

- There are **three key legal systems** or **underlying methodologies of law** operating in the world that have been adopted by different countries for different reasons: common law, civil law and Sharia law.

- Economics can be described as the ways in which society decides **what to produce**, **how to produce it** and **who to produce it for**. There are three basic kinds of economic system – planned, market and mixed economies.

- **Political systems affect legal systems.** There may be a **democracy** or a **dictatorship**, which generally influences the **nature of the rule of law** in the nation. In democratic systems there is usually **separation of powers** between the head of state, the executive, the legislature and the judiciary. In dictatorial systems some or all of these powers may be combined so that one person or party has total power.

- 'Legal systems' can be used in **two** senses: to describe the body of laws and mechanisms for their enforcement in a country, and to describe the underlying nature of a country's law.

- **Law** is the enforceable body of rules that govern any society. **Positive law** is the body of law imposed by the state.

- The main distinctions to be made between types of law are between **national** and **international** law, and between **criminal** and **civil** law.

- **Conflict of laws** occur when people from different legal jurisdictions trade with each other and their respective legal rules conflict. **International law** is the system of law regulating the interrelationship of sovereign states and their rights and duties with regard to one another.

- Sources of international law are **public** (treaties, custom and general legal principles) and **private** (a nation's own national laws which regulate international dealings).

- A **crime** is conduct prohibited by the law. It is usually **punished** by the state, which **prosecutes** the case, by means of **fines** or **imprisonment**. There is usually a **heavy burden of proof**.

- **Civil law** exists to regulate disputes about the rights and obligations of persons when dealing with each other. The state is not party to a civil case, and there is a lighter burden of proof.

- **Common law builds up over time**, added to by the legislature (statutes are presumed to add to, not alter, existing law) and by **judicial precedent**.

- Judges play two roles in building up **case law** in common law systems – by setting and applying **judicial precedent**, and, by **interpreting statutes**, they also perform the important function of **judicial review**.

- Civil law systems seek to ensure **comprehensibility** and **certainty** by means of **codification** via **statutes** and **administrative regulations**. In simple terms, so that common law and custom do not apply.

- In civil law systems, **judges simply apply the law** – they do not make law by means of judicial precedent, although they may perform **judicial review** to ensure that statutes etc are in line with the **constitution**.

- Sharia law is based on the religion of Islam. This means that the law extends into **areas of belief and religious practice** and that the **law is God-given** and so has **wider significance than social order**.

- The main sources of **Sharia** law are the **Quran** and the **Sunnah**. The secondary sources of law are the Madhab.

- In Sharia law, judges may need to **interpret** the law (it cannot be changed). They do this in line with the **Sunnah Ahadith** (sayings of the Prophet) that are varyingly reliable. **Fiqh** is the process of further legal interpretation, using **ijtihad**. Judges may also perform a form of judicial review.

Quick Quiz

1 **Fill in the blanks**.

   Law is the _enforceable body_ of _rules_ that govern any society.

2 Principles of English law do not become inoperative through lapse of time.

   True   [X]

   False   [ ]

3 The four rules associated with applying a judicial precedent are:

   (1) _a precedent must be based on a decision of law, not of fact_

   (2) _material facts must be the same_

   (3) _preceding court must have had superior status_

   (4) _it must form a part of ratio decidendi of the case_

4 **Fill in the blanks**.

   In the civil law tradition, _codification_ is the process of putting _all_ the law on a specific area together in a _code_.

5 French law is usually drafted as general principles and in simple language to ensure that the law is accessible.

   True   [X]

   False   [ ]

Answers to Quick Quiz

1 **Law** is the **enforceable body** of **rules** that govern any society.

2 True. They do not become inoperative due to age.

3 (1) A precedent must be based on a decision of law, not of fact
    (2) It must form part of the *ratio decidendi* of the case
    (3) The material facts of each case must be the same
    (4) The preceding court must have had a superior status to the court using the precedent

4 In the civil law tradition, **codification** is the process of putting **all** the law on a specific area together in a **code**.

5 True. Simple language is used so all members of the public can understand it.

Now try the questions below from the Practice Question Bank

Number
1, 2, 3, 4

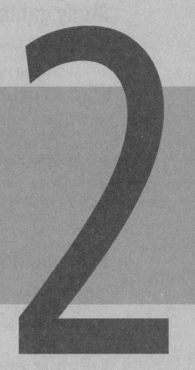

International trade, legal regulation and conflict of laws

Topic list	Syllabus reference
1 Public and private international law	A2(a)
2 Conflict of laws and the need for international regulation	A2(a), A2(b)
3 Role of international organisations in trade	A2(c)

Introduction

In the last chapter, we made reference to **international law**, and began to suggest why its development has been considered necessary. This is basically because of the problem of **conflict of laws**.

In this chapter, we shall look specifically at the acts and events which increasingly give rise to **international co-operation** in the area of law. Although we shall consider acts of international significance, such as war crimes and abuses of human rights, the issue of major significance for our syllabus is **international trade and commerce**. We shall begin to look at the issues surrounding this.

The need for international regulation has been recognised by a number of **international bodies** in various ways. We shall introduce some of these bodies and in general terms, discuss their history and their aims. Some have been active in producing model laws and codes that we shall be looking at later in the Study Text.

Lastly in this chapter we shall consider some of the international institutions which exist to **adjudicate international legal disputes**.

Study guide

		Intellectual level
A	**Essential elements of legal systems**	
2	**International trade, international legal regulation and conflict of laws**	
(a)	Explain the need for international legal regulation in the context of conflict of laws	1
(b)	Explain the function of international treaties, conventions and model codes	1
(c)	Explain the roles of international organisations, such as the UN, the ICC, the WTO, the OECD, UNIDROIT, UNCITRAL and courts in the promotion and regulation of international trade	1

Exam guide

Questions on these topics are most likely to focus on the role of the different bodies involved in the operation and development of international law, and on the features of international commerce that make such development necessary.

1 Public and private international law

FAST FORWARD

Public international law governs the relations between states and international organisations. **Private international law** regulates cases where there is a conflict of laws.

International law is the system regulating the interrelationship of sovereign states and their rights and duties with regard to one another. We need to break international law down further.

(a) **Public international law** consists of rules and principles which apply in general to the conduct of sovereign states and international organisations and the relationships between them.

(b) **Private international law** regulates cases which involve the national laws of two or more states where a different result will ensue depending on which state's law is applied.

PO1 requires you to continually review legislation and regulations that affect your working environment. The contents of this Study Text should help you identify common legal and regulatory requirements.

2 Conflict of laws and the need for international regulation

Public international law is to do with the **recognition of states**, or **wars**, or the aftermath of wars; that is, events which are considered of **international significance**. Part of international law is therefore dealing with matters such as **war crimes** and other **human rights abuses**.

However, our syllabus is only concerned with situations where individuals or corporations interact or act on the basis of international commerce; that is **private international law**.

Economics, politics and law all affect **international trade**. Given the differences between economic and political systems in nations, there are therefore significant barriers to free international trade.

2.1 Barriers to free international trade

FAST FORWARD

Barriers to free trade exist to **protect** markets from outside competition. They include tariffs or customs duties, import quotas, embargoes, hidden subsidies for exporters and domestic producers, import restrictions, as well as the barriers created by differences in laws.

In practice many barriers to free trade exist because governments try to protect home industries against foreign competition. **Protectionism** can be practised by a government in several ways.

2.1.1 Tariffs or customs duties

Tariffs or customs duties are taxes on **imported goods**. The effect of a tariff is to raise the price paid for the imported goods by domestic consumers, while leaving the price paid to foreign producers the same, or even lower. The difference is transferred to the government sector.

2.1.2 Import quotas

Import quotas are restrictions on the **quantity** of a product that is allowed to be imported into the country. The quota has a similar effect on consumer welfare to that of import tariffs, but the overall effects are more complicated.

- Both domestic and foreign suppliers enjoy a higher price, while consumers buy less at the higher price.

- Domestic producers supply more.

- There are fewer imports (in volume).

- The government collects no revenue.

2.1.3 Embargo

An **embargo** on imports from one particular country is a total ban, ie effectively a zero quota.

2.1.4 Hidden export subsidies and import restrictions

There is a range of **government subsidies** and **assistance** for exports and deterrents against imports. Some examples include:

(a) **For exports** – export credit guarantees (insurance against bad debts for overseas sales), financial help (such as government grants to the aircraft or shipbuilding industry) and general state assistance.

(b) **For imports** – complex import regulations and documentation, or special safety standards demanded from imported goods and so on.

2.1.5 Differences in law

In addition to economic problems there are legal barriers to trading between nations. For instance, take a moment to try and define what a contract is. A contract is something **defined by the law**, and so, as the law varies from country to country, may be one thing in one country and a different thing in the other. It may have different legal consequences in different parts of the world.

For example, the following definition of contract could be given.

Key term

> A **contract** is a legally binding agreement.

However, **what makes an agreement 'legally binding'** is **likely to vary** from country to country. In one country, a legally binding agreement may be formed by two people making an agreement and shaking hands on it. In another, the agreement may have to be committed to writing and evidenced by witnesses.

In some countries, it may be the case that an agreement does not become legally binding unless **other conditions** are fulfilled. For example, in England, there is a legal doctrine known as consideration. Under this doctrine parties have to exchange promises, acts or forfeitures of value to create a contract. Such a legal doctrine is unknown in other parts of the world.

This raises a problem. People wanting to engage in **international trade**, say A (from country Z) wants to trade with B (from country Y). If the relationship breaks down, the following issues could arise:

- A could claim that under Z's law, no contract was ever formed.
- B could claim that under Y's law, no contract was ever formed.
- Both parties could claim that the contract is not legally enforceable in their country.
- The remedies available for broken contracts in the different countries may differ.
- The parties might disagree on the choice of country in which to seek legal resolution.
- They might seek legal resolutions in their countries and be unable to enforce them.

These are all issues arising from **conflict of laws**.

2.2 Conflict of laws

Conflict of laws is where parties from different nations have a legal dispute, and it is necessary to determine which national law governs the validity of the legal situation.

2.2.1 Example: Conflict of laws

A contract is made in England, but the contract is to be fulfilled in India. The relationship between the parties breaks down and legal resolution is sought. But should this be under English law or Indian law?

2.2.2 International conventions, treaties and model laws

International co-operation is required to ensure that solutions can be found to issues such as the conflict of laws. Otherwise, the parties may be able to avoid each other and any solutions sought may not be enforceable.

Countries have sought solutions to these problems by coming to **agreements** with each other and by enacting various **conventions** and **treaties** that **regulate international practice**. UN Conventions are agreements which are binding under international law on states and other entities.

For instance, the **Rome Convention 1980** set out policy on what law should govern the validity of international contracts. It sets down the general principle that if the parties have a **written contract** and have **expressed preference** for a particular law in that written contract, that law should govern the contract. This is known as **choice of laws**.

The **New York Convention 1958** set out the agreement of countries relating to referring cases to arbitration.

However, the conventions have not necessarily solved all the problems presented by conflict of laws completely. The United Nations has also developed **model laws** that countries may adopt into their own national laws. These make practices uniform on an international basis and iron out any remaining problems.

3 Role of international organisations in trade

Important bodies associated with international law include the UN, the ICC, the WTO, the OECD, UNIDROIT and UNCITRAL.

BPP
LEARNING MEDIA

3.1 The United Nations (UN)

Almost every independent state in the world is a member of the **United Nations (UN)**. The UN started in 1945 when the then-members ratified the UN charter. The purposes of the UN are to:

- Maintain peace and security
- Develop friendly relations among nations
- Co-operate in solving economic, social, cultural and humanitarian problems
- Promote respect for human rights and international freedoms

The UN Charter states that member nations should **develop and codify international law**. Currently, there are over 500 UN conventions, treaties and standards which legally bind the states that ratify them. There are **two bodies** in the UN involved in **drafting international law**: The **International Law Commission** and the **UN Commission on International Trade Law (UNCITRAL)**.

3.2 UN Commission on International Trade Law (UNCITRAL)

UNCITRAL is the **core legal body** within the United Nations in the field of international trade law. It was established in 1966, when the General Assembly recognised that disparities in national laws governing international trade created obstacles to the flow of trade. UNCITRAL was given the task of harmonising and unifying the law of international trade by:

- **Co-ordinating** the work of organisations active in the field and encouraging their co-operation.

- **Promoting** wider participation in **existing international conventions** and **wider acceptance** of existing model and uniform laws.

- **Preparing** or promoting the adoption of **new international conventions**, **model laws** and **uniform laws**. The promotion of, codification and acceptance of international trade terms, provisions, customs and practices in collaboration with the organisations operating in this field.

- **Promoting** ways and means of ensuring a **uniform interpretation** and **application** of international conventions and uniform laws in the field of international trade.

- **Collecting** and **disseminating information** on national legislation and modern legal developments, including case law, in the field of international trade law.

- **Establishing** and **maintaining a close collaboration** with the United Nations Conference on Trade and Development.

- **Maintaining liaison** with other **UN organs** and **other agencies** concerned with international trade.

- **Taking any other action** it may deem useful to fulfil its functions.

A total of 60 member states are elected by the UN General Assembly to form UNCITRAL. It is structured so as to be **representative** of the world's various geographic regions, economic and legal systems. The Commission carries out its work at annual sessions, held in alternate years at United Nations' headquarters in New York and in Vienna. Members of the Commission are elected for terms of six years and half the members' terms expire every thee years.

The Commission operates through **six working groups**, composed of all member states of the Commission. The six working groups and their current topics are as follows:

- Working group I – Micro, small and medium-sized enterprises
- Working group II – Arbitration and conciliation
- Working group III – Online dispute resolution
- Working group IV – Electronic commerce
- Working group V – Insolvency law
- Working group VI – Security interests

Non-members of the Commission and other interested international organisations are invited to attend sessions of the Commission and of its working groups, as **observers**. They can participate in any discussions to the same extent as members.

UNCITRAL has achieved the following outcomes, among others:

- **UN Convention on Contracts for the International Sale of Goods**. This Convention established a comprehensive code of legal rules governing the formation of contracts for the international sale of goods. This includes the obligations of the buyer and seller, remedies for breach of contract and other aspects of the contract.

- **UN Convention on the Carriage of Goods by Sea** (The Hamburg rules). This Convention established a uniform legal regime governing the rights and obligations of shippers, carriers and consignees under a contract of carriage of goods by sea.

- **UN Convention on International Bills of Exchange and International Promissory Notes**. This Convention provides a comprehensive code of legal rules governing international instruments for use in international commercial transactions.

- **UNCITRAL Model Law on International Commercial Arbitration**. These provisions are designed to assist states in reforming and modernising their laws on arbitral procedure so as to take into account the particular features and needs of international commercial arbitration.

- **UNCITRAL Model Law on Electronic Commerce**. This Model Law, adopted in 1996, is intended to facilitate the use of modern means of communications and storage of information.

- **UNCITRAL Model Law on Cross-Border Insolvency**. This Model Law seeks to promote fair legislation for cases where an insolvent debtor has assets in more than one state.

3.3 International Chamber of Commerce (ICC)

The **International Chamber of Commerce (ICC)** was formed in 1919 'to serve world business by promoting trade and investment, open markets for goods and services, and the free flow of capital'.

It was originally created by business leaders from Belgium, UK, France, Italy and the United States. Now it is a **world wide** business organisation with thousands of member companies and associations from 130 countries.

The ICC makes representations to governments on issues related to **international trade**. It also develops **codes of practice** to encourage businesses to operate with a minimum of government intervention. The ICC co-operates with, and advises, the **United Nations** and provides **practical services to businesses** and seeks to **combat commercial crime**.

Another important aspect of the ICC is that it set up the **International Court of Arbitration** in 1923.

3.4 World Trade Organisation (WTO)

The **World Trade Organisation** is the newest of the various international organisations we are looking at. It was formed in 1995 as successor to the General Agreement on Tariffs and Trade (GATT), which was set up after World War II. It is an organisation that devotes itself entirely to international trade in goods, services, traded inventions, creations and intellectual property.

The WTO has 162 members and these represent 97% of international trade. The organisation seeks to **promote the free flow of trade** by removing obstacles to trade, and to make sure that individuals, companies and governments know what these rules are. The WTO:

- Administers trade agreements
- Is a forum for trade agreements
- Settles trade disputes
- Reviews national trade policies
- Assists developing countries in trade policy issues (training/technical assistance)
- Co-operates with other international organisations

GATT is the WTO's main **guidelines on international trade** in goods. It is the result of negotiations between nations and is subject to updating and revision, such as when the WTO was set up and when GATT was extended to **intellectual property**, **services**, **dispute settlement** and other areas.

The WTO agreements contain the principles of **liberalisation** of **free trade**. They include commitments by each country to lower customs tariffs and other trade barriers, and to open and keep open services markets. They also set procedures for settling disputes.

The current set of agreements is the outcome of the 1986–94 Uruguay Round GATT negotiations which set up a non-discriminatory trading system that spells out each country's **rights** and **obligations**. Each country receives guarantees that its exports will be treated fairly and consistently in members' markets and promises to do the same for imports into its own market. There is some latitude towards 'developing' countries in how they implement their commitments. There are limited permitted exceptions negotiated on a country-by-country basis.

All WTO members must **notify** the WTO about laws in force and measures adopted. They must undergo periodic scrutiny, each review containing reports by the country concerned and the WTO Secretariat.

Decisions of the WTO are made by the **entire membership**, usually on the basis of consensus. The structure of the WTO is as follows.

(a)   The **Secretariat** is based in Geneva, with around 600 staff under a director-general. The Secretariat's role is to supply technical support for the various councils and committees and the ministerial conferences. It also provides technical assistance for developing countries, analyses world trade, explains WTO affairs to the public and media and provides some form of legal assistance in the dispute settlement process.

(b)   The **Ministerial Conference** is the WTO's top-level decision-making body, meeting at least once every two years.

(c)   The **General Council** meets several times a year in Geneva, sometimes as the Trade Policy Review Body and the Dispute Settlement Body.

(d)   **Special councils** such as the Goods Council, Services Council and Intellectual Property (TRIPS) Council report to the General Council.

(e)   **Committees**, working groups and working parties deal with the individual agreements and other areas such as the environment, development, membership applications and regional trade agreements.

Through the **Dispute Settlement Body** (DSB), the WTO operates a dispute settlement procedure for resolving trade quarrels between member countries. If this proves unsuccessful, the parties engage in a stage-by-stage procedure that may eventually result in a binding ruling by a **panel of experts** appointed by the Body in each dispute, subject to an **appeal**. The panel's judgements are based on interpretations of the agreements and individual countries' commitments.

The **Dispute Settlement Body** can accept or reject the panel's findings or the results of an appeal on a point of law only. It monitors how the rulings and recommendations are implemented, and it can authorise sanctions when a country does not comply with a ruling.

The **panel of experts** is appointed by the DSB in consultation with the countries in dispute. Only if the two sides cannot agree does the WTO director-general appoint them. Panels consist of three (possibly five) experts from different countries, who examine the evidence and decide who is right and who is wrong. The panel's report is passed to the Dispute Settlement Body, which can only reject the report by consensus. Panellists for each case are chosen from a permanent list of well-qualified candidates, or from elsewhere, but they serve in their individual capacities and cannot receive instructions from any government.

Any **appeal** is heard by three members of a permanent seven-member Appellate Body set up by the Dispute Settlement Body and broadly representing the range of WTO membership. Members of the Appellate Body have to be individuals with recognised standing in the field of law and international trade, and must not be affiliated with any government. The appeal can uphold, modify or reverse the panel's legal findings and conclusion but the final decision rests with the Dispute Settlement Body, which has to accept or reject the appeals report within 30 days. Rejection is only possible by consensus.

Exam focus point	Questions on this area may focus on the various roles of the respective organisations.

3.5 Organisation for Economic Co-operation and Development (OECD)

The **Organisation for Economic Co-operation and Development (OECD)** is a **group of member countries**. It originally comprised countries in North American and Europe but has expanded to include such countries as Japan, Australia, Mexico and Korea. **It has members from most of the continents**.

The OECD developed in **1961** out of an organisation set up to administer American and Canadian aid to Europe after World War II.

Its purpose is to be 'a forum to **discuss, develop and refine economic and social policies**'. It has created both **legally binding agreements** (for instance in relation to bribery) and also **non-binding agreements** (such as guidelines for multinational enterprises).

The OECD invites **non-member countries** to subscribe to its agreements as well as members, and is involved in a further 70 countries, including China, Russia, Brazil and some countries in Africa.

3.6 International Institute for the Unification of Private Law (UNIDROIT)

The **International Institute for the Unification of Private Law** is an **independent intergovernmental organisation** which studies the need for, and how to modernise, harmonise and co-ordinate, private international law, and in particular trade law. It is based in Rome and has operated since 1926.

Membership of UNIDROIT is restricted to 63 states which have signed up to the UNIDROIT Statute. They represent all five continents and a variety of different legal, economic and political systems.

UNIDROIT is structured as follows:

(a)   The **Secretariat** is responsible for the day-to-day running of UNIDROIT's work programme. There is a Secretary-General plus a staff of international civil servants and various ancillary staff.

(b)   The **Governing Council** supervises UNIDROIT's policy. It draws up the work programme and supervises how the Secretariat is carrying it out. It comprises the President of the Institute and 25 elected members, typically eminent judges, practitioners, academics and civil servants.

(c)   The **General Assembly** is the ultimate decision-making organ of UNIDROIT, approving the annual budget, approving the work programme and electing the Governing Council. Each member government has one representative.

UNIDROIT's basic objective is to prepare modern, harmonised and uniform rules of **private international law**. Sometimes it strays into public international law, especially in areas where hard and fast lines of demarcation are difficult to draw or where the laws are very complicated and interlinked. Uniform rules prepared by UNIDROIT are concerned with substantive law rules; they will only include uniform conflict of law rules incidentally.

The need for harmonised rules is usually driven by new technologies and commercial practices. States specifically ask for new solutions or transactions which are **transnational** by their very nature. UNIDROIT will assess whether states are willing to accept change to their municipal law rules in favour of a new international solution on that subject before embarking on the process. Some rules are restricted to truly cross-border situations or relations while others are extended to cover purely internal situations or relations.

Because UNIDROIT is an intergovernmental structure, its rules have traditionally tended to take the form of **international conventions**. These apply automatically in preference to a state's national law once they have been implemented. Conventions are needed where:

- The scope of rules affects third parties as well as the parties to a contract, or
- The interests of third parties or the public interest are at stake, as in the law of property.

BPP LEARNING MEDIA

Since states often drag their heels in **implementing conventions**, UNIDROIT has more recently favoured alternatives such as:

- **Model laws** to be taken into consideration when drafting domestic legislation on the subject covered

- **General principles** addressed directly to judges, arbitrators and contracting parties, who are then left free to decide whether to use them or not

- **Legal guides**, typically on new business techniques, on new types of transaction or on the framework for the organisation of markets at both the domestic and the international level

UNIDROIT has, over the years, prepared over seventy studies and drafts. Many of these have resulted in **international instruments**, and its work has also served as the basis for international instruments adopted under the auspices of other international organisations already in force. For example, the UNCITRAL Convention on Contracts for the International Sale of Goods.

Chapter Roundup

- **Public international law** governs the relations between states and international organisations. **Private international law** regulates cases where there is a conflict of laws.

- Barriers to free trade exist to **protect** markets from outside competition. They include tariffs or customs duties, import quotas, embargoes, hidden subsidies for exporters and domestic producers, import restrictions, as well as the barriers created by differences in laws.

- **Conflict of laws** is where parties from different nations have a legal dispute, and it is necessary to determine which national law governs the validity of the legal situation.

- **Important bodies** associated with international law include the UN, the ICC, the WTO, the OECD, UNIDROIT and UNCITRAL.

UN
ICC — International Chamber of Commerce
WTO — World Trade Organization
OECD — Organisation for Economic Co-operation and Development
UNIDROIT — International Institute for the Unification of Private Law
UNCITRAL — UN Commission on International Trade Law

Quick Quiz

1   What is meant by the term conflict of laws?

2   The core legal body of the UN is UNIDROIT.

    True   ☐

    False ☒

3   The International Chamber of Commerce (ICC) established the International Court of Arbitration (ICA).

    True   ☒

    False ☒

4   The four aims of the United Nations are:

    (1)   maintain peace and security

    (2)   develop friendly relations among nations

    (3)   co-operate in solving economic, social, cultural and humanitarian problems

    (4)   promote respect for human rights & international freedoms

5   The two bodies of the UN which are involved in drafting international law are:

    (1)   the International Law Commission

    (2)   the UN Commission on International Trade Law (UNCITRAL)

Answers to Quick Quiz

1   Conflict of laws is a problem that arises when people from different nation states enter into a legal relationship with each other, and it is not clear whose national law will govern that legal relationship.

2   False. The core legal body of the UN is UNCITRAL.

3   True. The ICC established the ICA in 1923.

4   The aims of the UN:

   (1)   Maintain peace and security
   (2)   Develop friendly relations among nations
   (3)   Co-operate in solving economic, social, cultural and humanitarian problems
   (4)   Promote respect for human rights and international freedoms

5   (1)   The International Law Commission
   (2)   The UN Commission on International Trade Law (UNCITRAL)

Now try the questions below from the Practice Question Bank

Number
5, 6, 7

Court-based adjudication and alternative dispute resolution mechanisms

Topic list	Syllabus reference
1 Court-based adjudication	A3(a)
2 Role of international courts	A3(b)
3 Alternative dispute resolution (ADR)	A3(a)
4 UNCITRAL Model Law on International Commercial Arbitration	A3(c)
5 Arbitration agreement	A3(c)
6 Arbitral tribunal	A3(d)
7 Conduct of arbitral proceedings	A3(c)
8 Award enforcement	A3(e)

Introduction

We have already considered the concept of **arbitration**. In this chapter we shall look at the detail of the UNCITRAL **Model Law on International Commercial Arbitration**. We shall look at four aspects contained within the Model Law:

- What constitutes an arbitration agreement
- The arbitral tribunal
- How proceedings are conducted
- Awards and their enforcement

Many cases relating to the Convention for **the International Sale of Goods**, which we will look at in detail in the next chapters, are submitted to arbitration under this model agreement.

NOTE – This chapter and the three that follow are based on various UN Model Laws and Conventions. References are made to some of their Articles (subsections). This is purely for information purposes and to help you follow the structure of the rules.

Study guide

		Intellectual level
A	**Essential elements of legal systems**	
3	**Alternative dispute resolution mechanisms**	
(a)	Explain the operation, and evaluate the distinct merits, of court-based adjudication and alternative dispute resolution mechanisms	2
(b)	Explain the roles of the international courts of trade, including the International Court of Arbitration	1
(c)	Explain and apply the provisions of the UNCITRAL Model Law on International Commercial Arbitration	2
(d)	Describe the arbitral tribunal	2
(e)	Explain arbitral awards	2

Exam guide

Given its practical nature and the fact there is a Model Law on it, arbitration is a highly examinable topic in this exam. The detailed rules could easily be examined in a scenario question.

1 Court-based adjudication

Legal disputes, of whatever nature, have **traditionally** been **settled in courts**. In fact, as we have seen, in the common law system courts have a key role in settling disputes, and in so doing, creating legal precedent, and therefore, creating law.

Most countries have a **system of courts**, with lower-level courts for minor matters and higher-level courts for more serious matters, and also to hear appeals when court decisions are disputed.

FAST FORWARD

> Court-based adjudication depends on a **system of courts** which settle disputes. A **court of first instance** is a court where a case is heard for the first time. An **appellate court**, or **court of appeal**, is a higher court where the previous decision of a lower court can be re-heard, due to a dispute over a point of law or point of fact in a decided case. Civil and criminal cases tend to have different court structures and procedures.

Most legal systems will have a system of courts that, in its most basic form, involves cases starting in a **court of first instance** and moving up to an **appeal court** if the decision is contested. Cases may be appealed on a point of law or point of fact.

However, in most countries, the court system will be **more complicated** than this. Most countries will have different courts to deal with civil and criminal law, and may also have different courts within those systems to deal with major and minor cases. The number of judges, and the existence of a jury, will differ between those courts as well.

We shall continue our studies by using the **example of the English court system**.

1.1 English system of courts

FAST FORWARD

> In England there is a **different court structure** for **civil** and **criminal** law, although some of the higher courts have jurisdiction over both types of law.

The system is **decentralised** through a **system of local courts**, so that smaller matters can be dealt with where they have occurred. However, the largest cases are tried in the major courts in the capital city, London.

There is a system of review to higher courts. The English legal system contains a series of **appeal courts**. Cases in either type of law may be appealed up through the system. The highest court within England is the **Supreme Court**. However, this court only deals with cases whose outcome will have a significant impact on the country's laws. Due to the UK's membership of the EU, the highest court of appeal is the **European Court of Justice**.

1.1.1 Civil court structure

The following diagram sets out the **civil court structure** for England.

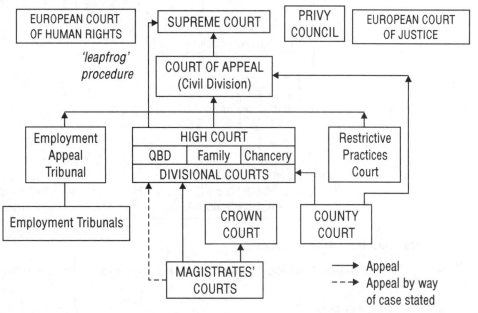

The **key courts** in the civil system are:

- The **County Court**, which only has civil jurisdiction and which deals with almost every type of civil case at a local level.

- The **High Court**, which deals with the most major cases at first instance and is sometimes a court of appeal from the County Court.

- The **Court of Appeal**, which is the major appeal court in civil matters.

The **County Court** is manned by **circuit judges**, who must be barristers (qualified legal advocates) of at least 10 years' standing.

The **High Court** is manned by **puisne judges**, who must also be barristers of ten years' standing. They hear cases at first instance alone, but at least two judges must hear appeal cases.

The **Court of Appeal** is manned by **Lord Justices of Appeal**, who are judges promoted from the High Court. Three judges, normally, sit together, and cases are decided by a majority.

1.1.2 Criminal court structure

The diagram below sets out the English **criminal court structure**.

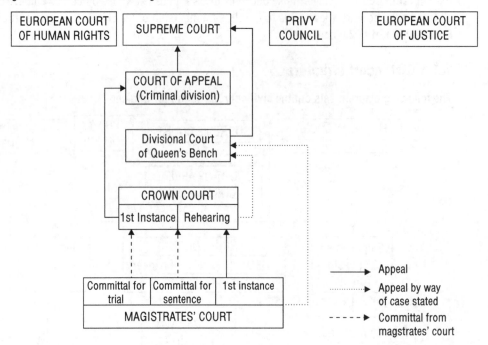

The **key courts** in the **criminal system** are:

- The **Magistrates' Court** and the **Crown Court**, which are local courts hearing the bulk of criminal cases

- The **Court of Appeal**

The **Crown Court** hears cases at first instance and is an appeal court from the magistrates' court. Cases are appealed from the Crown Court to the Court of Appeal.

There are two types of magistrate: **lay magistrates**, who are not legally qualified and sit part-time, and **district judges**, who are solicitors (legally qualified persons) or barristers of at least seven years' standing. Most magistrates are lay magistrates and two or three of them must sit together to hear a case. District judges sit alone.

The **Crown Court** is staffed by **circuit judges** or, sometimes, **lay magistrates**.

Key terms

> **Indictable offences** are more serious offences that can only be heard in a Crown Court.
>
> **Summary offences** are minor crimes, only triable summarily in magistrates' courts.
>
> Some offences are **'triable either way'**.

1.1.3 Making a civil claim

Civil procedure in England has been reformed in recent years to try and reduce the cost and time involved in taking a matter to court. Therefore, it is possible to take small claims to court under a small claims procedure, where it is not necessary to engage a legal professional, and the case should be heard reasonably quickly.

However, for **larger cases** in the County Court or High Court, the **cost and time involved can be substantial**. In larger cases, it is practice for the parties to appoint **solicitors** (qualified legal professionals) to establish the facts in the case. In addition, the solicitors will often appoint **barristers** (qualified legal advocates) to present the case.

Taking a case to court can be a slow process; if a case is appealed, it is likely to take **years** rather than **months** to reach final settlements.

An important feature of the English system is the concept of **pre-trial disclosure**. This is the practice of disclosing documents relevant to the case to the other party before trial proceedings.

Pre-trial disclosure can result in a lot of **expense**, as it can involve a significant amount of time and, therefore, legal cost.

1.2 Advantages and disadvantages of court-based adjudication

FAST FORWARD

Court is generally **expensive** and **slow**, but offers a wider range of better, more enforceable solutions.

It is usually more **expensive** to go to court than to submit your case to arbitration, mediation or conciliation (see later). The main reason for this is the cost of legal professionals, court fees and, in common law systems, the cost of pre-trial disclosure, which can be high.

Another disadvantage is the **time scale** involved. The UK government has sought to make court action more accessible to the public, but taking a legal dispute to court can still be a lengthy and very costly business, particularly if the matter is subject to appeal.

A related disadvantage is the **waiting period** before a case comes to trial. This can be substantial, due to the large number of cases going through the court system and, in common law systems, the time it takes to conduct pre-trial disclosure.

However, going to court can provide helpful legal **solutions** and settlements, such as a **court order** to prevent someone from behaving in a certain way or an order for **compensation**. In some cases, parties may want a **decision** made about which party is legally 'right'.

Additionally, because **judicial precedent** establishes **legal rules for the future**, similar future cases may be resolved before legal action is required, saving future generations the time and expense of going to court.

2 Role of international courts

FAST FORWARD

International adjudicators include **international courts** (ECJ) and international venues for **arbitration** (ICA). They can sort out **conflicts of law** and the **enforcement** of settlements.

When international legal problems need solving, problems can arise due to the issue of **conflicts between the participants' laws** and the problems of **enforcing punishment or settlement** on persons in different countries. However, states may (and often do) co-operate with one another, for example by **extraditing** criminals from one country to another.

International adjudication and arbitrations are also important, especially in the promotion and regulation of international trade. We shall look at the **European Court of Justice** (ECJ) which came into being as a result of the treaties between the European nations forming the European Union.

There are various international venues for **arbitration** in various countries in the world. We shall look, in particular, at the International Court of Arbitration (ICA).

ECJ - European Court of Justice

2.1 European Court of Justice (ECJ)

The European Union's (EU) **European Court of Justice** is part of the legal system of each member state.

The ECJ is ordered along **civil law lines**, but an unofficial system of **precedent** can arise where national states are reluctant to refer similar cases to the ECJ once a clear decision has been made.

The **ECJ is the highest court in the EU** and is the result of the treaties between the member states of the EU. It is the highest court of appeal in each member state of the EU.

2.2 International Court of Arbitration (ICA)

The **International Court of Arbitration** is a body set up by the International Chamber of Commerce in 1923. It is composed of members from every continent in the world.

The ICA has been instrumental in developing the use of international commercial arbitration and initiated the 1958 New York Convention. This is an important **multilateral treaty,** by which ratifying states agreed to recognise written arbitration agreements and not submit such disputes to national courts.

Exam focus point

You should not let the name of this institution confuse you in the exam. It is called a court of arbitration, but is not a court in the sense of the courts we looked at earlier. It is an arbitration body, which applies rules of arbitration set out by the International Chamber of Commerce.

Arbitration is a useful tool for settling **international commercial disputes**, when people trade in states where the legal system is very different from their own and legal decisions may not seem fair.

The ICA oversees all aspects of the **arbitration process**, such as:

- Appointment of arbitrators
- Confirmation of appointment of arbitrators
- Deciding on challenges to arbitrators
- Approving arbitral awards
- Fixing arbitrators' fees

The ICA is assisted in appointing arbitrators by the member nations of the ICC, which have **national selection committees** maintaining details of potential arbitrators. However, arbitrators do not have to be selected from pre-existing lists. This means the ICA maintains the flexibility of arbitration and the benefit to the parties of being able to select their own arbitrator.

3 Alternative dispute resolution (ADR)

FAST FORWARD

It is increasingly common practice in commercial contracts or agreements to include a clause providing that the dispute is to be settled by **arbitration**. Arbitration is one example of **alternative dispute resolution**, which also includes **mediation** and **conciliation.**

Key term

Alternative Dispute Resolution is any type of procedure or combination of procedures voluntarily used to resolve differences, other than court-based adjudication. ADR procedures may include, but are not limited to, conciliation, facilitation, mediation, early neutral evaluation, adjudication and arbitration.

3.1 Arbitration

Key term

Arbitration is settlement of a dispute by an independent person, usually chosen by the parties themselves.

Arbitration can produce **different solutions** to court-based adjudication. For example, it could produce the following results:

- A change in the way a person or organisation behaves
- A promise that a person or company won't do something
- An apology
- An explanation for what happened
- A mistake corrected
- Compensation

An **agreement** between parties to submit any dispute that may arise to **arbitration** is a **contract**, which is subject to the rules of contract law.

We shall look later on at the **UN's model arbitration law**, but it is useful now to identify that it is founded on the following **principles**:

- The need to obtain a fair resolution by means of an independent tribunal without unnecessary delay or expense

- The fact that parties are free to agree how arbitration should work, subject to such safeguards as are necessary to protect the public

- The fact that courts should not intervene except as necessary to protect the public interest

Although ideally there is no room for courts in a dispute submitted to arbitration, there should still be room for **appeals to courts**.

3.1.1 Arbitration in Islamic law

Arbitration is highly recommended in Islamic law. Islamic arbitration is known as **takhim** and arbitrators are called **hakam**.

The law concerning who may be an **arbitrator** is strict, like the law concerning who may be a judge. The qualifications needed are similar, particularly that the arbitrator must be Muslim, male, just, learned in Sharia and free from any defects that could affect his ability to arbitrate.

3.2 Mediation and conciliation

Mediation and **conciliation** involve the use of an independent third party to assist the parties in coming to their own solution of the problem. Mediation agreements are usually not legally binding on the parties.

Concepts of mediation or conciliation are found in **Islamic law**; **solh** is conciliation and **wasta is** mediation.

3.3 Advantages and disadvantages of alternative dispute resolution

A major advantage of ADR is that the parties are involved in choosing the person who is going to settle their dispute. This means that they can gain the services of an **expert** in the particular commercial field that they are in.

It is sometimes argued that ADR is **cheaper** than court action, although this will depend on the practices of the nation in which proceedings are being taken. For example, in England and the US, the cost of going to court is high, due to the high cost of legal representation. It might be cheaper to go to arbitration, where legal representation is not always necessary.

However, in other countries, where the cost of court action is not so high, it might be more expensive to go to arbitration, such as when the costs of the arbitrator and the venue must be met. In comparison, judges and court costs are provided by the state.

Another advantage is that ADR is usually **private**, unless the parties want the proceedings to be public. If the dispute is over a commercially sensitive matter, this may be essential to the parties. Even if the matter is more routine, the parties may not want any publicity about their dispute process. Court proceedings, on the other hand, are usually kept on record and open to the public.

ADR is **informal** and **quicker** than court proceedings.

4 UNCITRAL Model Law on International Commercial Arbitration

FAST FORWARD

Arbitration is the settlement of disputes by an independent party usually chosen by the parties themselves.

The **United Nations Commission on International Trade Law** adopted the Model Law on International Commercial Arbitration in 1994. It is not a Convention, but a set of rules to be adopted into national laws so as to make international practice uniform.

4.1 International commercial arbitration

FAST FORWARD

An arbitration is international if the parties have their places of business in **different states**; and commercial if it arises from matters of a **commercial nature** (that is, relating to trade).

The Model Law defines what makes arbitration both **international** and **commercial** in character.

Article 1

Arbitration is international if:

(a)   The parties to the arbitration agreement have their places of business in different states.

(b)   The parties' places of business are in the same state but the place designated for arbitration is in a different state, or the obligations of the commercial relationship are to be performed in a different state.

(c)   The parties have expressly agreed that the subject matter of the arbitration agreement relates to more than one country.

Arbitration is **commercial** if it covers matters arising from all relationships of a commercial nature, that is, relating to **trade**, whether there is a contract or not. This should be interpreted widely.

The Model Law gives the following as **examples of commercial transactions**:

- Supply/exchange of goods and services
- Distribution agreement
- Commercial representation
- Agency
- Factoring
- Leasing
- Construction of works
- Consulting
- Carriage of goods by air/sea/road/rail
- Carriage of passengers by the same
- Engineering
- Licensing
- Investment
- Financing
- Banking
- Insurance
- Exploitation agreement or concession
- Joint venture
- Other industrial/business co-operation

If a party has **more than one place of business**, the relevant place of business for the purpose of the arbitration agreement is the place with the closest relationship to the arbitration agreement.

4.2 Written communications

The Model Law sets out a general rule about **receipt of written communications** which will be in force in any arbitration agreement, unless the parties agree otherwise.

Article 3

Any written communication is deemed to have been received if it is delivered to the addressee personally or if it is delivered at his place of business, habitual residence or mailing address; if none of these can be found after making a reasonable inquiry, a written communication is deemed to have been received if it is sent to the addressee's last-known place of business, habitual residence or mailing address by registered letter or any other means which provide a record of the attempt to deliver it.

The communication is deemed to have been received on the day it is so delivered.

4.3 Role of the courts

The Model Law specifies that **courts shall not intervene** in matters governed by the Model Law, except where stated within the Model Law: Article 5. Each state that adopts the Model Law should specify a court or other authority within the adopted law which will perform necessary functions (for example, default appointment of arbitrators) if necessary: Article 6.

5 Arbitration agreement

FAST FORWARD

An arbitration agreement is an agreement by the parties to submit **disputes** arising under a contract to arbitration.

Key term

An **arbitration agreement** is an agreement by the parties to submit to arbitration all or certain disputes which have arisen or which may arise between them in respect of a defined legal relationship, whether contractual or not: Article 7(1). An arbitration agreement may be in the form of an arbitration clause or in the form of a separate agreement.

5.1 Form of the arbitration agreement

FAST FORWARD

The **Model Law** requires that an arbitration agreement be in **writing**, but this may be by written reference to a clause in another document.

An **arbitration agreement** may be a separate agreement, or may be a clause in another agreement. For example, a contract for the international sale of goods or other commercial relationships.

Exam focus point

When answering scenario questions in the area of commercial arbitration always look for an arbitration agreement; remember that one is required before the parties can go to arbitration.

The Model Law requires that **the arbitration agreement be in writing**: Article 7(2). What constitutes writing is explained in the Model Law.

Key term

A **written arbitration agreement** is one contained in a document signed by the parties or in an exchange of communications which provide a record of the agreement. It may also be in an exchange of statements of claim and defence in which the existence of an agreement is alleged by one party and not denied by another. The reference in a contract to a document containing an arbitration clause constitutes an arbitration agreement, provided that the contract is in writing and the reference is such as to make that clause part of the contract.

As you can see from the key term, an **agreement can be 'in writing'** in three ways:

(a) It is **contained in a document** providing written evidence of the agreement.

(b) It is **referred to** by a party **in documents relating to legal proceedings** and the other party does not deny its existence.

(c) A written contract between the parties **makes reference** to another document containing an arbitration agreement.

5.1.1 Example: form of arbitration agreement

To illustrate the point in (c) above, the following situation could arise:

A and B, whose places of business are in different states, are contracting for the sale of goods by A to B in June 20X9. They have contracted on a similar basis before, in December 20X7. The December 20X7 contract contained significant detail about the relationship that was to exist between the parties, including an arbitration agreement. The December 20X7 contract was in writing.

BPP
LEARNING MEDIA

Part A Essential elements of legal systems | **3: Court-based adjudication and alternative dispute resolution mechanisms**   **45**

The June 20X9 contract could be a much shorter document, detailing the goods and the price, and it might state that all other conditions of the contract are to be the same as the December 20X7 contract.

In this case, the June 20X9 contract contains an **arbitration agreement**, because it makes reference to a **previous document** containing an arbitration agreement.

5.2 Court proceedings

The Model Law sets out how arbitration **interacts** with the court system.

If an action is brought before a court in relation to a matter which is subject to an arbitration agreement, the court should **refer the matter to arbitration**, unless they find that the clause is null and void, for example, if it was not in writing: Article 8(1).

Arbitral proceedings may be commenced where a matter is subject to arbitration, even if court proceedings have been initiated and are continuing in respect of the agreement: Article 8(2).

UN Case 57

The facts: A Hong Kong company which was a subsidiary of a Korean company (Company A) had an agreement with another Hong Kong company (Company B). The contract contained an arbitration clause providing for arbitration in a third country, under the rules of that third country and in accordance with the rules of the International Commercial Arbitration Association.

Company B sued for damages in the Hong Kong courts under the contract, claiming that the arbitration clause was null and void because it referred by mistake to an unspecified third country, or inoperative because it referred to a non-existent organisation and non-existent rules.

Decision: The court found that the clause sufficiently indicated the parties' intention to arbitrate. The references did not make it impossible to perform, because it could be performed in any country other than where the parties had their place of business and under the law of arbitration of that place.

---

6 Arbitral tribunal

6.1 Composition of the arbitral tribunal

The **number of arbitrators** in the arbitral tribunal may be agreed by the parties but will otherwise be three. If the parties do not agree on how to appoint the arbitrators, each shall appoint one and the two so appointed will appoint a third arbitrator.

The **parties may determine the number of arbitrators** to make up the arbitral tribunals. **If the parties do not do so**, the Model Law states that **there will be three arbitrators**: Article 10.

The **parties may agree on how the arbitrators are to be appointed**. If they do not agree on a method, the Model Law sets out how arbitrators are to be appointed. However, even if the parties agree on their own method, there are a number of **rules** which **must be observed**: Article 11.

(a) A person will not be stopped from being an arbitrator on the grounds of his nationality.

(b) If the parties fail to appoint arbitrators by the agreed procedure, any party may request that the relevant authority or court, specified in their national law, appoint an arbitrator.

(c) If any of the arbitrators or relevant third parties to the agreement fails to perform his functions properly, any party may apply to the relevant authority or court to take action.

(d) Any decision taken by the relevant authority or court in relation to (b) and (c) will not be subject to appeal.

Appointment of the arbitrator: Article 11	
Arbitration with three arbitrators	Each party to the agreement will appoint one arbitrator. This should be done within 30 days of the request to do so. The two appointed arbitrators shall appoint a third arbitrator. This should be done within 30 days of the appointment of the first two arbitrators.
Arbitration with sole arbitrator	If the parties have agreed that there shall be a sole arbitrator, they shall agree on who that arbitrator will be. If the parties cannot agree on the sole arbitrator, either party may request that the relevant authority or court specified in their national law shall appoint the arbitrator.

6.2 Independent and impartial arbitrators

FAST FORWARD

The arbitrators should be **independent** and **qualified**. They should disclose any relevant facts that might make them not independent or impartial.

The arbitrator should be **independent** and **impartial** in relation to the matter. He should also possess any qualifications specified in the arbitration agreement: Article 11(5).

When someone is asked to be an arbitrator, they must **disclose any relevant facts** that **might make them not independent or impartial** in relation to the matter being arbitrated. They should continue to do this throughout the process of arbitration, if relevant circumstances arise: Article 12.

Under Article 12, a party may **challenge the appointment of the arbitrator** if he feels the arbitrator:

- Is **not independent and impartial**
- **Does not possess the qualifications required** by the arbitration agreement

6.2.1 Challenging an arbitrator

A person **cannot** challenge an arbitrator in whose appointment they were involved on the grounds of matters of which they were aware at the time of the appointment: Article 12.

The parties may agree on the **procedures for challenging an arbitrator**. If they do not, the Model Law sets out a challenge procedure: Article 13.

If the challenge procedure agreed upon is not successful, the challenging party may **refer the matter to the relevant authority or court** within 30 days. The arbitral tribunal (including the challenged arbitrator) may continue the arbitration while such action is pending.

Challenging the appointment of an arbitrator
Any party who intends to challenge the appointment of an arbitrator must send a **written statement** of their challenge to the arbitral tribunal within 15 days of becoming aware of the grounds for a challenge.
The challenged arbitrator may **withdraw** from office as a result of the challenge.
The other party may **agree to the challenge**, in which case the challenged arbitrator must withdraw.
If the arbitrator does not withdraw and the other party does not agree with the challenge, the **arbitral tribunal** must decide on the challenge.
If a challenge is unsuccessful, the challenger has a further **30 days** to ask the court to decide on the challenge.
Once the court has decided on the challenge, **no further appeal** may be made.
While the challenge is proceeding the original arbitral tribunal, including the challenged arbitrator, may **continue** the arbitral proceedings and make an award.

6.2.2 Arbitrator unable to act

If it becomes impossible for the arbitrator to act, his appointment is **terminated** if he withdraws from office or if the parties agree that it is terminated: Article 14. If there is any controversy about whether an arbitrator is still validly appointed, any party may **refer the matter to the relevant authority or court**. Where an arbitrator has withdrawn, a **substitute arbitrator** can be appointed on the same basis that the original arbitrators were appointed: Article 15.

6.3 Jurisdiction of the arbitral tribunal

FAST FORWARD

The tribunal can rule on **anything in its jurisdiction**.

If the arbitration agreement is a clause in a different contract, the arbitration clause shall be treated as being an independent part of the contract. This means that if the **arbitral tribunal** concludes that the contract is null and void, this does not affect the arbitration clause, and therefore the fact that the dispute should be settled in arbitration. The arbitral tribunal may rule on anything in its jurisdiction, including on **whether an agreement contains an arbitration agreement**: Article 16.

7 Conduct of arbitral proceedings

FAST FORWARD

The parties may agree on the **procedure** to be followed. If they do not, the tribunal shall **conduct proceedings as they see fit**.

The following general rules apply to arbitration tribunal proceedings:

(a)   The parties shall be treated with **equality** and each party shall be given a **full opportunity to present his case**: Article 18

(b)   The **parties are free to agree on the procedure** to be followed, subject to the requirements of the Model Law: Article 19

(c)   **If the parties do not agree** on a procedure, the **arbitral tribunal shall conduct the arbitration in a manner which it considers fit**: Article 19

Arbitration proceedings: general points		
Place (Art 20)	(a)	The parties shall agree on the place of arbitration.
	(b)	If the parties do not agree, the arbitral tribunal shall determine where the arbitration takes place. They shall consider the circumstances of the case and the convenience for the parties.
Commencement (Art 21)	(a)	The parties shall agree upon when arbitral proceedings commence.
	(b)	If the parties do not agree on when arbitral proceedings commence, then they commence when the request for referral to arbitration is received by the respondent.
Language (Art 22)	(a)	The parties may agree what language proceedings are to be conducted in.
	(b)	If they do not so agree, the arbitral tribunal may determine the language that will be used.
		The arbitral tribunal may order that documentary evidence be accompanied by translations into the language being used for the proceedings.
Experts (Art 26)		Unless the parties agree not to, the arbitral tribunal may appoint one or more experts to report to it on relevant, specific issues determined by the tribunal. If the tribunal considers it necessary, the expert may be questioned by the parties, and expert witnesses may testify.
Court assistance (Art 27)		The arbitral tribunal itself, or one of the parties, with permission from the arbitral tribunal may request assistance in taking evidence from a competent court.

7.1 Statements of claim and in defence

The claimant must make a **statement of claim** and the defendant shall make a **statement in defence**.

The **claimant** (person referring the matter to arbitration) shall state, under Article 23,

- The **facts** supporting his claim
- The **points at issue**
- Any **remedy** sought

The defendant shall state their **defence** in respect of these particulars.

7.1.1 Timing

The **statements of both claim and in defence** shall be made within the period of time agreed by the parties. If they have not come to an agreement on when the statements shall be made, the arbitral tribunal may decide.

7.1.2 Other documents

The parties may include documents that they consider to be **relevant with their claims**, or make reference to them. The parties may also supplement their statements during proceedings.

7.1.3 Failure to provide written statements

If the claimant fails to provide a **statement of claim** within the time period, the arbitral tribunal shall terminate proceedings. However, if the defendant fails to provide a **statement of defence**, the arbitral tribunal shall not treat this as admission of guilt in itself and will continue with proceedings.

7.2 Hearings and written proceedings

Proceedings may be **oral** or **written**.

Unless the parties have made any **agreements to the contrary**, the arbitral tribunal shall decide under Article 24 whether:

- To hold **oral hearings** for the presentation of evidence, or
- To conduct proceedings on the basis of **documents**.

If the parties have not agreed otherwise, the arbitral tribunal shall carry out **oral hearings if requested** by one of the parties.

The parties shall be given **advance warning** of hearings or any inspection of goods or documents by the arbitral tribunal.

All statements, documents and other information from one party shall be **publicised** to the other. Any material, such as expert evidence, used by the tribunal in coming to its decision shall be made available to both parties.

If either of the parties **fails to appear** at a hearing or produce documentary evidence the arbitral tribunal will continue with the case, and will make its decision on the basis of evidence available to it: Article 25.

7.3 Challenging the jurisdiction of the arbitral tribunal

There are rules on when and how the jurisdiction of the arbitral tribunal may be **challenged**.

If a party wants to **challenge the jurisdiction** of the tribunal to conduct proceedings, such a plea must be raised before the statement of defence is submitted: Article 16(2).

Any party may challenge the jurisdiction of the tribunal, regardless of whether they have **participated** in appointing an arbitrator.

If the arbitral tribunal concludes that it does have jurisdiction, any party may **apply to the relevant authority or court** to decide whether this decision is valid. However, it must do so within 30 days of hearing the tribunal's decision concerning its jurisdiction: Article 16(3).

7.4 Termination of proceedings

FAST FORWARD

Proceedings end either with an **award** or with a **termination order**.

The proceedings are terminated under Article 32 when:

- An **award** is made
- An **order** of the arbitral tribunal is made to terminate proceedings.

7.4.1 Termination by order

The arbitral tribunal makes an **order to terminate proceedings** when:

- The claimant **withdraws** their claim (unless the defendant with a legitimate interest in continuing with proceedings objects)

- The parties **agree to terminate** proceedings

- The arbitration has become **unnecessary** or **impossible**

8 Award enforcement

8.1 Interim measures of protection

FAST FORWARD

Interim measures of protection may be ordered from either party while the arbitration proceeds.

The arbitral tribunal may order either party to undertake **interim measures of protection** while arbitration is proceeding: Article 17.

8.2 Deciding the dispute

FAST FORWARD

The **decision** must be a majority one, applying the law as necessary.

The arbitral tribunal shall make its decision according to the **rules of law chosen by the parties**. If the law of a particular state is designated, the tribunal shall make its decision according to the substantive laws of that state: Article 28(1).

If the parties do not specify the appropriate laws, the arbitral tribunal may make its decision according to **the law that it sees fit to apply**: Article 28(2). In any case, the arbitral tribunal shall make its decision in accordance with custom associated with the trade applicable to the transaction: Article 28(4).

The decision shall be concluded by a **majority of the arbitrators**: Article 29.

If the **parties settle the dispute** before the arbitrators take their decision, the arbitral tribunal shall end the arbitration and **record the settlement as if it had been an arbitral award**: Article 30.

8.3 Form and content of the arbitral award

FAST FORWARD

The award should be in **writing** and signed and dated by the arbitrators. It should also state the **place** of arbitration.

Under Article 31 the arbitral award shall:

- Be in **writing**
- Be **signed by the arbitrators** (or a majority of them if there are three or more)
- State the **reasons** behind the award
- State the **date** of the award and the **place** of arbitration
- **Be copied** and these copies sent to each party

A party may, with notice to the other party, request that any **error in computation or typing** in the award be corrected by the tribunal, or that an explanation or interpretation of a point be made: Article 33. Such a request must be made within an agreed time, or within 30 days if no such time has been agreed. The tribunal may make such correction without prompting within 30 days of the award being made.

If the tribunal believes that the request is justified, it must **make the correction**, or give the explanation within 30 days of receipt of the request. The correction or interpretation becomes part of the award.

8.4 Additional award

A party may request that the arbitral tribunal make an **additional award** that has been referred to during proceedings, but not included within the final award: Article 33. This must also be requested within 30 days of the receipt of the award. The tribunal may make the additional award within 60 days, if it considers the request to be justified.

8.5 Recourse against arbitral award

FAST FORWARD

Parties may apply to have the award **set aside** if they can show certain factors existed.

Under Article 34, parties may apply to the relevant court or authority (as previously specified) to have the arbitral award **set aside** if:

(a) A party to the arbitration agreement was under some **incapacity** or the agreement is not valid under the laws to which the parties have subjected it

(b) A party was **not given proper notice** of an arbitrator's appointment or of the proceedings or that party was otherwise unable to present his case

(c) The award **deals with a matter not contemplated** by the parties or not falling within the terms of the arbitration agreement

(d) The **composition** of the tribunal was **incorrect**

(e) The subject matter of the dispute is **not capable of being settled by arbitration** under the law of the State

(f) The award conflicts with **public policy** in that State. However an application must be made within **three months** after the award was made, or a request under Article 33 to amend the award was rejected.

Courts may **suspend** (for any time period) a **setting-aside proceeding**. This allows the tribunal to resume the original proceedings or take other actions that eliminate the need for a setting-aside proceeding.

Exam focus point

Exam questions may be set on the procedure for appointing members of an arbitration panel, the grounds for challenging the appointment of an arbitrator and the procedure to be followed by an arbitration panel in reaching its decision.

8.6 Recognition and enforcement of an arbitral award

An arbitral award is **binding**.

Regardless of which country an arbitral award was made in, **it shall be recognised as binding**: Article 35. To **enforce an award**, a party should make written application to the court specified under Article 36. They should supply the court with the original award made by the arbitral court or with a certified copy. If the award was not made in the official language of the state, they should provide a certified translation.

Under **Article 36**, the **court may only refuse an application** for **recognition** or enforcement if:

(a) At the request of the party against whom it is invoked, if that party furnishes to the competent court where recognition or enforcement is sought, proof that:

   (i) A party to the arbitration agreement referred to in article 7 was under some **incapacity**; or the said agreement is not valid under the law to which the parties have subjected it or, failing any indication thereon, under the law of the country where the award was made; or

   (ii) The party against whom the award is invoked was not given **proper notice** of the appointment of an arbitrator or of the arbitral proceedings or was otherwise unable to present his case; or

   (iii) The award deals with a dispute **not contemplated** by or not **falling within the terms** of the submission to arbitration, or it contains decisions on matters beyond the scope of the submission to arbitration, provided that, if the decisions on matters submitted to arbitration can be separated from those not so submitted, that part of the award which contains decisions on matters submitted to arbitration may be recognised and enforced; or

   (iv) The **composition of the arbitral tribunal** or the **arbitral procedure** was not in accordance with the agreement of the parties or, failing such agreement, was not in accordance with the law of the country where the arbitration took place; or

   (v) The **award has not yet become binding** on the parties or has been set aside or suspended by a court of the country in which, or under the law of which, that award was made; or

(b) If the court finds that:

   (i) The **subject-matter of the dispute** is not capable of settlement by arbitration under the law of this state; or

   (ii) The recognition or enforcement of the award would be **contrary to the public policy** of this state.

You can see that the grounds for **setting aside** a decision are very similar to those related to **recourse against an award**. However, there are some **practical differences** between the two procedures.

(a) A **setting-aside** procedure is **effective in all states** involved in the arbitration. This contrasts with an award for **recognition** or **enforcement** which is **only valid in the state where the party seeks recognition or enforcement**.

(b) There may be **differences in the public policy grounds** under a setting-aside procedure and a recognition/enforcement procedure, because different states are involved in the decisions.

- Court-based adjudication depends on a **system of courts** which settle disputes. A **court of first instance** is a court where a case is heard for the first time. An **appellate court**, or **court of appeal**, is a higher court where the previous decision of a lower court can be re-heard, due to a dispute over a point of law or point of fact in a decided case. Civil and criminal cases tend to have different court structures and procedures.

- In England there is a **different court structure** for **civil** and **criminal** law, although some of the higher courts have jurisdiction over both types of law.

- **Court** is generally **expensive** and **slow**, but offers a wider range of better, more enforceable solutions.

- **International adjudicators** include **international courts** (ECJ) and international venues for **arbitration** (ICA). They can sort out **conflicts of law** and the **enforcement** of settlements.

- It is increasingly common practice in commercial contracts or agreements to include a clause providing that the dispute is to be settled by **arbitration**. Arbitration is one example of **alternative dispute resolution** (ADR), which also includes **mediation** and **conciliation**.

- **Arbitration** is the settlement of disputes by an independent party usually chosen by the parties themselves.

- An arbitration is international if the parties have their places of business in **different states** and commercial if it arises from matters of a **commercial nature** (that is, relating to trade).

- An arbitration agreement is an agreement by the parties to submit **disputes** arising under a contract to arbitration.

- The **Model Law** requires that an arbitration agreement be in **writing**, but this may be by written reference to a clause in another document.

- The Model Law sets out how arbitration **interacts** with the court system.

- The **number of arbitrators** on the arbitral tribunal may be agreed by the parties but will otherwise be three. If the parties do not agree on how to appoint the arbitrators, each shall appoint one and the two so appointed will appoint a third arbitrator.

- The arbitrators should be **independent** and **qualified**. They should disclose any relevant facts that might make them not independent or impartial.

- The tribunal can rule on **anything in its jurisdiction**.

- The parties may agree on the **procedure** to be followed. If they do not, the tribunal shall **conduct proceedings as they see fit**.

- The claimant must make a **statement of claim** and the defendant shall make a **statement in defence**.

- Proceedings may be **oral** or **written**.

- There are rules on when and how the jurisdiction of the arbitral tribunal may be **challenged**.

- Proceedings end either with an **award** or with a **termination order**.

- **Interim measures of protection** may be ordered from either party while the arbitration proceeds.

- The **decision** must be a majority one, applying the law as necessary.

- The award should be in **writing** and signed and dated by the arbitrators. It should also state the **place** of arbitration.

- Parties may apply to have the award **set aside** if they can show certain factors existed.

- An arbitral award is **binding**.

Quick Quiz

1   An arbitration agreement must be in writing.

      True   ☒

      False   ☐

2   An arbitral award must be in writing.

      True   ☒

      False   ☐

3   **Fill in the blanks** in the statements below, using the words in the box.

      The distinction between (1) ....._criminal_..... and (2) ....._civil_........... liability is central to most legal systems.

      (3) ....._Arbitration_.............. allows parties to bring their dispute before a non-legal independent expert so that he may decide the case.

• criminal	• arbitration	• civil

4   The two types of court that can be found in most legal systems are:

      (1)   ....._~~civil~~_...... _courts of first instance_ ....

      (2)   ....._~~criminal~~_...... _appellate courts_ ....

5   **Fill in the blanks** in the sentence below.

      ....._ADR (Alternative dispute resolution)_.......... is any type of procedure or combination of

      procedures ....._voluntarily_.... used to resolve differences in controversy, other than court-based adjudication.

54   **3: Court-based adjudication and alternative dispute resolution mechanisms** | Part A Essential elements of legal systems

BPP
LEARNING MEDIA

Answers to Quick Quiz

1   True. Agreements must be written

2   True. Awards must be written

3   (1) criminal (2) civil (3) arbitration

4   (1)   Courts of first instance
     (2)   Appellate courts

5   **Alternative dispute resolution** is any type of procedure or combination of procedures **voluntarily** used to resolve differences in controversy, other than court-based adjudication.

Now try the questions below from the Practice Question Bank

Number
8, 9, 10

3: Court-based adjudication and alternative dispute resolution mechanisms | Part A Essential elements of legal systems

International
business transactions

Contracts for the international sale of goods

Topic list	Syllabus reference
1 Contracts for the International Sale of Goods (UNCISG)	B1(a)
2 Ratification of the Convention	B1(a)
3 Formation of a contract for the international sale of goods	B1(b)
4 Offer	B1(b)
5 Acceptance	B1(b)
6 Counter-offer	B1(b)
7 Communication of acceptance	B1(b)
8 Modification or termination of the contract	B1(b)
9 ICC Incoterms	B1(c)

Introduction

In this chapter we introduce **contracts for the international sale of goods**. We mentioned previously that the United Nations has a Convention on the sale of goods which applies to parties in member states.

In this and the next two chapters we shall look at the provisions of the **Convention** and some of the cases that have been decided on the basis of it.

We have already discussed some of the problems of contracting with people in other states. Different nations will have different requirements as to what constitutes a contract. The Convention sets out requirements about **offer** and **acceptance**, which we shall examine here.

Study guide

		Intellectual level
B	**International business transactions**	
1	**Introduction to the UN Convention on Contracts for the International Sale of Goods and ICC Incoterms**	
(a)	Explain the sphere of application and general provisions of the convention	1
(b)	Explain and be able to apply the rules for creating contractual relations under the Convention	2
(c)	Explain the meaning and effect of the ICC Incoterms	1

Exam guide

Application of the Convention is likely to come up in a scenario question in every exam, so you should regard this topic as highly examinable.

1 Contracts for the International Sale of Goods (UNCISG)

FAST FORWARD

The UN Convention on Contracts for the International Sale of Goods (UNCISG) applies to contracts for the sale of goods between parties whose **places of business** are in different states, when the states are **contracting states**, or the rules of **private international law** lead to the application of the law of a contracting state.

We have already introduced the **UN Convention on Contracts for the International Sale of Goods** (UNCISG). Throughout this part of the Text we shall be referring in detail to its Articles.

Unless excluded by the parties (Article 6), the UNCISG applies to contracts of **sales of goods** between parties whose **places of business are in different states**,

(a)   When the states are **contracting states**, or

(b)   When the rules of **private international law** lead to the application of the law of a contracting state: Article 1

Its basic principles are that it is: **international**, **uniform** and **based on good faith**: Article 7.

The fact that the parties have their **places of business** in different states is disregarded, if it does not appear either from the contract or from dealings between them at any time before or at the conclusion of the contract. The nationalities of the parties and their civil or commercial character, or that of the contract, are **not** taken into account when determining whether or not the contract applies.

Parties to a contract covered by the Convention are bound by any **usage** or custom to which they have agreed and by any practices established between themselves: Article 9. These practices may be those commonly accepted in a particular trade.

1.1 Example: Application of the Convention

If the contract was between parties in a contracting state and a non-contracting state, and the parties agreed that the **relevant law** for the contract is the national law of the contracting state, the Convention would apply to that contract.

The Convention does not apply to the **liability of the seller for death or personal injury** caused by the goods to any person: Article 5.

1.2 Sales of goods

FAST FORWARD

A **sale of goods** is an agreement by which the seller transfers, or agrees to transfer, the property in goods to a buyer for monetary compensation, called the price.

Key terms

Sales of goods can be defined as a contract by which the seller transfers, or agrees to transfer, the property in goods to a buyer in exchange for monetary compensation, called the price.

'**Property**' in this context means legal title.

Under **Article 2**, the **Convention does not apply to sales of goods bought for personal, family or household use**. This is unless the seller neither knew, or ought to have known, that the goods were bought for that use. It also does not apply to:

- Goods bought by auction
- Goods bought on execution of/by authority of law
- Stocks, shares, investment securities, negotiable instruments or money
- Ships, vessels, hovercraft or aircraft
- Electricity

Exam focus point

It is vital that you appreciate that due to Article 2, **the Convention does not apply to sales of commodities for personal use**.

If you are asked to identify commodities that fall under the scope of the Convention, then you should choose them carefully. If you stick to examples of machinery or industrial materials then you won't go far wrong.

The Convention **does not apply** to the **supply of services**, or contracts where the **main obligation** of one of the parties is the **provision of labour**. It also does not apply to contracts of manufacture where the **buyer provides the substantial part of the materials** for manufacture or production: Article 3.

UN Case 105

The facts: An Austrian company ordered brushes and brooms from a company in the former Yugoslavia but provided the materials for the production.

Decision: The Convention was not applicable because the Yugoslav company was predominantly providing labour under the contract.

The Convention applies only to the formation of **contracts of sale**, and the rights and obligations of the buyer and seller arising from them. It is not usually concerned with the contract's validity or usage, nor with the effect of the contract on the property in goods sold: Article 4.

1.3 Place of business

You should note that the Convention refers to **place of business**, not nationality. If either of the parties to the contract has **more than one place of business** and these places of business are in different states, the relevant place of business will be the **one most closely connected to the contract** and its performance: Article 10.

If either of the parties does not have a place of business, the relevant place will be the party's **habitual residence**: Article 10.

2 Ratification of the Convention

2.1 Example: states in territories with different laws

If a state has two or more territorial units in which different laws are applicable (for example, the UK has England and Scotland) it may declare whether this Convention extends to **all its territorial units** or **just some of them**.

The UNCISG has to be **ratified**, **accepted** or **approved** by member states. When doing so, member states may declare that they are not bound by parts of the Convention. If they make such a declaration, they are not considered to be contracting states so Article 1(1) does not apply: Article 92.

Two or more contracting states may ratify the Convention but '**opt out**' of the Convention in relation to each other, or in relation to persons whose places of business are in each other's states: Article 94.

Contracting states whose national legislation requires contracts to be in writing may effectively **disapply** the UNCISG in respect of its provisions which allow contracts not to be in writing: Article 96.

> **FAST FORWARD**
>
> A state which ratifies the Convention may declare itself **not bound** by certain provisions, in which case it is not a contracting state. However, declaring that contracts must still be in writing because that is the national law does not prevent it being a contracting state.

3 Formation of a contract for the international sale of goods

> **FAST FORWARD**
>
> A contract for the international sale of goods is formed when a valid offer is **validly accepted**.

A contract for the international sale of goods is concluded when **acceptance of an offer** becomes effective.

The Convention states that a contract for the sale of international goods **does not have to be in or evidenced by writing**. There are no other requirements as to form, and it can be proved by any means, including witnesses: Article 11. This may be disapplied if one of the parties is in a contracting state which requires writing: Articles 12 and 96. 'Writing' includes telegram and telex: Article 13.

4 Offer

> **FAST FORWARD**
>
> 'Offer' is a **sufficiently definite proposal** for concluding a contract addressed to one or more persons. An offer is sufficiently definite when it indicates the goods in question and makes provision for quantity and price. An offer becomes effective when it reaches the offeree and can be ended by being withdrawn, revoked or rejected.

Key terms

> An **offer** is a proposal for concluding a contract addressed to one or more specific persons that is sufficiently definite and that indicates the intention of the offeror to be bound by acceptance: Article 14.
>
> An **invitation to treat** or to make offers is any other proposal, unless the person making it clearly indicates to the contrary: Article 14.

4.1 'Sufficiently definite'

An offer is **sufficiently definite** when:

- It indicates the goods in question, and
- It makes provisions for price and quantity of the goods: Article 14

> **UN Case 53**
>
> *The facts:* A US company carried out extensive negotiations with a Hungarian company to manufacture aircraft engines. The US company made two alternative offers and did not quote an exact price.
>
> *Decision:* The court of first instance decided that a valid contract had been concluded. However, on appeal, the US Supreme Court found that the offer and acceptance were both vague. They didn't explicitly, or by implication, fix the price or make provision for that price to be determined. The acceptance was merely an expression of the intention of the Hungarian company to conclude a contract. Therefore the main requirements of an offer were not met and so no valid contract had been formed.

4.2 Commencement of offer

The offer becomes **effective when it reaches the offeree**: Article 15. An offer 'reaches' the offeree when

- It is made orally to him
- It is delivered by other means to him personally, at his place of business or mailing address
- If there is no business or mailing address, it is delivered to him personally at his habitual residence: Article 24.

This 'reaching' rule applies to **offer**, **acceptance** and any other indication of **intention**, such as withdrawal or revocation. A delay or error in the transmission of the communication, or its failure to arrive, does not deprive that party of the right to rely on the communication: Article 27.

4.3 End of offer

An offer may come to an end in the following ways:

- Withdrawal
- Revocation
- Rejection

Even an irrevocable offer may be **withdrawn** if the withdrawal reaches the offeree before or at the same time as the offer: Article 15. Remember, the rules for the withdrawal reaching the offeree are the same as for the offer reaching the offeree.

An offer may be **revoked** if the revocation reaches the offeree before acceptance is despatched: Article 16.

There are certain instances in which an offer may **not be revoked**: Article 16. These are where:

- The offer was irrevocable, or
- It was reasonable to assume the offer was irrevocable, and the offeree acted on that assumption

Key term

> An **irrevocable offer** is one that indicates that it is, whether by means of it stating a fixed time for acceptance or otherwise.

An offer, even one which is irrevocable, is terminated by **rejection** when rejection reaches the offerer: Article 17. As we shall see later, acceptance which contains additions or limitations or other modifications to the offer is a **counter-offer**, which rejects the offer and terminates it: Article 19.

5 Acceptance

FAST FORWARD

> 'Acceptance' is a statement **made by the offeree**, or other conduct of the offeree that indicates assent to an offer. Assent must be a statement or an act. Silence or inactivity cannot be acceptance. Acceptance becomes effective **when it reaches the offeror**.

'**Acceptance**' is a statement made by the offeree, or other conduct of the offeree, that indicates assent to an offer: Article 18.

Acceptance must be a **statement** or **an act**, such as the despatch of goods or payment of an agreed price. Silence or inactivity does **not** constitute acceptance.

UN Case 95

The facts: A Swiss buyer sent an order to an Austrian seller. The seller had sent the buyer a written confirmation. The buyer failed to react. When the seller sued for the price, it argued that a contract had been concluded.

Decision: The court decided that the letter of confirmation constituted acceptance under both Swiss and Austrian law, and the parties should have known that. The exchange of confirmations was also consistent with how the parties had dealt with each other in the past. Acceptance was therefore valid, and a contract had been concluded and the seller was entitled to payment.

5.1 Commencement of acceptance

Acceptance becomes **effective the moment that the indication of assent reaches the offeror**: Article 18. The **exceptions** to this rule are that **acceptance is not effective** when:

- Acceptance has not reached the offeror within a fixed timescale (if relevant)
- Acceptance has not reached the offeror within **reasonable time**

5.1.1 Reasonable time

Reasonable time will be judged in relation to the **method of communication** that was used by the offeror. An **oral offer** must be **accepted immediately** unless the circumstances indicate otherwise: Article 18.

5.1.2 Example

If an offeror made an offer by post, it is **reasonable** that acceptance could take several days, as it would be reasonable for acceptance to be posted in return.

5.1.3 Acceptance by an act

When an offer or the past transactions between the offeror and offeree indicate that the offeree may indicate his assent by performing an act, **acceptance is effective as soon as the act is performed**. Such acceptance is only effective if the act is performed in the correct time period: Article 18.

6 Counter-offer

A **counter-offer** is a reply to an offer which **purports to be acceptance** but which **varies the terms** of the offer. **Minor variations** to the offer may not be a counter-offer, unless the offeror **objects to them** without undue delay.

A **counter-offer** is a reply to an offer which purports to be acceptance but which contains additions, limitations or other modifications to the terms of the offer: Article 19.

An indication that contains such additions, limitations or modifications that **do not materially alter the terms of the offer is an acceptance of that offer**. The terms that form part of the contract will be the altered terms.

If the **offeror objects** to the new terms, without undue delay, either orally or by notice, the acceptance will not be effective.

Examples of what might constitute material alteration of the terms would be a **significant change to the price** or the **quantity** of goods being provided, the **time** or **place of delivery** or a change to **how disputes are to be settled**.

However, if the offeror had mistakenly used an old price and in the buyer's confirmation they had replaced it with the more up-to-date price, this is a **small modification** and would stand unless the offeror objected.

7 Communication of acceptance

FAST FORWARD

Acceptance must reach the offeror within the time specified by the contract or within a reasonable time. There are certain rules governing **communication of acceptance**.

An acceptance is only valid if it reaches the offeror in **reasonable time or within a time fixed by the contract**: Article 18. The period of time commences:

- From the moment the telegram containing the offer is handed in
- From the date shown in the letter containing the offer or on the envelope
- When an offer contained in instantaneous communication reaches the offeree: Article 20

Official holidays and **non-business days** are included within the time period. If acceptance cannot be delivered because the last day of the time period is a non-business day or a holiday, an extra business day is given to effect delivery.

However, **late acceptance** can be valid, if the offeror orally accepts it without delay or dispatches a notice to that effect: Article 21. Also, if there has been a problem with delivery of acceptance, late acceptance is valid unless the offeror orally informs the offeree that the offer has lapsed, or dispatches a notice to that effect.

7.1 Withdrawal of acceptance

Acceptance may be **withdrawn** if the withdrawal reaches the offeror before or at the same time as the acceptance would have become effective: Article 22.

8 Modification or termination of the contract

FAST FORWARD

A contract may be **modified or terminated at any time** provided the parties agree.

Under Article 29, a contract once formed may be **modified** or **terminated** by the mere agreement of the parties. However, if a contract is in writing then any modification or termination must also be in writing.

The UNCISG governs the formation of the **contracts** and **obligations** of the parties in those contracts to which it applies. It does not set out any internationally agreed terms for the contract and to the relative risks and responsibilities of the parties in getting goods from one part of the world to another.

9 ICC Incoterms

FAST FORWARD

Seller and buyer may include an **Incoterm** in their contract, defining the **risks and responsibilities** borne by the parties in getting goods from one part of the world to another or from one part of a country or trading bloc to another. They cover issues to do with **carriage, insurance, risk, customs documentation and duties/taxes**.

You will remember that the ICC is the **International Chamber of Commerce**. It has developed 'Incoterms', ('**International Commercial Terms**') which are **standard terms of trade** commonly incorporated in international trading contracts. They also apply to contracts for domestic trade.

There are **11** Incoterms divided into two categories: those relevant to contracts involving **any mode or modes of transport** (including cases where maritime (sea-going) transport is used in part) and those relevant to cases which only involve **maritime transport**.

The main **issues in international trade** that are addressed by deciding to use particular Incoterms are:

- Who pays the **costs of carriage** from the seller to the buyer?
- Who bears the **risk** that damage will occur to the goods at any point in time?
- Who bears the **cost of insuring** the goods?
- Where does **property** in the goods pass?
- Where does **risk** pass?
- Who pays customs duties: ie how far are **customs costs** included in the contract price?
- Who raises **customs documentation**?

The Incoterms range from the **most basic deal** (**EXW**, where the seller simply makes goods available at its premises in the country of export) to the **most all-encompassing deal** (**DDP**, where the seller delivers to a place in the country of import named by the buyer, having sorted out all the insurance and customs issues, and having paid all the tax, insurance and carriage costs). The **level of service** should be reflected in the **contract price** agreed between buyer and seller, but that is for the parties to agree. **Incoterms determine responsibilities, not the amount of the contract price**.

It is important to note that the **obligations** associated with contracts using Incoterms are not legal requirements, they will affect the rights and duties of parties if incorporated into the contract.

9.1 Terms relevant to any mode or modes of transport

The following **seven terms** can be used where the contract involves any mode of transportation.

9.1.1 Ex works (EXW)

Under such a contract, the seller has **minimum obligations** with respect to delivery. They simply have to make the goods available to the buyer at the seller's own place of business (works).

9.1.2 Free carrier (FCA)

Under this term, the seller fulfils their obligations when the goods have been **cleared for export** and handed over to the carrier named by the buyer at a named point.

9.1.3 Carriage paid to (CPT)

This is where the seller pays for carriage to a **named location**. The risk for the goods passes from seller to buyer when the goods are handed over to the first carrier.

9.1.4 Carriage and insurance paid to (CIP)

This is where **carriage and insurance** are paid by the seller up to a named destination; thereafter, the buyer assumes costs, such as import duties and other taxes. The buyer bears the risk once the goods have been passed to the first carrier.

9.1.5 Delivered at terminal (DAT)

Under this term, the seller pays for carriage costs to a **named terminal** at a **named destination**, and for unloading from the arriving means of transport and placing the goods at the buyer's disposal. A terminal can be any place, whether it is referred to as a terminal or not, for example a quay, warehouse, container yard, or road, rail or air cargo terminal. The seller bears all the risks in delivering to and unloading the goods at the terminal, and undertakes and pays all export clearance tasks, but the obligation to clear the goods for import, pay any import duty or carry out any import customs formalities is the buyer's.

9.1.6 Delivered at place (DAP)

The seller discharges their responsibilities and is no longer liable for any risks only once the goods are ready for unloading by the **buyer at** the agreed **destination**. The buyer has responsibility for import clearance etc.

9.1.7 Delivered duty paid (DDP)

This is, in effect, the opposite to the EXW term, which represents the minimum obligation for the seller. DDP means that the seller bears all the risk and is obliged to **deliver goods** to a **named place** in the **country the goods are being imported** to, **with all duties relating to that importation paid**.

9.2 Terms relevant to maritime transport only

The following **four terms** are only valid for maritime (sea-going) transportation, that is where the point of delivery and the place to which the goods are carried to the buyer are both ports.

9.2.1 Free alongside ship (FAS)

The seller discharges their obligations when the goods have been placed **alongside the ship** at a named port of shipment in the country of export. The buyer bears all risk from that moment. This term should not be used if the buyer is not capable of carrying out export formalities.

9.2.2 Free on board (FOB)

The **buyer** makes arrangements for shipping and the **seller** discharges their duty by putting the goods on board the ship in the country of export. The seller does **not** have obligations in respect of carriage or insurance of the goods after they have placed them on board the vessel. However, they are required to provide any export licence or other authorisation required at their own expense and bear the risk and expense of the goods until they are on board the vessel. Thereafter, the buyer must bear responsibility for risk of the goods from when they are on board the vessel and obtain any **import licences** required.

9.2.3 Cost and freight (CFR)

The seller **pays for all costs and freight** (carriage) to take the goods to a named port of destination in the country of import, but once the goods are on board the vessel in the exporting country port, the goods become the risk of the buyer. The seller is, therefore, required to clear the goods for export, and the buyer arranges and pays for marine insurance.

9.2.4 Cost, insurance and freight (CIF)

The seller is required to **bear the cost of insurance** and **freight** (carriage) for the goods. They must contract for carriage on the usual terms for the goods to the **named port of destination** in the country of import by the usual route and in the way normally used for such goods.

In terms of **insurance**, they must obtain insurance for the goods that enables the buyer to claim directly from the insurers in the event of loss. This should be with an insurance company of good repute. The minimum insurance cover should be that which is stated in the contract plus 10%.

Exam focus point

> An article on ICC Incoterms appeared in *Student Accountant* and is available on the ACCA website.

Chapter Roundup

- The UN Convention on Contracts for the International Sale of Goods (UNCISG) applies to contracts for the sale of goods between parties whose **places of business** are in different states, when the states are **contracting states**, or the rules of **private international law** lead to the application of the law of a contracting state.

- A **sale of goods** is an agreement by which the seller transfers, or agrees to transfer, the property in goods to a buyer for monetary compensation, called the price.

- A state which ratifies the Convention may declare itself **not bound** by certain provisions, in which case it is not a contracting state. However, declaring that contracts must still be in writing because that is the national law does not prevent it being a contracting state.

- A contract for the international sale of goods is formed when a valid offer is **validly accepted**.

- 'Offer' is a **sufficiently definite proposal** for concluding a contract addressed to one or more persons. An offer is sufficiently definite when it indicates the goods in question and makes provision for quantity and price. An offer becomes effective when it reaches the offeree and can be ended by being withdrawn, revoked or rejected.

- 'Acceptance' is a statement **made by the offeree**, or other conduct of the offeree that indicates assent to an offer. Assent must be a statement or an act. Silence or inactivity cannot be acceptance. Acceptance becomes effective **when it reaches the offeror**.

- A **counter-offer** is a reply to an offer which **purports to be acceptance** but which varies the terms of the offer. **Minor variations** to the offer may not be a counter-offer, unless the offeror **objects to them** without undue delay.

- **Acceptance** must reach the offeror within the time specified by the contract or within a reasonable time. There are certain rules governing **communication of acceptance**.

- A contract may be **modified or terminated at any time** provided the parties agree.

- Seller and buyer may include an **Incoterm** in their contract, defining the **risks and responsibilities** borne by the parties in getting goods from one part of the world to another or from one part of a country or trading bloc to another. They cover issues to do with **carriage, insurance, risk, customs documentation and duties/taxes**.

BPP
LEARNING MEDIA

1 **Fill in the blanks**.

..........*Sale of goods*.......... can be defined as a contract by which the seller transfers, or agrees to transfer, the ....*property*.... in goods to a buyer in exchange for ....*monetary*....compensation, called the ....*price*

2 An offer is sufficiently definite when:

(1) ....~~the~~ *it indicates the goods in question*...and

(2) *it makes provisions for price & quantity of the goods*...................................

3 **Fill in the blanks**.

A ....*counter-offer*.... is a reply to an offer which purports to be acceptance but which contains
additions, limitations.......... or other *modifications*.. to the terms of the offer.

4 Acceptance is effective when the indication of assent reaches the offeror, except when:

(1) *acceptance has not reached the offeror within a fixed timescale (if relevant)*......

(2) ..*—//—*................................*within reasonable time*.........................

5 Acceptance may be withdrawn if the withdrawal reaches the offeror before or at the same time as the acceptance.

True ☒

False ☐

Answers to Quick Quiz

1   **Sales of goods** can be defined as a contract by which the seller transfers, or agrees to transfer, the **property** in goods to a buyer in exchange for **monetary** compensation, called the **price**.

2   (1)   It indicates the goods in question, and
    (2)   It makes provisions for price and quantity of the goods

3   A **counter-offer** is a reply to an offer which purports to be acceptance but which contains **additions, limitations** or other **modifications** to the terms of the offer.

4   (1)   Acceptance has not reached the offeror within a fixed timescale (if relevant)
    (2)   Acceptance has not reached the offeror within reasonable time

5   True. This is also true of an offer.

Now try the questions below from the Practice Question Bank

Number
11, 12, 13

Obligations and risk in contracts for international sales

Topic list	Syllabus reference
1 Obligations of the seller	B2(a)
2 Buyer's remedies for seller's breach of contract	B2(a)
3 Obligations of the buyer	B2(b)
4 Seller's remedies for buyer's breach of contract	B2(b)
5 Damages	B2(c)(ii)
6 Breach of contract	B2(c)(i)
7 Instalment contracts	B2(c)(i)
8 Interest	B2(c)(iii)
9 Exemptions: unexpected impediment to performance	B2(c)(iv)
10 Effects of avoidance	B2(c)(v)
11 Preservation of the goods	B2(c)(vi)
12 Passage of risk	B2(d)

Introduction

In this chapter we look at the **obligations** of the parties, the **remedies** available when parties default and the issue of when **risk** (for example, the risk of loss or damage to the goods) passes from the seller to the buyer.

The obligations of the seller fall into two key categories, **delivery** and **quality**. Delivery is a particular issue in international contracts, because contracts will often involve carriage, possibly with more than one carrier. Risk is a significant issue when goods are being carried, say at sea, or by more than one party.

If the seller fails to meet their obligations, the buyer may have **remedies**. **Damages** is a remedy common to both the buyer and seller.

The obligations of the buyer and the rights of the seller if the buyer does not meet their obligations are important. The buyer's obligations fall into the categories of **payment**, and **acceptance of delivery**.

We shall also look at the common provisions in relation to **anticipatory breach**, **instalment contracts**, **interest**, **exemption**, **effects of avoidance** and **preservation of goods**.

Study guide

		Intellectual level
B	**International business transactions**	
2	**Obligations of the seller and buyer, and provisions common to both**	
(a)	Explain and be able to apply the rules relating to the obligations of the seller under the Convention: (i) Delivery of goods and handing over documents (ii) Conformity of the goods and third party claims (iii) Remedies for breach of contract by the seller	2
(b)	Explain and be able to apply the rules relating to the obligations of the buyer under the Convention: (i) Payment of the price (ii) Taking delivery (iii) Remedies for breach of contract by the buyer	2
(c)	Explain and be able to apply the rules relating to the provisions common to both the seller and the buyer under the Convention: (i) Breach of contract and in particular anticipatory breach and instalment contracts (ii) Damages (iii) Interest (iv) Exemptions (v) Effects of avoidance (vi) Preservation of the goods	2
(d)	Explain and be able to apply the rules relating to the passing of risk under the Convention	2

Exam guide

Questions on this chapter may involve a fairly complex scenario. However the question is styled, you need to know the details of the Convention to answer it effectively.

1 Obligations of the seller

> **FAST FORWARD**
>
> The key obligations of the seller relate to **delivery** and **quality**.

The rules concerning the obligations of the seller are found in Chapter II of Part III of the Convention. There are two key areas for the rules, **delivery**, **quality** and **conformity**. Also in Chapter II are a number of remedies for breach of the rules, and therefore the contract, by the seller.

1.1 Delivery

> **FAST FORWARD**
>
> The seller is required to deliver the goods in **accordance with the contract** or, if no specifications are made, in accordance with the Convention.

> **Article 30**
>
> The seller must deliver the goods, hand over any documents relating to them and transfer the property in the goods as required by the contract and this Convention: Article 30.

1.1.1 Place of delivery

The terms of the contract between the buyer and seller may **specify a place** where the goods are to be delivered. If so, the goods must be delivered to that place: Article 31.

If the contract does not specify the place, the Convention implies the following terms into the contract:

(a) **Contract involving carriage**

A contract involving carriage is one where the goods have to be transported to the buyer as part of the contract.

The seller discharges their obligation to deliver the goods by handing the goods over to the first carrier for transmission to the buyer. The carrier is the person or entity transporting the goods to the buyer, or to the next carrier, if there are several involved.

(b) **Specific goods/identified goods drawn from specific stock**

If the parties know that the goods are in a particular place at the time the contract is made, then the seller discharges their obligations by placing the goods at the buyer's disposal at that place.

Key terms

> **Specific goods** are those which are identified as the goods to be sold at the time when the contract is made.
>
> **Identified goods from specific stock** are goods which are not specific but that are part of a larger, specific stock of goods.

(c) **Other instances**

If the contract does not fall into the categories of (a) or (b) then the seller discharges their obligation of delivery if they place the goods at the buyer's disposal at the place where the seller had their business at the time the contract was concluded: Article 31.

1.1.2 Contracts involving carriage

If the **goods in carriage are not clearly identified** to the contract, the seller must give the buyer **notice of the consignment**, specifying the goods: Article 32. The goods could be identified to the contract by markings on the goods, shipping documents or otherwise.

The **means of transport** chosen by the seller must be reasonable in the circumstances and according to the usual terms of transportation for such goods.

1.1.3 Example

It would not be reasonable to send **perishable goods** on a ship if the journey will take four weeks.

When the contract involves carriage, the parties will determine which of them should **insure** the goods while in transit. **If the contract does not require the seller to insure** the goods and the **buyer requests information** from the seller so that they may insure the goods, the **seller must give the buyer the available information**: Article 32.

1.2 Time of delivery

FAST FORWARD

Delivery should take place at the **time stated by the contract**.

Delivery should take place **on the date**, or within the period, **specified in the contract**: Article 33.

If the contract specifies a period within which delivery may take place, but makes it clear that the **buyer is entitled to determine** the delivery date, delivery should take place on the date which the buyer determines.

If no date or time period is specified in the contract, delivery should take place within **reasonable time** of the contract being formed: Article 33.

1.2.1 Handing over of documents

If the contract also requires **documents** to be handed over to the buyer by the seller (for example, shipping documents), these should be handed over at the time and place specified by the contract: Article 34. If the seller hands the documents over **before the required time**, and the documents do not correctly conform to the documents required by the contract, they may correct them before the time specified in the contract for original delivery. This is unless this causes the buyer unreasonable expense: Article 34.

1.3 Quality and conformity

FAST FORWARD

> The seller must deliver goods which are of the **quantity**, **quality** and **description** required by the contract and that are contained or packaged in the manner required by the contract.

Article 35

The seller must deliver goods which are of the quantity, quality and description required by the contract and which are contained or packaged in the manner required by the contract: Article 35.

If the contract does not state what the required level of quantity and quality is, and the goods are not described in the contract, the following **conformity requirements** must be met.

1.3.1 Conformity requirements

Conformity requirements: Article 35(2)
The goods are **fit for the purposes** for which **goods of the same description** would **ordinarily be used**.
The goods are fit for **any particular purpose expressedly or impliedly made known to the seller at the time of forming the contract**. This is unless circumstances show that the buyer did not rely on, or that it was unreasonable to rely on, the seller's skill and judgement.
The goods **possess the qualities of any sample or model** held out by the seller to the buyer.
The goods are **contained or packaged in the manner usual for such goods**, or where there is no such manner, in a manner adequate to preserve and protect the goods.

The seller is **not** obliged under Article 35(2) to sell goods which conform to all statutory or other public provisions in force in the buyer's state (such as health and safety regulations) unless either:

(a)   The same provisions apply in the seller's state, or
(b)   The buyer told the seller about the provisions and then relied on the seller's expert knowledge, or
(c)   The seller knew of the provisions due to special circumstances.

UN Case 84

The facts: The seller, a Swiss company, sold New Zealand mussels to the buyer, a German company. The buyer refused to pay because the mussels had been found by the Federal Health Office to be unsafe because they contained a cadmium concentration in excess of the statutory limit.

Decision: The supply of mussels with higher cadmium composition did not constitute a fundamental breach of contract justifying avoidance of the contract and a refusal of the buyer to pay the purchase price. The high cadmium composition did not constitute lack of conformity of the mussels with contract specifications under CISG 35(2), and the mussels were still fit for eating. It was also held that, even if the buyer had established faulty packaging of the goods as it had tried to do, the contract could not be avoided. In order to justify avoidance of the contract in these circumstances, faulty packaging must be a fundamental breach of contract, and must be easily detectable. This would enable the buyer to declare avoidance of the contract within a reasonable time after receiving delivery. The buyer was ordered to pay the purchase price plus interest.

The **seller is not liable for a lack of conformity** in the goods **if**, at the time of forming the contract, the **buyer knew**, or could not have been unaware, that the goods did not conform: Article 35(3).

The **seller is liable for any lack of conformity** which exists at the time when risk passes to the buyer, even though the lack of conformity becomes apparent only after that time: Article 36(1). The seller is also liable for any lack of conformity which occurs after risk passed and which is due to a breach of any of their obligations. This includes a breach of any guarantee that for a period of time the goods will remain fit for their ordinary purpose or for some particular purpose, or will retain specified qualities or characteristics: Article 36(2).

When the seller has delivered goods before the date for delivery but there is a shortfall of quantity or some other **non-conformity**, they may deliver any missing part or make up any deficiency, up until the agreed date for delivery. This is provided it does not cause the buyer unreasonable expense or inconvenience. In such cases, the buyer may still seek damages: Article 37.

1.3.2 Buyer's duty to examine the goods

The buyer must examine the goods to ensure **conformity** as soon as possible after delivery: Article 38.

(a) If the contract involves **carriage**, the buyer should examine the goods as soon as possible after their arrival.

(b) If the goods are being **despatched immediately by the buyer** and the seller knows that, the goods may be examined on their arrival at the next destination: Article 38.

The buyer loses the right to rely on a **lack of conformity** of the goods **if they do not give notice to the seller** specifying the lack of conformity **within a reasonable time** after they discovered it or ought to have discovered it: Article 39. If they do not inform the seller within two years of goods being handed over, the right is usually lost: Article 39.

UN Case 48

The facts: A German buyer of fresh cucumbers wanted to obtain a reduction of the price because the goods did not conform with contract specifications.

Decision: The court of first instance dismissed the application because the buyer had inspected the goods at the place of delivery in Turkey and had found them to be in good order. The appellate court found that the UN Convention was applicable as part of German law and it upheld the decision of the first court. The buyers had lost the right to rely on non-conformity because they waited seven days, until the goods arrived in Germany, to give notice of the non-conformity.

The seller cannot rely on Articles 38 and 39 to relieve them of responsibility regarding lack of conformity if the lack of conformity relates to facts of which they **knew or could not have been unaware**, and which they did not disclose to the buyer: Article 40.

1.4 Third-party rights

FAST FORWARD

The Convention sets out the position regarding third-party rights to goods, especially with regard to **intellectual property**.

Article 41

The seller must deliver goods which are free from any right or claim of a third party, unless the buyer agreed to take the goods subject to that right or claim. However, if such right or claim is based on industrial property or other intellectual property, the seller's obligation is governed by article 42.

> **Article 42**
>
> The seller must deliver goods which are free from any right or claim of a third party based on industrial property or other intellectual property, of which at the time of the conclusion of the contract the seller knew or could not have been unaware, provided that the right or claim is based on industrial property or other intellectual property:
>
> (a) Under the law of the state where the goods will be resold or otherwise used, if it was contemplated by the parties at the time of the conclusion of the contract that the goods would be resold or otherwise used in that state; or
>
> (b) In any other case, under the law of the state where the buyer has their place of business.

Key term

> **Intellectual property** is a term covering a number of distinct rights which provide the owner with a form of limited monopoly or a degree of exclusivity.

Intellectual property includes:

- Trade marks
- Patents
- Copyright

In other words, if the goods are subject to such a right or claim, the buyer must have **agreed** that they are to receive goods subject to such claims.

Notice that the qualification is that the buyer **must have been aware**, or **could not have been unaware of, the right to claim**. An arbitral tribunal might conclude that a party could not have been unaware of a global branding feature, such as the Coke dynamic ribbon. The seller is also relieved from liability where the right or obligation results from the seller's compliance with technical drawings, designs, formulae or other such specifications made by the buyer: Article 42.

The buyer must notify the seller of third-party rights and claims within a **reasonable time** of becoming aware of it: Article 43. This does not apply if the seller is already aware of the claim.

2 Buyer's remedies for seller's breach of contract

FAST FORWARD

> If the **seller breaches the contract**, the buyer has the right to **require performance**, **declare** the **contract avoided**, **reduce the price** in proportion to the non-conformity and **seek damages**.

Key terms

> **Breach of contract** is **where a party fails to perform their obligations** under the contract.
>
> **Fundamental breach of contract** is where a breach results in such detriment to the other party so as to substantially deprive them of what they are entitled to expect under the contract. This is unless the party in breach did not foresee such a result, and a reasonable person in the same kind of circumstances would not have foreseen it: Article 25.

The buyer is given a number of **rights** under the Convention if the seller breaches the contract.

- Specific rights given in the Convention
- Damages

2.1 Specific rights of the buyer under the Convention

The buyer is given a number of **rights** in articles 46 – 52 of the Convention.

- Article 46: Right to require performance
- Article 49: Right to declare the contract avoided
- Article 50: Right to reduce price in relation to non-conformity of goods

When only **part of the goods** has been delivered, or only part of them is in conformity, Articles 46–50 apply to the undelivered or non-conforming parts: Article 51.

Remember that the exercise of any of these rights **does not exclude the buyer's right to claim damages**: Article 45.

2.2 Performance

The buyer may require **performance of the contract** by the seller: Article 46.

The buyer may not require the seller to perform if they have already resorted to remedy that is **inconsistent** with performance (for example, declaring the contract avoided).

The buyer may set an **additional period of time** for the contract to be performed: Article 47. If they do so, they may not resort to another remedy for breach in that additional time period. Of course, they are still entitled to make a claim for damages after the additional time period. Note that a court does not have to enter a judgement of **specific performance** against any party unless it would do so in local cases under the law of its own contracting state: Article 28.

2.2.1 Lack of conformity of the goods

If the **goods delivered** by the seller **do not conform** to the contract or Convention requirements, the buyer may require the seller to:

(a)   Deliver **substitute goods** (if the breach of that term of the contract was fundamental).

(b)   **Repair the goods** (if the lack of conformity is slight, and the request to repair is not unreasonable): Article 46.

Subject to the remedy of avoidance, even after the date for performance the **seller may remedy** their own **failure to perform** at their own expense under Article 48 if:

*   There is no unreasonable delay.

*   It does not cause the buyer unreasonable inconvenience or uncertainty as to whether expenses advanced to the seller by the buyer will be reimbursed: Article 48.

In order to take such action, the seller should **give notice to the buyer** of their intentions. This notice is **deemed** to **include a request** that the buyer should contact the seller to let them know whether late performance is **acceptable**. This deemed notice is only effective if the buyer receives it. If the buyer receives the deemed notice and does not reply, the seller can assume that this means the late performance is acceptable and carry on with their **performance**. Remember that the buyer retains the right to claim **damages**.

2.2.2 Early delivery

If the seller **delivers the goods early**, the buyer may take delivery or refuse to take delivery at that time: Article 52.

2.2.3 Excess delivery

If the seller **delivers more than was ordered**, the buyer may take delivery of some or all of the excess, or not, as they choose: Article 52. If they do accept additional goods, however, **they must pay for them** at the contract price.

2.3 Avoidance

The buyer may declare the contract avoided if a failure by the seller to perform is a **fundamental breach of contract**: Article 51. They may also declare the contract avoided, in case of non-delivery, if the seller does not deliver in the additional time period fixed by the buyer, or declares that they will not be able to deliver in a fixed time period: Article 49. A declaration of avoidance is effective only if made by notice to the other party: Article 24.

2.3.1 Example: fundamental breach of contract

Failure to perform might be a fundamental breach of contract in a contract where time is of the essence. For example, when the goods are needed at a certain stage in the buyer's production, or for a particular point in time.

The buyer **loses the right to declare a contract avoided** if the goods are delivered, unless:

(a) Delivery is late (and they do so within a reasonable time of discovering the goods have been delivered).

(b) The seller commits another breach of contract (and they do so within a reasonable time after they knew or ought to have known of the breach, and after any additional time periods fixed): Article 49.

2.4 Reduction of the price

If the goods do not conform to the requirements of the contract the **buyer is entitled to reduce the price in proportion to the lack of conformity**. This is unless the seller corrects the lack of conformity in the contract time period or the buyer refuses to accept correction which is in line with Articles 37 and 48: Article 50. In the following case, the seller did not correct within the time period, and was not entitled to do so after that time period.

> *UN Case 56*
>
> *The facts*: A Swiss retailer refused to pay the seller, an Italian manufacturer of furniture, the purchase price, claiming that the goods did not conform to the contract.
>
> *Decision*: The court held that as the buyer has resold some of the goods without notifying the seller in time about that resale, the buyer had lost its right to rely on the non-conformity of those goods. However, with regard to the rest of the goods, the buyer was granted a reduction in the price as he had notified the seller of the defects promptly and the seller had refused to remedy them. The seller offered to pay the repair costs instead, but the court held that the intention of the convention was not to cover repair costs. It was to reduce the purchase price in relation to what value the delivered goods had in comparison to the value that conforming goods would have had.

The buyer may also reduce the price if the buyer has a **reasonable excuse** for failing to give notice of third-party rights under Article 43: Article 44.

Exam focus point

> Although exam questions may focus on the remedies available to a seller for a buyer's breach of contract, it is important not to overlook a buyer's remedies if the seller is in default.

3 Obligations of the buyer

FAST FORWARD

> The buyer has obligations in respect of **taking delivery of the goods and making payment**.

The rules concerning the obligations of the buyer are found in Chapter III of Part III of the Convention. There are two key areas for the rules, **payment** and **taking receipt of delivery**. Also in Chapter III are a number of remedies for breach of the rules, and therefore the contract, by the seller.

3.1 Payment

Article 53

> The buyer must pay the price for the goods and take delivery of them as required by the contract and this Convention: Article 53.

This general requirement includes a duty to take steps to **comply with any formalities** to enable to payments to be made: Article 54.

The following provisions also apply:

(a) **Price not concluded**: Where the contract has been formed without reference to the price, the buyer and seller are deemed to have, by implication, made reference to the price generally charged at the time the contract was formed: Article 55.

(b) **Price determined accorded to weight**: Where the price is to be fixed according to weight, if there is doubt, the price is to be determined by net weight: Article 56.

3.1.1 Where price is to be paid

The contract may specify **where the price is to be paid**. If it does not, the buyer must:

- Pay it at the **seller's place of business**, or

- If payment is to be made when goods or documents are handed over, at the **place where the goods or documents are handed over**: Article 57

If the seller changes their place of business after the contract has been formed, and it costs the buyer more to make payment as a result, the seller should bear that increase in price: Article 57.

3.1.2 When the price is to be paid

The contract may specify **when the price is to be paid**. If it does not, the buyer must pay the price when the seller places the goods and/or documents at the buyer's disposal, although:

- The buyer is **not obliged** to pay until they have **examined** the goods. This is unless the procedures for delivery or payment agreed upon by the parties are inconsistent with the buyer having that opportunity

- The seller may make payment a **condition** of handing over the goods

- If the contract includes **carriage**, the seller may **despatch** the goods on the condition that they will not be released unless **payment is made**: Article 58

If a **fixed date for payment** has been set, the buyer must pay the price without the seller needing to request that they do so: Article 59.

3.2 Taking delivery

The **buyer's obligation** to take delivery consists of the buyer:

- Doing all acts which could reasonably be expected of them in order to enable the seller to make delivery

- Taking over the goods: Article 60

4 Seller's remedies for buyer's breach of contract

FAST FORWARD

If the buyer breaches the contract the seller has the right to require **payment** and **acceptance** of the goods, **declare** the **contract avoided** and **seek damages**.

The seller is given a number of **rights** under the Convention by Article 61 if the buyer breaches the contract. These fall into two categories:

- Specific rights given in the Convention in Articles 62 to 65
- Damages

If a seller seeks a remedy for **breach of contract** the court may not grant the buyer any period of grace: Article 61.

4.1 Specific rights under the Convention

The seller is given a number of **rights** in Articles 61–65 of the Convention.

(a)   Article 62: Right to require payment and acceptance of goods

(b)   Article 64: Right to declare the contract avoided

Point to note

> Remember that the exercise of any of these rights does not exclude the seller's right to claim damages: Article 61.

4.2 Right to require payment and acceptance of the goods

The **seller has the right to require the buyer to make payment, take delivery or perform their other obligations**, unless they have resorted to a remedy which is incompatible with this: Article 62.

The seller may fix an **additional time period** within which the buyer should perform their obligations: Article 63. This should be of **reasonable** length. The seller may not resort to any remedy for breach of contract during this time period. The seller is not deprived, however, of the right to claim damages for delay in performance.

4.3 Avoidance

The seller may **declare the contract avoided**:

- If the buyer's failure to perform is a **fundamental breach**, or

- If the **buyer does not accept the goods** and/or **pay for them** in the additional time period allowed by the seller; or

- The buyer **declares that they will not accept the goods and pay for them** in that time: Article 64.

Where the **buyer has paid for the goods**, the seller loses the right to declare it avoided, unless they do so:

- In respect of **late performance** by the buyer, before the seller becomes aware that performance has been rendered.

- In respect of **any other breach** by the buyer, within a reasonable time of knowing of the breach, or in the expectation of additional time allowed: Article 65.

4.4 Buyer's failure to specify

The contract may state that the buyer is to specify the **form**, **measurement** or other **features** of the goods. If they fail to do so, the seller may make the specification, taking into account the buyer's known requirements: Article 65. They must inform the buyer of this and fix a reasonable time by which the buyer can make amendments. Further failure by the buyer to act means that the seller's specification is binding.

5 Damages

FAST FORWARD

> An injured party is **always entitled to claim damages** under the Convention, regardless of any other remedy sought or obtained, though they are required to **mitigate** (seek to limit) the extent of their loss. Damages is a monetary remedy equal to the **loss suffered by the injured party** as a result of the breach.

Exam focus point

> Remember that an **injured party** is **always entitled to claim damages**, **regardless** of any **other claims** they make under the Convention.

Key term

> **Damages** is a monetary sum equal to the loss (including loss of profit) suffered by the injured party as a consequence of the breach: Article 74.

The **amount** of damages may not be greater than the loss which the party in breach foresaw (or should have foreseen) at the time of the contract being formed, in the light of known facts then.

If the buyer has avoided the contract for the seller's breach and has bought **replacement goods** they may claim the value of these as damages: Article 75.

If the seller has avoided the contract for the buyer's breach, and has sold the goods to another party, the **proceeds of this sale** should be deducted from any damages awarded: Article 75.

If the contract is avoided and there is a **current price for** the goods, the party claiming damages may, if they have not made a purchase or resale, recover the difference between the price fixed by the contract and the current price at the time of avoidance, as well as any further damages recoverable.

However, if the party claiming the damages has **avoided the contract** after taking over the goods, the current price at the time of such taking over shall be applied instead of the current price at the time of avoidance: Article 76.

The **'current price'** is the **price prevailing at the place where delivery of the goods should have been made** or, if there is no current price at that place, the price at such other place as serves as a reasonable substitute, making due allowance for differences in the cost of transporting the goods.

5.1 Mitigation of the loss

Article 77 requires an injured party to take **reasonable measures** to mitigate the loss, including loss of profit, resulting from the breach.

Examples of **mitigation** include:

- Selling goods rejected by the buyer to a **third party**
- Buying **replacement goods** from a third party when the seller has failed to deliver

If a party fails to mitigate their loss, damages may be **reduced** by the amount in which the loss should have been mitigated: Article 77.

The following English case illustrates the operation of the **doctrine of mitigation of loss**.

> *Payzu Ltd v Saunders 1919*
>
> *The facts:* The parties had entered into a contract for the supply of goods to be delivered and paid for by instalments. The claimants failed to pay for the first instalment when due, one month after delivery. The defendants declined to make further deliveries unless the claimants paid cash in advance with their orders. The claimants refused to accept delivery on those terms. The price of the goods rose, and they sued for breach of contract.
>
> *Decision:* The seller had no right to repudiate the original contract. But the claimants should have mitigated their loss by accepting the seller's offer of delivery against cash payment. Damages were limited to the amount of their assumed loss if they had paid in advance, which was interest over the period of pre-payment.

6 Breach of contract

FAST FORWARD

A party may **suspend performance** if they have reason to believe that the other party will not perform a substantial part of the contract. A party suspending performance should give notice to the other party, and if the other party assures performance, the suspension should not be carried out. In cases of **fundamental breach**, the contract may be **avoided**.

Attention!

Remember, **breach of contract** is defined as the failure of one party to perform their obligations under the contract.

6.1 Anticipatory breach: suspension of performance

The Convention gives parties the right to **suspend performance** in certain situations. The general rule is as follows: a party may suspend performance if, after the contract starts, it becomes apparent that the other party will not perform a substantial part of their obligations due to:

- A serious deficiency in their ability to perform, or their creditworthiness
- Their conduct in preparing to perform/performing the contract: Article 71

What this means is that a party may suspend performance if the other party is in **anticipatory breach**. In other words, it is clear that the party will breach the contract, even if the time for performance has not arrived.

In order to suspend performance, the person suspending performance must give the other party **notice** of their actions. If the other party gives adequate **assurance** that they are going to perform the contract, then the suspending party must **not suspend performance**, but must **carry on** with it: Article 71.

If the seller has already dispatched the goods before grounds for believing the buyer will be in anticipatory breach become evident, they may **prevent the goods being handed over** to the buyer. This may be even though the buyer holds documents of title: Article 71.

6.2 Fundamental breach: avoidance of the contract

In order for a breach of contract to be classified as fundamental, it must result in **such detriment** to the other party as to **substantially deprive** them of what they are **entitled to expect under the contract**. The consequences must be foreseeable by the party in breach or by a reasonable person in similar circumstances: Article 25

If it becomes clear that the other party is going to commit a fundamental breach of contract, the other party may **declare the contract avoided**: Article 72. If time allows, they must give reasonable notice of avoiding the contract in order to give the other party time to provide adequate assurance of performance. This is unless the other party has declared that they will not perform their obligations: Article 72.

7 Instalment contracts

> **FAST FORWARD**
>
> Failure to perform an **instalment** of a contract may allow the other party to avoid that instalment or the whole contract.

It may be that the contract is set up to be in **instalments** (of delivery or payment) under Article 73.

If a party fails to perform their obligations in relation to any instalment and this causes the instalment or whole contract to be fundamentally breached, the other party has certain rights. They may declare the contract **avoided** with respect to that instalment (Article 73(1)) **or** in respect of the whole contract (Article 73(2)). The latter is the case where failure to perform one instalment gives the other party a reasonable basis to assume the rest of the contract won't be fulfilled. The party may declare the contract avoided in respect of future deliveries if they do so within a reasonable time: Article 73(2). If deliveries are interdependent, and so the purpose contemplated when the contract was formed is frustrated, the contract may also be avoided: Article 73(3).

8 Interest

> **FAST FORWARD**
>
> A party who fails to pay the price or any sum in arrears will be required to pay **interest** on the overdue sum at a statutory rate.

If a party fails to pay the price or any sum that is in arrears, the other party is entitled to receive **interest on that overdue sum**: Article 78. This interest would be at an applicable statutory rate, and would not prejudice any claim for damages.

9 Exemptions: unexpected impediment to performance

Parties are not liable for non-performance due to **unexpected impediments** out of their control.

A party to an international contract is **not** liable to pay damages for a failure to perform any of their obligations if they can prove that the failure was due to an **impediment beyond their control**: Article 79(1). They must also show that they could not **reasonably have been expected to have taken the impediment into account at the time** of the conclusion of the contract, or to have avoided or overcome the impediment or its consequences. The exemption from liability only has effect for the period during which the impediment exists: Article 79(3).

Sometimes the party who suffered the impediment did so because of a **failure by a third party** (sub-contractor) whom they had engaged to perform the whole or part of the contract's obligations. In this case, the party is only exempt from liability under Article 79(2) if they can prove that both they themselves and the sub-contractor would be exempt under the terms of Article 79(1).

Where a party who fails to perform because of an impediment wishes to benefit from **exemption** under Article 79, they must give **notice** of the impediment to the other party and its effect on their ability to perform. However, this notice must be received by the other party within a reasonable time after the defaulting party knew or ought to have known of the impediment. If there is delay in this respect then the defaulting party is liable for damages resulting from the injured party's non-receipt of notice: Article 79(4).

Article 79 affects **only the parties' rights in respect of damages** under the Convention. Any other right available under the Convention, such as reduction of the price, is unaffected by Article 79: Article 79(5).

If one party's **act or omission** causes failure of the other party to perform, the first party may not rely on the second party's failure to perform: Article 80.

10 Effects of avoidance

Avoidance of the contract releases both parties from their obligations, but does not affect the parties' rights to apply for damages, any provisions for the settlement of disputes or the ability to claim restitution.

Avoiding the contract releases both parties from their obligations under the contract: Article 81. This does not affect:

- The parties' right to make a claim for **damages**

- Any provisions in relation to the **settlement of disputes**

- Any other provisions in the contract governing the parties' rights and obligations in the event of avoidance

- The right to claim **restitution of the goods** by a party who has performed the contract wholly or in part

You should note that the right to avoid the contract is lost if **restitution of the goods cannot take place** (for example, if they have been sold on to a third party): Article 82. The buyer can still claim damages: Article 83. When both parties are bound to make restitution, they must do so concurrently.

However, despite **impossibility of restitution**, one party may still avoid the contract or require delivery of substitute goods if:

- The impossibility of restitution is not due to their act or omission,

- The goods have deteriorated or perished because of examination by the buyer, or

- The goods have been sold, consumed or transformed by the buyer before they discovered their lack of conformity: Article 82.

When the buyer cannot claim restitution or avoid the contract, but has paid the price, the seller must **refund the price plus interest**: Article 84. Whether or not they make restitution of the goods, the buyer must account to the seller for all benefits they have derived from the goods: Article 84.

11 Preservation of the goods

Both parties have a duty to take reasonable steps to **preserve the goods** when they are in their possession.

Both parties have a duty to take reasonable steps to **preserve the condition of goods** belonging to the **other party** which are in their possession. In some cases, if the only reasonable step to take is to sell the goods to a third party and realise their value, both parties may take this step if they have given notice to the other party. The duty falls particularly on the parties in the following situations:

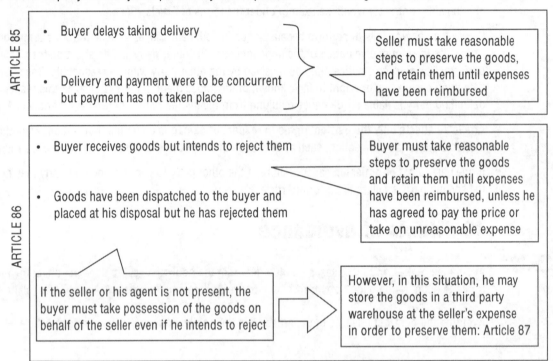

ARTICLE 85

- Buyer delays taking delivery

- Delivery and payment were to be concurrent but payment has not taken place

Seller must take reasonable steps to preserve the goods, and retain them until expenses have been reimbursed

ARTICLE 86

- Buyer receives goods but intends to reject them

- Goods have been dispatched to the buyer and placed at his disposal but he has rejected them

Buyer must take reasonable steps to preserve the goods and retain them until expenses have been reimbursed, unless he has agreed to pay the price or take on unreasonable expense

If the seller or his agent is not present, the buyer must take possession of the goods on behalf of the seller even if he intends to reject

However, in this situation, he may store the goods in a third party warehouse at the seller's expense in order to preserve them: Article 87

A party who is bound to preserve the goods may **sell** them by any appropriate means. They can do this if there has been an unreasonable delay by the other party in taking possession of the goods, in taking them back, or in paying the price or the cost of preservation, provided that reasonable notice of the intention to sell has been given to the other party: Article 88.

Where goods are subject to rapid **deterioration**, or their preservation would involve **unreasonable expense**, the party **must** take reasonable measures to sell them, and to give notice of this to the other party if possible. Any party selling goods in these circumstances can retain amounts from the proceeds of sale to cover **preservation and selling expenses**, but must account for the balance to the other party: Article 88.

12 Passage of risk

In contracts **involving carriage**, if not otherwise specified by the parties, risk passes to the buyer **when the goods are given to the first carrier**. In contracts **not involving carriage**, if not otherwise specified by the parties, risk passes to the buyer **when they take over the goods**.

Article 66

Loss of or damage to the goods after risk has passed to the buyer does not discharge them from their obligation to pay the price, unless loss or damage is due to an act or omission of the seller: Article 66.

A key issue for parties to contracts for sales of goods is **'when does risk pass?'** In other words, when does the risk of loss or damage to the goods pass from the seller to the buyer? The answer falls into three parts, depending on whether the contract includes **carriage** or not and whether the goods are sold when already in transit.

12.1 Contract including carriage

The **contract may specify the place** at which risk passes to the buyer. If it does, then the **risk passes** to the buyer **when the goods are transferred to the carrier at that place** (even if the seller is authorised to retain documentation at that time): Article 67.

If the **contract does not specify** the place at which risk passes to the buyer, then **risk passes** when the **goods are transferred to the first carrier** for transmission to the buyer: Article 67.

However, in either case, **risk does not pass** to the buyer **unless** the **goods are clearly identified** to the contract, by markings, shipping documents, notice or otherwise.

12.2 Contracts for goods sold in transit

Goods may sometimes be sold when they have already been put in **transit** from the place of manufacture (say, Korea) to some distribution centre (say, Hamburg). The risk in goods sold in transit passes to the buyer from the time the contract is concluded. This is when the circumstances are such that the risk is assumed by the buyer from the time the goods were handed over to the carrier who issued the documents embodying the contract of carriage. Nevertheless, if at the time of the conclusion of the contract of sale the seller knew or should have known that the goods had been lost or damaged and did not tell the buyer, the seller keeps the risk: Article 68.

12.3 Contracts not including carriage

Risk passes to the buyer when they take over the goods, or the goods are **placed at their disposal** and they commit breach by not taking delivery of them: Article 69.

If the buyer is bound to take over the goods at a place **other than the seller's place of business**, risk passes to the buyer when delivery is due and the **buyer is aware** that the **goods have been placed at their disposal**: Article 69. When the seller has committed a fundamental breach of contract, the rules on risk in Articles 67-69 do not affect the buyer's remedies for breach: Article 70.

12.4 Risk and non-conformity of the goods

If the **goods do not conform** to the required standards of **quality**, **quantity** and **description** and this is not discovered until after risk has passed to the buyer, the seller is still liable for this lack of conformity if it is due to a breach of their obligations: Article 36.

PO11 requires you to identify and manage financial risk. Knowledge of the passage of risk will enable you to appreciate risk of loss in international sales and to identify ways of managing it.

Chapter Roundup

- The key obligations of the seller relate to **delivery** and **quality**.

- The seller is required to deliver the goods in **accordance with the contract** or, if no specifications are made, in accordance with the Convention.

- **Delivery** should take place at the **time stated by the contract**.

- The seller must deliver goods which are of the **quantity**, **quality** and **description** required by the contract and that are contained or packaged in the manner required by the contract.

- The Convention sets out the position regarding third-party rights to goods, especially with regard to **intellectual property**.

- If the **seller breaches the contract**, the buyer has the right to **require performance**, **declare** the **contract avoided**, **reduce the price** in proportion to the non-conformity and **seek damages**.

- The buyer has obligations in respect of **taking delivery of the goods and making payment**.

- If the buyer breaches the contract, the seller has the right to require **payment** and **acceptance** of the goods, **declare** the **contract avoided** and **seek damages**.

- An injured party is **always entitled to claim damages** under the Convention, regardless of any other remedy sought or obtained, though they are required to **mitigate** (seek to limit) the extent of their loss. Damages is a monetary remedy equal to the **loss suffered by the injured party** as a result of the breach.

- A party may **suspend performance** if they have reason to believe that the other party will not perform a substantial part of the contract. A party suspending performance should give notice to the other party, and if the other party assures performance, the suspension should not be carried out. In cases of **fundamental breach**, the contract may be **avoided**.

- Failure to perform an **instalment** of a contract may allow the other party to avoid that instalment or the whole contract.

- A party who fails to pay the price or any sum in arrears will be required to pay **interest** on the overdue sum at a statutory rate.

- Parties are not liable for non-performance due to **unexpected impediments** out of their control.

- **Avoidance** of the contract releases both parties from their obligations, but does not affect the parties' rights to apply for damages, any provisions for the settlement of disputes or the ability to claim restitution.

- Both parties have a duty to take reasonable steps to **preserve the goods** when they are in their possession.

- In contracts **involving carriage**, if not otherwise specified by the parties, risk passes to the buyer **when the goods are given to the first carrier**. In contracts **not involving carriage**, if not otherwise specified by the parties, risk passes to the buyer **when they take over the goods**.

Quick Quiz

1   Name two conformity requirements for goods sold that are set out in the Convention.

   (1) *fit for the purpose*

   (2) *possess qualities of any sample*

2   When the contract does not refer to price, the buyer and seller are deemed to have made reference to the price generally charged at the time the contract was formed.

   True ☒

   False ☐

3   What does the buyer's obligation to take delivery consist of?

   (1) *doing all acts that could reasonably be expected of him to take delivery*

   (2) *taking over the goods*

4   **Fill in the blanks**.

A party may suspend performance if, after the contract starts, it becomes apparent that the other party will not perform a ...*substantial*... part of their obligations because of:

A ...*serious deficiency*... in their ability to perform or creditworthiness

Their ...*conduct*.... in preparing to perform the contract

5   In what circumstances does the seller have a duty to take reasonable steps to preserve the goods?

   (1) *the buyer delays taking delivery*

   (2) *the payment & delivery were meant to be concurrent, but the buyer has not made payment*

Answers to Quick Quiz

1   (1)   Fit for the purpose for which goods of that description would ordinarily be used
    (2)   Fit for any purpose express or implied to the seller at the time of the contract
    (3)   Possess qualities of any sample or model used to obtain the sale
    (4)   Contained/packaged in a manner usual for such goods

2   True. The price generally charged at the time the contract was formed will apply if a contract does not refer to a price.

3   (1)   Doing all acts that could reasonably be expected of him to take delivery
    (2)   Taking over the goods

4   A party may suspend performance if, after the contract starts, it becomes apparent that the other party will not perform a **substantial** part of their obligations because of:

    - A **serious deficiency** in their ability to perform or creditworthiness
    - Their **conduct** in preparing to perform the contract

5   (1)   The buyer delays taking delivery
    (2)   The payment and delivery were due to be concurrent, but the buyer has not made payment

Now try the questions below from the Practice Question Bank

Number
14, 15, 16, 17

Transportation and payment of international business transactions

Transportation documents and means of payment

Topic list	Syllabus reference
1 Bills of lading	C1(a)
2 Means of payment	C1(b)
3 International bank transfers	C1(b)
4 UNCITRAL Model Law on International Credit Transfers	C1(c)
5 Bills of exchange	C1(d)
6 UN Convention on International Bills of Exchange and International Promissory Notes	C1(d)
7 Letters of credit	C1(e)
8 Letters of comfort	C1(e)

Introduction

In this chapter we shall look at some practical issues relating to **transportation and payment**.

We have made reference in previous chapters to the importance of carriage in an international sale of goods contract. Here we shall look at the issue of transportation documents, specifically **bills of lading**. These are documents issued by the physical carrier of the goods to the person with whom the shipper has contracted to transport the goods.

When contracts for the international sale of goods have been concluded, as we have seen in the previous chapter, **payment of the price** must take place. Making payments internationally is more complicated than making payments within your own country. For example, a British cheque will not be acceptable to an American supplier.

However, increasing globalisation of banks and banking methods means that making **international payments** is more straightforward than it has ever been. We shall look at three methods - **bank transfers**, **bills of exchange** and **letters of credit**.

UNCITRAL has treaties in existence setting out international law for the use of **credit transfers** and **bills of exchange** which we shall cover.

Study guide

		Intellectual level
C	**Transportation and payment of international business transactions**	
1	**Transportation documents and means of payment**	
(a)	Define and explain the operation of bills of lading	1
(b)	Explain the operation of bank transfers	1
(c)	Explain and be able to apply the rules of UNCITRAL Model Law on International Credit Transfer	2
(d)	Explain and be able to apply the rules of the UN Convention on International Bills of Exchange and International Promissory Notes	2
(e)	Explain the operation of letters of credit and letters of comfort	2

Exam guide

Transportation documents and payment are likely to be examined in multiple choice questions, but there is nothing stopping the issues in this chapter from cropping up in scenario questions in the exam.

1 Bills of lading

FAST FORWARD

Carriage is an important feature of international contracts for the sale of goods. The **bill of lading** is therefore an important document because it is evidence of when the goods have passed to the carrier. This is a sign that risk has passed to the buyer.

Goods will usually be transported to the buyer by a third party — a courier or shipping company. This may be **complicated** by the fact that delivery is obtained through one third party and subcontracted or otherwise carried out by another different party. This is illustrated in the following diagram.

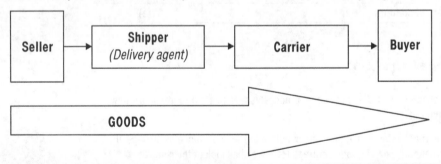

FAST FORWARD

Bills of lading may be **negotiable** or **non-negotiable**, and they may take the form of an inland, ocean or through bill of lading, or an airway bill.

An important document associated with the transfer of goods from the buyer to the seller in this arrangement is a **bill of lading**.

Key term

A **bill of lading** is a document which is issued by a carrier to the shipper, acknowledging that the carrier has received the shipment of goods and that they have been placed on board a particular vessel, bound for a particular destination.

The **bill of lading** does three things:

(a)   It provides **evidence** that the goods described in it have been **received by the carrier** (and, if it is a shipped bill of lading, that they have been shipped).

(b)   It either provides evidence of, or contains within it, the **contract of carriage** and the terms on which the goods are to be carried.

(c)   It can be a **document of title** to the goods being shipped.

It will also usually state **to whom the goods are being shipped**. The seller is responsible for ensuring that a bill of lading is delivered to the buyer with the goods.

The bill of lading is important when you consider the **passing of risk** under the contract that we discussed previously. You will remember that if no other provision is made, **risk passes to the buyer when the goods pass to the carrier**. The **bill of lading is evidence that that has happened**, so it is evidence of when risk passes to the buyer.

A bill of lading may be one of **four types**:

(a)   An **inland bill of lading** relates to a contract for transporting goods overland to the seller's international carrier (say, from the factory to the port).

(b)   An **ocean bill of lading** relates to a contract for carriage of goods from a seller in one country to a specified port in another country.

(c)   A **through bill of lading** combines the contracts for inland and marine carriage. It covers transport from one specified point to another.

(d)   An **airway bill** relates to a contract for carriage of goods by air (both domestic and international) from one point to another.

A **very important distinction** between types of bills of lading is between those that are negotiable and those that are non-negotiable.

(a)   With a **negotiable bill of lading**, the person who legally owns the bill of lading owns the goods and has the right to re-route them. A negotiable bill is issued to the seller's order, rather than to a named recipient of the goods. The carrier holds the goods until it receives an original bill of lading endorsed by the seller, which has been presented by the seller to the bank for payment.

(b)   With a **non-negotiable bill of lading** (which includes all airway bills), the bill of lading names a recipient to whom the carrier must deliver the goods.

2 Means of payment

Payment may be undertaken by various methods including international bank transfers, international bills of exchange or letters of credit.

In a normal sale of goods, payment is effected in **cash**, by **cheque** or by **automatic clearing** between one bank and another. These methods operate perfectly effectively when the parties and their banks are in one country. International sales of goods are more complicated, and necessitate payment using: **international bank transfers**, **international bills of exchange**, or **letters of credit**.

3 International bank transfers

A common and straightforward method of making an international payment is to carry out an **international bank transfer**. Essentially, this is where the buyer orders **their bank (in Country A) to transfer money to a receiving bank (in Country B)** where it will be credited to the seller. The transfer is carried out electronically. The transaction just described, buyer to seller, is an international credit transfer. These are the most common types of bank transfer, and UNCITRAL has set out a **Model Law on international credit transfers**.

3.1 Advantages of bank transfers

Bank transfers are **straightforward** to arrange and carry out. They are contained within the systems of the bank as they are carried out **electronically** and do not require reliance on any other systems, such as the postal system.

3.2 Disadvantages of bank transfers

As bank transfers do not have to be arranged in person, there is scope for **fraudulent payments** being made if a person comes into possession of the authentication procedures for the transfers. As bank transfers are quicker than bills of exchange there is not the same **cancellation period**, should the parties become aware of such fraudulent activity.

4 UNCITRAL Model Law on International Credit Transfers

FAST FORWARD

> The **UNCITRAL Model Law on International Credit Transfers** sets out the terms on which funds are transferred from a buyer to a seller through the international banking system, and the rights and liabilities that ensue.

The **UNCITRAL Model Law on International Credit Transfers** was prepared in response to a major change in the means by which funds transfers are made internationally. This change involved the increased use of payment orders sent by electronic means rather than on paper.

The Model Law applies to credit transfers where any **sending bank** and its **receiving bank** are in different states: Article 1. The term 'bank' here refers to banks plus other entities who execute payment orders in the manner of a bank.

For the purpose of the Model Law, **branches** of a bank in different states are **separate banks**.

Key terms

> **Originator**: issuer of the first payment order: Article 2.
>
> **Sender**: the person who issues a payment order, including the originator and the sending bank: Article 2.

'Credit transfer' means the series of operations beginning with the originator's payment order, made for the purpose of placing funds at the disposal of a beneficiary. The term includes any payment order issued by the originator's bank or any intermediary bank intended to carry out the originator's payment order: Article 2.

'Payment order' means an **unconditional instruction**, in any form, by a sender to a receiving bank to place at the disposal of a beneficiary a fixed or determinable amount of money if:

(a)   The receiving bank is to be reimbursed by debiting an account of (or otherwise receiving payment from) the sender, and

(b)   The instruction does not provide that payment is to be made at the request of the beneficiary: Article 2.

A **payment order** can simply direct the beneficiary's bank to hold the funds: Article 2.

If an instruction to pay is made subject to a condition but the bank executes it by issuing an **unconditional payment order**, it thereafter becomes a full credit transfer: Article 3.

An international credit transfer is thus the **execution of an unconditional instruction** by a person to a bank to make payment to a beneficiary in another country. Clearly the person giving the instruction must make funds available to be passed down the line.

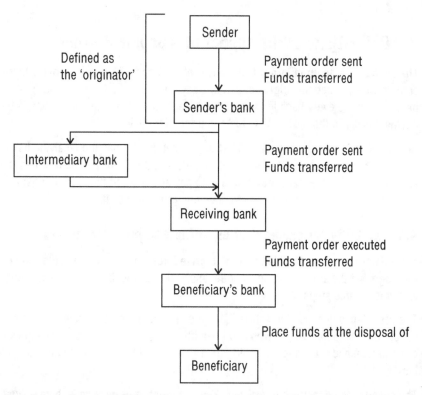

At its simplest an **international credit transfer** would involve the Sender in Country A instructing their Bank X (the sending bank) to send a payment order and fund directly to Bank Y in Country B (the receiving and the beneficiary's bank) where the Beneficiary has an account. Often, however, the receiving and the beneficiary's bank are not the same, and indeed there may be intermediary banks along the way.

4.1 Categories of transaction covered by the Model Law

The Model Law applies to **international credit transfers**, not debit transfers. It is not restricted to credit transfers made by electronic means, nor to credit transfers only by businesses. Many credit transfers, both domestic and international, begin with a paper-based payment order from the originator to its bank to be followed by an interbank payment order in electronic form.

Many credit transfers require the services of not only the **originator's bank** and the **beneficiary's bank** but also one or more **intermediary banks**. In such a case the credit transfer is initiated by a **payment order** issued by the originator to the originator's bank, followed by payment orders from the originator's bank to the intermediary bank and from the intermediary bank to the beneficiary's bank. The credit transfer also requires payment by each of the three senders to its receiving bank.

Therefore the definition of a credit transfer includes the **entire**

> 'series of operations, beginning with the originator's payment order, made for the purpose of placing funds at the disposal of a beneficiary, not just to the payment order that passed from a bank in one country to a bank in another country'.

4.2 Scope of the Model Law

Article 4 provides that **'Except as otherwise provided in this law, the rights and obligations of parties to a credit transfer may be varied by their agreement.'** This means that, in principle, the Model Law is **not** mandatory law. The parties to a credit transfer may vary their rights and obligations by agreement, with some exceptions which we shall see.

4.3 Obligations of the sender of a payment order

The **sender of a payment order** is the buyer of the goods. They are normally therefore the originator of the credit transfer, since the originator sends a payment order to the originator's bank. However, it may also be a bank, since every bank in the credit transfer chain, except the beneficiary's bank, must send its own payment order to the next bank in the credit transfer chain.

Article 5(6) sets out the one real obligation of a sender, 'to pay the receiving bank for the payment order when the receiving bank accepts it'. There is a **special rule** for payment orders that contain a future execution date. In that case the obligation to pay arises when the receiving bank accepts the payment order, but payment is not due until the beginning of the execution period.

4.3.1 Liability for payment of unauthorised payment orders

In an electronic payment order, an **unauthorised person** may have acted as 'sender' and sent the message, but the authentication by code, encryption or the like would be accurate. The Model Law deals with this in three steps.

The **first step** is described in Article 5(1): 'A sender is bound by a payment order ... if it was issued by the sender or by another person who had the authority to bind the sender'. The question as to whether the other person had the authority to bind the sender is left to the appropriate legal rules outside the Model Law.

The **second step** described in Article 5(2) is the **most important**, as it is an obligation that the receiving bank cannot avoid by agreement to the contrary.

'When a payment order ... is subject to **authentication** [by agreement between the sender and the receiving bank], a purported sender ... is ... bound if

(a)   The authentication is in the circumstances a commercially reasonable method of security against unauthorised payment offers, and

(b)   The receiving bank complied with the authentication.'

In the case of an electronic payment order, it is assumed that the receiving bank determines the **authentication procedures** it is prepared to implement. Therefore, the bank bears all the risk of an unauthorised payment order when the authentication procedures are not, at a minimum, 'commercially reasonable'.

The determination of what is **commercially reasonable** will vary from time to time and from place to place depending on the technology available, including the cost of implementing the technology in comparison with the risk, and such other factors as may be applicable at the time. If the authentication procedure is 'a mere comparison of signature', Article 5(2) does not apply.

If the authentication procedure was **commercially reasonable** and the bank followed the procedure, the purported sender is bound by the payment order. This is justified as follows.

(a)   The bank has no means to distinguish the authorised use of the authentication from the unauthorised person's use of the authentication. Banks would be unable to offer electronic credit transfers at an acceptable price if they bore the risk that payment orders that were properly authenticated were nevertheless unauthorised.

(b)   If the authentication procedure is commercially reasonable and the bank can show that it followed the procedure, the chances are that it was the sender's fault that some unauthorised person learned how to authenticate the payment order.

'The **third step** is the sender or receiving bank, as the case may be, is responsible for any **unauthorised payment** order that could be shown to have been sent as a result of the fault of that party.

Many students struggle with international credit transfers because there are many definitions to learn and the procedure for making the transfer is complicated. However, it is important not to neglect this important topic because it could come up in many different types of question.

4.4 How does the sender make payment to the receiving bank?

An **originator** may not have an account with the originator's bank and may therefore pay the amount of the credit transfer, plus the applicable fees, to the originator's bank in cash. This is often the case when an individual originates the payment order. In most cases, however, the originator will have an account with the sending bank, which will have an account for the originator at the receiving bank.

In any such case, payment to the receiving bank will normally be made by a debit to the account of the sender held by the **receiving bank**. The receiving bank is in a position to **determine** whether there is a **sufficient credit balance** in the account, or whether it is **willing to extend credit** to the sender to the extent of the resulting debit balance. Therefore, Article 6(a) provides that payment is made when the debit is made.

The reverse situation may also occur. The receiving bank maintains an account with the sending bank. Alternatively, both the sending bank and the receiving bank may maintain accounts with a third bank. Then the **sending bank** can **pay** the **receiving bank** by **crediting** the **receiving bank's account** or by instructing the third bank to credit the receiving bank's account, as the case may be. The result in either of those two situations is that the credit balance of the receiving bank (with the sending bank or with the third bank) is increased, with a concurrently larger credit risk.

Normally that would be acceptable to the receiving bank. However, on occasion the **credit balance**, and the resulting **credit risk**, may be more than the receiving bank was willing to have with the sending bank or the third bank. Therefore, the Model Law provides in Article 6(b)(i) and (ii) that payment takes place when the credit

> 'is used [by the receiving bank] or, if not used, on the banking day following the day on which the credit is available for use and the receiving bank learns of that fact'.

In other words, if the **receiving bank** does not use the credit and **does not wish to bear the credit risk**, it has a **short period** of time to **notify** the sending bank that the payment is not acceptable to it.

The receiving bank may also seek to net the obligation of the sending bank with other obligations arising out of other payment orders. The netting may be based on a **bilateral 'netting agreement'** between the two banks, or on the rules of a funds transfer system that provides for the settlement of obligations among participants, either bilaterally or multilaterally.

If netting takes place under any of these circumstances, Article 6(b)(iv) provides that payment to the various receiving banks for each of the individual payment orders occurs when **final settlement** is made in favour of the receiving bank, in accordance with the agreement or the rules. The Model Law does not take a position as to whether a netting agreement is valid or effective under the applicable law.

4.5 Obligations of the receiving bank

The obligations of a **receiving bank** are divided into the **obligations** that are part of a **successful credit transfer** and the **obligations** that **arise** when **something goes wrong**. Most payment orders that are received by a bank are executed promptly and the credit transfer is completed successfully. In a real sense, a receiving bank in such a credit transfer never has an unexecuted obligation in regard to the payment order.

4.5.1 Obligations to execute a payment order

Articles 8(2) and 10(1) set out the obligations of a **receiving bank** to execute a payment order that it 'accepts'. The **obligation** of a receiving bank other than the beneficiary's bank is to **issue a payment order** that will **properly implement the payment order** received. The **obligation** of the **beneficiary's bank** is to **place the funds** at the **disposal** of the **beneficiary**. Until the receiving bank 'accepts' the payment order, it has no obligation to execute it.

In most cases a **receiving bank** (that is, not the beneficiary's bank) **accepts** a **payment order** at the point when it **issues it own payment order** intended to carry out the payment order received. A **beneficiary's bank accepts** a payment order at the point **when it credits the account of the beneficiary**.

In those two situations the receiving bank and the beneficiary's bank undertake their primary obligation and discharge that obligation by the same act. However, a receiving bank may **accept** a payment order in some other way before it executes the payment order received.

(a) Some funds **transfer systems** have a rule that a receiving bank is required to execute all payment orders it receives from another member of the funds transfer system. In such a case the receiving bank accepts the payment order when it receives it.

(b) A receiving bank **may debit the account** of the **sender** as the means of **receiving payment** or may notify the sender that it accepts the payment order. It therefore accepts the payment order when it debits the account or gives the notice.

(c) The philosophy of the Model Law is that a bank that receives a payment order and payment for it must either **implement the payment** order or **give notice of rejection**. If the receiving bank neither implements the payment order nor rejects it within the required time, the receiving bank is deemed to have accepted the payment order and the associated obligations. Article 11 provides that normally the receiving bank must execute the payment order by the banking day after it is received and for value as of the day of receipt.

4.5.2 Obligations of the receiving bank when something goes wrong

The receiving bank also has **obligations** when something goes wrong. Some payment orders may be **defective**. A message received may contain insufficient data to be a payment order or a payment order may not be executed because of insufficient data. For example, a payment order that expresses the amount of money to be transferred in two different ways, such as in words and in figures, may indicate the amount in an inconsistent manner. The same thing may occur in identifying the beneficiary, for example, by name and by account number. Where there is **insufficient data**, or an **inconsistency in the data** which the receiving bank detects, the receiving bank is obligated to notify the sender.

The receiving bank may have issued a conforming payment order but completion may be delayed and neither the originator nor the beneficiary knows what has happened. Article 13 provides that each receiving bank is requested to **assist the originator** and to seek the assistance of the next receiving bank to complete the banking procedures of the credit transfer.

If the **credit transfer is not completed**, Article 14(1) provides that

> 'the originator's bank is obligated to refund to the originator any payment received from it, with interest from the day of payment to the day of refund'.

The originator's bank can in turn recover what it paid to its receiving bank, with interest, and that bank can recover from its receiving bank. The **chain of responsibility** for refunding stops at the bank that is unable to complete the credit transfer.

4.6 Liability of any bank for delaying payment

The liability of a bank in the chain for causing delay is to pay interest: Article 17. It is current practice in many credit transfer arrangements for a bank that delays implementing a payment order receiving to issue its payment order for the amount of the transfer plus the appropriate amount of interest for the delay. If the bank does so, its receiving bank is obligated to pass on that interest to the beneficiary. Since the delaying bank has acted in a manner calculated to **compensate the beneficiary**, the delaying bank is discharged of its liability. If the interest is not passed on to the beneficiary as contemplated by Article 17, the beneficiary has a direct right to recover the interest from the bank that holds it.

The remedy of **recovery of interest** is the **only remedy available** to the originator or the beneficiary, except when the failure to execute the payment order, or to execute it properly occurred

> '(a) with the specific intent to cause loss, or (b) recklessly and with actual knowledge that loss would be likely to result'.

In those unusual circumstances, **recovery may be based on whatever doctrines may be available** in the legal system outside the Model Law: Article 18.

4.7 Completion of credit transfer and its consequences

A **credit transfer is completed** when the beneficiary's bank accepts a payment order for the benefit of the beneficiary: Article 19. At that point the banking system has completed its obligations to the originator. The beneficiary's bank's subsequent failure to act properly, if that should occur, is the beneficiary's concern. It is not covered by the Model Law but is left to the law otherwise regulating the account relationship.

In many credit transfers the **originator** and the **beneficiary are the same person**. The bank customer is merely shifting its funds from one bank to another. In such a case completion of the credit transfer obviously does not change the legal relationship between the customer as originator and the originator's bank and between the customer as beneficiary and the beneficiary's bank.

5 Bills of exchange

the drawer, the drawee and the payee

FAST FORWARD

The parties to a bill of exchange are the **drawer**, the **drawee** (the bank) and the **payee** initially. The drawee may become its acceptor by accepting the bill. The payee may become an endorser by endorsing the bill to another holder, or the bearer.

Key terms

According to Article 3 of the UN Convention an international **bill of exchange** is a written instrument which:

becomes acceptor by accepting the bill

(a) Contains an unconditional order whereby the drawer directs the drawee to pay a **definite sum** of money to the **payee** or to their order

(b) Is **payable on demand** or at a **definite time**

bank becomes endorser by endorsing the bill to another holder, or the bearer

(c) Is dated

(d) Is signed by the drawer

The fact that is it an international bill of exchange must be clearly stated: Article 1. It should therefore contain the words 'International bill of exchange (UNCITRAL Convention)'.

The **drawee** is a person (usually a bank) on whom a bill is drawn and who has not accepted it.

The **drawer** is the person (or persons) making the payment (the buyer).

The **payee** is the person (or persons) in whose favour the drawer has directed payment (the seller).

Often the bill is presented to the drawee before it is actually payable, so that the drawee can 'accept' the bill in writing (normally just by a signature). On an **accepted bill of exchange** the principal debtor liable to pay is the drawee (the bank) rather than the drawer. Practically speaking, a bill of exchange which has been accepted means that the drawer has irrecoverably made funds available for payment to the bank.

A bill of exchange may be transferred from the payee to another 'holder' by **endorsement** – by signing it. This signature may be 'in blank' (just a signature), which means that the bill is then payable to bearer, ie any person who presents it for payment. Alternatively, the endorsement may be 'special', eg 'pay X, signed Y (the payee)'. In this case, X becomes the holder of the bill and may present it for payment.

A **cheque** is a common example of a bill of exchange, defined as a bill of exchange drawn on a banker and payable on demand but **international bills of exchange** must be used in international situations.

6 UN Convention on International Bills of Exchange and International Promissory Notes

FAST FORWARD

> The **UN Convention on International Bills of Exchange and International Promissory Notes** sets out the terms on which buyers may pay sellers by means of a written instrument. A bill of exchange represents a right to receive payment, and this right can be transferred.

Key term

> An **international bill of exchange** (according to Article 2 of the Convention) is a bill of exchange (as defined in Article 3 – **not** a cheque) which specifies at least two of the following places and indicates that any two so specified are situated in different states:
>
> (a)   The place where the bill is drawn
> (b)   The place indicated next to the signature of the drawer
> (c)   The place indicated next to the name of the drawee
> (d)   The place indicated next to the name of the payee
> (e)   The place of payment

6.1 Example: International bill of exchange

International Bill of Exchange (UNCITRAL Convention)

On behalf of Buyer Inc of Country A, I order Barchester Bank plc of London, UK$_{(c)}$ to pay the sum of \$30,000 to Seller SA of Country B$_{(d)}$ at the Smalltown branch of Country B$_{(e)}$.

Signed ......*Peter Barket Julie Sharman*...... on behalf of Buyer Inc, Country A

Date ......*19 August 20X4*......

At ......*Largetown, Country A*...... (a)(b)

In this example, the letters (a) to (e) indicate the **requirements** set out in the key term above. As the bill of exchange designates three different states (Country A, UK and Country B), and it states that it is, this is an international bill of exchange.

A bill that states it is an **international bill of exchange** (UNCITRAL Convention) and which bears the signature of the drawer or the acceptance of the drawee, but which lacks other elements, may still be completed. It will then be effective as a bill: Article 12(1).

If such a bill is completed without authority then a party who signed the instrument before the completion may invoke such lack of authority as a defence against a person who had knowledge of such a **lack of authority** when he became a holder. But a party who signed the instrument after the completion is liable according to the terms of the instrument so completed: Article 12(2).

We shall look now in detail at some of the terms used in the **UN Convention**, and at the rights and liabilities the Convention sets out.

6.2 How much the bill is for

The sum payable on a bill is deemed to be a **definite sum**. This is even if the bill states that it is to be paid:

- With interest
- By instalments
- According to a rate of exchange indicated in the bill
- To be determined as directed by the bill
- In a currency other than the currency in which the sum is expressed in the bill: Article 7

If there is a **discrepancy** between the sum expressed in words and the sum expressed in figures, the sum payable by the instrument is the sum expressed in words: Article 8(1).

If a bill states that the sum is to be **paid with interest**, without specifying the date from which interest is to run, interest runs from the date of the bill: Article 8(4). The rate at which interest is to be paid may be expressed either as a definite rate or as a variable rate.

6.3 When the amount is payable

A bill is **payable on demand** if it states that it is payable at sight or on demand or on presentation, or if no time of payment is expressed: Article 9(1). The time of payment of a bill payable on demand is the date on which the instrument is presented for payment: Article 9.

A bill which is payable at a **definite time** and which is accepted or endorsed or guaranteed after maturity is a bill payable on demand as regards the acceptor, the endorser or the guarantor.

According to Article 9(3) a bill is deemed to be payable at a **definite time** if it states that it is payable:

(a)   On a stated date, or at a fixed period after a stated date, or at a fixed period after the date of the instrument

(b)   At a fixed period after sight (determined by the date of acceptance or, if the bill is dishonoured by non-acceptance, by the date of protest or, if protest is dispensed with, by the date of dishonour)

(c)   By instalments.

6.4 Parties to the bill

6.4.1 The payee

The **payee** is the person or persons to whom the bill's drawer has instructed payment to be made.

A bill may be drawn payable to **two or more payees**: Article 10(1). In this case it is payable to any one of them.

6.4.2 The drawer

The **drawer** is the person who has instructed payment to be made. The drawer is initially principally blank on the bill, since a person is liable on a bill once they or their agent signs it: Article 33. However, a **forged signature** does not impose any liability on the person whose signature was forged, unless they consent to be bound by the forged signature or represents that it is their own.

The drawer agrees that if a bill is **dishonoured** by non-acceptance or by non-payment and it is protested as necessary, they will pay the bill to the holder, or to any endorser or any endorser's guarantor who takes up and pays the bill: Article 38(1).

The drawer may exclude or limit their **own liability** for acceptance or for payment by an express stipulation in the bill, if another party is or becomes liable on the bill: Article 38(2).

6.4.3 The drawee and the acceptor

The **drawee** is the person – nearly always a bank – who is instructed by the drawer to pay the payee.

The drawee (or another person) may, before the bill is due for payment, 'accept' liability to pay it. The **acceptor** becomes principally liable on the bill, above the drawer.

The drawee is not liable on a bill until they accept it: Article 40(1). The acceptor engages that they will pay the bill in accordance with the terms of their acceptance to the holder, or to any party who takes up and pays the bill: Article 40(2).

An **acceptance** must be written on the front or back of the bill and may be effected: Article 41:

(a)   By the signature of the drawee accompanied by the word 'accepted' or similar import, or

(b)   By the signature alone of the drawee.

A bill may be accepted before, at or after **maturity**, or after it has been dishonoured by non-acceptance or by non-payment: Article 42(2).

An acceptance must be **unqualified**. An acceptance is qualified if it is conditional or varies the terms of the bill, for instance if it accepts only part of the sum payable: Article 43(1). If the drawee stipulates in the bill that his acceptance is subject to qualification:

(a)   They are nevertheless bound according to the terms of their qualified acceptance

(b)   The bill is dishonoured by non-acceptance.

Any bill may be **presented for acceptance**, and it must be presented for acceptance:

(a)   If the drawer has stipulated so in the bill, or

(b)   If the bill is payable at a fixed period after sight, or

(c)   If the bill is payable elsewhere than at the residence or place of business of the drawee, unless it is payable on demand: Article 49.

A bill is duly presented for acceptance if it is **presented in accordance with the following rules**: Article 51:

(a)   The holder must present the bill to the drawee on a business day at a reasonable hour.

(b)   Presentation for acceptance may be made to a person or authority other than the drawee if that person or authority is entitled under the applicable law to accept the bill.

(c)   If a bill is payable on a fixed date, presentation for acceptance must be made before or on that date.

(d)   A bill payable on demand or at a fixed period after sight must be presented for acceptance within one year of its date.

(e)   A bill in which the drawer has stated date or time-limit for presentation for acceptance must be presented on the stated date or within the stated time-limit.

If a bill which must be presented for acceptance is not so presented, the drawer, the endorsers and their guarantors are **not liable** on the bill. However, failure to present a bill for acceptance does not discharge the guarantor of the drawee of liability on the bill: Article 53.

A bill is considered to be **dishonoured by non-acceptance** under Article 54 if the drawee, upon due presentation, expressly refuses to accept the bill. This will also be the case if acceptance cannot be obtained with reasonable diligence or if the holder cannot obtain the acceptance to which he is entitled under this Convention.

The holder may then exercise an immediate right of **recourse** against the drawer, the endorsers and their guarantors. The holder may then claim payment from the guarantor of the drawee upon any necessary protest.

If a bill payable on demand is presented for acceptance, but acceptance is **refused**, it is not considered to be dishonoured by non-acceptance: Article 54(3).

BPP
LEARNING MEDIA

6.4.4 The guarantor

Payment of a bill, whether or not it has been accepted, **may be guaranteed**, as to the whole or part of its amount, for the account of a party or the drawee. A guarantee may be given by any person, who may or may not already be a party: Article 46. A guarantee must be written on the instrument or on a slip affixed therefore *('allonge')*, and it may be effected by a signature alone on the front of the bill. A signature alone on the front of the bill, other than that of the drawer or the drawee, is a guarantee.

A guarantor may specify the person for whom he has become guarantor. In the absence of such specification, the person for whom he has become guarantor is the acceptor or the drawee.

The **liability** of a guarantor on the bill is of the same nature as that of the party for whom they have become guarantor: Article 47.

The guarantor who pays the bill may **recover** from the party for whom they have become guarantor, and from the parties who are liable on it to that party, the amount paid and any interest: Article 48(2).

6.5 Transferring an international bill of exchange

Instead of presenting the bill to the acceptor for payment, the payee may instead choose to **transfer** the right to receive payment to another person (for instance, a supplier they owe money to). The transfer is effected by the process of endorsement with the payee becoming the **endorser**, and the supplier becoming the **endorsee**.

A bill is **transferred** by endorsement and delivery of the bill by the endorser to the endorsee, or by mere delivery of the instrument if the last endorsement is in blank: Article 13.

An instrument may be transferred in this way after maturity, except by the drawee, or the acceptor: Article 24.

6.5.1 Endorsement

An **endorsement** must be written on the instrument or on a slip affixed thereto *('allonge')*. It must be signed: Article 14(1). An endorsement may be:

(a)   **In blank**, that is, by a signature alone or by a signature accompanied by a statement to the effect that the bill is payable to a person in possession of it;

(b)   **Special**, that is, by a signature accompanied by an indication of the person to whom the bill is payable.

A **signature alone**, other than that of the drawee, is an endorsement only if placed on the back of the bill.

If the drawer has inserted in the instrument, such words as **'not negotiable'**, **'not transferable'**, **'not to order'**, **'pay (x) only'**, or similar, the bill may not be transferred except for purposes of collection. Any endorsement, even if it does not contain words authorising the endorsee to collect the instrument, is deemed to be an endorsement for collection: Article 17(1).

An **endorsement must be unconditional**: Article 18. A conditional endorsement transfers the bill whether or not the condition is fulfilled. The condition is ineffective as to those parties and transferees who are subsequent to the endorsee.

An endorsement in respect of a **part of the sum due** under the instrument is ineffective as an endorsement: Article 19. If there are **two or more endorsements**, it is presumed, unless the contrary is proved, that each endorsement was made in the order in which it appears on the instrument: Article 20.

If an endorsement contains the words **'for collection'**, **'for deposit'**, **'value in collection'**, **'by procuration'**, **'pay any bank'**, or words of similar import authorising the endorsee to collect the instrument, the endorsee is a holder who, according to Article 21(1):

(a)   May exercise all rights arising out of the instrument
(b)   May endorse the instrument only for purposes of collection
(c)   Is subject only to the claims and defences which may be set up against the endorser

The endorser for collection is **not liable** on the bill to any subsequent holder.

If an endorser contains the words **'value in security'**, **'value in pledge',** or any other words indicating a pledge, then according to Article 22, the endorsee is a holder who:

(a)   May exercise all rights arising out of the bill

(b)   May endorse the bill only for purposes of collection

If such an endorsee endorses for collection, he is **not liable** on the instrument to any subsequent holder.

If an **endorsement is forged**, the person whose endorsement is forged, or a party who signed the bill before the forgery, has the right to recover compensation for any damage that he may have suffered because of the forgery against:

(a)   The forger

(b)   The person to whom the instrument was directly transferred by the forger

(c)   A party or the drawee who paid the instrument to the forger directly or through one or more endorsees for collection: Article 25(1)

An **endorsee** for collection is not liable however if he is **without knowledge** of the forgery at the time they pay the principal, or advises them of the receipt of payment, or at the time they receive payment, if this is later. This is unless their lack of knowledge is due to their **failure to act in good faith** or to exercise reasonable care: Article 25(2).

The **drawee** who pays a bill is also not liable if, at the time they pay the instrument, they are **without knowledge** of the forgery, unless their lack of knowledge is due to their **failure to act in good faith** or to exercise reasonable care.

6.5.2 Liability of the endorser

Endorsers agree that upon dishonour of the bill by non-acceptance or by non-payment, and upon any necessary protest, they will pay the bill to the holder, or to any subsequent endorser or any endorser's guarantor who takes up and pays the bill: Article 44(1). An endorser may exclude or limit their own liability by an express stipulation on the bill. Such a stipulation is effective only with respect to that endorser.

Unless otherwise agreed, **a person who transfers a bill by endorsement** and delivery, or by mere delivery, represents to the holder to whom he transfers the bill (the transferee) that:

(a)   It does not bear any forged or unauthorised signature

(b)   It has not been materially altered

(c)   At the time of transfer, they have no knowledge of any fact which would impair the right of the transferee to payment of the bill against the acceptor or, in the case of an unaccepted bill, the drawer: Article 45(1)

The **transferor is liable** only if the transferee took the instrument without knowledge of the matter giving rise to such liability.

If the transferor is liable the **transferee may recover,** even before maturity, the amount paid by them to the transferor, with interest.

6.5.3 The holder of a bill

Because a bill is transferred either by endorsement or simply by transfer, the person to whom it is transferred is known as the **holder** of the bill.

A person is a **holder** if they are:

(a)   The payee in possession of the bill, or

(b)   In possession of a bill which has been endorsed to them, or on which the last endorsement is in blank, and on which there appears an uninterrupted series of endorsements. This is even if any endorsement was forged or was signed by an agent without authority: Article 15(1)

If an **endorsement in blank is** followed by another endorsement, the person who signed this last endorsement is deemed to be an endorsee by the endorsement in blank.

A **person may still be a holder** even if the bill was obtained by them or any previous holder under circumstances, including incapacity or fraud, duress or mistake of any kind, that would give rise to a claim to, or a defence against liability on, the bill.

The holder of a bill on which the **last endorsement** is in blank may:

(a) Further endorse it either by an endorsement in blank or by a special endorsement

(b) Convert the blank endorsement into a special endorsement by indicating in the endorsement that the bill is payable to themselves or to some other specified person, or

(c) Transfer the bill merely by delivery: Article 16

The holder of an instrument has all the **rights** conferred on them by this Convention against the parties to the instrument, and may transfer them as above: Article 27.

The **transfer of an instrument** by a protected holder vests in any subsequent holder the rights to and on the instrument which the protected holder had: Article 31.

6.6 Presenting the bill for payment

To obtain payment of the bill, it must be duly '**presented for payment**'. This means that the holder must present the bill to the drawee or the acceptor on a business day at a reasonable hour: Article 55.

A bill which is **not payable on demand** must be presented for payment **on the date of maturity** or on **one of the two** business days which follow. A bill which is **payable on demand** must be presented for payment within **one year** of its date.

A **bill must be presented** for payment:

(a) At the place of payment specified in it

(b) If no place of payment is specified, at the address of the drawee or the acceptor indicated in it, or

(c) If no place of payment is specified and the address of the drawee or the acceptor is not indicated, at the principal place of business or habitual residence of the drawee or the acceptor

An instrument which is presented at a **clearing house** is duly presented for payment if the law of the place where the clearing house is located or the rules or customs of that clearing house so provide.

The requirement to **present for payment** may be dispensed with in some cases, most notably where it has been protested for dishonour by non-acceptance: Article 56(3). In all other cases, if an instrument is not duly presented for payment, the drawer, the endorsers and their guarantors are not liable on it: Article 57(1). Failure to present an instrument for payment does not however discharge the acceptor, and their guarantors, or the guarantor of the drawee, of liability on it.

6.6.1 Dishonour for non-payment

A **bill is dishonoured by non-payment** under Article 58:

(a) If payment is refused upon due presentation or if the holder cannot obtain the payment to which they are entitled

(b) If presentation for payment is dispensed with and the instrument is unpaid at maturity

If a bill is dishonoured by non-payment, the holder may, subject to the rules on protests, **exercise a right of recourse** against the endorsers and their guarantors.

6.7 Protesting the bill for dishonour

If an instrument is dishonoured by non-acceptance or by non-payment, the holder may exercise a right of recourse only after the instrument has been duly **protested for dishonour**: Article 59.

A protest is a **statement of dishonour drawn** up at the place where the bill has been dishonoured and signed and dated by a person authorised in that respect by the law of that place.

The statement of dishonour must specify:

(a) The person at whose request the bill is protested

(b) The place of protest

(c) The demand made and the answer given, if any, or the fact that the drawee or the acceptor could not be found: Article 60. A protest may be made on the instrument or *'allonge'*, or as a separate document.

Protest for dishonour must be made on the day on which the bill is dishonoured or on one of the four business days which follow: Article 61.

If a bill which must be protested for non-acceptance or for non-payment is **not duly protested**, the drawer, the endorsers and their guarantors are **not liable** on it (Article 63), but it does not discharge the acceptor or the guarantor of the drawee of liability on it.

The holder, upon dishonour of a bill by non-acceptance or by non-payment, must give **notice** of such dishonour:

(a) To the drawer and the last endorser

(b) To all other endorsers and guarantors whose addresses the holder can ascertain on the basis of information contained in the bill: Article 64

Notice of dishonour operates for the benefit of any party who has a right of recourse on the instrument against the party notified.

If a person who is required to give notice of dishonour fails to give it to a party who is entitled to receive it, they are liable for any **damages** which that party may suffer from such failure: Article 68.

6.8 How much is payable by the liable party?

The holder may **exercise their rights** on the bill against any one party, or several, or all parties, liable on it and is not obliged to observe the order in which the parties have become bound. Any party who takes up and pays the bill may exercise their rights in the same manner against parties liable to them: Article 69(1).

At maturity the amount payable to the holder is the amount of the instrument with interest, if interest has been stipulated: Article 70.

After maturity, the amount payable to the holder is the amount of the bill with interest, if interest has been stipulated for, to the date of maturity at the rate stipulated plus any expenses of protest and of the notices given by them. The amount payable on a bill paid **before maturity** is often subject to a discount from the date of payment to the date of maturity.

A court may award **damages** or **compensation** for additional loss caused to the holder by reason of delay in payment.

Under Article 71 a party who pays a bill and is thereby **discharged** in whole or in part of their liability on it may recover from the parties liable to them:

(a) The entire sum which he has paid
(b) Interest on that sum from the date on which they made payment
(c) Any expenses of the notices given by them

An instrument must be paid in the **currency** in which the sum payable is expressed: Article 75.

A party is discharged of liability on the bill when they **pay the holder**, or a party subsequent to themselves who has paid the bill and is in possession of it, the amount due:

(a) At or after maturity, or
(b) Before maturity, upon dishonour by non-acceptance: Article 72(1)

6.9 Advantages of international bills of exchange

(a) They provide a **convenient method** of **collecting payments** from buyers in a different state.

(b) The seller can seek **immediate finance**, using term bills of exchange, instead of having to wait until the period of credit expires (ie until the maturity of the bill). At the same time, the buyer is allowed the full period of credit before payment is made.

(c) On payment, the foreign buyer keeps the bill as **evidence of payment**, so that a bill of exchange also serves as a receipt.

(d) If a bill of exchange is dishonoured, it may be used by the drawer to **pursue payment** by means of legal action in the drawee's country.

(e) The buyer's bank might add its name to a bill to indicate that it **guarantees** payment at maturity.

7 Letters of credit

A basic **letter of credit** is issued by the issuing bank at the request of the buyer, and advised to the seller's advising bank. Provided the requisite documents are presented by the seller, payment is made by the advising bank and reimbursed by the issuing bank.

Letters of credit are **irrevocable** unless otherwise stated. They may also take a variety of forms.

Letters of credit provide a method of payment in international trade which gives the seller a risk-free method of obtaining payment, and which ensures for the buyer that the seller complies to the letter with the terms of the underlying sales contract.

(a) The **seller receives immediate payment** of the amount due to them, less any discount, instead of having to wait until the end of the credit period for payment. To obtain payment, the seller must present documents which comply strictly with the terms of the letter of credit.

(b) The buyer is able to get a **period of credit** before having to pay for the imports.

The procedure is as follows.

(a) The buyer and the seller first of all agree a **contract for the sale of the goods**, which provides for payment through a letter of credit.

(b) The **buyer** (the **applicant**) then requests a bank in his country to issue a **letter of credit** in favour of the seller. This bank which issues the letter of credit is known as the **issuing bank**.

(c) The issuing bank, by issuing its letter of credit, **guarantees payment** to the **seller** (the beneficiary/payee), provided the seller complies with the requirements as to documentation. Banks are involved in the credits, not in the underlying contracts.

(d) The issuing bank asks the seller's bank in the seller's country to **advise the credit** to the seller.

(e) The **advising bank** establishes the authenticity of, and agrees to **handle, the credit** (on terms arranged with the issuing bank).

(f) The advising bank (in the seller's country) might be required by the issuing bank to add its own **'confirmation'** to the credit. The advising bank would then be adding its own guarantee of payment to the guarantee already provided by the issuing bank.

(g) A **letter of credit arrangement** must be made between the seller, the buyer and participating banks **before the sale takes place**.

Once the **advising bank** informs the seller of the letter of credit, and/or confirms it, the seller may ship the goods. The documents called for in the letter of credit, such as the invoice or bill of lading, are presented by the seller to the advising bank. If they comply with the letter of credit, the seller is paid and the advising bank forwards the documents to the issuing bank.

Once the latter has **checked the documents**, it pays the advising bank. It then releases the documents to the buyer so the latter can claim the goods from the carrier. Letters of credit are **slow to arrange**, and **administratively cumbersome**. However, they are usually essential where the **risk of non-payment is high**, or when **dealing for the first time with an unknown buyer**. There are various **types of letter of credit**.

(a) **Confirmed letter of credit**: the advising bank (for a fee) confirms that payment will be made to the seller provided the requisite documents are presented by the seller, payment being made by the advising bank even if the issuing bank or buyer fails to reimburse the payment.

(b) **Unconfirmed letter of credit**: the advising bank does not guarantee payment even in the event of default by the issuing bank, but confirms that the letter of credit is authentic.

(c) **Revocable letter of credit**: can be amended or cancelled by the buyer at any time without notice to the seller. They are rarely used since they give little protection to the seller.

(d) **Irrevocable letter of credit**: it cannot be amended or called without agreement of all parties.

(e) **Standby letters of credit** are used in cases where another, less secure, method of payment has been agreed. If the other method fails then the seller can claim payment under the standby. These are subject to the UN Convention on Independent Guarantees and Standby Letters of Credit.

(f) **Revolving letters of credit** are used where there is a course of dealings between buyer and seller, so it is easier to keep a letter of credit open at all times which may revolve automatically or subject to certain conditions.

(g) The letter of credit may be **time-revolving**, which means it is reinstated after use for the next regular shipment, until the amount of the credit has been used up. If it is **value-revolving**, once its value has been used it can be reinstated in the same amount, for further shipments.

(h) A **transferable letter of credit** allows the seller to transfer the right to receive payment to another person who was not party to the original contract, such as the original supplier of the goods.

(i) Alternatively, a **back-to-back letter of credit** allows the seller to use the buyer's letter of credit as security to issue a second letter of credit from him as buyer to the original supplier or seller.

8 Letters of comfort

FAST FORWARD

A **letter of comfort** purports to assure a creditor that a third party will ensure payment of its debtor's debts, but it has no legal effect.

A letter of comfort is a letter issued to a **third-party lender** by a **parent company**. The letter acknowledges the parent company's approval of a **subsidiary company's** attempt at raising finance. The letter of comfort does not guarantee the loan given to the subsidiary company. It merely gives reassurance to the lender that the parent company is aware of, and approves of, the situation.

The importance of letters of comfort comes to the fore when the subsidiary nears **insolvency**, or actually becomes insolvent. At such a time lenders, other creditors and indeed the directors of the insolvent subsidiary look to the parent company and its letter of comfort, usually unsuccessfully as the cases decided to date enforce the rule that they are not binding on the parent.

Re Augustus Barnett & Son Ltd 1986

The facts: An action for fraudulent trading in an insolvency was brought against a company and against its parent company. The court refused to lift the corporate veil and identify the insolvent subsidiary with its parent company, which had issued and frequently confirmed letters of comfort to the subsidiary's creditors.

Decision: In this case the subsidiary's directors had not been fraudulent, and anyway the parent's directors had not been involved in management, so the action failed. However, it raised the suggestion that the veil of incorporation could be lifted if the parent's conduct indicated an assumption of liability.

Kleinwort Benson Ltd v Malaysia Mining Corporation Berhad 1989

The facts: Kleinworts lent £5m to a Malaysian mining company, and requested a letter of comfort from the borrower's parent company. The parent wrote: '...It is our policy to ensure that the business of (the borrower) is conducted in such a way that (it) is at all times in a position to meet its liabilities to you...', and Kleinworts evidently placed reliance on this when advancing the funds. There was a subsequent liquidity crisis in the tin industry and Kleinworts made a demand on the parent, based on the letter of comfort.

Decision: The Court of Appeal reasoned that the statement as to 'ensuring' the subsidiary's ability to meet its obligations did not constitute a promise to maintain the parent's supportive policy in the future, and there was no express promise to pay. There is some debate over this decision, and certainly the wording in letters of comfort has to be very precisely phrased if the parent is to avoid liability.

Chapter Roundup

- **Carriage** is an important feature of international contracts for the sale of goods. The **bill of lading** is therefore an important document because it is evidence of when the goods have passed to the carrier. This is a sign that risk has passed to the buyer.

- Bills of lading may be **negotiable** or **non-negotiable**, and they may take the form of an inland, ocean or through bill of lading, or an airway bill.

- **Payment** may be undertaken by various methods including international bank transfers, international bills of exchange or letters of credit.

- **The UNCITRAL Model Law on International Credit Transfers** sets out the terms on which funds are transferred from a buyer to a seller via the international banking system, and the rights and liabilities that ensue.

- The parties to a bill of exchange are the **drawer**, the **drawee** (the bank) and the **payee** initially. The drawee may become its acceptor by accepting the bill. The payee may become an endorser by endorsing the bill to another holder, or the bearer.

- **The UN Convention on International Bills of Exchange and International Promissory Notes** sets out the terms on which buyers may pay sellers by means of a written instrument. A bill of exchange represents a right to receive payment, and this right can be transferred.

- A basic **letter of credit** is issued by the issuing bank at the request of the buyer, and advised to the seller's advising bank. Provided the requisite documents are presented by the seller, payment is made by the advising bank and reimbursed by the issuing bank.

- Letters of credit are **irrevocable** unless otherwise stated. They may also take a variety of forms.

- A **letter of comfort** purports to assure a creditor that a third party will ensure payment of its debtor's debts, but it has no legal effect.

BPP
LEARNING MEDIA

1   When the contract covers transport from one specified place to another, the bill of lading is most likely to be in the form of *a through bill of lading*

2   The legal owner of a negotiable bill of lading has the right to re-route them.

True   ☒

False   ☐

3   In what particular circumstances might you chose to use letters of credit to receive payment?

(1)   *high risk of non - payment* , or

(2)   *new buyer unknown to you*

4   In issuing a letter of credit, the issuing bank unconditionally guarantees payment to the seller.

True   ☐

False   ☒

5   If the buyer issues a letter of credit to a seller who in turn needs to pay his own supplier, the form of the letter of credit should be either:

(1)   *a transferable letter of credit*

(2)   *a back-to-back letter of credit*

1   When the contract covers transport from one specified place to another, the bill of lading is most likely to be in the form of **a through bill of lading**.

2   True. A legal owner can re-route.

3   (1)   If the buyer was new and unknown to you
         (2)   If there was a large risk of non-payment

4   False. The seller must comply with the requirements as to presentation of documents to receive payment.

5   (1)   A transferable letter of credit, or
         (2)   A back-to-back letter of credit.

Now try the questions below from the Practice Question Bank

Number
18, 19, 20, 21

Formation and constitution of business organisations

7

Agency law

Topic list	Syllabus reference
1 Role of agency and agency relationships	D1(a)
2 Formation of agency	D1(b)
3 Authority of the agent	D1(c)
4 Relations between agents and third parties	D1(d)

Introduction

In this chapter we examine how an **agency relationship** arises and how the **agent's authority** is acquired and defined. Agency is the foundation of most business relationships where more than one person engages in commerce together. Examples include **partnerships** and **companies**, which we shall introduce in the next chapter.

'Agents' are employed by **'principals'** to perform tasks which the principals cannot or do not wish to perform themselves. This is often because the principal does not have the time or expertise to carry out the task.

If businesspeople did not employ the services of agents, they would be weighed down by the contractual details, and would probably get little else done!

When parties enter into an **agency arrangement**, the principal gives a measure of authority to the agent to carry out tasks on their behalf. The agent **contracts and deals with third parties** on behalf of the principal.

Study guide

		Intellectual level
D	**Formation and constitution of business organisations**	
1	**Agency law**	
(a)	Define the role of the agent and give examples of such relationships paying particular regard to partners and company directors	2
(b)	Explain the formation of the agency relationship	2
(c)	Define the authority of the agent	2
(d)	Explain the potential liability of both principal and agent	2

Exam guide

Agency may form a multiple choice question requiring you to identify types of agent, how agency relationships are established and an agent's authority and liability to others.

1 Role of agency and agency relationships

FAST FORWARD

Agency is a relationship which exists between two legal persons (the **principal** and the **agent**) in which the function of the agent is to form a **contract between their principal and a third party**. Partners, company directors, factors, brokers and commercial agents are all acting as agents.

Agency is a very important feature of **modern commercial life**. It can be represented diagrammatically as follows:

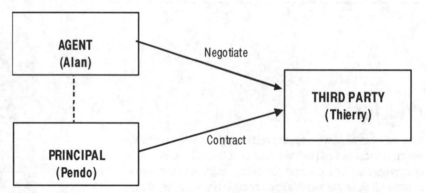

For instance Pendo may ask Alan to take Pendo's shoes to be repaired. Pendo and Alan expressly agree that Alan is to do this on Pendo's behalf. In other words, Alan becomes the agent in negotiating a contract between Pendo and Thierry, the shoe repairer, for Pendo's shoes to be mended.

1.1 Types of agent

In practice, there are many **examples of agency relationships** you are probably aware of in everyday life, although you might not know that they illustrate the law of agency. The most important agency relationships for the F4 syllabus are those of partners and company directors.

Types of agent	
Partners	This is a particularly important example of agents in your syllabus: accountants who own and run an accountancy practice together are partners, and are therefore agents of each other.
Company directors	This is another important example of agency in your syllabus. Company directors act as agents of their company.
Promoters	A promoter is someone (except professionals acting in their professional capacity) who undertakes to form a company.
Factors	A factor, sometimes called a mercantile agent, is a person whose job is to sell or buy goods on behalf of another person. For example, motor dealers are often factors.
Brokers	A broker may operate in many trades. They are essentially intermediaries who arrange contracts in return for commission. For example, an insurance broker.
Auctioneers	Auctioneers are agents authorised to sell property at auction on behalf of the seller. When an auctioneer accepts a bid from a buyer, they become the agent of the buyer for the purpose of making a record of the sale.
Commercial agents	A commercial agent is an independent agent who has continuing authority in connection with the sale or purchase of goods.

2 Formation of agency

FAST FORWARD

The relationship of principal and agent is created by **mutual consent** in the vast majority of cases. This **agreement does not have to be formal or written**.

The mutual consent comes about usually by **express agreement**, even if it is informal. However, it may also be **implied agreement**, due to the **relationship** or **conduct** of the parties.

2.1 Express agreement

This is where the agent is **expressly appointed** by the principal. This may be orally or in writing. In most commercial situations, the appointment would be made in writing to ensure that everything was clear. An agent expressly appointed by the principal has **actual authority** of the principal to act on their behalf.

2.2 Implied agreement

An agency relationship between two people may be implied by their **relationship** or by their **conduct**.

For example, if an employee's duties include making contracts for their employer, say by ordering goods on their account, then they are, by implied agreement, the agent of the employer for this purpose. An agent authorised in this way is said to have 'implied authority'.

2.3 Ratification of an agent's act: retrospective agreement

FAST FORWARD

A principal may **ratify** an act of an agent retrospectively.

An agency relationship may be created **retrospectively**, by the 'principal' **ratifying** the act of the 'agent'. Therefore it is created after the 'agent' has formed a contract on behalf of the 'principal'. If the principal agrees to the acts of the agent after the event, they may approve the acts of the agent and make it as if they had been principal and agent at the time of the contract.

The **conditions for ratification** are:

- The principal must have **existed** at the time of the contract made by the agent
- The principal must have had **legal capacity** at the time the contract was made
- The ratification must take place **within reasonable time**

- They ratify the contract in its **entirety**
- They **communicate** their ratification to the third party sufficiently clearly

Once a contract has been ratified by the principal, the effect is that it is as if the agency relationship had been **expressly formed before** the contract made by the agent took place.

2.4 Formation of agency agreement without consent

An agency may be created, or an agent's authority may be extended, without express consent. This happens **by estoppel**, when the principal **'holds out'** a person to be their agent, and when there is an **agent of necessity**.

2.4.1 Implied agreement

In some cases, an agency created by implied agreement might result in the agent having **more implied authority** than the principal might have consented to.

2.4.2 Agent by estoppel

An agency relationship may be formed by implication when the **principal holds out to third parties** that a person is their agent, even if the principal and the 'agent' do not agree to form such a relationship. In such a case, the principal is estopped from denying the agent's apparent/ostensible authority, hence the name **'agent by estoppel'**. An agency relationship is not so formed if it is the 'agent' who creates the impression that they are in an agency relationship with a 'principal'.

2.4.3 Agent by necessity

In some rare situations, it may be necessary for a person to take action in respect of someone else's goods in an **emergency situation**. That person can become an **agent of necessity** of the owner of the goods, as they take steps in respect of the goods.

Illustration

A seller is shipping frozen goods to a buyer in another country. While the ship is docked, the freezers in the ship break down and the relevant part required to fix them cannot be obtained. If the ship's captain (acting as the agent of necessity) cannot make contact with the owner of the goods, they might, of necessity, sell the goods while they are still frozen, rather than allow them to spoil by defrosting.

This is particularly rare, because it would only occur when the 'agent' could not make contact with the principal, which in the modern world is **extremely unlikely**.

This principle is a historic part of English shipping and merchant law and you should be aware that it might be possible, but do not worry about the other details of the doctrine.

3 Authority of the agent

If an agent acts within the limits of their authority, any contract they make on the principal's behalf is **binding** on both principal and third party. The extent of the agent's authority may be **express, implied** or **ostensible**. Express and implied authority are both forms of **actual authority**.

A principal does not give the agent unlimited authority to act on their behalf. A **contract** made by the agent is **binding** on the principal and the other party **only if** the **agent was acting within the limits of their authority** from their principal.

In analysing the **limits of an agent's authority**, three distinct sources of authority can be identified:

- Express authority
- Implied authority
- Ostensible authority

3.1 Express authority

Express authority is a matter between principal and agent. This is authority explicitly given by the principal to the agent to perform particular tasks, along with the powers necessary to perform those tasks.

The extent of the agent's express authority will depend on the **construction of the words used on their appointment**. If the appointment is in **writing**, then the document will need to be examined. If it is oral, then the scope of the agent's authority will be a matter of evidence. If the agent contracts outside the scope of their express (actual) authority, they may be **liable** to the principal and the third party for **breach of warrant of authority**.

Illustration

A board of directors may give an individual director express authority to enter the company into a specific contract. The company would be bound to this contract, but not to one made by the individual director outside the express authority.

3.2 Implied authority

Where there is no express authority, authority may be **implied** from the **nature** of the agent's activities or from what is **usual** or **customary** in the **circumstances**. Between principal and agent, the latter's express authority is paramount. The agent cannot contravene the principal's express instructions by claiming that they had implied authority for acting in the way they did. As far as **third parties** are concerned, they are entitled to assume that the agent has implied usual authority unless they know to the contrary.

Watteau v Fenwick 1893

The facts: The owner of a hotel (F) employed the previous owner (H) to manage it. F forbade H to buy cigars on credit but H did buy cigars from W. W sued F for payment but F argued that he was not bound by the contract, since H had no actual authority to make it. W believed that H still owned the hotel.

Decision: It was within the usual authority of a manager of a hotel to buy cigars on credit and F was bound by the contract (although W did not even know that H was the agent of F) since his restriction of usual authority had not been communicated.

Hely-Hutchinson v Brayhead Ltd 1968

The facts: The chairman and chief executive of a company acted as its *de facto* managing director, but he had never been formally appointed to that position. Nevertheless, he purported to bind the company to a particular transaction. When the other party to the agreement sought to enforce it, the company claimed that the chairman had no authority to bind it.

Decision: Although the director derived no authority from his position as chairman of the board, he did acquire authority from his position as chief executive. Therefore the company was bound by the contract as it was within the implied authority of a person holding such a position.

A principal employs a stockbroker to sell shares. It is an implied term of the arrangement between them that the broker shall have **actual authority** to do what is usual in practice for a broker selling shares for a client. Any person dealing with the broker is entitled to assume (unless informed to the contrary) that the broker has the usual authority of a broker acting for a client.

3.3 Actual authority

Express and implied authority are sometimes referred to together as **actual authority**. This distinguishes them from **apparent** or **ostensible authority**.

Key term

> **Actual authority** is a legal relationship between principal and agent created by a consensual agreement between them.

3.4 Apparent/ostensible authority

FAST FORWARD

> An agent's **apparent** or **ostensible authority** may be greater than their express or implied authority. This occurs where a **principal** holds it out to be so to a third party, who relied on the representation and altered their position as a result. It may be **more extensive** than what is usual or incidental.

The **apparent** (or **ostensible**) authority of an agent is what a principal **represents** to other persons that they have given to the agent (authority by '**holding out**'). As a result, an agent with **express** or **implied** authority which is limited can be held, in practice, to have a more extensive authority.

Apparent/ostensible authority usually **arises** either

(a)   Where the **principal** has **represented** the agent as having authority even though they have not actually been appointed

(b)   Where the **principal** has **revoked** the agent's **authority** but the **third party** has **not had notice** of this.

3.4.1 The extent of ostensible authority

Ostensible authority is not restricted to what is usual and incidental. The principal may expressly or by inference from their conduct **confer on the agent any amount of ostensible authority**.

3.4.2 Example: partnership

A **partner** has considerable but **limited implied authority** by virtue of being a partner. If, however, the other partners allow them to exercise greater authority than is implied, they have represented that they have wider authority. They will be bound by the contracts which they make within the limits of this **ostensible authority**.

3.4.3 Example: companies

> *Freeman & Lockyer v Buckhurst Park Properties (Mangal) Ltd 1964*
>
> *The facts:* K and H carried on business as property developers through a company which they owned in equal shares. Each appointed another director, making four in all. H lived abroad and the business of the company was left entirely under the control of K. As a director K had no actual or apparent authority to enter into contracts as agent of the company, but he did make contracts as if he were a managing director, without authority to do so. The other directors were aware of these activities but had not authorised them. The claimants sued the company for work done on K's instructions.

Decision: There had been a representation by the company through its board of directors that K was the authorised agent of the company. The board had authority to make such contracts and also had power to delegate authority to K by appointing him to be Managing Director. Although there had been no actual delegation to K, the company had, by its acquiescence, led the claimants to believe that K was an authorised agent and the claimants had relied on it. The company was bound by the contract made by K under the principle of 'holding out' (or estoppel). The company was estopped from denying (that is, not permitted to deny) that K was its agent, although K had no actual authority from the company.

It can be seen that it is the **conduct** of the '**principal**' which **creates ostensible authority**. It does not matter whether there is a pre-existing agency relationship or not.

Exam focus point

This is important – ostensible authority arises in two distinct ways. It may arise where a **person makes a representation to third parties** that a particular person has the authority to act as their agent, without actually appointing them as their agent. Alternatively, it may arise where a **principal has previously represented to a third party** that an agent has authority to act on their behalf.

3.4.4 Representations creating ostensible authority

The **representation must be made by the principal or an agent acting on their behalf.** It cannot be made by the agent who is claiming ostensible authority.

It must be a **representation of fact, not law**, and must be **made to the third party**. This distinguishes ostensible authority from actual authority, where the third party need know nothing of the agent's authority.

3.4.5 Reliance on representations

It must be shown that the **third party relied on the representation**. If there is no causal link between the third party's loss and the representation, the third party will not be able to hold the principal as liable.

 Illustration

If the third party did not believe that the agent had authority, or if they positively knew they did not, then ostensible authority cannot be claimed. This is true even if the agent appeared to have authority.

3.4.6 Alteration of position following a representation

It is enough that the third party **alters their position as a result of reliance on the representation**. They do not have to suffer any detriment as a result, but damages would in such an event be minimal.

3.5 Revocation of authority

Where a principal has represented to a third party that an agent has authority to act, and has subsequently **revoked the agent's authority**, this may be **insufficient to escape liability**. The principal should inform third parties who have previously dealt with the agent of the change in circumstances. This is particularly relevant to partnerships and the position when a partner leaves a partnership.

3.6 Termination of agency

FAST FORWARD Agency is terminated by **agreement** or by **operation of law** (death, insanity, insolvency).

Agency is terminated when the **parties agree** that the relationship should end.

It may also be terminated by **operation of law** in the following situations:

- Principal or agent dies
- Principal or agent becomes insane
- Principal becomes bankrupt, or the agent becomes bankrupt and this interferes with their position as agent

Termination brings the **actual authority** of the agent to an end. However, third parties are allowed to enforce contracts made later by the 'agent' until they are actively or constructively informed of the termination of the agency relationship.

4 Relations between agents and third parties

FAST FORWARD

An agent usually has **no liability** for a contract entered into as an agent, nor any **right to enforce it**. Exceptions to this: when an agent is **intended** to have liability; where it is **usual business practice** to have liability; when the agent is actually acting on their own behalf; where agent and principal have joint liability.

A third party to a contract entered into with an agent acting outside their ostensible authority can sue for breach of **warranty of authority**.

4.1 Liability of the agent for contracts formed

An agent contracting for their principal within their actual and/or apparent authority generally **has no liability** on the contract and **is not entitled to enforce it**. However, there are **circumstances** when the **agent will be personally liable** and can enforce it.

(a) When they **intended to undertake personal liability** – for example, where they sign a contract as party to it without signifying that they are an agent.

(b) Where it is **usual business practice or trade custom** for an agent to be liable and entitled.

(c) Where the agent **is acting on their own behalf** even though they purport to act for a principal.

Where an agent enters into a **collateral contract** with the third party (with whom they have contracted on the principal's behalf) there is separate liability and entitlement to enforcement on that collateral contract.

It can happen that there is **joint liability** of agent and principal. This is usually the case where an agent did not disclose that they acted for a principal.

4.2 Breach of warranty of authority

An agent who **exceeds their ostensible authority** will generally have **no liability to their principal**, since the latter will not be bound by the unauthorised contract made for him. But the agent **will be liable** in such a case **to the third party** for breach of warranty of authority.

Chapter Roundup

- **Agency** is a relationship which exists between two legal persons (the **principal** and the **agent**) in which the function of the agent is to form a **contract between their principal and a third party**. Partners, company directors, factors, brokers and commercial agents are all acting as agents.

- The relationship of principal and agent is created by **mutual consent** in the vast majority of cases. This **agreement does not have to be formal or written**.

- The mutual consent comes about usually by **express agreement**, even if it is informal. However, it may also be **implied agreement**, due to the **relationship** or **conduct** of the parties.

- A principal many **ratify** an act of an agent retrospectively.

- An agency may be created, or an agent's authority may be extended, without express consent. This happens **by estoppel**, when the principal 'holds out' a person to be their agent, and when there is an **agent of necessity**.

- If an agent acts within the limits of their authority, any contract they make on the principal's behalf is **binding** on both principal and third party. The extent of the agent's authority may be **express, implied** or **ostensible**. Express and implied authority are both forms of **actual authority**.

- An agent's **apparent** or **ostensible authority** may be greater than their express or implied authority. This occurs where a **principal** holds it out to be so to a third party, who relied on the representation and altered their position as a result. It may be **more extensive** than what is usual or incidental.

- Agency is terminated by **agreement** or by **operation of law** (death, insanity, insolvency).

- An agent usually has **no liability** for a contract entered into as an agent, nor any **right to enforce it**. Exceptions to this: when an agent is **intended** to have liability; where it is **usual business practice** to have liability; when the agent is actually acting on their own behalf; where agent and principal have joint liability.

- A third party to a contract entered into with an agent acting outside their ostensible authority can sue for breach of **warranty of authority**.

Quick Quiz

1   **Fill in the blanks** in the statements, using the words in the boxes below.

Agency is the (1)...~~relationship~~... which exists between two (2).......~~legal~~......... persons. They are the (3).~~principal~~... and the agent, in which the function of the agent is to form a (4)...~~contract~~... between their (5)...~~principal~~... and a (6)..~~third party~~

• relationship	• contract	• legal
• third party	• principal	• principal

2   A principal may, in certain circumstances, ratify the acts of the agent which has retrospective effect.

True   ☒

False   ☐

3   What is the best definition of ostensible authority?

(a)   The authority which the principal represents to other persons that they have given to the agent.
(b)   The authority implied to other persons by the agent's actions.

4   What point of law is explained in the case of *Freeman & Lockyer v Buckhurst Park Properties (Mangal) Ltd 1964?*

5   Which of the following are circumstances where an agent may enforce a contract?

(a)   Where the agent is intended to take personal liability
(b)   Where it is usual business practice to allow enforcement
(c)   Where the agent acts on their own behalf even if they purport to act for a principal

(i)   (a), (b)
(ii)   (b), (c)
(iii)   (a), (c)
(iv)   (a), (b) and (c)

Answers to Quick Quiz

1   (1)   relationship   (2)   legal   (3)   principal
     (4)   contract   (5)   principal   (6)   third party

2   True. Principals may ratify retrospectively.

3   (a). The key word is represents.

4   A director may have ostensible authority to contract if, although they do not have their express permission, the other directors are aware that contracts are being made and do nothing to prevent it.

5   (iv). They are all valid circumstances.

Now try the questions below from the Practice Question Bank

Number
22, 23

Partnerships

Topic list	Syllabus reference
1 Partnerships	D2(a)
2 Forming an unlimited liability partnership	D2(b)
3 Terminating an unlimited liability partnership	D2(e)
4 Authority of partners in an unlimited liability partnership	D2(c)
5 Liability of partners in an unlimited liability partnership	D2(d)
6 Limited liability partnerships	D2(a – e)

Introduction

Partnerships are a common form of business organisation and are commonly used for **small businesses** and some **professional businesses**, for example accountants.

Partnerships are groups of individuals who have an **agency** relationship with each other. We shall look at how partnerships are **formed** and later **terminated**, then at how **relationships** with other partners and with third parties work.

Study guide

		Intellectual level
D	**Formation and constitution of business organisations**	
2	**Partnerships**	
(a)	Demonstrate a knowledge of the legislation governing the partnership, both unlimited and limited	1
(b)	Discuss the formation of a partnership	2
(c)	Explain the authority of partners in relation to partnership activity	2
(d)	Analyse the liability of various partners for partnership debts	2
(e)	Explain the termination of a partnership and partners' subsequent rights and liabilities	2

Exam guide

Partnership is highly suited to scenario questions where you may be required to identify who is liable for partnership debts.

1 Partnerships

FAST FORWARD

Partnership is defined as 'the relation which subsists between persons carrying on a business in common with a view of profit'. A partnership is *not* a separate legal person distinct from its members, it is merely a 'relation' between persons. Each partner (there must be at least two) is **personally liable** for all the debts of the firm.

Partnership is a common form of business association. It is **flexible**, because it can either be a **formal** or **informal** arrangement, so can be used for large organisations or a small husband and wife operation.

Partnership is normal practice in the **professions** as most professions prohibit their members from carrying on practice through limited companies, though some professions permit their members to trade as limited liability partnerships, which have many of the characteristics of companies. Businesspeople are not so restricted and generally prefer to trade through a limited company for the advantages this can bring.

Applying the law on partnerships and companies to meet the needs of your clients is a way of meeting the requirement of PO1 for those working in public practice. You need to keep your knowledge of partnership and company law up-to-date in order to provide the best possible advice to clients.

Exam focus point

Your syllabus requires you to demonstrate knowledge of the legislation governing both limited and unlimited liability partnerships. You should therefore make careful note of the rules regarding the Partnership Act 1890, the Limited Partnership Act 1907 and the Limited Liability Partnership Act 2000.

1.1 Definition of partnership

Key term

Partnership is the relation which subsists between persons carrying on a business in common with a view of profit.

We shall look at some points raised by this definition now.

1.1.1 The relation which subsists between persons

'Person' includes a corporation such as a **registered company** as well as an **individual** living person.

There must be at least **two** partners. If, therefore, two people are in partnership, one dies and the survivor carries on the business, that person is a sole trader. There is no longer a partnership.

1.1.2 Carrying on a business

Business can include **every trade**, **occupation** or **profession**. But three points should be noted.

(a) A business is a **form of activity**. If two or more persons are merely the passive joint owners of revenue-producing property, such as rented houses, that fact does not make them partners.

(b) A business can consist of a **single transaction**. These situations are often described as 'joint ventures'.

(c) Carrying on a business must have a **beginning and an end**. A partnership begins when the partners agree to conduct their **business activity** together.

1.1.3 In common

Broadly this phrase means that the partners must be associated in the business as **joint proprietors**. The evidence that this is so is found in their taking a share of the profits, especially **net profit**.

1.1.4 A view of profit

If persons enter into a partnership with a **view of making profits** but they actually suffer losses, it is still a partnership. The test to be applied is one of **intention**. If the intention of trading together is just to gain experience, for example, there is no partnership.

1.2 Consequences of the definition

In most cases there is no doubt about the existence of a partnership. The partners declare their intention by such steps as signing a **written partnership agreement** and adopting a **firm name**. These outward and visible signs of the existence of a partnership are not essential however – a partnership can exist without them.

1.2.1 Terminology

firm vs company

The word 'firm' is correctly used to denote a partnership. It is **not** correct to apply it to a registered company (though the newspapers often do so).

The word 'company' may form part of the name of a partnership, for example, 'Smith and Company'. But 'limited company' or 'registered company' is **only** applied to a properly registered company.

1.3 Liability of the partners

Every partner is liable **without limit** for the debts of the partnership. This means that a creditor can require a partner to settle an invoice if the partnership fails to pay, and partners must make good the partnership's debts if the partnership is terminated and does not have sufficient assets to pay what it owes.

It is possible to register a limited partnership in which one or more individual partners have limited liability, but the limited partners may not take part in the management of the business.

The **limited partnership** is useful where one partner wishes to invest in the activities of the partnership without being involved in its day-to-day operation. Such partners are entitled to inspect the accounts of the partnership.

Under the **Limited Liability Partnership Act 2000** it is possible to register a partnership with limited liability (an LLP).

LLP

2 Forming an unlimited liability partnership

FAST FORWARD

Partnerships can be **formed** very informally, but there may be complex formalities to ensure clarity.

A partnership can be a very **informal arrangement**. This is reflected in the procedure to form a partnership.

A partnership is **formed when two or more people agree to run a business together**. Partnerships can be formed in any trade or occupation or profession.

In order to be a partnership, the business must be **'carried on in common'**, meaning that all parties must have **responsibility** for the business. In other words, there is **more than one proprietor**. A husband and wife who run a shop together are partners, but a shop owner and their employee are not. In law then, the formation of a partnership is essentially straightforward. People **make an agreement** together to run a business, and **carry that agreement out**.

2.1 Common formation formalities

In practice, the formalities of setting up a partnership may be more **complex** than simple agreement. Many professional people use partnerships. These business associations can be vast organisations with substantial revenue and expenditure, such as the larger accountancy firms and many law firms.

Such organisations have so many partners that the relationships between them have to be **regulated**. Thus forming some partnerships can involve creating **detailed partnership agreements** which lay out terms and conditions of partnership.

2.2 The partnership agreement

A **written partnership agreement** is **not legally required**. In practice there are advantages in setting down, in writing, the terms of their association.

(a)   It **fills** in the **details** which the law would not imply – the nature of the firm's business, its name, and the bank at which the firm will maintain its account, for instance.

(b)   A written agreement serves to **override terms,** otherwise implied by the Partnership Act 1890, which are inappropriate to the partnership. The Act, for example, implies that partners share profits equally.

(c)   Additional clauses can be developed. **Expulsion clauses** are an example and they provide a mechanism to expel a partner where there would be no ability to do so otherwise.

3 Terminating an unlimited liability partnership

FAST FORWARD

Partnerships may be **terminated** by passing of time, termination of the underlying venture, death or bankruptcy of a partner, illegality, notice, agreement or by order of the court.

Termination is, quite simply, when the partnership comes to an end.

Illustration

Alison, Ben, Caroline and David are in partnership as accountants. Caroline decides to change career and become an interior designer. In her place, Alison, Ben and David invite Emily to join the partnership.

As far as third parties are concerned, a partnership offering accountancy services still exists. In fact, however, the old partnership (ABCD) has been dissolved, and a new partnership (ABDE) has replaced it.

3.1 Events causing termination

The **Partnership Act 1890** states that partnership is terminated in the following instances.

- **Passing of time**, if the partnership was entered into for a fixed term
- **Termination of the venture**, if entered into for a single venture
- The **death or bankruptcy** of a partner (partnership agreement may vary this)
- **Subsequent illegality**
- **Notice** given by a partner if it is a partnership of indefinite duration
- **Order of the court** granted to a partner
- **Agreement** between the partners

In the event of the **termination** of a partnership, the partnership's **assets are realised** and the proceeds applied in this order.

- Paying off **external debts**
- Repaying to the **partners** any **loans** or **advances**
- Repaying the partners' **capital contribution**
- Anything left over is then **repaid** to the **partners** in the **profit-sharing ratio**.

The partnership agreement can exclude some of these provisions and can **avoid dissolution** in the following circumstances.

- **Death** of a partner
- **Bankruptcy** of a partner

It is wise to make such provisions to give **stability** to the partnership.

4 Authority of partners in an unlimited liability partnership

FAST FORWARD

The **authority** of partners to bind each other in contract is based on the principles of agency.

In simple terms, a partner is the **agent of the partnership and their co-partners**. This means that some of their acts bind the other partners, either because they have, or because they appear to have, authority. The **Partnership Act 1890 defines** the **authority** of a partner to make contracts as follows.

Authority of a partner

Every partner is an **agent** of the firm and their other partners for the purpose of the business of the partnership, and the acts of every partner who does any act for carrying on the **usual way** of business if the kind carried on by the firm of which they are a member **bind the firm** and their partners, **unless** the partner so acting has **in fact no authority** to act for the firm in the particular matter, **and the person with whom they are dealing** either **knows that they have no authority**, or **does not know or believe them to be a partner**.

Where a partner pledges the credit of the firm for a **purpose apparently not connected** with the firm's ordinary course of business, the **firm is not bound, unless** they are in fact **specially authorised** by the other partners: but this section does not affect any personal liability incurred by an individual.

If it has been **agreed between the partners** that any **restriction** shall be placed on the power of any one or more of them to bind the firm, **no act** done in contravention of the agreement is **binding** on the firm with respect to **persons having notice of the agreement**.

The key point to note about authority of partners is that, other than when the partner has actual authority, the authority often **depends on the perception of the third party**. If the third party genuinely believes that the partner has authority, the partner is likely to bind the firm. Partners are also **jointly liable** for **crimes** and **torts** committed by one of their number in the course of business.

5 Liability of partners in an unlimited liability partnership

FAST FORWARD

> Partners are **jointly liable** for all partnership debts that result from contracts that the partners have made which bind the firm.

Partners are **jointly liable** for all partnership debts that result from contracts made by other partners which bind the firm. The **Civil Liability Act 1978** provides that judgement against one partner does not prevent subsequent actions against other partners. The link between authority and liability can be seen in the following diagram.

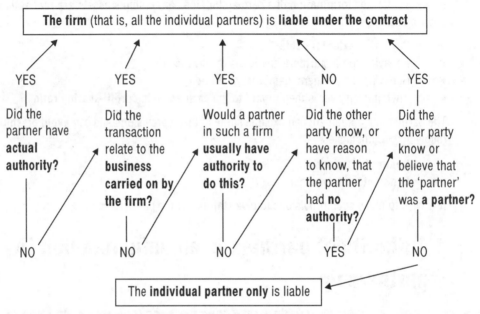

There are particular rules on liability for new and retiring partners.

Partner	Partner liability
New partners	A new partner admitted to an existing firm is liable for **debts incurred** only **after** they become a partner. They are not liable for debts incurred before they were a partner unless they agree to become liable.
Retiring partners	A partner who retires is still **liable** for any **outstanding debts** incurred while they were a partner, unless the creditor has agreed to release them from liability. They are also **liable** for debts of the firm **incurred after their retirement** if the creditor knew them to be a partner (before retirement) and has not had **notice** of their retirement.
	Therefore, it is **vital** on retirement that a partner **gives notice** to all the creditors of the firm. The retiring partner may have an indemnity from the remaining partners with respect to this issue.

5.1 Supervision and regulation

There is **no formal statutory supervision** or **regulation** of partnerships. Their accounts need not be in prescribed form nor is an audit necessary. The public has no means or legal right of inspection of the firm's accounts or other information such as companies must provide. If, however, the partners carry on business under a firm name which is not the surnames of them all, say, 'Smith, Jones & Co', they are required to disclose the **names** of the **partners** on their letterheads and at their places of business. They are required to make a **return** of their **profits** for income tax and **usually** to **register** for VAT.

5.2 Property

Partnerships **can** grant a **mortgage** or **fixed charge** over property, but **cannot** grant **floating changes**.

6 Limited liability partnerships

FAST FORWARD

> A **limited liability partnership** combines the features of a traditional partnership with the limited liability and creation of legal personality more usually associated with limited companies.

6.1 Definition of limited liability partnership

Another form of partnership commonly used in England, particularly for professional partnerships, is the **limited liability partnership (LLP)**. This type of business association was created by the Limited Liability Partnership Act 2000.

LLPs are similar to limited companies in that they have separate legal identity and unlimited liability for debts, but the liability of the individual partners (or members) is **limited to the amount of their capital contribution**.

LLPs have similar requirements for **governance** and **accountability** as limited companies. They are generally set up by firms of professionals such as accountants and lawyers, who are required by the rules of their professions to operate as partnerships but who seek to have the protection of limited liability.

Key term

> A **limited liability partnership (LLP)** is a corporate body which has separate legal personality from its members and therefore some of the advantages and disadvantages of a company.

The **main advantage of an LLP** over a traditional partnership is that the LLP will be liable for its own debts rather than the partners. All contracts with third parties will be with the LLP.

6.2 Formation

A limited liability partnership may be formed by persons associating to carry on lawful business with a view to profit, but it **must be incorporated** to be recognised. LLPs can have an unlimited number of partners. To be incorporated, the subscribers must send an **incorporation document** and a **statement of compliance** to the Registrar of Companies.

The **document must be signed** and **state** the following:

- The **name** of the LLP
- The **location** of its **registered office** (England and Wales/Wales/Scotland)
- The **address** of the registered office
- The name and address of all the **members** of the LLP
- Which of the members are to be **designated members**

A **registration fee** is also payable to Companies House.

6.3 Internal regulation

LLPs are more **flexible** than companies as they provide **similar protection** for the owners, but **with less statutory rules** on areas such as meetings and management. No board of directors is needed. As can be seen in the incorporation procedures, LLPs come under the supervision of the **Registrar of Companies** (the Registrar). The members of the LLP are those who **subscribe** to the original incorporation document, and those admitted afterwards in accordance with the terms of the partnership agreement.

The **rights and duties** of the **partners** will usually be set out in a **partnership agreement**. In the absence of a partnership agreement, the rights and duties are set out in regulations under the Act. LLPs must have **two designated members**, who take responsibility for the publicity requirements of the LLP.

Examples of **duties** of an LLP's **designated members** include:

- **Filing** certain notices with the Registrar, such as when a member leaves
- Signing and filing **accounts**
- Appointing **auditors** if appropriate

The Registrar will maintain a file containing the **publicised documents** of the LLP at Companies House.

6.4 External relationships

Every member is an **agent** of the LLP. As such, where the member has authority, the LLP will be bound by the acts of the member.

The **LLP will not be bound by the acts of the member where**:

- They have no authority and the third party is aware of that fact
- They have ceased to be a member, and the third party is aware of that fact

6.5 Dissolution

An LLP **does not dissolve when a member leaves** in the same way that a traditional partnership does. Where a member has died or (for a corporate member) been wound up, that member ceases to be a member, but the LLP continues in existence.

An **LLP must therefore be wound up** when the time has come for it to be dissolved. This is achieved under provisions **similar to company winding-up** provisions.

6.6 Limited partnership

The other form of partnership that is seen, rarely, in the UK is the **limited partnership**. Under the Limited Partnership Act 1907, a partnership may be formed in which at least one partner (the general partner) must have **full, unlimited liability**. The other partners have **limited liability** for the debts of the partnership beyond the extent of the capital they have contributed. The rules are as follows:

- Limited partners may not withdraw their capital
- Limited partners may not take part in the management of the partnership
- Limited partners cannot bind the partnership in a contract with a third party without losing the benefit of limited liability
- The partnership must be registered with Companies House

Exam focus point

Partnership questions in scenarios often revolve around a partner's authority to enter into contracts and the liability of all the partners when debts are incurred.

Chapter Roundup

- **Partnership** is defined as 'the relation which subsists between persons carrying on a business in common with a view of profit'. A partnership is *not* a separate legal person distinct from its members, it is merely a 'relation' between persons. Each partner (there must be at least two) is **personally liable** for all the debts of the firm.

- Partnerships can be **formed** very informally, but there may be complex formalities to ensure clarity.

- Partnerships may be **terminated** by passing of time, termination of the underlying venture, death or bankruptcy of a partner, illegality, notice, agreement or by order of the court.

- The **authority** of partners to bind each other in contract is based on the principles of agency.

- Partners are **jointly liable** for all partnership debts that result from contracts that the partners have made which bind the firm.

- **A limited liability partnership** combines the features of a traditional partnership with the limited liability and creation of a legal personality more usually associated with limited companies.

Quick Quiz

1   Which one of the following statements about traditional (unlimited) partnerships is **incorrect**?

    A   In England a partnership has no existence distinct from the partners.
    B   A partnership must have a written partnership agreement.
    C   A partnership is subject to the Partnership Act.
    D   Each partner is an agent of the firm.

2   An LLP dissolves when a member leaves.

    True   ☐

    False   ☒

3   Which one of the following statements about the liability of a new partner in a partnership is **correct**?

    A   New partners automatically assume liability for existing partnership debts when they join the firm and for new debts incurred after they join.
    B   New partners are only liable for partnership debts that they personally authorise.
    C   New partners are not liable for existing partnership debts when they join but are liable for new partnership debts incurred after they join.
    D   New partners become liable for new partnership debts when they meet the creditors personally.

4   It is the LLP itself, rather than the partners personally, that enjoys the benefit of limited liability.

    True   ☐

    False   ☒

5   There is no legal requirement for an LLP to be audited.

    True   ☐

    False   ☒

Answers to Quick Quiz

1   B. A written agreement is not needed.

2   False. LLPs are only dissolved when they cease to trade.

3   C. New partners are only liable for partnership debts incurred after they join a firm.

4   False. It is the partners of an LLP that enjoy limited liability.

5   False. An LLP may be required to appoint auditors if it fulfils certain criteria.

Now try the questions below from the Practice Question Bank

Number
24, 25

Corporations and legal personality

Topic list	Syllabus reference
1 Sole traders' and companies' legal identities	D3(a)
2 Limited liability of members	D3(b)
3 Types of company	D3(c)
4 Additional classifications	D3(c)
5 Effect of legal personality	D3(d)
6 Ignoring separate personality	D3(e)
7 Comparison of companies and partnerships	D3(a)

Introduction

Companies, as business vehicles, are distinct from sole traders and
partnerships. The key difference between them is the concept of **separate legal
personality**. This chapter outlines this doctrine, and also discusses its
implications (primarily **limited liability** for members) and the exceptions to it
(lifting the **veil of incorporation**).

*The Companies Act 2006 and the Small Business, Enterprise and Employment
Act 2015 apply to this and all chapters unless otherwise stated.*

Study guide

		Intellectual level
D	**Formation and constitution of business organisations**	
3	**Corporations and legal personality**	
(a)	Distinguish between sole traders, partnerships and companies	1
(b)	Explain the meaning and effect of limited liability	2
(c)	Analyse different types of companies, especially private and public companies	1
(d)	Illustrate the effect of separate personality and the veil of incorporation	2
(e)	Recognise instances where separate personality will be ignored (lifting the veil of incorporation)	2

Exam guide

You must be able to compare and contrast companies and partnerships, and to identify which business vehicle would be the best form of business organisation in a particular situation.

Two articles on the Companies Act 2006 appeared in *Student Accountant* and are available on the ACCA website.

1 Sole traders' and companies' legal identities

FAST FORWARD

In a **sole tradership**, there is no legal distinction between the individual and the business.

1.1 Sole traders

A **sole trader owns** and **runs a business**. They contribute capital to start the enterprise, run it with or without employees, and earn the profits or stand the losses of the venture.

Sole traders are found mainly in the **retail trades** (local newsagents), **small-scale service industries** (plumbers), and **small manufacturing** and **craft industries**. An accountant may operate as a sole trader.

1.2 Legal status of the sole trader

Whilst the business is a separate accounting entity the business is **not legally distinct** from the person who owns it. In law, the person and the business are viewed as the same entity.

The **advantages** of being a sole trader are as follows.

(a) **No formal procedures** are required to set up in business. However, for certain classes of business a licence may be required (eg retailing wines and spirits), and VAT registration is often necessary.

(b) **Independence** and **self-accountability**. A sole trader does not need to consult anybody about business decisions and is not required to reveal the state of the business to anyone (other than the tax authorities each year).

(c) **Personal supervision** of the business by the sole trader should ensure its effective operation. Personal contact with customers may enhance commercial flexibility.

(d) **All** the **profits** of the business **accrue** to the sole trader. This can be a powerful motivator, and satisfying to the individual whose ability/energy results in reward.

The **disadvantages** of being a sole trader include the following.

(a) If the business gets into debt, a sole trader's **personal wealth** (for example, private house) might be lost if the debts are called in, as they are the same legal entity.

(b) Expansion of the business is usually only possible by **ploughing back** the **profits** of the business as further capital, although loans or overdraft finance may be available.

(c) The business has a **high dependence** on the **individual** which can mean long working hours and difficulties during sickness or holidays.

(d) The **death** of the proprietor may make it **necessary** to **sell** the **business** in order to pay the resulting tax liabilities, or family members may not wish to continue the business anyway.

(e) The **individual** may **only have one skill**. A sole trader may be, say, a good technical engineer or craftsman but may lack the skills to market effectively or to maintain accounting records to control the business effectively.

(f) Other **disadvantages** include lack of diversification, absence of economies of scale and problems of raising finance.

1.3 Companies

A company has a **legal personality** separate from its owners (known as members). It is a formal arrangement, surrounded by formality and publicity, but its chief advantage is that members' **liability** for the company's debts is typically **limited**.

A company is the most popular form of **business association** and, by its nature, it is more **formal** than a partnership or a sole trader. There is often substantially **more legislation** on the formation and procedures of companies than any other business association.

The key reason why the company is a popular form of business association is that the **liability of its members to contribute to the debts of the entity is significantly limited**. For many people, this benefit outweighs the disadvantage of the formality surrounding companies, and encourages them not to trade as sole traders or (unlimited) partnerships.

1.4 Definition of a company

Key terms

For the purposes of this Study Text, a **company** is an entity registered as such under the Companies Act 2006.

The key feature of a company is that it has a **legal personality** (existence) distinct from its members and directors.

1.5 Legal personality

A person possesses **legal rights** and is subject to **legal obligations**. In law, the term 'person' is used to denote two categories of legal person.

- An individual human being is a **natural person**. A sole trader is a natural person, and there is legally no distinction between the individual and the business entity in sole tradership.

- The law also recognises **artificial persons** in the form of companies and limited partnerships. Unlimited partnerships are not artificial persons.

Key term

Corporate personality is a common law principle that grants a company a legal identity, separate from the members who comprise it. It follows that the property of a company belongs to that company, debts of the company must be satisfied from the assets of that company, and the company has perpetual succession until wound up.

A corporation is a **legal entity** separate from the natural persons connected with it, for example as members or directors.

2 Limited liability of members

FAST FORWARD

The fact that a company's members – not the company itself – have **limited liability** for its debts **protects the members** from the company's creditors and ultimately from the full risk of business failure.

A key consequence of the fact that the company is distinct from its members is that its members have **limited liability**.

Key term

> **Limited liability** is a protection offered to members of certain types of company. In the event of business failure, the members will only be asked to contribute identifiable amounts to the assets of the business.

2.1 Protection for members against creditors

The **company** itself is **liable without limit for its own debts**. If the company buys plastic from another company, for example, it owes the other company money.

Limited liability is a benefit to members. They own the business, so might be the people whom the creditors logically ask to pay the debts of the company if the company is unable to pay them itself.

Limited liability prevents this by stipulating the **creditors** of a limited company **cannot demand payment of the company's debts** from members of the company.

2.2 Protection from business failure

As the company is liable for all its own debts, limited liability only becomes an issue in the event of a business failure when the **company is unable to pay its own debts**.

This will result in the **winding up** of the company and enables the creditors to be paid from the proceeds of any assets remaining in the company. It is at winding up that limited liability becomes most relevant.

2.3 Members asked to contribute identifiable amounts

Although the creditors of the company cannot ask the members of the company to pay the debts of the company, there are some amounts that **members are required to pay in the event of a winding up**.

Type of company	Amount owed by member at winding up
Company limited by shares	Any **outstanding amount** from when they originally purchased their shares from the company.
	If the member's shares are fully paid, they **do not have to contribute anything in the event of a winding up**.
Company limited by guarantee	The **amount they guaranteed** to pay in the event of a winding up

2.4 Liability of the company for tort and crime

As a company has a **separate legal identity**, it may also have liabilities in **tort** and **crime**. Criminal liability of companies in particular is a topical area but is outside the scope of your syllabus.

3 Types of company

Most companies are those **incorporated** under the **Companies Act**. However there are other types of company such as **corporations sole**, **chartered corporations**, **statutory corporations** and **community interest companies**.

Corporations are **classified** in one of the following categories.

Categories	Description
Corporations sole	A corporation sole is an **official position** which is filled by one person who is replaced from time to time. The Public Trustee and the Treasury Solicitor are corporations sole.
Chartered corporations	These are usually **charities** or bodies such as the Association of Chartered Certified Accountants, formed by Royal Charter.
Statutory corporations	Statutory corporations are formed by special Acts of Parliament. This method is little used now, as it is slow and expensive. It was used in the nineteenth century to form railway and canal companies.
Registered companies	Registration under the Companies Act is the normal method of incorporating a commercial concern. Any body of this type is properly called a company.
Community Interest Companies (CICs)	A special form of company for use by 'social' enterprises pursuing purposes that are beneficial to the community, rather than the maximisation of profit for the benefit of owners, created by the Companies (Audit, Investigation and Community Enterprise) Act 2004.

3.1 Limited companies

The meaning of limited liability has already been explained. It is the **member**, not the company, whose liability for the company's debts may be limited.

3.1.1 Liability limited by shares

Liability is usually **limited by shares**. This is the position when a company which has share capital states in its constitution that 'the liability of members is limited'.

3.1.2 Liability limited by guarantee

Alternatively a company may be **limited by guarantee.** Its constitution states the amount which each member **undertakes** to **contribute** in a winding up (also known as a liquidation). A creditor has no direct claim against a member under their guarantee, nor can the company require a member to pay up under their guarantee until the company goes into liquidation.

Companies limited by guarantee are appropriate to **non-commercial activities**, such as a charity or a trade association which is non-profit making but wishes to have a form of reserve capital if it becomes insolvent. They do not have **share capital**.

3.2 Unlimited liability companies

Key term

An **unlimited liability company** is a company in which members do not have limited liability. In the event of business failure, the liquidator can require members to contribute as much as may be required to pay the company's debts in full.

An unlimited company **can only be a private company**; by definition, a **public company is always limited.** An unlimited company need not **file** a copy of its **annual accounts** and reports with the Registrar, unless during the relevant accounting reference period:

(a) It is (to its knowledge) a **subsidiary** of a limited company.

(b) **Two** or more **limited companies** have **exercised rights** over the **company**, which (had they been exercised by only one of them) would have **made** the **company** a **subsidiary** of that one company.

(c) It is the **parent company** of a limited liability company.

The unlimited company certainly has its uses. It provides a **corporate body** (a separate legal entity) which can conveniently hold assets to which liabilities do not attach.

3.3 Public and private companies

A company may be **private** or **public**. Only the latter may offer its share to the public.

Key terms

A **public company** is a company whose constitution states that it is public and that it has complied with the registration procedures for such a company.

A **private company** is a company which has not been registered as a public company under the Companies Act. The major practical distinction between a private and public company is that the former may not offer its securities to the public.

A **public** company is a company registered as such under the Companies Act with the Registrar. **Any company not registered as public is a private company**. A public company may be one which was **originally incorporated** as a public company or one which re-registered as a public company having been previously a private company.

3.4 Conditions for being a public company

To trade, a public company must hold a **Registrar's trading certificate** having met the requirements, including **minimum capital** of £50,000.

3.4.1 Registrar's trading certificate

Before it can trade, a company originally incorporated as a public company must have a **trading certificate** issued by the Registrar. The conditions for this are:

- The **name** of the company identifies it as a public company, by ending with the words 'public limited company' or 'plc' or their Welsh equivalent, 'ccc', for a Welsh company.

- The **constitution** of the company states 'the company is a public company' or words to that effect.

- The **allotted share capital** of the company is at least the authorised minimum, which is £50,000.

- It is a **company** limited by shares.

With regard to the **minimum share capital** of £50,000.

- A company originally incorporated as a public company will not be permitted to trade until its **allotted** share capital is at least £50,000.

- A private company which re-registers as a public company will not be permitted to trade until it has **allotted** share capital of at least £50,000; this needs only be paid up to one-quarter of its nominal value (plus the whole of any premium).

- A private company which has share capital of £50,000 or more may, of course, continue as a private company; it is always **optional** to become a public company.

A **company limited by guarantee** which has no share capital, and an **unlimited company**, **cannot** be **public companies**.

3.4.2 Minimum membership and directors

A **public company** must have a minimum of **one member**. This is the same as a private company. However, unlike a private company it must have at least **two directors**. A private company must have just one. Directors do not usually have liability for the company's debts.

3.5 Private companies

A **private company** is the **residual category** and so does not need to satisfy any special conditions. They are generally small enterprises in which some, if not all, shareholders are also directors and **vice versa**. Ownership and management are combined in the same individuals.

Therefore, it is unnecessary to impose on the directors complicated restrictions to safeguard the interests of members and so the number of rules that apply to public companies are reduced for private companies.

3.6 Differences between private and public companies

FAST FORWARD

The main differences between public and private companies relate to: **capital**, **dealings** in **shares**, **accounts**, **commencement of business**, **general meetings**, **names**, **identification** and **disclosure requirements**.

The more **important differences** between public and private companies relate to the following factors.

3.6.1 Capital

The **main differences** are:

(a) There is a minimum amount of **£50,000** for a **public company**, but **no minimum** for a **private** company.

(b) A public company may **raise capital** by **offering** its **shares** or debentures to the public; a **private** company is **prohibited** from doing so.

(c) Both **public** and **private companies** must generally **offer** to **existing members first** any ordinary shares to be allotted for cash. However a **private** company **may permanently disapply** this rule.

3.6.2 Dealings in shares

Only a **public company** can obtain a listing for its shares on the **Stock Exchange** or other investment exchange. To obtain the advantages of listing, the company must agree to elaborate conditions contained in particulars in a **listing agreement** with the Stock Exchange. However, not all public companies are listed.

3.6.3 Accounts

(a) A **public company** has **six months** from the end of its accounting reference period in which to produce its statutory audited accounts. The period for a **private company** is **nine months**.

(b) A **private** company, if qualified by its size, may have **partial exemption** from various **accounting provisions**. These exemptions are not available to a public company or to its subsidiaries (even if they are private companies).

(c) A **listed public company** must publish its full accounts and reports on its **website**.

(d) **Public companies** must **lay their accounts** and reports before a **general meeting annually**. Private companies have no such requirement.

3.6.4 Commencement of business

A **private** company can commence business **as soon** as it is **incorporated**. A **public** company, if incorporated as such, must first **obtain a trading certificate from the Registrar**.

3.6.5 General meetings

Private companies are not required to hold annual general meetings (AGMs). **Public companies** must hold one within six months of their financial year end.

3.6.6 Names and Identification

The **rules on identification** as public or private are as follows.

- The word **'limited'** or **'Ltd'** in the name denotes a private company; **'public limited company'** or **'plc'** must appear at the end of the name of a public company.

- The **constitution** of a **public** company must state that it is a public company. A **private company** should be identified as private.

3.6.7 Disclosure requirements

There are **special disclosure and publicity requirements** for public companies.

The **main advantage** of carrying on business through a public, rather than a private, company is that a public company, by the issue of listing particulars, may obtain a **listing** on the Stock Exchange and so mobilise capital from the investing public generally.

Attention!

There is an important distinction between public companies and **listed public companies**. Listed (or quoted) companies are those which trade their shares (and other securities) on stock exchanges. Not all public companies sell their shares on stock exchanges (although, in law, they are entitled to sell their shares to the public). **Private** companies are not entitled to sell shares to the public in this way.

In practice, only public companies meeting certain criteria would be allowed to obtain such a listing by the Stock Exchange.

Private companies may be broadly **classified** into two groups: **independent** (also called **free-standing**) private companies and **subsidiaries** of other companies.

4 Additional classifications

FAST FORWARD

There are a number of other ways in which companies can be **classified**.

4.1 Parent (holding) and subsidiary companies

There is a distinction between an 'accounting' definition of a parent company, and a 'legal' definition under the Companies Act. A company will be the **parent (or holding) company** of another company, its **subsidiary company**, according to the following rules.

Key term

Parent company

(a) It holds a **majority of the voting rights** in the subsidiary.

(b) It **is a member of the subsidiary and has the right to appoint or remove a majority of its board of directors**.

(c) It **has the right to exercise a dominant influence over the subsidiary**:

    (i)   By virtue of provisions contained in the subsidiary's articles.

    (ii)   By virtue of a control contract.

(d) **It is a member of the subsidiary and controls alone**, under an agreement with other members, **a majority of the voting rights in the company.**

(e) **A company is also a parent if:**

   (i)   It has the power to exercise, or actually exercises, a dominant influence or control over the subsidiary

   (ii)   It and the subsidiary are managed on a unified basis

(f) **A company is also treated as the parent of the subsidiaries of its subsidiaries.**

A company (A Ltd) is a **wholly owned subsidiary** of another company (B Ltd) if it has no other members except B Ltd and its wholly owned subsidiaries, or persons acting on B Ltd's or its subsidiaries' behalf.

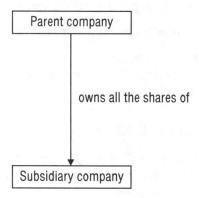

The diagram illustrates a **simple group**. In practice, such groups might be much larger and much more complex.

The **importance** of the **parent** and **subsidiary company relationship** is recognised in company law in a number of rules.

(a) A parent company must generally prepare **group accounts** in which the financial situation of parent and subsidiary companies is consolidated as if they were one person.

(b) A subsidiary may **not ordinarily be a member** of its parent company.

(c) Since directors of a parent company can **control** its **subsidiary**, some rules designed to regulate the dealings of companies with directors also apply to its subsidiaries, particularly loans to directors.

PO7 requires you to prepare financial statements in accordance with legal and regulatory requirements. This section will help you to identify whether a group (or combined entity) exists. This should assit you in preparing financial statements which are appropriate to the type of entity concerned.

4.2 Quoted companies

As we have seen public companies may seek a listing on a **public exchange**. This option is not open to private companies, who are not allowed to offer their shares for sale to the public. Listed companies are sometimes referred to as **quoted companies** (because their shares are quoted publicly).

4.3 Small companies regime

Small companies benefit from the **small companies regime's** reduced legal requirements in terms of filing accounts with the Registrar and obtaining an audit. The definitions of a small company for the purposes of accounting and auditing are almost identical.

In **accounting terms**, a company is small if it meets two of the following applicable criteria:

(a)   Balance sheet total of not more than £5.1 million
(b)   Turnover of not more than £10.2 million
(c)   50 employees or fewer on average

For **audit purposes**, a company is classed as small if it qualifies on the above criteria, but must **meet both** of conditions (a) and (b).

4.4 Micro-entities regime

A **micro-entity** has to option to take advantage of certain **accounting exemptions**. These include using **simple profit and loss accounts** and **balance sheets** and only providing a **minimum of accounting information** (referred to in the regulations as minimum accounting terms).

An **entity** is classed as **'micro'** if it meets at least **two** of the following **conditions**:

(a)   Annual turnover must be not more than £632,000
(b)   The balance sheet total must be not more than £316,000
(c)   The average number of employees must be not more than 10

4.5 Multinational companies

The vast majority of companies will simply operate in one country. However, some of the larger companies in the world will operate in more than one country. Such companies are **multinational**.

Key term

> A **multinational company** is a company that produces and markets its products in more than one country.

4.5.1 Examples: multinational companies

Some examples of well-known multinational companies include Walmart, Royal Dutch Shell, Exxon Mobil and Toyota.

5 Effect of legal personality

FAST FORWARD

> The case of *Salomon v Salomon & Co Ltd 1897* clearly demonstrates the **separate legal personality** of companies.

Salomon v Salomon & Co Ltd 1897

The facts: The claimant, S, had carried on business for 30 years. He decided to form a limited company to purchase the business, so he and six members of his family each subscribed for one share.

The company then purchased the business from S for £38,782, the purchase price being payable to the claimant by way of the issue of 20,000 £1 shares, the issue of £10,000 of debentures and £8,782 in cash.

The company did not prosper and was wound up a year later, at which point its liabilities exceeded its assets. The liquidator, representing unsecured trade creditors of the company, claimed that the company's business was in effect still the claimant's (he owned 20,001 of 20,007 shares). Therefore he should bear liability for its debts and that payment of the debenture debt to him should be postponed until the company's trade creditors were paid.

Decision: The House of Lords held that the business was owned by, and its debts were liabilities of, the company. The claimant was under no liability to the company or its creditors, his debentures were validly issued and the security created by them over the company's assets was effective. This was because the company was a legal entity separate and distinct from S.

The **principle of separate legal personality** was confirmed in the following case.

Lee v Lee's Air Farming Ltd 1960

The facts: Mr Lee, who owned the majority of the shares of an aerial crop-spraying business, and was the sole working director of the company, was killed while piloting the aircraft.

Decision: Although he was the majority shareholder and sole working director of the company, he and the company were separate legal persons. Therefore he could also be an employee with rights against it when killed in an accident in the course of his employment.

The following is a more **recent case** on separate legal personality which confirms the previous case law is still valid.

MacDonald v Costello 2011

The facts: Mr and Mrs Costello entered into an agreement with MacDonald (a firm of builders) to develop land which they owned. For tax purposes, the Costellos used a special purpose vehicle (Oakwood Residential Limited) to finance the work and the contract was between Oakwood and MacDonald. Oakwood had been used in previous dealings between the parties. Oakwood failed to pay some invoices when there was disagreement about the work which had been done. MacDonald was awarded a payment order against Oakwood and an award in restitution against the Costellos personally for unjust enrichment. The Costellos appealed the award for unjust enrichment.

Decision: Although the Costellos had been enriched by the work done by MacDonald, it was decided that the award against them should not be upheld. They were not party to the contract and, as shareholders of Oakwood, they were protected by the veil of incorporation.

5.1 Veil of incorporation

FAST FORWARD

Incorporation 'veils' members from outsiders' view but this veil may be lifted in **some circumstances**, so creditors and others can seek redress directly from members. The veil may be lifted: by statute to enforce the law; to prevent the evasion of obligations; and in certain situations where companies trade as a group.

Because a company has **separate legal personality** from the people who own or run it (the members/shareholders/directors), people can look at a company and not know who or what owns or runs it.

The fact that members are 'hidden' in this way is sometimes referred to as the '**veil of incorporation**': the members are 'veiled' from view.

6 Ignoring separate personality

FAST FORWARD

It is sometimes necessary by law to look at who the owners of a company are. This is referred to as '**lifting the veil**'.

Separate personality can be **ignored** to:

- **Identify** the **company** with its **members** and/or directors.
- Treat a **group of companies** as a **single commercial entity** (if a company is owned by another company).

The more important of these two reasons is the first one, although the second reason can sometimes be more complex. The main instances for lifting the veil are to **enforce the law**, **prevent evasion of obligations** and in some **group situations**. However, with the establishment of the concept of **corporate manslaughter** it is likely that directors will increasingly face prosecution and custodial sentences where they are found personally accountable for a death where the death can be connected with how they ran their business. The veil of incorporation will no longer protect them: *R v OLL Ltd 1994*.

6.1 Lifting the veil by statute to enforce the law

Lifting of the veil is **permitted under a number of statutes** to enforce the law.

6.1.1 Liability for trading without trading certificate

A public company must obtain a trading certificate from the Registrar before it may commence to trade. Failure to do so leads to **personal liability** of the directors for any loss or damage suffered by a third party resulting from a transaction made in contravention of the trading certificate requirement. They are also liable for a fine.

6.1.2 Fraudulent and wrongful trading

When a company is wound up, it may appear that its business has been carried on with **intent** to **defraud creditors** or others. In this case the court may decide that the persons (usually the directors) who were knowingly parties to the **fraudulent trading** shall be **personally responsible** under civil law for debts and other liabilities of the company: s 213 Insolvency Act 1986.

Fraudulent trading is also a criminal offence. Under the Companies Act 2006 any person guilty of the offence, even if the company has not been or is not being wound up, is liable for a fine or imprisonment for up to ten years.

If a company in insolvency proceedings is found to have traded when there is no reasonable prospect of avoiding insolvent liquidation, its directors may be liable under civil law for **wrongful trading**. Again a court may order such directors to make a contribution to the company's assets: s 214 Insolvency Act 1986.

6.1.3 Disqualified directors

Directors who participate in the management of a company in contravention of an order under the Company Directors Disqualification Act 1986 will be **jointly** or **severally liable** along with the company for the company's debts.

6.1.4 Abuse of company names

In the past there were a number of instances where directors of companies which went into **insolvent liquidation** formed another company with an identical or similar name. This new company bought the original company's business and assets from its liquidator.

The Insolvency Act 1986 makes it a criminal offence, and the directors personally liable, where they are a director of a company that goes into insolvent liquidation and they become involved with the directing, managing or promoting of a business which has an **identical name** to the original company, or a **name similar** enough to suggest a connection.

Exam focus point

> Questions in this area may require the identification of circumstances where the veil of incorporation will be lifted.

6.2 Lifting the veil to prevent evasion of obligations

A company may be identified with those who control it, for instance to determine its residence for tax purposes. The courts may also ignore the distinction between a company and its members and managers if the latter use that distinction to **evade** their **existing legal obligations**.

Gilford Motor Co Ltd v Home 1933

The facts: The defendant had been employed by the claimant company under a contract which forbade him to solicit its customers after leaving its service. After the termination of his employment he formed a company of which his wife and an employee were the sole directors and shareholders. However, he managed the company and through it evaded the covenant that prevented him from soliciting customers of his former employer.

Decision: An injunction requiring observance of the covenant would be made both against the defendant and the company which he had formed as a 'a mere cloak or sham'.

6.2.1 Public interest

In time of war a company is not permitted to trade with '**enemy aliens**'. The courts may draw aside the veil if, despite a company being registered in the UK, it is suspected that it is controlled by aliens: *Daimler Co Ltd v Continental Tyre and Rubber Co (GB) Ltd 1917*. The question of nationality may also arise in peacetime, where it is convenient for a foreign entity to have a British **facade** on its operations.

Re F G Films Ltd 1953

The facts: An English company was formed by an American company to 'make' a film which would obtain certain marketing and other advantages from being called a British film. Staff and finance were American and there were neither premises nor employees in England. The film was produced in India.

Decision: The British company was the American company's agent and so the film did not qualify as British. Effectively, the corporate entity of the British company was swept away and it was exposed as a 'sham' company.

6.2.2 Evasion of liabilities

The veil of incorporation may also be lifted where directors **ignore** the separate legal personality of two companies and transfer assets from one to the other in disregard of their duties, in order to avoid an existing liability.

Re H and Others 1996

The facts: The court was asked to rule that various companies within a group, together with the minority shareholders, should be treated as one entity in order to restrain assets prior to trial.

Decision: The order was granted. The court thought there was evidence that the companies had been used for the fraudulent evasion of excise duty.

6.2.3 Evasion of taxation

Courts may lift the veil of incorporation where it is being used to **conceal** the nationality of the company.

Unit Construction Co Ltd v Bullock 1960

The facts: Three companies, wholly owned by a UK company, were registered in Kenya. Although the companies' constitutions required board meetings to be held in Kenya, all three were, in fact, managed entirely by the holding company.

Decision: The companies were resident in the UK and liable to UK tax. The Kenyan connection was a sham, the question being not where they ought to have been managed, but where they were actually managed.

6.2.4 Quasi-partnership

An application to wind up a company on the 'just and equitable' ground under the Insolvency Act 1986 may involve the court lifting the veil to reveal the company as a **quasi-partnership.** This may happen where the company only has a few members, all of whom are actively involved in its affairs. Typically the individuals have operated contentedly as a company for years, but then fall out, and one or more of them seeks to remove the others.

The courts are willing in such cases to treat the **central relationship** between the directors as being that of partners, and rule that it would be unfair, therefore, to allow the company to continue with only some of its original members. This is illustrated by the case of *Ebrahimi v Westbourne Galleries Ltd 1973*.

6.3 Lifting the veil in group situations

The principle of the veil of incorporation extends to the holding (parent) company/subsidiary relationship. Although holding companies and subsidiaries are part of a group under company law, they retain their **separate legal personalities**. There is also some precedent for treating separate companies as a group (*DHN Food Distributors v Tower Hamlets LBC 1976*) although doubt has since been cast on this by subsequent cases.

In *Adams v Cape Industries plc 1990*, three reasons were put forward for identifying the companies as one, and lifting the veil of incorporation. They are:

- The subsidiary is acting as **agent** for the holding company
- The group is to be treated as a **single economic entity** because of statutory provision
- The **corporate structure** is being used as a **facade** (or sham) to conceal the truth

---

Adams v Cape Industries plc 1990

The facts: Cape, an English company, headed a group which included many wholly owned subsidiaries. Some of these mined asbestos in South Africa, and others marketed the asbestos in various countries including the USA.

Several hundred claimants had been awarded damages by a Texas court for personal injuries suffered as a result of exposure to asbestos dust. The defendants in Texas included one of Cape's subsidiaries, NAAC. The courts also considered the position of AMC, another subsidiary, and CPC, a company linked to Cape Industries.

Decision: The judgement would not be enforced against the English holding company, either on the basis that Cape had been 'present' in the US through its local subsidiaries or because it had carried on business in the US through the agency of NAAC. Slade LJ commented in giving the judgement that English law 'for better or worse recognises the creation of subsidiary companies ... which would fail to be treated as separate legal entities, with all the rights and liabilities which would normally be attached to separate legal entities'.

Whether desirable or not, English law allowed a group structure to be used so that legal liability fell on an individual member of a group rather than the group as a whole.

Exam focus point

Lifting the veil in group situations is easily forgotten. Ensure you know the *Cape Industries* case and the three reasons for lifting the veil in groups which it sets out.

6.4 Summary of situations in which the veil can be lifted

The instances in which the veil will be lifted are as follows.

Lifting the veil by statute to enforce the law	• Liability for trading without a trading certificate • Fraudulent and wrongful trading • Disqualified directors • Abuse of company names
Evasion of obligations	• Evasion of legal obligations • Public interest • Evasion of liabilities • Evasion of taxation • Quasi-partnership
Group situations	• Subsidiary acting as agent for the holding company • The group is to be treated as a single economic entity • The corporate structure is being used as a sham

6.5 Lifting the veil and limited liability

The above examples of lifting the veil include examples of where, if they have broken the law, **directors** can be made **personally liable** for a company's debts. This is very rare. If those directors are also members, then limited liability **does not apply**. This is the only time that limited liability is overridden and that the **member** becomes **personally liable** for the company's debts **due to their actions as a director**.

7 Comparison of companies and partnerships

FAST FORWARD

Because it is a separate legal entity, a company has a number of features which are different from a partnership. The most important difference between a company and a traditional partnership is that a company has a **separate legal personality** from its members, while a traditional partnership does not.

7.1 The differences

The **separate legal personality** of a company gives rise to a number of characteristics which mark it out from a traditional partnership. **Revise** this table when you have studied the rest of the book and know more of the details concerning the distinctive factors of companies.

Factor	Company	Traditional partnership
Entity	Is a legal entity separate from its members	Has no existence outside of its members
Liability	Members' liability can be limited	Partners' liability is usually unlimited
Size	May have any number of members (at least one)	Some partnerships are limited to 20 members (professional partnerships excluded)
Succession	Perpetual succession – change in ownership does not affect existence	Partnerships are dissolved when any of the partners leaves it
Owners' interests	Members own transferable shares	Partners cannot assign their interests in a partnership
Assets	Company owns the assets	Partners own assets jointly
Management	Company must have at least one director (two for a public company)	All partners can participate in management
Constitution	Company must have a written constitution	A partnership may have a written partnership agreement, but also may not

Factor	Company	Traditional partnership
Accounts	A company must usually deliver accounts to the Registrar	Partners do not have to send their accounts to the Registrar
Security	A company may offer a floating charge over its assets	A partnership may not usually give a floating charge on assets
Withdrawal of capital	Strict rules concerning repayment of subscribed capital	More straightforward for a partner to withdraw capital
Taxation	Company pays tax on its profit Directors are taxed through PAYE system Shareholders receive dividends which are taxed ten months after the tax year	Partners extract 'drawings' weekly or monthly. No tax is deducted as income tax is payable on final profit for the year.
Management	Members elect directors to manage the company	All partners have a right to be involved in management

Chapter Roundup

- In a **sole tradership**, there is no legal distinction between the individual and the business.

- A company has a **legal personality** separate from its owners (known as members). It is a formal arrangement, surrounded by formality and publicity, but its chief advantage is that members' **liability** for the company's debts is typically **limited**.

- The fact that a company's members – not the company itself – have **limited liability** for its debts **protects** the **members** from the company's creditors and ultimately from the full risk of business failure.

- Most companies are those **incorporated** under the **Companies Act**. However there are other types of company such as **corporations sole**, **chartered corporations**, **statutory corporations** and **community interest companies**.

- A company may be **private** or **public**. Only the latter may offer its shares to the public.

- To trade, a public company must hold a **Registrar's trading certificate** having met the requirements, including **minimum capital** of **£50,000**.

- The main differences between public and private companies relate to: **capital**, **dealings** in **shares**, **accounts**, **commencement of business**, **general meetings**, **names**, **identification** and **disclosure requirements**.

- There are a number of other ways in which companies can be **classified**.

- The case of *Salomon v Salomon & Co Ltd 1897* clearly demonstrates the **separate legal personality** of companies.

- Incorporation 'veils' members from outsiders' view but this veil may be lifted in **some circumstances**, so creditors and others can seek redress directly from members. The veil may be lifted: by statute to enforce the law; to prevent the evasion of obligations; and in certain situations where companies trade as a group.

- It is sometimes necessary by law to look at who the owners of a company are. This is referred to as **'lifting the veil'**.

- Because it is a separate legal entity, a company has a number of features which are different from a partnership. The most important difference between a company and a traditional partnership is that a company has a **separate legal personality** from its members, while a traditional partnership does not.

1   Which two of the following statements is true? A private company

A   Is defined as any company that is not a public company

B   Sells its shares on the junior stock market known as the Alternative Investment Market and on the Stock Exchange

C   Must have at least one director with unlimited liability

D   Is a significant form of business organisation in areas of the economy that do not require large amounts of capital

2   Under which circumstance would a member of a limited company have to contribute funds on winding up?

A   Where there is not enough cash to pay the creditors

B   Where they have an outstanding amount from when they originally purchased their shares

C   To allow the company to repurchase debentures it issued

D   Where the company is a community interest company and the funds are required to complete a community project

3   The minimum share capital of a public limited company is

A   £12,500

B   £50,000

C   £100,000

D   £500,000

4   Which two of the following are correct? A public company or plc

A   Is defined as any company which is not a private company

B   Has a legal personality that is separate from its members or owners

C   Must have at least one director with unlimited liability

D   Can own property and make contracts in its own name

5   Businesses in the form of sole traders are legally distinct from their owners.

True   ☐

False   ☒

Answers to Quick Quiz

1   A and D are correct. A private company cannot sell its shares to the public on any stock market, so B is incorrect. Directors need not have unlimited liability, so C is incorrect.

2   B   Members only have a liability for any outstanding amounts of share capital partly paid for.

3   B   £50,000 is the minimum.

4   B and D are correct. A public company has to be defined as such in its constitution so A is incorrect. No directors *need* have unlimited liability, so C is incorrect.

5   False. Sole trader businesses are not legally distinct from their owners.

Now try the questions below from the Practice Question Bank

Number
26, 27

Company formation

Topic list	Syllabus reference
1 Promoters and pre-incorporation contracts	D4(a)
2 Pre-incorporation expenses and contracts	D4(b)
3 Registration procedures	D4(c)
4 Statutory books and records	D4(d)
5 Confirmation statements	D4(d)

Introduction

This chapter concentrates on the **procedural aspects** of **company formation**. Important topics in these sections include the **formalities** that a company must observe in order to be formed, and the liability of **promoters for pre-incorporation contracts**.

This chapter also considers the concept of the **public accountability** of **limited companies** in terms of the records they must keep and returns they must make.

Study guide

		Intellectual level
D	**Formation and constitution of business organisations**	
4	**The formation and constitution of a company**	
(a)	Explain the role and duties of company promoters, and the breach of those duties and remedies available to the company	2
(b)	Explain the meaning of, and the rules relating to, pre-incorporation contracts	2
(c)	Describe the procedure for registering companies, both public and private, including the system of streamlined company registration	1
(d)	Describe the statutory books, records and returns, including the confirmation statement and the register of people with significant control, that companies must keep or make	1

Exam guide

Questions could be set on the procedures that need to be followed in order to set up a private or public limited company. You may also be tested on the potential liability of a promoter.

1 Promoters and pre-incorporation contracts

FAST FORWARD

A promoter **forms** a company. They must act with **reasonable skill** and **care**; if shares are to be allotted they are the agent of the prospective shareholders, with an agent's fiduciary duties.

A company cannot form itself. The person who forms it is called a '**promoter**'. A promoter is an example of an **agent**.

Key term

A **promoter** is one who undertakes to form a company with reference to a given project and to set it going and who takes the necessary steps to accomplish that purpose.

In addition to the person who takes the procedural steps to get a company incorporated, the term 'promoter' includes anyone who makes **business preparations** for the company. **However**, a person who acts **merely** in a **professional capacity** in company formation, such as a solicitor or an accountant, **is not** on that account a **promoter**.

1.1 Duties of promoters

Promoters have a general duty to exercise **reasonable skill and care**.

If the **promoter** is to be the **owner** of the company there is **no conflict of interest** and it does not matter if the promoter obtains some advantage from this position, for example, by selling their existing business to the company for 100% of its shares.

If, however, **some or all the shares** of the company when formed **are to be allotted to other people**, the promoter acts as their **agent**. This means they have the customary **duties** of an agent and the following fiduciary duties.

(a) A promoter must account for any **benefits obtained** through acting as a promoter.

(b) Promoters must not put themselves in a position where their own **interests conflict** with those of the company.

(c)   A promoter must provide **full information** on their transactions and account for all monies arising from them. The promoter must, therefore, make **proper disclosure** of any personal advantage to **existing** and **prospective** company **members** or to an **independent board of directors**.

A promoter may make a **profit** as a result of their position.

(a)   A **legitimate** profit is made by a promoter who acquires interest in property **before promoting** a company and then makes a profit when they sell the property to the promoted company, provided they disclose it.

(b)   A **wrongful** profit is made by a promoter who enters into, and makes a profit personally from, a contract as a promoter. They are in breach of fiduciary duty.

A promoter of a public company makes their **disclosure of legitimate profit** through listing particulars or a prospectus. If they make proper disclosure of a legitimate profit, they may retain it.

1.1.1 Remedy for breach of promoter's fiduciary duty

If the promoter does not make a proper disclosure of legitimate profits, or if they make wrongful profits, the primary remedy of the company is to **rescind** the **contract** and **recover its money**: *Erlanger v New Sombrero Phosphate Co 1878*.

However, sometimes it is too late to rescind because the property can no longer be returned or the company prefers to keep it. In such a case the company can **only recover** from the promoter their **wrongful profit**, unless some special circumstances dictate otherwise.

Where shares are sold under a **prospectus offer**, promoters have a statutory liability to compensate any person (who acquires securities to which the prospectus relates) who suffered loss as a result of any untrue or misleading statement or omission. **Statutory** and **listing regulations**, together with **rigorous investigation** by merchant banks, have greatly lessened the problem of the dishonest promoter.

2 Pre-incorporation expenses and contracts

FAST FORWARD

> A promoter has **no automatic right** to be reimbursed **pre-incorporation expenses** by the company, though this can be expressly agreed.

2.1 Pre-incorporation expenses

A promoter usually incurs **expenses** in preparations, such as drafting legal documents, made before the company is formed. They have **no automatic right to recover these 'pre-incorporation expenses'** from the company. However, they can generally arrange that the first directors, of whom they may be one, **agree** that the company shall pay the bills or refund to them their expenditure. They could also include a special article in the company's constitution containing an indemnity for the promoter.

2.2 Pre-incorporation contracts

FAST FORWARD

> Pre-incorporation contracts **cannot** be ratified by the company. A new contract on the same or similar terms must be expressly created.

Key term

> A **pre-incorporation contract** is a contract purported to be made by a company or its agent at a time before the company has been formed.

In agency law a principal may ratify a contract made by an agent retrospectively. However, a company can **never ratify** a contract made on its behalf **before it was incorporated**. This is because it did not exist when the pre-incorporation contract was made, so one of the conditions for ratification fails.

A company may enter into a **new contract** on the **same** or **similar terms** after it has been incorporated (**novation**). However, there must be **sufficient evidence** that the company has made a new contract. Mere recognition of the pre-incorporation contract by performing it, or accepting benefits under it, is not the same as making a new contract.

2.3 Liability of promoters for pre-incorporation contracts

A company's **promoter** is **liable** on all contracts to which they are deemed to be a party. This means they may also be entitled to enforce such contracts against the other party and so they could transfer the right to **enforce** the contract to the company.

2.4 Other ways of avoiding liability as a promoter for pre-incorporation contracts

There are various other ways for **promoters** to **avoid liability** for a **pre-incorporation contract**.

(a)   The contract remains as a **draft** (so not binding) until the company is formed. The promoters are the directors, and the company has the power to enter the contract. Once the company is formed, the directors take office and the company enters into the contract.

(b)   If the contract has to be finalised before incorporation it should contain a clause that the personal liability of promoters is to cease if the company, when formed, enters a **new contract** on the same or similar terms. This is known as **novation**.

(c)   A common way to avoid the problem concerning pre-incorporation contracts is to buy a company **'off the shelf'**. Even if a person contracts on behalf of the new company before it is bought, the company should be able to ratify the contract since it existed 'on the shelf' at the time the contract was made.

Exam focus point

You should consider the status of pre-incorporation contracts as a highly examinable topic.

3 Registration procedures

FAST FORWARD

A **company** is **formed and registered** under the Companies Act 2006 when it is issued with a **certificate of incorporation** by the Registrar, after submission to the Registrar of a number of documents and a fee.

Most companies are **registered** under the Companies Act 2006.

A company is formed under the Companies Act 2006 by one or more persons **subscribing to a memorandum of association**, who comply with the requirements regarding registration. A company may not be formed for an unlawful purpose.

3.1 Documents to be delivered to the Registrar

To obtain r**egistration** of a company limited by shares, an **application for registration**, **various documents** and a **fee** must be sent to the Registrar (usually electronically).

3.1.1 Application for registration

The Companies Act requires an **application for registration** to be made and submitted to the Registrar.

The **application** must contain:

- The company's **proposed name**
- The **location** of its **registered office** (England and Wales, Wales, Scotland or Northern Ireland)
- That the **liability of members** is to be **limited** by **shares** or **guarantee**
- Whether the company is to be **private** or **public**
- A statement of the **intended address** of the **registered office**

Documents to be delivered	Description
Memorandum of association	This is a **prescribed form** signed by the subscribers. The memorandum states that the subscribers wish to form a company and they agree to become members of it. If the company has share capital each subscriber agrees to subscribe for at least one share.
Articles of association (only required if the company does not adopt model articles)	Articles are signed by the same subscriber(s), dated and witnessed. **Model articles** are provided by statute and can be adopted by a new company if: • No other articles are registered, or • If the articles supplied do not exclude or modify the model articles.
Statement of proposed officers	The statement gives the particulars of the proposed **director(s)** and **company secretary** if applicable. The persons named as directors must consent to act in this capacity. When the company is incorporated they are deemed to be appointed.
Statement of compliance	The statement that the **requirements** of the **Companies Act** in respect of registration have been **complied** with.
Statement of capital and initial shareholdings (only required for companies limited by shares)	A statement of capital and initial shareholdings must be delivered by all companies with **share capital**. Alternatively, a statement of guarantee is required by companies limited by guarantee.
Registration fee	A **registration fee** is also payable on registration.

Exam focus point

Questions on incorporation could require you to identify the documents which should be sent to the Registrar.

3.2 Certificate of incorporation

The Registrar considers whether the documents are formally in order. If satisfied, the company is given a 'registered number'. A **certificate of incorporation** is issued and notice of it is publicised.

A company is registered by the inclusion of the company in the register, and the issue of a **certificate of incorporation** by the Registrar. The certificate:

- Identifies the company by its **name** and **registered number**
- States that it is **limited** (if appropriate) and whether it is a **private** or **public** company
- States whether the **registered office** is in England and Wales, Wales, Scotland or Northern Ireland
- States the **date of incorporation**
- Is **signed** by the **Registrar**, or authenticated by the Registrar's official seal

Key term

A **certificate of incorporation** is a certificate issued by the Registrar which denotes the date of incorporation, 'the subscribers, together with any persons who from time to time become members, become a body corporate capable of exercising all the functions of an incorporated company'.

The **certificate of incorporation** is **conclusive evidence** that:

- All the **requirements** of the **Companies Act** have been **followed**.
- The company is a **company authorised** to be **registered** and has been **duly registered**.
- If the certificate states that the company is a **public company**, it is conclusive.

If irregularities in formation procedure or an error in the certificate itself are later discovered, the certificate is nonetheless **valid** and **conclusive**: *Jubilee Cotton Mills Ltd v Lewes 1924*.

Upon incorporation persons named as **directors** and **secretary** in the statement of proposed officers automatically become such officers.

3.3 Companies 'off the shelf'

Buying a company '**off the shelf**' avoids the administrative burden of registering a company.

Despite the **Small Business, Enterprise and Employment Act 2015** introducing changes to streamline company administration, the registration of a new company can be a lengthy business and it is often easiest for people wishing to operate as a company to purchase an **'off-the-shelf' company**.

This is possible by contacting enterprises specialising in registering a **stock of companies**, ready for sale when a person comes along who needs the advantages of incorporation.

Normally the persons associated with the company formation enterprise are registered as the company's subscribers, and its first secretary and director. When the company is purchased, the **shares** are **transferred** to the **buyer**, and the Registrar is notified of the director's and the secretary's resignation.

The principal **advantages** for the purchaser of purchasing an off-the-shelf company are as follows.

(a)   The **following documents** will **not need** to be **filed** with the Registrar by the purchaser:

       (i)   Memorandum and articles (unless the articles are not model articles)
       (ii)   Application for registration
       (iii)   Statement of proposed officers
       (iv)   Statement of compliance
       (v)   Statement of capital and initial shareholdings
       (vi)   Fee

       This is because the specialist has already registered the company. It will therefore be a quicker and, very possibly, cheaper way of incorporating a business.

(b)   There will be **no risk** of **potential liability** arising from pre-incorporation contracts. The company can trade without needing to worry about waiting for the Registrar's certificate of incorporation.

The **disadvantages** relate to the changes that will be required to the off-the-shelf company to make it compatible with the members' needs.

(a)   The off-the-shelf company is likely to have **model articles**. The directors may wish to amend these.

(b)   The directors may want to **change** the **name** of the company.

(c)   The **subscriber shares** will need to be **transferred**, and the transfer recorded in the register of members. Stamp duty will be payable.

3.4 Re-registration procedures

A **private company** with share capital may be able to re-register as a **public company** if the share capital requirement is met. A public company may re-register as a private one.

Note. For a private company to re-register as a public company it must fulfil the share capital requirement of a public company: allotted share capital must be at least £50,000, of which a quarter must be paid up, plus the whole of any premium.

	Re-registering as a public company	Re-registering as a private company
Resolution	The **shareholders must agree** to the company going public • Convene a general meeting • Pass a **special resolution** (75% majority) – Alters the constitution	The **shareholders must agree** to the company going private • Convene a general meeting • Pass a **special resolution** (75% majority of those present and voting) – Alters the constitution

Application	The **company must** then **apply** to the Registrar to go public
	
	• Send application to the Registrar
	
	• Send additional information to the Registrar, comprising
	
	  – Copy of the special resolution
	
	  – Copy of proposed new public company articles
	
	  – Statement of the company's proposed name on re-registration
	
	  – Statement of proposed company secretary
	
	  – Balance sheet and related auditors' statement which states that at the balance sheet date the company's net assets are not less than its called-up share capital and undistributable reserves.
	
	  – Statement of compliance
	
	  – Valuation report regarding allotment of shares for non-cash consideration since the balance sheet date
		The **company must** then **apply** to the Registrar to go private
		
		• Send the application to the Registrar
		
		• Send additional information to the Registrar, comprising
		
		  – Copy of the special resolution
		
		  – Copy of altered new private company articles
		
		  – Statement of compliance
		
		  – Statement of the company's proposed name on re-registration

Approval	The Registrar must accept the statement of compliance as sufficient evidence that the company is entitled to be re-registered as public. A certificate of incorporation on re-registration is issued.	The Registrar issues a certificate of incorporation on re-registration.
Compulsory re-registration	If the **share capital** of a public company **falls below £50,000**, it must re-register as a private company.	There is **no such compulsion** for a private company.

3.4.1 Limited company to unlimited company re-registration

Although less common, it is also possible for a **private limited company to re-register as an unlimited**. This requires the **approval of all the members** of the company and is only permitted if the company has not previously re-registered as a limited company. On application to the Registrar, the company must submit its proposed name, the resolution, proposed new articles and a statement of compliance that the requirements for re-registration have been complied with.

3.4.2 Unlimited company to limited company re-registration

An **unlimited company may re-register as limited** if it passes a **special resolution** to that effect and is only permitted if the company has not previously re-registered as unlimited. The company should then

apply to the Registrar, submitting a copy of the resolution (which must state whether the company is to be limited by shares or guarantee), its proposed name, a statement of guarantee (if the company is to be limited by guarantee), a statement of capital (if the company has share capital) and a statement of compliance that confirms the requirements for re-registration have been complied with.

3.5 Commencement of business rules

FAST FORWARD

To **trade** or **borrow**, a public company needs a **trading certificate**. Private companies may commence business on **registration**.

3.5.1 Public companies

A **public company** incorporated as such may not do business or exercise any borrowing powers unless it has obtained a **trading certificate** from the Registrar. This is obtained by sending an application to the Registrar. A private company which is re-registered as a public company is not subject to this rule.

The **application**:

- States the nominal value of the allotted share capital is not less than £50,000, or prescribed euro equivalent

- States the particulars of preliminary expenses and payments or benefits to promoters

- Must be accompanied by a statement of compliance.

If a public company does business or borrows before obtaining a certificate the other party is protected since the **transaction is valid**. However, the company (and any officer in default) have committed an offence **punishable** by a **fine**. They may also have to indemnify the third party.

Under the Insolvency Act 1986 a court may **wind up** a public company which does not obtain a trading certificate within **one year** of incorporation.

3.5.2 Private company

A **private company** may do business and exercise its borrowing powers from the date of its incorporation. After registration the following procedures are important.

(a)   A **first meeting** of the directors should be held at which the chairman, secretary and sometimes the auditors are appointed, shares are allotted to raise capital, authority is given to open a bank account and other commercial arrangements are made.

(b)   A **return of allotments** should be made to the Registrar.

(c)   The company may give notice to the Registrar of the **accounting reference date** on which its annual accounts will be made up. If no such notice is given within the prescribed period, companies are deemed to have an accounting reference date of the **last day of the month** in which the **anniversary of incorporation** falls.

4 Statutory books and records

4.1 The requirement for public accountability

FAST FORWARD

The price of limited liability is greater **public accountability** by means of the Companies Registry, registers, the *London Gazette* and company letterheads.

Under company law the **privileges of trading** through a separate corporate body are matched by the duty to provide information which is available to the public about the company.

Basic sources of information on UK companies
The Registrar keeps a file at **Companies House** which holds all documents delivered by the company for filing. Any member of the public, for example someone who intends to do business with the company, may inspect the file (usually electronically).
The **registers and other documents** which the company is required to hold at its registered office (or another registered address).
The *London Gazette*, a specialist publication, in which the company itself or the Registrar is required to publish certain notices or publicise the receipt of certain documents.
The **company's letterheads** and other forms, which must give particulars of the company's place of registration, its identifying number and the address of its office.

4.2 The Registrar of Companies

The **Registrar of Companies** (the Registrar) and the Registrar's department within the government is usually called Companies House (in full it is 'the Companies Registration Office').

For **English** and **Welsh** companies the Registrar is located at Companies House in **Cardiff**; for **Scottish** companies the Registrar is in **Edinburgh**.

The company is identified by its **name** and **serial number** which must be stated on every document sent to Companies House for filing.

On incorporation, the company's file includes a copy of its **certificate of incorporation** and the **original documents** presented to secure its incorporation.

Once a company has been in existence for some time the **file is likely to include** the following.

- Certificate of incorporation
- Public company trading certificate
- Each year's annual accounts and return
- Copies of special and some ordinary resolutions
- A copy of the altered articles of association, if applicable
- Notices of various events, such as a change of directors or secretary
- If a company issues a prospectus, a signed copy with all annexed documents

4.3 Statutory books

FAST FORWARD

A company must keep **registers** of certain aspects of its constitution, including the registers of members, and directors.

Various people are entitled to have access to **registers** and copies of records that the company must keep. To enable the documents to be found easily the company must keep them at its **registered office** or a **single alternative inspection location** (SAIL) which is registered with Companies House. All documents may be kept at either location or a combination of the two. Companies are not permitted to have more than one single alternative inspection location.

Private companies are permitted to file their registers of members, directors and secretaries, people with significant control (PSC) and directors' residential addresses at **Companies House** instead of a registered office or SAIL.

Register/copies of records
Register of **members**
Register of **people with significant control**
Register of **directors (and secretaries)**
Register of **directors' residential addresses**
Records of **directors' service contracts and indemnities**
Records of **resolutions and meetings** of the company
Register of **debentureholders**
Register of disclosed **interests** in shares (public company only)

4.4 Register of members

Every company must keep a **register of members**. It must contain:

(a) The **name** and **address** of **each member**

(b) **The shareholder class** (if more than one) to which they belong, unless this is indicated in the particulars of their shareholding

(c) If the company has a share capital, the **number of shares** held by each member. In addition:

    (i) If the shares have **distinguishing numbers**, the members' shares must be identified in the register by those numbers

    (ii) If the company has more than one class of share, the members' shares must be **distinguished** by their **class**, such as preference, ordinary, or non-voting shares

(d) The date on which each member **became**, and eventually the date on which they **ceased** to be, a member

Any member of the company can inspect the **register of members** of a company without charge. A member of the public must pay, but has the right of inspection.

A company with more than **50 members** must keep a separate index of those members, unless the register itself functions as an index.

4.5 Register of people with significant control (PSC)

All private and public companies are required to keep a **register of people with significant control**. This register contains information on individuals who own or control over 25% of a company's shares or voting rights, or who exercise control over the company and its management in other ways (for example through the ability to appoint or remove directors).

The information which is required to be collected includes the individual's **name**, **date of birth**, **nationality** and **service address** and **details of their interest in the company**. This information will be checked and updated each year when the company submits its confirmation statement and is available for public inspection. It an **offence** not to comply with the requirement to file this register.

4.6 Register of directors

The **register of directors** must contain the following details for all directors.

- **Present** and **former** forenames and surnames
- A **service address** (may be the company's registered address rather than their home address)
- **Residency** and **nationality**
- **Business occupation** (if any)
- **Date of birth**

The register does not include shadow directors and it must be **open to inspection** by a member (free of charge), or by any other person (for a fee). Note the company must keep a separate **register** of **directors' residential addresses** but this is not available to members or the general public.

4.7 Records of directors' service contracts

The company should keep **copies** or written memoranda of all **service contracts** for its directors, including contracts for services which are not performed in the capacity of director. Members are entitled to view these copies for free, or request a copy on payment of a set fee.

Key term

> A director's **service contract** means a contract under which:
>
> (a) A director of the company undertakes personally to perform services (as director or otherwise) for a company, or for a subsidiary of the company, or
>
> (b) Services (as director or otherwise) that a director of the company undertakes personally to perform which are made available by a third party to the company, or to a subsidiary of the company.

4.8 Register of debentureholders

Companies with debentures issued nearly always keep a **register of debentureholders** but there is no statutory compulsion to do so.

4.9 Accounting records

FAST FORWARD

Companies must keep **sufficient accounting records** to explain the company's transactions and its financial position; in other words, so a profit and loss account and balance sheet can be prepared.

A company is required to keep **accounting records** sufficient to **show and explain** the company's transactions. At any time, it should be possible:

- To **disclose**, with reasonable accuracy, the **company's financial position** at intervals of not more than six months

- For the directors to ensure that any accounts required to be prepared **comply** with the **Companies Act 2006** and **International Accounting Standards**

Certain **specific records** are required by the Act.

(a) Daily entries of **sums paid** and **received**, with details of the source and nature of the transactions

(b) A **record** of **assets** and **liabilities**

(c) **Statements of stock** held by the company at the end of each financial year

(d) **Statements of stocktaking** to back up the records in (c)

(e) **Statements of goods bought and sold** (except retail sales), together with details of buyers and sellers sufficient to identify them

The requirements (c) to (e) above apply only to businesses involved in **dealing in goods**.

Accounting records must be kept for **three** years (in the case of a **private** company), and **six** years in that of a **public** one.

Accounting records should be kept at the company's **registered office** or at some other place thought fit by the directors. Accounting records should be open to **inspection** by the **company's officers**. Shareholders have **no statutory rights** to inspect the records, although they may be granted the right by the articles.

Failure in respect of these duties is an **offence** by the officers in default.

4.10 Annual accounts

FAST FORWARD

A registered company must prepare **annual accounts** showing a true and fair view, lay them and various reports before members, and file them with the Registrar following directors' approval.

For each **accounting reference period** (usually 12 months) of the company, the directors must prepare accounts. Where they are prepared in Companies Act format they must include a **balance sheet** and **profit and loss account** which give a **true and fair view** of the individual company's and the group's:

- Assets
- Liabilities
- Financial position
- Profit or loss

The accounts can either be in **Companies Act format** or prepared in accordance with **International Accounting Standards (IAS)**. Where international accounting standards are followed, a note to this effect must be included in the notes to the accounts. Most private companies are permitted to file **abbreviated accounts**.

The company's board of directors must **approve** the **annual accounts** and they must be signed by a director on behalf of the board. When directors approve annual accounts that do not comply with the Act or IAS they are **guilty** of an **offence**.

A public company is required to **lay its accounts**, and the **directors' report**, before **members** in **general meeting**. A quoted company must also lay the directors' remuneration report before the general meeting.

A company must file its annual accounts and its report with the **Registrar** within a maximum period reckoned from the date to which the accounts are made up. The standard permitted interval between the end of the accounting period and the filing of accounts is **six months** for a **public** and **nine months** for a **private company**.

The accounts must be **audited**. The **auditors' report** must be attached to the copies issued to members, filed with the Registrar or published. Exemptions apply to **small and dormant companies,** though members may require an audit. The accounts must also be accompanied by a **directors' report** giving information on a number of prescribed matters. These include (where an audit was necessary) a statement that there is no relevant information of which the auditors are unaware, and another statement from the directors that they exercised due skill and care in the period. Quoted companies must submit the **directors' remuneration report**.

Under the Companies Act 2006 (Strategic Report and Directors' Report) Regulations 2013, large companies must prepare a **strategic report** as part of their financial statements.

The purpose of the strategic report is to inform members of the company and help them **assess how the directors have performed** their duty to promote the success of the company.

The strategic report must contain a **fair review of the company's business**, and a description of the principal risks and uncertainties facing the company.

The review required is a **balanced and comprehensive analysis** of the development and performance of the company's business during the financial year, and the position of the company's business at the end of that year, consistent with the size and complexity of the business.

Each **member** and **debentureholder** is entitled to be sent a copy of the **annual accounts**, together with the directors' and auditor's reports. In the case of public companies, they should be sent at least 21 days before the meeting at which they shall be laid. In the case of private companies they should be sent at the same time as the documents are filed, if not earlier.

Anyone else entitled to **receive** notice of a general meeting, including the company's auditor, should **also receive** a copy. At any other time any member or debentureholder is entitled to a copy free of charge within **seven days** of requesting it.

All companies may prepare summary financial statements to be circulated to members instead of the full accounts, subject to various requirements as to form and content being met. However, members have the right to receive full accounts should they wish to.

Quoted companies must make their annual accounts and reports available on a website which identifies the company and is maintained on the company's behalf. The documents must be made available as soon as reasonably practicable and access should not be conditional on the payment of a fee or subject to other restrictions.

Where the company or its directors **fail to comply** with the Act, they may be subject to a **fine**.

PO7 requires you to prepare financial statements in accordance with relevant accounting standards, policies and legislation. This section will help you understand some legal requirements relating to when the financial reports should be published and their contents.

5 Confirmation statements

Every twelve months a company must send a **confirmation statement** to the Registrar.

Every company must send a **confirmation statement** to the Registrar. The statement can be sent at any time, but no more than twelve months may elapse between statement submissions.
The purpose of the **confirmation statement** is to keep the Registrar informed about certain changes to the company. Much of this information would have been submitted when the company is formed.

Confirmation statements are used to **confirm** that there have been **no changes** to the information held by the Registrar during the previous twelve months, if none have been made. If changes have been made, it records just the changes that have occurred.

Examples of information requiring confirmation are:

- The address of the **registered office** of the company

- The address (if different) at which the **register of members** or **debentureholders** is kept

- The type of company and its principal **business activities**

- The total number of **issued shares,** their **aggregate nominal value** and the amounts paid and unpaid on each share

- For each **class of share**, the **rights** of those shares, the **total number** of shares in that class and their **total nominal value**

- Particulars of **members** of the company

- Changes to the **Register of people with significant control**

- Particulars of those who have **ceased** to be members since the last return

- The number of shares of each **class** held by members at the return date, and transferred by members since incorporation or the last return date

- The particulars of **directors,** and **secretary (if applicable)**

Chapter Roundup

- A promoter **forms** a company. They must act with **reasonable skill** and **care**; if shares are to be allotted they are the agent of the prospective shareholders, with an agent's fiduciary duties.

- A promoter has **no automatic right** to be reimbursed **pre-incorporation expenses** by the company, though this can be expressly agreed.

- Pre-incorporation contracts **cannot** be ratified by the company. A new contract on the same or similar terms must be expressly created.

- A **company** is **formed and registered** under the Companies Act 2006 when it is issued with a **certificate of incorporation** by the Registrar, after submission to the Registrar of a number of documents and a fee.

- Buying a company **'off the shelf'** avoids the administrative burden of registering a company.

- A **private company** with share capital may be able to re-register as a **public company** if the share capital requirement is met. A public company may re-register as a private one.

- To **trade** or **borrow**, a public company needs a **trading certificate**. Private companies may commence business on **registration**.

- The price of limited liability is greater **public accountability** by means of the Companies Registry, registers, the *London Gazette* and company letterheads.

- A company must keep **registers** of certain aspects of its constitution, including the registers of members, and directors.

- Companies must keep **sufficient accounting records** to explain the company's transactions and its financial position; in other words, so a profit and loss account and balance sheet can be prepared.

- A registered company must prepare **annual accounts** showing a true and fair view, lay them and various reports before members, and file them with the Registrar following directors' approval.

- Every twelve months a company must send a **confirmation statement** to the Registrar.

1   A company can confirm a pre-incorporation contract by performing it or obtaining benefits from it.

   True   ☐

   False   ☒

2   If a public company does business or borrows before obtaining a trading certificate from the Registrar, the transaction is:

   A   Invalid, and the third party cannot recover any loss
   B   Invalid, but the third party may recover any loss from the directors
   C   Valid, and the directors are punishable by a fine
   D   Valid, but the third party can sue the directors for further damages

3   A company must keep a register of directors. What details must be revealed?

   Select all that apply.

   A   Full name
   B   Service address
   C   Nationality
   D   Date of birth
   E   Business occupation

4   An accountant or solicitor acting in their professional capacity during the registration of a company may be deemed a promoter.

   True   ☐

   False   ☒

5   If a certificate of incorporation is dated 6 March, but is not signed and issued until 8 March, when is the company deemed to have come into existence?   8 March   6 March   —

Answers to Quick Quiz

1   False. The company must make a new contract on similar terms.

2   C. The directors are punished for allowing the company to trade before it is allowed to.

3   All of them.

4   False. A person acting in a professional capacity will not be deemed a promoter.

5   6 March. The date on the certificate is conclusive.

Now try the questions below from the Practice Question Bank

Number
28, 29

11

Constitution of a company

Topic list	Syllabus reference
1 Memorandum of association	D4(e)
2 A company's constitution	D4(e), D4(f), D4(g)
3 Company objects and capacity	D4(e)
4 The constitution as a contract	D4(e)
5 Company name and registered office	D4(h)

Introduction

The **articles of association** is one of the documents that may be required to be submitted to the Registrar when applying for registration. The articles, together with any resolutions and agreements which may affect them, form the company's **constitution**.

The constitution sets out what the company does; if there are no restrictions specified then the company may do anything, provided it is legal. Clearly this includes the capacity to contract, an important aspect of legal personality. Also significant is the concept of **ultra vires**, a term used to describe transactions that are outside the scope of the company's capacity.

ultra vires = transactions that are outside the scope of the company's capacity

Study guide

		Intellectual level
D	**Formation and constitution of business organisations**	
4	**The formation and constitution of a company**	
(e)	Analyse the effect of a company's constitutional documents	2
(f)	Describe the contents of model articles of association	1
(g)	Explain how articles of association can be changed	2
(h)	Explain the controls over the names that companies may or may not use	2

Exam guide

A company's constitution could easily be examined in either a knowledge or an application question. You may be asked to explain any of the constitutional documents and how they may be altered.

1 Memorandum of association

> The memorandum is a **simple document** which states that the subscribers wish to form a company and become members of it.

Before the Companies Act 2006, the **memorandum of association** was an extremely important document containing information concerning the relationship between the company and the outside world – for example, its aims and purpose (its objects).

The position changed with the 2006 Act and much of the information contained in the old memorandum is now to be found in the 'articles of association', which we will come to shortly. The **essence** of the memorandum has been retained, although it is now a very simple historical document which states that the **subscribers** (the initial shareholders):

(a)   Wish to **form a company** under the Act, and

(b)   Agree to **become members** of the company and to take at least one share each if the company is to have share capital.

The memorandum must be in the **prescribed form** and must be **signed** by each subscriber.

It has been deemed by the Companies Act 2006 that companies which were incorporated under a **previous** Act and whose memorandum contains provisions now found in the articles, shall have these provisions interpreted as if they are part of the articles.

2 A company's constitution

> A **company's constitution** comprises the **articles of association** and any **resolutions and agreements** it makes which affect the constitution.

According to the Companies Act 2006, the constitution of a company consists of:

* The **articles of association**
* **Resolutions and agreements** that it makes that affect the constitution

We shall consider resolutions and agreements first. This will help explain how the articles of association are amended.

2.1 Resolutions and agreements

In addition to the main **constitutional document** (the articles of association), **resolutions** and **agreements** also form part of a company's constitution.

Resolutions are decisions passed by members that directly affect the company's constitution, as they are used to **introduce**, **amend** or **remove** provisions in the articles. **Agreements**, made for example between the company and members, are also deemed as amending the constitution.

Copies of resolutions or agreements that amend the constitution must be sent to the Registrar within **15 days** of being passed or agreed. If a company fails to do this then every officer who is in default commits an offence punishable by fine. Where a **resolution** or **agreement** which affects a company's constitution is **not in writing**, the company is required to send the registrar a **written memorandum** that sets out the terms of the resolution or agreement in question.

Articles of association

2.2 Articles of association

> The **articles of association** consist of the internal rules that relate to the management and administration of the company.

The articles contain detailed **rules** and **regulations** setting out how the company is to be **managed** and **administered**. The Act states that the registered articles should be contained in a **single document** which is divided into **consecutively numbered paragraphs**. Articles should contain rules on a number of areas, the most important being summarised in the table below.

Contents of articles	
Appointment and dismissal of directors	Communication with members
Powers, responsibilities and liabilities of directors	Class meetings
Directors' meetings	Issue of shares
General meetings; calling, conduct and voting	Transfer of shares
Members' rights	Documents and records
Dividends	Company secretary

2.2.1 Model articles

Rather than each company having to draft their own articles, and to allow companies to be set up **quickly** and **easily**, the Act allows the Secretary of State to provide **model** (or standard) **articles** that companies can adopt. Different models are available for different types of company; most companies would adopt model **private** or **public company** articles.

Companies are free to use **any** of the model articles that they wish to, by registering them on incorporation. If **no articles** are registered then the company will be **automatically incorporated** with the **default model articles** which are relevant to the type of company being formed. Model articles can be **amended** by the members and therefore tailored to the specific needs of the company.

Model articles are, effectively, a **'safety net'** which allow directors and members to take decisions if the company has failed to include suitable provisions in its registered articles, or registered no articles at all.

The following summarises the **model articles for a private limited company**. Do not try to learn the contents but use it to understand the type of information contained in them. Model articles are also available for **public limited companies**. These articles are different to those of a private limited company as they are **more appropriate** to the needs of a **plc**.

We shall cover a number of the **model articles** later in this Study Text.

Model articles for private companies limited by shares

Index to the articles

Part 4 Decision making by shareholders

Organisation of general meetings

37. Attendance and speaking at general meetings
38. Quorum for general meetings
39. Chairing of general meetings
40. Attendance and speaking by directors and non-shareholders
41. Adjournment

Voting at general meetings

42. Voting: general
43. Errors and disputes
44. Poll votes
45. Content of proxy notices
46. Delivery of proxy notices
47. Amendments to resolutions

Part 5 Administrative arrangements

48. Means of communication to be used
49. Company seals
50. No right to inspect accounts and other records
51. Provision for employees on cessation of business

Directors' indemnity and insurance

52. Indemnity
53. Insurance

2.2.2 Alteration of the articles

> **FAST FORWARD**
>
> The articles may be altered by a **special resolution**. The basic test is whether the alteration is for the **benefit of the company as a whole**.

Any company has a statutory power to alter its articles by **special resolution**. A private company may pass a **written resolution** with a **75% majority**. The alteration will be valid and binding on **all** members of the company. **Copies** of the amended articles must be sent to the **Registrar**, within 15 days of the amendment taking effect.

2.2.3 Making the company's constitution unalterable

There are devices by which some provisions of the company's constitution can be made **unalterable** unless the member who wishes to prevent any alteration consents.

(a)   The articles may give a member **additional votes** so that they can block a resolution to alter articles on particular points (including the removal of their weighted voting rights from the articles). However, to be effective, the articles must also limit the powers of members to alter the articles that give extra votes.

(b)   The articles may provide that when a meeting is held to vote on a proposed alteration of the articles the **quorum present must include** the **member concerned**. They can then deny the meeting a quorum by absenting themselves.

(c)   The Act permits companies to **'entrench' provisions** in their articles. This means specific provisions may only be **amended** or **removed** if certain **conditions** are met which are more restrictive than a special resolution such as agreement of all the members. However, such 'entrenched provisions' **cannot** be drafted so that the articles can never be amended or removed.

2.2.4 Restrictions on alteration

Even when it is possible to hold a meeting and pass a special resolution, alteration of the articles is **restricted** by the following principles.

(a) The alteration is **void** if it **conflicts with the Companies Act** or with general law.

(b) In various circumstances, such as to protect a minority, the **court may order** that an alteration be made or, alternatively, that an existing article shall not be altered.

(c) An existing **member may not be compelled** by alteration of the articles to **subscribe for additional shares** or to accept increased liability for the shares which they hold, unless they have given their consent.

(d) An alteration of the articles which varies the rights attached to a class of shares may only be made if the **correct rights variation procedure** has been followed to obtain the consent of the class. A 15% minority may apply to the court to cancel the variation.

(e) A person whose **contract** is contained in the articles cannot obtain an injunction to prevent the articles being altered, **but** they may be entitled to **damages** for breach of contract. Alteration cannot take away rights already acquired by performing the contract.

(f) An alteration may be **void** if the **majority** who approve it are **not acting *bona fide* in what they deem to be the interests of the company as a whole**.

The case law on the **bona fide test** is an effort to hold the balance between two principles:

(a) The **majority** are **entitled** to **alter articles**, even though a minority considers that the alteration is prejudicial to its interests.

(b) A minority is entitled to protection against an alteration which is intended to **benefit** the **majority** rather than the company, and which is **unjustified discrimination** against the minority.

Principle (b) tends to be **restricted** to cases where the majority seeks to expel the minority from the company.

The most elaborate analysis of this subject was made by the Court of Appeal in the case of *Greenhalgh v Arderne Cinemas Ltd 1950*. Two main propositions were laid down by the judge.

(a) **'Bona fide for the benefit of the company as a whole'** is a **single test** and also a **subjective test** (what did the majority believe?). The court will not substitute its own view.

(b) 'The company as a whole' means, in this context, **the general body of shareholders**. The test is whether every 'individual hypothetical member' would, in the honest opinion of the majority, benefit from the alteration.

If the purpose is to benefit the company as a whole the alteration is valid, even though it can be shown that the **minority does in fact suffer special detriment** and that other members escape loss.

2.2.5 Expulsion of minorities

Expulsion cases are concerned with:

- Alteration of the articles for the purpose of **removing** a **director from office**

- Alteration of the articles to permit a majority of members to **enforce** a **transfer** to themselves of the shareholding of a minority

The action of the majority in altering the articles to achieve 'expulsion' will generally be treated as **valid** even though it is discriminatory, if the majority were concerned to **benefit the company** or to remove some detriment to its interests.

If, on the other hand, the majority was **blatantly seeking** to secure an **advantage** to themselves by their discrimination, the alteration made to the articles by their voting control of the company will be invalid. The cases below illustrate how the distinctions are applied in practice.

> **Sidebottom v Kershaw, Leese & Co Ltd 1920**
>
> *The facts:* The articles were altered to enable the directors to purchase at a fair price the shareholding of any member who competed with the company in its business. The minority against whom the new article was aimed did carry on a competing business. They challenged the validity of the alteration on the ground that it was an abuse of majority power to 'expel' a member.
>
> *Decision:* There was no objection to a power of 'expulsion' by this means. It was a justifiable alteration if made *bona fide* in the interests of the company as a whole. On the facts this was justifiable.

> **Brown v British Abrasive Wheel Co 1919**
>
> *The facts:* The company needed further capital. The majority, who held 98% of the existing shares, were willing to provide more capital — but only if they could buy up the 2% minority. As the minority refused to sell, the majority proposed to alter the articles to provide for compulsory acquisition on a fair value basis. The minority objected to the alteration.
>
> *Decision:* The alteration was invalid since it was merely for the benefit of the majority. It was not an alteration 'directly concerned with the provision of further capital' and therefore not for the benefit of the company.

> **Dafen Tinplate Co Ltd v Llanelly Steel Co (1907) Ltd 1920**
>
> *The facts:* The claimant was a minority shareholder which had transferred its custom from the defendant company to another supplier. The majority shareholders of the defendant company sought to protect their interests by altering the articles to provide for compulsory acquisition of the claimant's shares.
>
> The new article was not restricted (as it was in *Sidebottom's* case above) to acquisition of shares on specific grounds where benefit to the company would result. It was simply expressed as a power to acquire the shares of a member. The claimant objected that the alteration was invalid, since it was not for the benefit of the company.
>
> *Decision:* The alteration was invalid because it 'enables the majority of the shareholders to compel any shareholder to transfer his shares'. This wide power could not 'properly be said to be for the benefit of the company'. The mere unexpressed intention to use the power in a particular way was not enough.

Therefore if the majority intend that the **power to acquire the shares of a minority** is to be **restricted** to specific circumstances for the benefit of the company, they should ensure that this restriction is included in the new article.

Exam focus point

> Scenario questions on this area of law may concern a majority wishing to amend the company's articles to allow the expulsion of a minority. If this is the case, pay close attention to the resolution as it may be invalid under one of the cases above.

2.2.6 Filing of alteration

Whenever any alteration is made to the articles, a copy of the altered articles must be delivered to the Registrar within **15 days**, together with a signed copy of the special resolution making the alteration.

2.2.7 Interaction of statute and articles

There are **two aspects** to consider.

(a)   The Companies Act may permit companies to do something **if** their **articles** also authorise it. For example, a company may reduce its capital if its articles give power to do this. If, however, they do not, then the company must **alter** the articles to include the **necessary power** before it may exercise the statutory power.

(b)   The Companies Act will **override** the articles:

(i)   If the Companies Act **prohibits something**

(ii)   If something is permitted by the Companies Act **only** by a **special procedure** (such as passing a special resolution in general meeting)

3 Company objects and capacity

FAST FORWARD

A **company's objects** are its aims and purposes. If a company enters into a contract which is outside its objects, that contract is said to be **ultra vires.** However, the rights of third parties to the contract are protected.

3.1 The objects

The objects are the **'aims'** and **'purposes'** of a company. Under previous companies legislation they were held in a specific clause within the memorandum of association. This clause set out everything the company could do, including being a 'general commercial company' which meant it could pretty much do anything.

The 2006 Act changed matters. The objects could now be found in the **articles**, but most articles will **not** mention any objects. This is because under the Act a company's objects are **completely unrestricted** (ie it can carry out any lawful activity). Only where the company wishes to restrict its activities is there an inclusion of those **restrictions** in the articles.

3.1.1 Alteration of the objects

As a company's objects are located in its articles, it may alter its objects by **special resolution** for any reason. The procedure is the same as for any other type of alteration.

3.2 Contractual capacity and *ultra vires*

FAST FORWARD

Companies may only act in accordance with their **objects**. If the directors permit an act which is restricted by the company's objects then the act is *ultra vires*.

Key terms

> **Ultra vires** is where a company exceeds its objects and acts outside its capacity.
>
> Companies which have **unrestricted objects** are highly unlikely to act *ultra vires* since their constitution permits them to do anything. Where a company has restrictions placed on its objects and it breaches these restrictions, then it would be acting *ultra vires*.

The approach taken by the Companies Act 2006 is to give **security** to commercial transactions for **third parties**, whilst preserving the rights of shareholders to restrain directors from entering an *ultra vires* action.

There are two important sections of the Companies Act 2006 concerning *ultra vires* contracts:

Section 39 provides as follows:

'the validity of an act done by a company shall not be called into question on the ground of lack of capacity by reason of anything in the company's constitution.'

Section 40 provides as follows:

'in favour of a person dealing with a company in good faith, the power of the directors to bind the company, or authorise others to do so, shall be deemed to be free of any limitation under the company's constitution.'

There are a number of **points to note** about s 40.

(a) The section applies in favour of the **person dealing with the company**; it does not apply to the members.

(b) In contrast with s 39, **good faith** is required on the part of the third party. The company has, however, to prove lack of good faith in the third party and this may turn out to be quite difficult.

(c) The **third party** is not required to **enquire** whether or not there are any **restrictions** placed on the power of directors. They are free to assume the directors have any power they profess to have.

(d) The section covers not only acts beyond the capacity of the company, but acts beyond '**any limitation under the company's constitution**'.

Whilst sections 39 and 40 deal with the company's transactions with **third parties**, the **members** may take action against the directors for permitting *ultra vires* acts. Their action will be based on the fact that the **objects specifically restricted** the particular act and **directors** have a statutory duty to **abide** by the **company's constitution**.

The main problem for **members** is that they are most likely to be **aware** of the *ultra vires* act only **after** it has occurred; they are not, therefore, normally in a position to prevent it, although in theory they could seek an **injunction** if they found out about the potential *ultra vires* act before it took place.

3.3 Transactions with directors

The Companies Act 2006 also applies when the company enters into a contract with one of its **directors**, or its holding company, or any **person connected** with such a director. Contracts made between the company and these parties are **voidable** by the company if the director acts outside their capacity.

Whether or not the contract is avoided, the party and any **authorising director is liable to repay any profit** they made or make good any losses that result from such a contract.

4 The constitution as a contract

FAST FORWARD

The articles **constitute a contract** between:

- Company and members
- Members and the company
- Members and members

The articles **do not constitute** a contract between the **company** and **third parties**, or members in a **capacity** other than as **members** (the *Eley* case).

4.1 Effect

A **company's constitution binds**:

- Members to company
- Company to members
- Members to members

The company's constitution does **not** bind the company to third parties.

This principle applies only to rights and obligations which affect members **in their capacity as members**.

> *Hickman v Kent or Romney Marsh Sheepbreeders Association 1915*
>
> *The facts:* The claimant (H) was in dispute with the company which had threatened to expel him from membership. The articles provided that disputes between the company and its members should be submitted to arbitration. H, in breach of that article, began an action in court against the company.
>
> *Decision:* The proceedings would be stayed since the dispute (which related to matters affecting H as a member) must, in conformity with the articles, be submitted to arbitration.

The principle that only rights and obligations of members are covered applies when an outsider who is also a member seeks to rely on the articles in support of a claim made as an **outsider**.

> *Eley v Positive Government Security Life Assurance Co 1876*
>
> *The facts:* E, a solicitor, drafted the original articles and included a provision that the company must always employ him as its solicitor. E became a member of the company some months after its incorporation. He later sued the company for breach of contract in not employing him as its solicitor.
>
> *Decision:* E could not rely on the article since it was a contract between the company and its members and he was not asserting any claim as a member.

The members are able to compel the company to obey the Articles: *Pender v Lushington 1877.*

4.2 Constitution as a contract between members

The Companies Act gives to the **constitution** contractual effect between (a) the **company** and (b) its **members individually**. It can also impose a contract on the members in their dealings with each other.

> *Rayfield v Hands 1958*
>
> *The facts:* The articles required that (a) every director should be a shareholder and (b) the directors must purchase the shares of any member who gave them notice of his wish to dispose of them. The directors, however, denied that a member could enforce the obligation on them to acquire his shares.
>
> *Decision:* There was 'a contract ... between a member and member-directors in relation to their holdings of the company's shares in its articles' and the directors were bound by it.

Articles and resolutions are usually **drafted** so that each stage is a dealing between the company and the members, so that:

(a)   A member who intends to transfer their shares must, if the articles so require, give notice of their intention to the company.

(b)   The company must then give notice to other members that they have an option to take up their shares.

4.3 Constitution as a supplement to contracts

FAST FORWARD

> The constitution can be used to **establish the terms** of a contract existing elsewhere.

If an **outsider** makes a **separate contract** with the company and that contract contains no specific term on a particular point but the constitution does, then the contract is deemed to incorporate the constitution to that extent.

If a contract incorporates terms of the articles it is subject to the company's **right** to **alter** its articles. However, a company's articles cannot be altered to deprive another person of a right already earned, say for services rendered **prior** to the alteration.

Point to note

> Remember the articles only create contractual rights/obligations in relation to rights **as a member**.

4.4 Shareholder agreements

FAST FORWARD

Shareholders' agreements sometimes supplement a company's constitution.

Shareholder agreements are concerned with the **running of the company**; in particular they often contain terms by which the shareholders agree how they will vote on various issues.

They offer more protection to the interests of shareholders than do the articles of association. Individuals have a **power of veto** over any proposal which is contrary to the terms of the agreement. This enables a minority shareholder to protect their interests against unfavourable decisions of the majority.

5 Company name and registered office

FAST FORWARD

Except in **certain circumstances** a company's name must end with the words limited (Ltd), public limited company (plc) or the Welsh equivalents.

A company's name is its **identity**. There are a number of rules which restrict the choice of name that a company may adopt.

5.1 Statutory rules on the choice of company name

FAST FORWARD

No company may use a name which is:

– The **same** as an existing company on the Registrar's index of company names
– A **criminal offence, offensive,** or **'sensitive'**
– Suggestive of a **connection** with the **government or local authority** (unless approved)

The **choice of name** of a limited company must conform to the following rules.

(a) The name must **end** with the word(s):

(i) **Public limited company** (abbreviated **plc**) if it is a public company

(ii) **Limited** (or Ltd) if it is a private limited company, unless permitted to omit 'limited' from its name

(iii) The **Welsh equivalents** of either (i) or (ii) may be used by a Welsh company

(b) No company may have a name which is the **same** as any other company appearing in the statutory index at Companies House. For this purpose two names are treated as 'the same' in spite of minor or non-essential differences: for instance, the word 'the' as the first word in the name is ignored. 'John Smith Limited' is treated the same as 'John Smith' (an unlimited company) or 'John Smith & Company Ltd'. Where a company has a name which is the same or too similar to another, the Secretary of State may direct the company to **change its name**.

(c) No company may have a name, the use of which would be a **criminal** offence or which is considered **offensive** or **'sensitive'** (as defined by the Secretary of State).

(d) Official approval is required for a name which, in the Registrar's opinion, suggests a **connection** with the **government** or a **local authority** or which is subject to **control**.

A name which suggests some professional expertise, such as 'optician', will only be permitted if the appropriate representative association has been consulted and raises no objection.

The general purpose of the rule is to **prevent** a company **misleading** the public as to its real circumstances or activities. Certain names may be approved by the Secretary of State on written application.

5.2 Omission of the word 'limited'

A **private company** which is a **charity** or a **company limited by shares** or **guarantee** and **licensed** to do so **before 25 February 1982** may omit the word 'limited' from its name if the following conditions are satisfied.

(a) The objects of the company must be the **promotion** of either commerce, art, science, education, religion, charity or any profession (or anything incidental or conducive to such objects).

(b) The memorandum or articles must require that the **profits** or other income of the company are to be **applied to promoting** its objects and no dividends or return of capital may be paid to its members. Also on liquidation the **assets** (otherwise distributable to members) are to be **transferred** to another body with similar objects. The articles must not then be altered so that the company's status to omit 'Limited' is lost.

5.3 Change of name

A company may decide to **change its name** by:

(a) Passing a **special resolution**

(b) By **any other means** provided for in the **articles** (in other words the company can specify its own procedure for changing its name).

Where a **special resolution** has been passed, the **Registrar** should be notified and a copy of the resolution sent. If the change was made by **any other procedure** covered by (b), the Registrar should be notified and a statement provided which states that the change has been made in accordance with the articles.

The change is effective from when a new **incorporation certificate is issued**, although the company is still treated as the same legal entity as before. The same limitations as above apply to adoption of a name by change of name as by incorporation of a new company.

5.4 Passing-off action

A person who considers that their rights have been infringed can apply for an injunction to restrain a company from using a name (**even if** the name has been duly registered). It can do this if the name suggests that the latter company is carrying on the business of the complainant or is otherwise connected with it.

A company can be **prevented** by an **injunction** issued by the court in a **passing-off action** from **using** its **registered name** if, in doing so, it causes its goods to be confused with those of the claimant.

> *Ewing v Buttercup Margarine Co Ltd 1917*
>
> *The facts:* The claimant had since 1904 run a chain of 150 shops in Scotland and the north of England through which he sold margarine and tea. He traded as 'The Buttercup Dairy Co'. The defendant was a registered company formed in 1916 with the name above. It sold margarine as a wholesaler in the London area. The defendant contended that there was unlikely to be confusion between the goods sold by the two concerns.
>
> *Decision:* An injunction would be granted to restrain the defendants from the use of its name since the claimant had the established connection under the Buttercup name. He planned to open shops in the south of England and, if the defendants sold margarine retail, there could be confusion between the two businesses.

If, however, the two companies' **businesses are different**, confusion is unlikely to occur, and hence the courts will refuse to grant an injunction. The complaint will also not succeed if the **claimant lays claim to the exclusive use of a word** which has a **general use**.

5.5 Appeal to the Company Names Adjudicators

A company which feels that another company's name is **too similar** to its own may object to the Company Names Adjudicator under the Companies Act. The adjudicator will review the case and, within **90 days**, will make a decision and provide the reasons for it in public. In most cases the adjudicator will require the offending company to **change its name** to one which does not breach the rules. In some cases the **adjudicator may determine** the new name.

An appeal against the decision may be made in court. The court may **reverse** the adjudicator's decision, **affirm** it and may even **determine** a new name.

5.6 Publication of the company's name

The **company's name** must **appear legibly** and **conspicuously**:

- **Outside** the **registered office** and all **places of business**

- On all **business letters, order forms**, notices and **official publications**

- On all **receipts** and **invoices** issued on the company's behalf

- On all **bills of exchange**, **letters of credit**, **promissory notes**, **cheques** and **orders** for money or goods purporting to be signed by, or on behalf, of the company

- On its **website**

5.7 Business names other than the corporate name

Key term

> A **business name** is a name used by a company which is different from the company's corporate name or by a firm which is different from the name(s) of the proprietor or the partners.

Most companies trade under their own **registered names**. However, a company may prefer to use some other name.

The rules require any person (company, partnership or sole trader) who carries on business under a **different name** from their own:

(a) To **state** its **name**, registered **number** and registered **address** on all **business letters (including emails)**, invoices, receipts, written orders for goods or services and written demands for payment of debts.

(b) To **display** its **name** and **address** in a **prominent position** in any **business premises** to which its customers and suppliers have access.

(c) On **request** from any **person** with whom it does business, to give **notice** of its name and address.

5.8 Registered office

The Companies Act 2006 provides that a company must at all times have a **registered office** to which all communications and notices can be sent. Its location in England and Wales or just in Wales or Scotland determines its domicile. A company may **change its registered office** (but not its domicile), but for a period of 14 days after notice is served any person may validly present documents to the previous address.

Chapter Roundup

- The memorandum is a **simple document** which states that the subscribers wish to form a company and become members of it.

- A **company's constitution** comprises the **articles of association** and any **resolutions and agreements** it makes which affect the constitution.

- The articles may be altered by a **special resolution**. The basic test is whether the alteration is for the **benefit of the company as a whole**.

- A **company's objects** are its aims and purposes. If a company enters into a contract which is outside its objects, that contract is said to be **ultra vires**. However, the rights of third parties to the contract are protected.

- Companies may only act in accordance with their **objects**. If the directors permit an act which is restricted by the company's objects then the act is *ultra vires*.

- The articles **constitute** a **contract** between:

    - Company and members
    - Members and the company
    - Members and members

- The articles **do not constitute** a contract between the **company** and **third parties**, or members in a **capacity** other than as **members** (the *Eley* case).

- The constitution can be used to **establish the terms** of a contract existing elsewhere.

- **Shareholders' agreements** sometimes supplement a company's constitution.

- Except in **certain circumstances** a company's name must end with the words limited (Ltd), public limited company (plc) or the Welsh equivalents.

- No company may use a name which is:

    - The **same** as an existing company on the Registrar's index of company names
    - A **criminal offence, offensive** or **'sensitive'**
    - Suggestive of a **connection** with the **government** or **local authority** (unless approved)

BPP
LEARNING MEDIA

1   Percy Limited has recently formed a contract with a third party, which is restricted by the objects in the company's constitution.

    Which of the following statements is/are correct?

    A   The validity of the act cannot be questioned on the grounds of lack of capacity by reason of anything in the company's constitution.

    B   The act may be restrained by the members of Percy Ltd.

    C   The act may be enforced by the third party.

    D   The directors have a duty to observe any limitation on their powers flowing from the company's constitution.

2   If a company wishes to restrict its objects, what kind of resolution is required?

    A   Special resolution
    B   Special resolution with special notice
    C   Ordinary resolution with special notice
    D   Ordinary resolution

3   A company has been formed within the last six months. Another long-established company considers that because of similarity between their names there may be confusion between it and the new company. The only action the long-established company can take is to bring a passing-off action if it is to prevent the new company using its name.

    True ☐

    False ☒

4   Which of the following persons are **not** bound to one another by the constitution?

    A   Members to company
    B   Company to members
    C   Members to members
    D   Company to third parties

5   How long does a company have to file amended articles with the Registrar if they have been altered?

    A   14 days
    B   15 days
    C   21 days
    D   28 days

Answers to Quick Quiz

1   A, C and D are correct. Members can only act before the contract is signed, so B is incorrect.

2   A. A special resolution is required to restrict the objects, as with any alteration to the articles in general.

3   False. The long-established company can also complain to the Company Names Adjudicator.

4   A, B and C are correct: s 33. D is incorrect, illustrated by *Eley v Positive Government Security Life Assurance Co Ltd 1876.*

5   B. A company has 15 days to file amended articles with the Registrar.

Now try the questions below from the Practice Question Bank

Number
30, 31, 32

Capital and the financing of companies

Share capital

Topic list	Syllabus reference
1 Members	E1(a)
2 The nature of shares and capital	E1(a)
3 Types of share	E1(b)
4 Allotment of shares	E1(c)
5 Issuing shares at a premium or at a discount	E1(d)

Introduction

In this chapter the nature of share capital is explained. You should note (and **not** confuse) the different types of capital that are important for company law purposes.

The rest of the chapter discusses procedural matters relating to the **issue** and **transfer** of shares. You will see that there are built-in safeguards to protect members' rights, **pre-emption rights** and the necessity for directors to be authorised to **allot** shares. There are also safeguards that ensure that a company receives **sufficient consideration** for its shares.

Study guide

		Intellectual level
E	**Capital and the financing of companies**	
1	**Share capital**	
(a)	Examine the different meanings of capital	2
(b)	Illustrate the difference between various classes of shares, including treasury shares, and the procedure for altering class rights	2
(c)	Explain allotment of shares and distinguish between rights issue and bonus issue of shares	2
(d)	Examine the effect of issuing shares at either a discount, or at a premium	2

Exam guide

Share capital is an important syllabus area that lends itself well to different types of question. You may be tested on the different types of share, what class rights are and how they can be altered.

1 Members

FAST FORWARD

A member of a company is a person who has **agreed to become a member**, and whose name has been **entered** in the **register of members**. This may occur by: subscription to the memorandum; applying for shares; the presentation to the company of a transfer of shares to the prospective member; applying as personal representative of a deceased member or a trustee of a bankrupt.

1.1 Becoming a member

Key term

A **member** of a company is a person who has agreed to be a member and whose name has been entered in the register of members.

Entry in the register is **essential**. Mere delivery to the company of a transfer of shares does not make the transferor a member – until the transfer is entered in the register.

1.2 Subscriber shares

Subscribers to the memorandum are deemed to have agreed to become members of the company. As soon as the company is formed their names should be entered in the register of members.

Other persons may **acquire shares** and become members:

- By **applying for**, and being allotted, shares
- By presenting to the company for registration a **transfer** of shares to them
- By applying as **personal representative** or **trustee** of a

    - Deceased member
    - Bankrupt member

1.3 Ceasing to be a member

FAST FORWARD

There are **eight** ways in which a member ceases to be so.

A **member ceases** to be a member in any of the following circumstances.

- They **transfer** all their shares to another person and the transfer is registered.
- The member **dies**.
- The **shares** of a bankrupt member are **registered** in the name of their trustee.
- A **member who is a minor repudiates their shares.**
- The **trustee** of a **bankrupt member disclaims** their shares.
- The **company forfeits** or **accepts** the **surrender of shares.**
- The **company** sells them in exercise of a lien.
- The **company is dissolved** and **ceases to exist**.

1.4 The number of members

FAST FORWARD

Public and **private companies** must have a minimum of **one** member. There is **no maximum** number.

Public and private companies must have a minimum **of one member**. There is **no maximum** number. Where a company has a sole member, the following rules will apply.

(a) The **register of members** must contain a statement that there is **only one member** and give their address.

(b) **Quorum**. The Act **automatically permits** a **quorum of one** for general meetings.

2 The nature of shares and capital

FAST FORWARD

A **share** is a transferable form of property, carrying rights and obligations, by which the interest of a member of a company limited by shares is measured.

2.1 Shares

Key term

A **share** is the interest of a shareholder in the company measured by a sum of money, for the purpose of a liability in the first place, and of interest in the second; but also consisting of a series of mutual covenants entered into by all the shareholders *inter se*.

The **key points** in this definition are:

- The share must be **paid for** ('liability'). The nominal value of the share fixes this liability: it is the base price of the share, eg a $1 ordinary share.
- It gives a **proportionate entitlement** to dividends, votes and any return of capital ('interest').
- It is a form of **bargain** ('mutual covenants') between shareholders which underlies such principles as majority control and minority protection.

Key term

A share's **nominal value** is its face value. So a $1 ordinary share for instance, has a nominal value of $1. No share can be issued at a value below its nominal value.

A **share** is a form of **personal property**, carrying **rights** and **obligations**. It is, by its nature, **transferable**.

A member who holds one or more shares is a **shareholder**. However, some companies (such as most companies limited by guarantee) do not have a share capital. So they have members who are not also shareholders.

Information about any **special rights** attached to shares is obtainable from one of the following documents which are on the file at Companies House:

- The **articles**, which are the normal context in which share rights are defined.

- A **resolution** or agreement incidental to the creation of a new class of shares (copies must be delivered to the Registrar).

- A **statement of capital** given to the Registrar within one month of **allotment**, together with the return of allotment.

2.2 Types of capital

The term **'capital'** is used in several senses in company legislation, to mean issued, allotted or called up share capital or loan capital.

2.2.1 Authorised share capital

Under previous company legislation, companies had to specify a **maximum authorised share capital** that it could issue. Under the 2006 Act, the concept of authorised share capital was removed.

2.2.2 Issued and allotted share capital

Key terms

Issued and **allotted share capital** is the type, class, number and amount of the shares issued and allotted to specific shareholders, including shares taken on formation by the subscribers to the memorandum.

A company need not issue all its share capital at once. If it retains a part, this is **unissued share capital**.

Issued share capital can be **increased** through the allotment of shares.

Rights issues and the issue of **bonus shares** will also increase the amount of a company's capital.

2.2.3 Called up and paid up share capital

Key terms

Called up share capital is the amount which the company has required shareholders to pay now or in the future on the shares issued.

Paid up share capital is the amount which shareholders have actually paid on the shares issued and called up.

For example, a company has issued and allotted 70 $1 (nominal value) shares, has received 25c per share on application and has called on members for a second 25c. Therefore its issued and allotted share capital is $70 and its **called up** share capital is $35 (50c per share). When the members pay the call, the **'paid up'** share capital is then $35 also. Capital not yet called is **'uncalled capital'**. Called capital which is not yet paid is termed **'partly paid'**; the company therefore has an outstanding claim against its shareholders and this debt is transferred to the new shareholder if the share is transferred.

As we saw earlier, on **allotment public companies** must receive at least **one quarter of the nominal value** of the shares paid up, plus the whole of any premium.

2.2.4 Loan capital

Key term

Loan capital comprises debentures and other long-term loans to a business.

Loan capital, in contrast with the above, is the term used to describe **borrowed money**, obtained usually by the issue of debentures. **It is nothing to do with shares**.

2.3 Market value

Shares of a public company are **freely transferable** (providing the appropriate procedures are followed) and, therefore, may be subsequently sold by some or all of the shareholders. The sale price will not necessarily be the nominal value; rather it will reflect the prospects of the company and therefore may be greater, or less, than the nominal value.

3 Types of share

FAST FORWARD

If the constitution of a company states no differences between shares, it is assumed that they are all **ordinary** shares with parallel rights and obligations. There may, however, be other types, notably **preference shares**.

3.1 Ordinary shares (equity)

If no differences between shares are expressed then all shares are equity shares with the **same rights**, known as ordinary shares.

Key terms

Equity is the residual interest in the assets of the company after deducting all its liabilities. It comprises issued share capital, excluding any part that does not carry any right to participate beyond a specified amount in a distribution.

Equity share capital is a company's issued share capital, less capital which carries preferential rights.

Ordinary shares are shares which entitle the holders to the remaining divisible profits (and, in a liquidation, the assets) after prior interests, such as creditors and prior charge capital, have been satisfied.

3.2 Class rights

Key term

Class rights are rights which are attached to particular types of shares by the company's constitution.

A company may, at its option, attach **special rights** to different shares regarding:

- Dividends
- Return of capital
- Voting
- The right to appoint or remove a director

Shares which have different rights from others are grouped together with other shares carrying identical rights to form a **class**. The most common types of share capital with different rights are **preference shares** and **ordinary shares**. There may also be ordinary shares with voting rights and ordinary shares without voting rights.

3.3 Preference shares

FAST FORWARD

The most common right of preference shareholders is a **prior right** to receive a fixed dividend. This right is not a right to **compel payment** of a dividend, but it is **cumulative** unless otherwise stated. Usually, preference shareholders **cannot participate** in a dividend over and above their fixed dividend and **cease to be entitled to arrears of undeclared dividends** when the company goes into liquidation.

Key term

Preference shares are shares carrying one or more rights, such as a fixed rate of dividend or preferential claim to any company profits available for distribution.

A preference share may, and generally will, carry a **prior right** to receive an annual dividend of fixed amount, say 6% of the share's nominal value. **Ordinary** and **preference shares** are **deemed** to have **identical rights**. However, a company's articles or resolutions may create differences between them.

As regards the **priority dividend entitlement**, four points should be noted.

(a) **The right is merely to receive a dividend at the specified rate before any other dividend may be paid or declared**. It is **not** a right to compel the company to pay the dividend. The company can decline to pay the dividend if it decides to transfer available profits to reserves, instead of using the profits to pay the preference dividend.

(b) **The right to receive a preference dividend is deemed to be cumulative unless the contrary is stated.** If, therefore, a 6% dividend is not paid in Year 1, the priority entitlement is normally carried forward to Year 2, increasing the priority right for that year to 12% – and so on.

When arrears of cumulative dividend are paid, the holders of the shares at **the time when the dividend is declared** are entitled to the whole of it, even though they did not hold the shares in the year to which the arrears relate. An intention that preference shares should not carry forward an entitlement to arrears is usually expressed by the word **'non-cumulative'**.

(c) **If a company which has arrears of unpaid cumulative preference dividends goes into liquidation, the preference shareholders cease to be entitled to the arrears unless:**

(i) A **dividend** has been **declared** though **not yet paid** when liquidation commences.

(ii) The **articles** (or other terms of issue) **expressly provide** that, in a liquidation, arrears are to be paid in priority to return of capital to members.

(d) **Holders of preference shares have no entitlement to participate in any additional dividend over and above their specified rate.** If, for example, a 6% dividend is paid on 6% preference shares, the entire balance of available profit may then be distributed to the holders of ordinary shares.

This rule also may be expressly overridden by the terms of issue. For example, the articles may provide that the preference shares are to receive a priority 6% dividend and are also to participate equally in any dividends payable after the ordinary shares have received a 6% dividend. Preference shares with these rights are called **participating preference shares**.

In all other respects preference shares carry the **same** rights as ordinary shares **unless otherwise stated**. If they do rank equally they carry the same rights, no more and no less, to return of capital, distribution of surplus assets and voting. In practice, it is **unusual** to issue preference shares on this basis. More usually, it is expressly provided that:

(a) The preference shares are to carry a **priority right** to **return of capital**.

(b) They are **not to carry a right to vote, or voting is permitted in specified circumstances**. For example failure to pay the preference dividend, variation of their rights or a resolution to wind up.

When preference shares carry a **priority right** to **return** of **capital** the result is that:

(a) The amount paid up on the preference shares, say $1 on each $1 share, is to be repaid in liquidation before anything is repaid to ordinary shareholders.

(b) Unless otherwise stated, the holders of the preference shares are **not** entitled to share in surplus assets when the ordinary share capital has been repaid.

3.3.1 Advantages and disadvantages of preference shares

The advantages of preference shares are **greater security of income** and (if they carry priority in repayment of capital) **greater security of capital**. However, in a period of persistent inflation, the benefit of entitlement to fixed income and to capital fixed in money terms is an illusion.

A number of other **drawbacks** and **pitfalls**, such as loss of arrears, winding up and enforced payment, have been indicated above. Preference shares may be said to fall between the two stools of risk and reward (as seen in ordinary shares) and security (debentures).

3.4 Redeemable shares

Redeemable shares are shares issued on terms that they may be bought back by a company, either at a future specific date or at the shareholder's or company's option.

3.5 Treasury shares

Treasury shares are created when a **private** or **public limited company** legitimately **purchases its own shares** out of **cash** or **distributable profit**. The purchased shares are then held by the company 'in treasury' which means the company can re-issue them without the usual formalities. They can only be sold for cash and the company cannot exercise the **voting rights** which attach to them.

3.5.1 Variation of class rights

FAST FORWARD

The holders of **issued** shares have **vested rights** which can only be varied by using a strict procedure. The standard procedure is by **special resolution** passed by at least **three-quarters** of the votes cast at a **separate class meeting** or by written consent.

Key term

A **variation of class rights** is an alteration in the position of shareholders with regard to those rights or duties which they have by virtue of their shares.

Examples of rights that attach to shares (**class rights**) include **voting rights**, a right to **dividends** and a right to a **return of capital** when a company is wound-up. Rights attach to a particular class of shares if the holders of shares in that class enjoy rights that are not enjoyed by the holders of shares in another class.

These class rights can only be varied by the company with the consent of all the shareholders in the class, or with such consent of a majority as is specified (usually) in the articles. The standard procedure for variation of class rights requires that a **special resolution** shall be passed by a **three-quarters majority** cast either at a **separate meeting** of the class, or by **written consent**. If any other requirements are imposed by the company's articles then these must also be followed.

3.5.2 When variation rules apply

FAST FORWARD

It is **not** a variation of class rights to issue shares to new members, to subdivide shares of another class, to return capital to preference shareholders, or to create a new class of preference shareholders.

It is only necessary to follow the variation of class rights procedure **if what is proposed amounts to a variation of class rights**. The following examples do not constitute a variation of class rights.

3.5.3 Examples: Not a variation of class rights

(a) **To issue shares of the same class to allottees who are not already members of the class** (unless the defined class rights prohibit this).

> *White v Bristol Aeroplane Co Ltd 1953*
>
> *The facts:* The company made a bonus issue of new ordinary and preference shares to the existing ordinary shareholders who alone were entitled under the articles to participate in bonus issues. The existing preference shareholders objected. They stated that reducing their proportion of the class of preference shares (by issuing the bonus of preference shares) was a variation of class rights to which they had not consented.
>
> *Decision:* This was not a variation of class rights since the existing preference shareholders had the same number of shares (and votes at a class meeting) as before.

(b) **To subdivide shares of another class with the incidental effect of increasing the voting strength of that other class**

> *Greenhalgh v Arderne Cinemas Ltd 1946*
>
> *The facts:* The company had two classes of ordinary shares, 50p shares and 10p shares. Every share carried one vote. A resolution was passed to subdivide each 50p share into five 10p shares, thus multiplying the votes of that class by five.
>
> *Decision:* The rights of the original 10p shares had not been varied since they still had one vote per share as before.

(c) **To return capital to the holders of preference shares**

(d) **To create and issue a new class of preference shares with priority over an existing class of ordinary shares**

The cases cited in the preceding paragraph illustrate the principle that without a '**literal variation**' of class rights there is no alteration of rights to which the safeguards of proper procedure and appeal to the court apply. The fact that the **value** of existing rights may be affected will not concern the court if the rights are unchanged.

Exam focus point

Knowledge of what does **not** constitute a variation of class rights is vital in this area.

3.5.4 Special situations

To deal with unusual **situations**, which in the past caused some difficulty, the following rules apply.

(a) If the class rights are set **by the articles and** they **provide** a **variation procedure**, that procedure must be followed for any variation, even if it is less onerous than the statutory procedure.

(b) If class **rights** are **defined otherwise than by the articles** and there is **no variation procedure**, consent of a **three-quarters majority** of the class is both necessary and sufficient.

The rules on **notice, voting, polls, circulation of resolutions** and **quorum** relating to general meetings relate also to class meetings when voting on alteration of class rights.

3.5.5 Minority appeals to the court for unfair prejudice

FAST FORWARD

A **dissenting minority** holding 15% or more of the issued shares may apply to the court within 21 days of class consent to have the variation cancelled as 'unfairly prejudicial'.

Whenever class rights are varied under a procedure contained in the constitution, a **minority of holders of shares of the class** may apply to the court to have the variation cancelled.

The **objectors together** must:

- Hold **not less** than **15%** of the **issued shares** of the class in question
- **Not** themselves have **consented** to or voted in favour of the variation
- **Apply** to the court within **21 days** of the consent being given by the class

The **court** can either **approve the variation** as made or cancel it as '**unfairly prejudicial**'. It cannot, however, modify the terms of the variation. To establish that a variation is 'unfairly prejudicial' to the class, the minority must show that the majority was seeking **some advantage** to themselves as **members** of a **different class**, instead of considering the interests of the class in which they were then voting.

3.6 Statement of capital and initial shareholdings

A return known as a **statement of capital and initial shareholdings** is required to be made to the **Registrar** when a company is registered, and therefore applies only to the **shares of the subscribers**. This statement must give the following details in respect of the company's **share capital** and be **up to date** as of the statement date.

(a)   The **total number of shares** of the company

(b)   The **aggregate nominal value of the shares**

(c)   For **each class** of share:

     (i)   The **prescribed particulars** of any rights attached
     (ii)   The **total number of shares** in the class
     (iii)   The **aggregate nominal value** of shares in the class

(d)   The **aggregate amount unpaid** on the **total number of shares**

(e)   **Information that identifies the subscribers to the memorandum of association**

(f)   In respect of **each subscriber**, the **number**, **nominal value** and **class of shares** taken by them on formation and the **amount** to be **paid up**

4 Allotment of shares

FAST FORWARD

Directors exercise the **delegated power** to allot shares, either by virtue of the articles or a resolution in general meeting.

4.1 Definition

Key term

Allotment of shares is the issue and allocation to a person of a certain number of shares under a contract of allotment. Once the shares are allotted and the holder is entered in the register of members, the holder becomes a member of the company. The member is issued with a share certificate.

The allotment of shares is a **form of contract**. The intending shareholder applies to the company for shares, and the company accepts the offer. The terms '**allotment**' and '**issue**' have different meanings.

(a)   A share is **allotted** when the person to whom it is allotted acquires an unconditional right to be entered in the register of members as the holder of that share. That stage is reached when the board of directors (to whom the power to allot shares is usually given) considers the application and formally resolves to allot the shares.

     However if the directors imposed a **condition**, for instance that the shares should be allotted only on receipt of the subscription money, the allotment would only take effect when payment was made.

(b)   The **issue** of shares is not a defined term but is usually taken to be a later stage at which the allottee **receives** a **letter of allotment** or share certificate issued by the company.

The allotment of shares of a **private company** is a **simple** and **immediate matter.** The name of the allottee is entered in the register of members soon after the allotment of shares and they become a member.

4.2 Public company allotment of shares

There are various **methods of selling shares** to the public.

Key terms

Public offer: where members of the public subscribe for shares directly to the company.

Offer for sale: an offer to members of the public to apply for shares, based on information in a prospectus

Placing: a method of raising share capital where shares are offered in a small number of large 'blocks', to persons or institutions who have previously agreed to purchase the shares at a predetermined price.

4.3 Private company allotment of shares

The **allotment of shares** in a **private company** is more **straightforward**. The rule to remember is that private companies cannot sell shares to the public. An application must be made to the directors directly. After that, shares are allotted and issued, and a return of allotment made to the Registrar, as for a public company.

4.3.1 Directors' powers to allot shares

Directors of **private companies** with **one class of share** have the **authority** to allot shares **unless restricted** by the articles.

Directors of **public companies** or **private companies with more than one class of share may not allot shares** (except to subscribers to the memorandum and to employees' share schemes) **without authority from the members.** Any director who allots shares **without authority** commits an **offence** under the Companies Act 2006 and may be fined. However, the allotment remains **valid**.

4.4 Pre-emption rights

FAST FORWARD

If the directors propose to allot 'equity securities' wholly for cash, there is a general requirement to offer these shares to **holders** of **similar shares** in proportion to their holdings.

Key term

Pre-emption rights are the rights of existing ordinary shareholders to be offered new shares issued by the company *pro rata* to their existing holding of that class of shares.

If a company proposes to allot ordinary shares wholly for cash, it has a **statutory obligation** to offer those shares first to holders of similar shares in **proportion to their holdings** and on the same or more favourable terms as the main allotment. This is known as a **rights issue**.

4.5 Rights issues

Key term

A **rights issue** is a right given to a shareholder to subscribe for further shares in the company, usually *pro rata* to their existing holding in the company's shares.

A rights issue must be made **in writing** (hard copy or electronic) in the same manner as a notice of a general meeting is sent to members. It must specify a period of **not less than 21 days** during which the offer may be accepted but may not be withdrawn. If not accepted or renounced in favour of another person within that period the offer is deemed to be declined.

Equity securities which have been offered to members in this way but are **not accepted** may then be allotted on the same (or less favourable) terms to non-members. If equity securities are allotted in breach of these rules the members to whom the offer should have been made may, within the ensuing two years, recover **compensation** for their loss from those in default. The allotment will generally be valid.

4.5.1 Exclusion of pre-emption rights

A **private** company may by its articles permanently exclude these rules so that there is no statutory right of first refusal.

4.5.2 Disapplication of pre-emption rights

Any company may, by special resolution, resolve that the statutory right of first refusal shall not apply. Such a resolution to 'disapply' the right may either:

(a) Be combined with the grant to directors of authority to allot shares, or

(b) Simply permit an offer of shares to be made for cash to a non-member (without first offering the shares to members) on a particular occasion

4.6 Bonus issues

Key term

> A **bonus issue** is the capitalisation of the reserves of a company by the issue of additional shares to existing shareholders, in proportion to their holdings. Such shares are normally fully paid-up with no cash called for from the shareholders.

A bonus issue is more correctly but less often called a 'capitalisation issue' (also called a 'scrip' issue). The articles of a company usually give it power to apply its reserves to paying up unissued shares wholly or in part, and then to allot these shares as a bonus issue to members.

5 Issuing shares at a premium or at a discount

FAST FORWARD

> In issuing shares, a company must fix a **price** which is **equal** to or **more than** the **nominal value of the shares**. It may not allot shares at a discount to the nominal value.

Every share has a **nominal value** and **may not be allotted at a discount** to that.

In allotting shares every company is required to obtain in money or money's worth, consideration of a value at least equal to the nominal value of the shares plus the whole of any premium. To issue shares **'at par'** is to obtain equal value, say, $1 for a $1 share.

> *Ooregum Gold Mining Co of India v Roper 1892*
>
> *The facts:* Shares in the company, although nominally £1, were trading at a market price of 12.5p. In an honest attempt to refinance the company, new £1 preference shares were issued and credited with 75p already paid, so the purchasers of the shares were actually paying twice the market value of the ordinary shares. When, however, the company subsequently went into insolvent liquidation the holders of the new shares were required to pay a further 75p.

If shares are allotted at a discount to their nominal value, the allottee, if they agree to the issue, must nonetheless pay the **full nominal value** with **interest** at the appropriate rate. Any subsequent holder of such a share who knew of the underpayment must make good the shortfall.

Consideration for shares	
Partly-paid shares	The no-discount rule only requires that, in allotting its shares, a company shall not fix a price which is less than the nominal value of the shares. It may leave part of that price to be paid at some later time. Thus $1 shares may be issued partly-paid: 75c on allotment and 25c when called for or by instalment. The unpaid capital passes with the shares. If transferred, they are a debt payable by the holder at the time when payment is demanded.
Underwriting fees	A company may pay underwriting or other commission in respect of an issue of shares if so permitted by its articles. This means that, if shares are issued at par, the net amount received will be below par value.
Bonus issue	The allotment of shares as a 'bonus issue' is for full consideration since reserves, which are shareholders' funds, are converted into fixed capital and are used to pay for the shares.
Money's worth	The price for the shares may be paid in **money** or **'money's worth'**, including goodwill and knowhow. It need not be paid in cash and the company may agree to accept a **'non-cash' consideration** of sufficient value. For instance, a company may issue shares in payment of the price agreed in the purchase of a property.

5.1 Private companies

Private companies may issue shares for **inadequate consideration** provided the directors are behaving reasonably and honestly.

A private company may allot shares for **inadequate consideration** by acceptance of goods or services at an overvalue. This loophole has been allowed to exist because in some cases it is very much a matter of opinion whether an asset is or is not of a stated value.

The **courts** therefore have **refused** to overrule directors in their valuation of an asset acquired for shares if it appears **reasonable** and **honest**. However, a blatant and unjustified overvaluation will be declared **invalid**.

5.2 Public companies

There are **stringent rules** on consideration for shares in public companies.

More **stringent rules** apply to **public companies**.

(a)   The company must, at the time of allotment, receive **at least one-quarter of the nominal value** of the shares and the **whole** of any premium.

(b)   Any **non-cash consideration** accepted must be **independently valued**.

(c)   **Non-cash consideration** may **not** be accepted as payment for shares if an undertaking contained in such consideration is to be, or may be, **performed more than five years after the allotment**. This relates to, say, a property or business in return for shares. To enforce the five-year rule the law requires that:

    (i)   At the time of the allotment the **allottee** must **undertake** to **perform** their side of the agreement within a specified period which must not exceed five years. If no such undertaking is given the **allottee** becomes **immediately liable** to pay cash for their shares as soon as they are allotted.

    (ii)   If the **allottee later fails** to **perform** their undertaking to transfer property at the due time, they become liable to pay **cash** for their shares when they default.

(d)   An **undertaking to do work or perform services is not to be accepted as consideration**. A public company may, however, allot shares to discharge a debt in respect of services already rendered.

    If a public company, against the above rule, accepts future services as consideration, the shareholder must pay the company, in cash, their **nominal value** plus any **premium** treated as paid-up, and **interest** at 5% on any such amount.

(e)   Within **two years of receiving its trading certificate**, a public company **may not receive a transfer of non-cash assets from a subscriber** to the memorandum, unless its value is less than 10% of the issued nominal share capital and it has been independently valued and agreed by an ordinary resolution.

5.2.1 Valuation of non-cash assets

When a public company allots shares for a non-cash consideration the company must usually obtain a **report on its value** from an independent valuer.

The **valuation report** must be made to the company within the six months before the allotment. On receiving the report the company must send a copy to the proposed allottee and later to the Registrar.

The independent valuation rule does not apply to an allotment of shares made in the course of a **takeover bid**.

5.3 Allotment of shares at a premium

> If shares are issued at a premium, the **excess** must be credited to a **share premium** account.

Key term

> **Share premium** is the excess received, either in cash or other consideration, over the nominal value of the shares issued.

An established company may be able to obtain consideration for new shares in excess of their nominal value. The excess, called 'share premium', must be credited to a **share premium account**.

Exam focus point

> Exam questions may test your knowledge of the meaning and effect of issuing shares at a premium and at a discount.

If a company obtains non-cash consideration for its shares which exceeds the nominal value of the shares the excess should also be credited to the **share premium account**.

5.3.1 Example: Using a share premium account

If a company allots its $1 (nominal) shares for $1.50 in cash, $1 per share is credited to the share capital account, and 50c to the share premium account.

 Illustration

We will use the above example to illustrate the effects of the transaction on the balance sheet. The company has issued 100 shares.

	Before share issue	After share issue
	$	$
Cash	100	250
Share capital	100	200
Share premium	–	50
	100	250

The general rule is that reduction of the share premium account is subject to the **same** restrictions as reduction of share capital. You should learn the fact that **a company cannot distribute any part of its share premium account as dividend**.

5.4 Uses of the share premium account

> Use of the share premium account is limited. It is most often used for **bonus issues**.

Under the Companies Act, the **permitted uses of share premium** are to pay:

- **Fully paid shares under a bonus issue** since this operation merely converts one form of fixed capital (share premium) into another (share capital)

- **Issue expenses** and **commission** in respect of a **new share issue**

Additionally, the share premium account may be used to finance any premium due when **redeemable shares** are redeemed.

Chapter Roundup

- A member of a company is a person who has **agreed to become a member**, and whose name has been **entered** in the **register of members**. This may occur by: subscription to the memorandum; applying for shares; the presentation to the company of a transfer of shares to the prospective member; applying as personal representative of a deceased member or a trustee of a bankrupt.

- There are **eight** ways in which a member ceases to be so.

- **Public** and **private companies** must have a minimum of **one** member. There is **no maximum** number.

- A **share** is a transferable form of property, carrying rights and obligations, by which the interest of a member of a company limited by shares is measured.

- The term **'capital'** is used in several senses in company legislation, to mean issued, allotted or called up share capital or loan capital.

- If the constitution of a company states no differences between shares, it is assumed that they are all **ordinary** shares with parallel rights and obligations. There may, however, be other types, notably **preference shares**.

- The most common right of preference shareholders is a **prior right** to receive a fixed dividend. This right is not a right to **compel payment** of a dividend, but it is **cumulative** unless otherwise stated. Usually, preference shareholders **cannot participate** in a dividend over and above their fixed dividend and **cease to be entitled to arrears of undeclared dividends** when the company goes into liquidation.

- The holders of **issued** shares have **vested rights** which can only be varied by using a strict procedure. The standard procedure is by **special resolution** passed by at least **three-quarters** of the votes cast at a **separate class meeting** or by written consent.

- It is **not** a variation of class rights to issue shares to new members, to subdivide shares of another class, to return capital to preference shareholders, or to create a new class of preference shareholders.

- A **dissenting minority** holding 15% or more of the issued shares may apply to the court within 21 days of class consent to have the variation cancelled as 'unfairly prejudicial'.

- Directors exercise the **delegated power** to allot shares, either by virtue of the articles or a resolution in general meeting.

- If the directors propose to allot 'equity securities' wholly for cash, there is a general requirement to offer these shares to **holders** of **similar shares** in proportion to their holdings.

- In issuing shares, a company must fix a **price** which is **equal** to or **more than** the **nominal value of the shares**. It may not allot shares at a discount to the nominal value.

- Private companies may issue shares for **inadequate consideration** provided the directors are behaving reasonably and honestly.

- There are **stringent rules** on consideration for shares in public companies.

- If shares are issued at a premium, the **excess** must be credited to a **share premium** account.

- Use of the share premium account is limited. It is most often used for **bonus issues**.

1   If a company fails to pay preference shareholders their dividend, they can bring a court action to compel the company to pay it.

True ☐

False ☒

2   Which two of the following are implied rights of preference shareholders?

A   The right to receive a dividend is cumulative.

B   If the company goes into liquidation, preference shareholders are entitled to claim all arrears of dividend from the liquidator.

C   As well as rights to their preference dividends, preference shareholders can share equally in dividends payable to ordinary shareholders.

D   Preference shareholders have equal voting rights to ordinary shareholders.

3   If a company issues new ordinary shares for cash, the general rule is that:

A   The shares must first be offered to existing members in the case of a public but not a private company.

B   The shares must first be offered to existing members whether the company is public or private.

C   The shares must first be offered to existing members in the case of a private but not a public company.

D   The shares need not be issued to existing members.

4   What is the minimum number of members that a plc must have?

A   One

B   Two

C   Three

D   Four

5   A share premium account can be used for bonus issues of shares or issue costs for new share issues.

True ☒

False ☐

Answers to Quick Quiz

1   False. The company may decide not to pay any dividend, or may be unable to because it does not have any distributable profits. What the preference shareholders have is a right to receive their dividends before other dividends are paid or declared.

2   A and D are implied rights; the others have to be stated explicitly.

3   B. The shares must be first offered to existing members whether the company is public or private.

4   A. All companies must have a minimum of one member.

5   True. Both are acceptable uses for the share premium account.

Now try the questions below from the Practice Question Bank

Number
33, 34

Loan capital

Topic list	Syllabus reference
1 Borrowing	E2(a)
2 Debentures and loan capital	E2(b), E2(c)
3 Charges	E2(d)
4 Registration of charges	E2(e)
5 Debentureholders' remedies	E2(b), E2(c)

Introduction

In this chapter on **borrowing** and **loan capital**, you should note that the interests and position of a lender are very different from that of a shareholder.

We shall be looking at how loan capital holders protect themselves, specifically through taking out **fixed or floating charges** over company assets. Charges give the lender the right to sell assets which are subject to the charge in order to recover money owed to them if the borrower does not repay the debt.

You need to understand the differences between fixed and floating charges, and also how they can protect loan creditors, for example by giving chargeholders the ability to appoint a **receiver**.

Study guide

		Intellectual level
E	**Capital and the financing of companies**	
2	**Loan capital**	
(a)	Define companies' borrowing powers	1
(b)	Explain the meaning of loan capital and debenture	2
(c)	Distinguish loan capital from share capital and explain the different rights held by shareholders and debentureholders	2
(d)	Explain the concept of a company charge and distinguish between fixed and floating charges	2
(e)	Describe the need and the procedure for registering company charges	2

Exam guide

Loan capital may crop up in questions involving insolvency and corporate finance in general. However, it is a topic that could also be examined in a scenario question. You may be required to identify instances where a company has exceeded its borrowing powers or the differences between types of charges.

1 Borrowing

FAST FORWARD Companies have an **implied power** to borrow for purposes incidental to their trade or business.

All companies registered under the Companies Act 2006 have an **implied power to borrow** for purposes **incidental to their trade or business**. A company formed under earlier Acts will have an implied power to borrow if its object is to carry on a trade or business. In delegating the company's power to borrow to the directors it is usual, and essential in the case of a company whose shares are quoted on the Stock Exchange, to impose a **maximum limit** on the **borrowing** arranged by directors.

A **contract** to **repay borrowed money** may in principle be **unenforceable** if either:

- It is money borrowed for an **ultra vires** (or restricted) purpose, and this is known to the lender.
- The directors **exceed their borrowing powers** or have no powers to borrow.

However:

- In both cases the lender will probably be **able** to **enforce** the contract.

- If the contract is within the capacity of the company, but beyond the delegated powers of the directors, the company may **ratify** the **loan contract**.

Case law has determined that if a company has power to borrow, it also has power to **create charges** over the company's assets as **security** for the loan.

1.1 Personal guarantees

Some lenders may require directors and/or members to agree to repay a loan out of their **personal wealth** should the company default on the debt. This is known as **requesting a personal guarantee**, which is a **promise by a person** (the directors or shareholders) to **assume a debt obligation** in the event of non-payment by the borrower (the company). Personal guarantees are a **means of protecting the lender** by preventing the shareholders/members from hiding behind the protection of limited liability. It is commonly used where the lender is very powerful (such as a bank) and the borrower (such as a new or small company) has no other source of funds .

2 Debentures and loan capital

2.1 Loan capital

FAST FORWARD

Loan capital comprises all the longer-term borrowing of a company. It is distinguished from share capital by the fact that, at some point, borrowing must be repaid. Share capital, on the other hand, is only returned to shareholders when the company is wound up.

A company's **loan capital** comprises all amounts which it borrows for the long term, such as **permanent overdrafts** at the bank, **unsecured loans** from a bank or other party and **loans secured** on assets, from a bank or other party. Companies often issue long-term loans as capital in the form of **debentures**.

2.2 Debentures

FAST FORWARD

A **debenture** is a document stating the terms on which a company has borrowed money. There are three main types.

- A **single debenture**

- **Debentures issued as a series** and usually registered

- **Debenture stock** subscribed to by a large number of lenders. Only this form requires a **debenture trust deed**, although the others may often incorporate one

Key term

A **debenture** is the written acknowledgement of a debt by a company, normally containing provisions as to payment of interest and the terms of repayment of principal. A debenture may be secured on some or all of the assets of the company or its subsidiaries.

A debenture may create a **charge** over the company's assets as security for the loan. However a document relating to an unsecured loan is also a debenture in company law.

2.3 Types of debenture

A debenture is usually a **formal legal document**. Broadly, there are **three main types**.

(a) **A single debenture**

If, for example, a company obtains a secured loan or overdraft facility from its bank, the latter is likely to insist that the company seals the **bank's standard form of debenture** creating the charge and giving the bank various safeguards and powers.

(b) **Debentures issued as a series and usually registered**

Different lenders may provide **different amounts** on **different dates**. Although each transaction is a separate loan, the intention is that the lenders should rank equally *(pari passu)* in their right to repayment and in any security given to them. Each lender therefore receives a debenture in identical form in respect of their loan. The debentures are **transferable securities**.

(c) **The issue of debenture stock subscribed to by a large number of lenders**

Only a public company may use this method to **offer its debentures to the public** and any such offer is a prospectus; if it seeks a listing on the Stock Exchange then the rules on listing particulars must be followed. Each lender has a right to be **repaid** their **capital** at the **due time** (unless they are perpetual) and to receive **interest** on it until **repayment**. This form of borrowing is treated as a single loan 'stock' in which each debenture stockholder has a specified fraction (in money terms) which they or some previous holder contributed when the stock was issued. Debenture stock is transferable in multiples of, say, $1 or $10.

A company must maintain a **register of all debenture holders** and register an allotment within two months.

One **advantage of debenture stock** over debentures issued as single and indivisible loan transactions is that the holder of debenture stock can sell part of their holding, say $1,000 (nominal), out of a larger amount.

Debenture stock must be created using a **debenture trust deed**, though single and series debentures may also use a debenture trust deed.

2.4 Debenture trust deed

Major elements of a debenture trust deed for debenture stock
The appointment usually of a trustee for prospective debenture stockholders. The trustee is usually a bank, insurance company or other institution, but may be an individual.
The nominal amount of the debenture stock is defined, which is the maximum amount which may be raised then or later. The date or period of repayment is specified, as is the rate of interest and half-yearly interest payment dates.
If the debenture stock is secured **the deed creates a charge or charges** over the assets of the company.
The trustee is authorised to **enforce the security** in case of default and, in particular, to appoint a receiver with suitable powers of management.
The company enters into **various covenants**, for instance to keep its assets fully insured or to limit its total borrowings. Breach is a default by the company.
There may be elaborate provisions for **transfer of stock** and **meetings** of debenture stockholders.

Advantages of a debenture trust deed for debenture stock
The **trustee** with appropriate powers can **intervene promptly** in case of default.
Security for the debenture stock in the form of charges over property can be **given to a single trustee**.
The **company** can **contact a representative of the debentureholders** with whom it can negotiate.
By calling a **meeting of debentureholders**, the trustee can consult them and obtain a decision binding on them all.
The **debentureholders** will be able to **enjoy the benefit of a legal mortgage** over the company's land.

2.5 Register of debentureholders

Company law does not specifically require a **register of debentureholders** be maintained. However, a company is normally required to maintain a register by the debenture or debenture trust deed when debentures are issued as a series or when debenture stock is issued.

When there is a register of debentureholders, the following **regulations** apply.

(a) The company is required by law to keep the **register** at its registered office, or at an **address** notified to the registrar.

(b) The register must be open to **inspection** by **any person** unless the constitution or trust deed provides otherwise. Any person may obtain a copy of the register or part of it for a fee. A holder of debentures issued under a trust deed may require the company (on payment) to supply them with a copy of the deed.

Under the Companies Act a company has **five days** to respond to an inspection request or seek exemption to do so from the court.

(c) The register should be **properly kept** in accordance with the requirements of the Companies Act.

2.6 Rights of debentureholders

The **position of debentureholders** is best described by **comparison** with that of **shareholders**. At first sight the two appear to have a great deal in common.

- Both **own transferable company securities,** which are usually long-term investments in the company.

- The **issue procedure** is much the same. An offer of either shares or debentures to the public is a 'prospectus' as defined by the Act.

- The **procedure** for **transfer** of registered shares and debentures is the same.

But there are **significant differences**.

Differences	Shareholder	Debentureholder
Role	Is a proprietor or owner of the company	Is a creditor of the company
Voting rights	May vote at general meetings	May not vote
Cost of investment	Shares may not be issued at a discount to nominal value	Debentures may be offered at a discount to nominal value
Return	Dividends are only paid • Out of distributable profits • When directors declare them	Interest must be paid when it is due
Redemption	Statutory restrictions on redeeming shares	No restriction on redeeming debentures
Liquidation	Shareholders are the last people to be paid in a winding up	Debentures must be paid back before shareholders are paid

From the investor's standpoint debenture stock is often **preferable to preference shares**. Although both yield a fixed income, debenture stock offers greater security.

2.6.1 Advantages and disadvantages of debentures (for the company)

Advantages	Disadvantages
Easily traded	May have to pay high interest rates to make them attractive
Terms clear and specific	Interest payments mandatory
Assets subject to a floating charge may be traded	Interest payments may upset shareholders if dividends fall
Popular due to guaranteed income	Debentureholders' remedies of liquidators or receivers may be disastrous for the company
Interest tax-deductible	Crystallisation of a floating charge can cause trading difficulties for a company
No restrictions on issue or purchase by a company	

3 Charges

FAST FORWARD

A charge over the assets of a company gives a creditor a **prior claim** over other creditors to payment of their debt out of these assets.

Charges may be either **fixed**, which attach to the relevant asset on creation, or **floating**, which attach on 'crystallisation'. For this reason it is not possible to identify the assets to which a **floating** charge relates (until **crystallisation**).

3.1 Definition

Key term

> A **charge** is an encumbrance upon real or personal property granting the holder certain rights over that property. They are often used as security for a debt owed to the charge holder. The most common form of charge is by way of legal mortgage, used to secure the indebtedness of borrowers in house purchase transactions. In the case of companies, charges over assets are most frequently granted to persons who provide loan capital to the business.

A charge **secured** over a company's assets gives to the creditor (called the 'chargee') a prior claim (over other creditors) to payment of their debt out of those assets. Charges are of two kinds, fixed and floating.

3.2 Fixed charges

Key term

> A **fixed charge** is a form of protection given to secured creditors relating to specific assets of a company. The charge grants the holder the right of enforcement against the identified asset (in the event of default in repayment or some other matter) so that the creditor may realise the asset to meet the debt owed. Fixed charges rank first in order of priority in liquidation.

Fixed (or specific) charges attach to the relevant asset as soon as the charge is created. By its nature a fixed charge is best suited to assets which the company is likely to retain for a long period. A mortgage is an example of a fixed charge.

If the company disposes of the charged asset it will either **repay the secured debt** out of the proceeds of sale so that the charge is discharged at the time of sale, or **pass the asset over to** the purchaser still subject to the charge.

3.3 Floating charges

Key term

> A **floating charge** has been defined, in case law, as:
>
> (a)   A charge on a class of assets of a company, present and future ...
>
> (b)   Which class is, in the ordinary course of the company's business, changing from time to time and ...
>
> (c)   Until the holders enforce the charge the company may carry on business and deal with the assets charged.

Floating charges do not attach to the relevant assets until the charge crystallises.

A floating charge is **not restricted** to assets such as **receivables** or **inventory**. A floating charge over 'the undertaking and assets' of a company (the most common type) applies to future as well as to current assets.

3.4 Identification of charges as fixed or floating

It is not always **immediately apparent** whether a charge is fixed or floating. Chargees often do not wish to identify a charge as being floating, as it may get paid later than preferential debts in insolvency proceedings.

A charge contract may declare the charge as fixed, or fixed and floating, whether it is or not. **The label attached** by parties in this way is **not a conclusive statement of the charge's legal nature**.

The general rule is that a **charge over assets will not be registered as fixed if it envisages that the company will still be able to deal with the charged assets without reference to the chargee**.

R in Right of British Columbia v Federal Business Development Bank 1988

The facts: In this Canadian case the Bank had a charge over the company's entire property expressed as 'a fixed and specific mortgage and charge'. Another term allowed the company to continue making sales from stock in the ordinary course of business until notified in writing by the bank to stop doing so.

Decision: The charge was created as a floating, not a fixed, charge.

However, the courts have found **exceptions** to the general rule concerning permission to deal.

(a)   In *Re GE Tunbridge Ltd 1995* it was held that the charge over certain fixed assets was a floating charge even though the company was required to obtain the chargee's permission before dealing with the assets.

(b)   In *Re Cimex Ltd 1994* the court decided that the charge in dispute was a fixed charge. The assets did not in the ordinary course of business change from time to time. This was despite the company being able to deal with the assets without the chargee's permission.

3.4.1 Charges over receivables

Charges expressed to be fixed which cover **present and future receivables** (book debts) are particularly tricky.

Again the general rule applies. If the company is allowed to deal with money collected from customers without notifying the chargee, the courts have decided that the charge is floating. If the money collected must be paid to the chargee, say in reduction of an overdraft, the courts have determined that the charge is fixed: *Siebe Gorman & Co Ltd v Barclays Bank Ltd 1979*.

In 2005 the House of Lords held in *Re Spectrum Plus* that there can be no fixed charge over a company's book debts.

3.5 Creating a floating charge

A **floating charge** is **often created by express words**. However no special form of words is essential. If a **company** gives to a chargee rights over its assets while **retaining freedom to deal with them in the ordinary course of business** until the charge crystallises, that will be a charge which 'floats'. The particular assets subject to a floating charge cannot be identified until the charge attaches by crystallisation.

3.6 Crystallisation of a floating charge

FAST FORWARD

Floating charges **crystallise** or harden (convert into a fixed charge) on the happening of certain relevant events.

ey term

Crystallisation of a floating charge occurs when it is converted into a fixed charge: that is, a fixed charge on the assets owned by the company at the time of crystallisation.

Events causing crystallisation
The **liquidation** of the company
Cessation of the company's **business**
Active intervention by the chargee, generally by way of appointing a receiver
If the **charge contract so provides**, when notice is given by the chargee that the charge is converted into a fixed charge (on whatever assets of the relevant class are owned by the company at the time of the giving of notice)
The **crystallisation** of **another floating charge** if it causes the company to cease business

Floating charge contracts sometimes make provision for '**automatic crystallisation**'. This is where the charge is to crystallise when a **specified event** – such as a breach of some term by the company – occurs, regardless of whether:

- The chargee learns of the event
- The chargee wants to enforce the charge as a result of the event

Such clauses have been accepted by the courts if they state that, on the event happening, the floating charge is **converted** to a fixed one. Clauses which provide only that a company is to cease to deal with charged assets on the occurrence of a particular event have been rejected.

3.7 Comparison of fixed and floating charges

FAST FORWARD

Floating charges rank **behind** a number of other creditors on liquidation, in particular preferential creditors such as employees.

A **fixed charge** is normally the more satisfactory form of security since it **confers immediate rights** over identified assets. A **floating charge** has some advantage in being applicable to **current assets which may be easier to realise** than long-term assets subject to a fixed charge. If, for example, a company becomes insolvent it may be easier to sell its inventory than its empty factory.

The principal disadvantages of floating charges
The **holder** of a floating charge **cannot be certain** until the charge crystallises which assets will form their security.
Even when a floating charge has crystallised over an identified pool of assets the **chargeholder** may find themself **postponed** to the claim of **other creditors** as follows.
(a) A **judgement creditor or landlord** who has seized goods and sold them may retain the proceeds if received before the appointment of the debentureholder's receiver.
(b) **Preferential debts** such as wages may be paid out of assets subject to a floating charge unless there are other uncharged assets available for this purpose.
(c) The **holder** of a **fixed charge** over the same assets will usually have priority over a floating charge on those assets, even if that charge was created before the fixed charge.
(d) A creditor may have sold goods and delivered them to the company on condition that they are to retain legal ownership until they have been paid (a **Romalpa** clause).
A **floating charge** may become **invalid automatically** if the company creates the charge to secure an existing debt and goes into liquidation within a year thereafter. The period is only six months with a fixed charge.

3.8 Priority of charges

FAST FORWARD

If more than one charge exists over the **same class of property** then legal rules must be applied to see which takes priority in the event the company goes into liquidation.

Different charges over the **same** property may be given to different creditors. It will be necessary in such cases to determine which party's claim has **priority**.

Illustration

If charges are created over the same property to secure a debt of $5,000 to X and $7,000 to Y and the property is sold yielding only $10,000, either X or Y is paid in full and the other receives only the balance remaining out of $10,000 realised from the security.

Priority of charges
Fixed charges rank according to the **order of their creation**. If two successive fixed charges over the same factory are created on 1 January and 1 February the earlier takes priority over the later one.
A floating charge created before a fixed charge will only take priority if, when the latter was created, the **fixed chargee** had **notice** of a clause in the floating charge that prevents a later prior charge.
A **fixed charge created before** a **floating one** has **priority**.
Two floating charges take priority according to the **time of creation**.

If a floating charge is existing and a fixed charge over the same property is created later the fixed charge has priority. This is unless the fixed chargeholder knew of the floating charge. The **fixed** charge ranks **first** since it attached to the property at the time of **creation** but the **floating** charge attaches at the time of **crystallisation**. Once a floating charge has crystallised it becomes a fixed charge and a fixed charge created subsequently ranks after it.

3.8.1 Negative pledge clauses

A floating chargeholder may seek to protect themselves against losing their priority by including in the terms of their floating charge a prohibition against the company creating a fixed charge over the same property (sometimes called a **'negative pledge clause'**).

If the company **breaks that prohibition** the creditor to whom the fixed charge is given nonetheless obtains priority, unless at the time when their charge is created they have **actual** knowledge of the prohibition.

3.8.2 Sale of charged assets

If a company sells a charged asset to a **third party** the following rules apply.

- A chargee with a fixed charge still has recourse to the property in the hands of the third party – the **charge** is **automatically** transferred with the property.

- Property only remains charged by a floating charge if the **third party** had **notice** of it when they acquired the property.

Exam focus point

You should be prepared to work out the priority of charges in a scenario.

4 Registration of charges

To be valid and enforceable, charges must be **registered**, within **21 days** of creation, with the Registrar.

Certain types of **charge** created by a company **should be registered** within **21 days** with the Registrar by either the company or a person interested in it (eg the debenture trustee). Charges securing a **debenture issue** and **floating charges** are **specifically registrable**.

Other charges that are **registrable** include charges on:

- Uncalled share capital or calls made but not paid
- Land or any interest in land, other than a charge for rent
- Receivables (book debts)
- Goodwill or any intellectual property
- Ships or aircraft or any share in a ship

4.1 The registration process

The **company is responsible for registering the charge** but the charge **may** also **be registered** as a result of an application **by another person** interested in the charge.

The Registrar should be sent **the instrument** by which the charge is created or evidenced. The Registrar also has to be sent **prescribed particulars of the charge**.

- The date when the charge was created
- The amount of the debt which it secures
- Short particulars of the property to which the charge applies
- The person entitled to it

The Registrar files the particulars in the company's 'charges' register and notes the date of delivery. They also issue a **certificate** which is **conclusive evidence** that the **charge had been duly registered**.

The 21-day period for registration runs from the **creation** of the **charge**, or the acquisition of property charged, and not from the making of the loan for which the charge is security. Creation of a charge is usually effected by **execution of a document**.

4.2 Rectification of register of changes

A **mistake** or **omission** in registered particulars can only be rectified by the court ordering an extension of the period for registration, and with the subsequent rectification of the register. The court will only make the order if the error or omission was accidental, or if it is just and equitable to do so.

4.3 Failure to deliver particulars

The duty to deliver particulars falls upon the **company** creating the charge; if no one delivers particulars within 21 days, the **company and its officers are liable to a fine**.

Non-delivery in the time period results in the **charge** being **void** against an administrator, liquidator or any creditor of a company.

Non-delivery of a charge means that the sum secured by it is **payable forthwith on demand**.

4.3.1 Late delivery of particulars

The rules governing late delivery are the **same** as governing registration of **further particulars**, that is, a **court order** is required for registration.

A **charge** can only be **registered late** if it **does not prejudice the creditors** or **shareholders of the company**. Therefore, a correctly registered fixed charge has priority over a fixed charge created earlier but registered after it, if that charge is registered late.

4.4 Register of charges

As you already know, every company is under an obligation to keep a copy of documents creating charges, and a register of charges, at its **registered office** or **single alternative inspection location**.

5 Debentureholders' remedies

5.1 Rights of unsecured debentureholders

A debentureholder **without security** has the same rights as any other creditor.

Any **debentureholder** is a **creditor** of the company with the normal remedies of an unsecured creditor. They could:

- **Sue** the company for debt and seize its property if their judgement for debt is unsatisfied
- Present a petition to the court for the **compulsory liquidation** of the company
- Apply to the court for an **administration order**, that is, a temporary reprieve to try and rescue a company

5.2 Rights of secured debentureholders

A **secured** debentureholder may enforce the security if the company defaults on payment of interest or repayment of capital. They may take possession of the asset subject to the charge and sell it or apply to the court for its transfer to their ownership by a foreclosure order. They may also appoint a receiver or administrator. A floating charge holder may place the company into administration.

A **secured** debentureholder (or the trustee of a debenture trust deed) may enforce the security. They may:

- Take **possession of the asset** subject to the charge if they have a fixed charge (if they have a floating charge they may only take possession if the contract allows)
- **Sell it** (provided the debenture is executed as a deed)
- Apply to the court for its **transfer** to their ownership by foreclosure order (rarely used and only available to a legal chargee)
- Appoint a **receiver** of it, provided an **administration order** is not in effect or (in the case of floating charge holders), appoint an administrator without needing to apply to the court

Chapter Roundup

- Companies have an **implied power** to borrow for purposes incidental to their trade or business.

- **Loan capital** comprises all the longer-term borrowing of a company. It is distinguished from share capital by the fact that, at some point, borrowing must be repaid. Share capital on the other hand is only returned to shareholders when the company is wound up.

- A **debenture** is a document stating the terms on which a company has borrowed money. There are three main types.

    - A **single debenture**
    - **Debentures issued as a series** and usually registered
    - **Debenture stock** subscribed to by a large number of lenders. Only this form requires a **debenture trust deed**, although the others may often incorporate one

- A charge over the assets of a company gives a creditor a **prior claim** over other creditors to payment of their debt out of these assets.

- Charges may be either **fixed**, which attach to the relevant asset on creation, or **floating**, which attach on 'crystallisation'. For this reason it is not possible to identify the assets to which a **floating** charge relates (until **crystallisation**).

- Floating charges **crystallise** or harden (convert into a fixed charge) on the happening of certain relevant events.

- Floating charges rank **behind** a number of other creditors on liquidation, in particular preferential creditors such as employees.

- If more than one charge exists over the **same class of property** then legal rules must be applied to see which takes priority in the event the company goes into liquidation.

- To be valid and enforceable, charges must be **registered** within **21 days** of creation, with the Registrar.

- A debentureholder **without security** has the same rights as any other creditor.

- A **secured** debentureholder may enforce the security if the company defaults on payment of interest or repayment of capital. They may take possession of the asset subject to the charge and sell it or apply to the court for its transfer to their ownership by a foreclosure order. They may also appoint a receiver or administrator. A floating charge holder may place the company into administration.

1   Which of the following are correct statements about the relationship between a company's ordinary shares and its debentures?

Select all that apply.

A   Debentures do not confer voting rights, whilst ordinary shares do.

B   The company's duty is to pay interest on debentures, and to pay dividends on ordinary shares.

C   Interest paid on debentures is deducted from pre-tax profits, dividends are paid from net profits.

D   A debentureholder takes priority over a member in liquidation.

2   A fixed charge

A   Cannot be an informal mortgage

B   Can be a legal mortgage

C   Can only attach to land, shares or book debts

D   Cannot attach to land

3   Company law requires a company to maintain a register of charges, but not a register of debentureholders.

True   ☒

False   ☒

4   In which of the following situations will crystallisation of a floating charge occur?

Select all that apply.

A   Liquidation of the company

B   Disposal by the company of the charged asset

C   Cessation of the company's business

D   After the giving of notice by the chargee if the contract so provides

5   Certain types of charges need to be registered within 28 days of creation.

True   ☐

False   ☒

Answers to Quick Quiz

1   A, C and D are correct. Whilst the company has a contractual duty to pay interest on debentures, there is no duty on it to pay dividends on shares. B is therefore incorrect.

2   B. A mortgage is an example of a fixed charge. It can extend to, for instance, plant and machinery as well as land.

3   True. A register of charges must be kept, a register of debentureholders is not required to be kept by the Act.

4   A, C and D are true. As the charge does not attach to the asset until crystallisation, B is untrue.

5   False. Certain charges such as charges securing a debenture issue and floating charges need to be registered within 21 days.

Now try the questions below from the Practice Question Bank

Number
35, 36

Capital maintenance and dividend law

Topic list	Syllabus reference
1 Capital maintenance	E3(a)
2 Reduction of share capital	E3(a)
3 Distributing dividends	E3(b)

Introduction

The capital which a limited company obtains from its members as consideration for their shares is sometimes called **'the creditors' buffer'**. No one can prevent an unsuccessful company from losing its capital by trading at a loss. However, whatever capital the company does have must be held for the payment of the company's debts and may not be returned to members except under procedures which safeguard the interest of creditors. That is the price which members of a limited company are required to pay for the protection of limited liability. This principle has been developed in a number of detailed applications.

- Capital may only be distributed to members under the formal procedure of a **reduction** of **share capital** or a **winding up** of the company.
- **Dividends** may only be paid out of distributable profits.

Study guide

		Intellectual level
E	**Capital and the financing of companies**	
3	**Capital maintenance and dividend law**	
(a)	Explain the doctrine of capital maintenance and capital reduction	2
(b)	Explain the rules governing the distribution of dividends in both private and public companies	2

Exam guide

Capital maintenance can be a difficult area. The different components could all be examined separately in multiple choice questions, or as part of a scenario question.

1 Capital maintenance

FAST FORWARD

The rules which dictate how a company is to manage and maintain its capital exist to maintain the delicate balance between the **members' enjoyment of limited liability** and the **creditors' requirements that the company shall remain able to pay its debts**.

Key term

Capital maintenance is a fundamental principle of company law that limited companies should not be allowed to make payments out of capital to the detriment of company creditors. Therefore the Companies Act contains many examples of control upon capital payments. These include provisions restricting dividend payments, and capital reduction schemes.

Exam focus point

The rules affecting the possible threats to capital are complicated in certain areas. However, provided you know the rules, questions on capital maintenance tend to be straightforward.

2 Reduction of share capital

FAST FORWARD

Reduction of capital can be achieved by: **extinguishing/reducing liability on partly-paid shares; cancelling paid-up share capital**; or **paying off part of paid-up share capital**. Court confirmation is required for public companies. The court considers the interests of creditors and different classes of shareholder. There must be power in the articles and a special resolution.

A limited company is permitted without restriction to cancel **unissued shares** as that change does not alter its financial position.

If a limited company with a share capital wishes to **reduce** its **issued share capital** it may do so, if:

- The **power to do so has not been restricted by the company's articles** (if it does not have power in the articles, these may be amended by a **special resolution**)
- It passes a **special resolution**. (If the articles have been amended, this is another special resolution)
- It obtains **confirmation** of the reduction **from the court**

A company's **share premium account** and **capital redemption reserve** are treated as share capital and can therefore be reduced using the above procedure. This allows the company to clean up its capital by removing old balances.

2.1 Solvency statement

A private company need not apply to the court if it supports its special resolution with a solvency statement.

> A **solvency statement** is a declaration by the directors, provided 15 days in advance of the meeting where the special resolution is to be voted on. It states there is no ground to suspect the company is currently unable, or will be unlikely to be able, to pay its debts for the next 12 months. All possible liabilities must be taken into account and the statement should be in the prescribed form, naming all the directors.

It is an **offence** for directors to deliver to the Registrar a solvency statement without having **reasonable grounds** for the opinions expressed in it.

The **benefits** to a private company of using a solvency statement, rather than going to court, to reduce its share capital include the **faster speed of** the procedure and the **lower cost** of filing documents, rather than involving expensive legal representation in court.

2.2 Why reduce share capital?

A company may wish to **reduce its capital** for one or more of the **following reasons**.

- The company has suffered a **loss** in the **value** of its **assets** and it reduces its capital to reflect that fact.

- The company wishes to **extinguish** the **interests** of some members entirely.

- The capital reduction is part of a **complicated arrangement** of capital which may involve, for instance, replacing share capital with loan capital.

There are **three basic methods of reducing share capital** specified in the Companies Act.

Method	What happens	Effects
Extinguish or reduce liability on partly paid shares	Eg Company has nominal value $1 shares 75c paid up. Either (a) reduce nominal value to 75c; or (b) reduce nominal value to a figure between 75c and $1	Company gives up claim for amount not paid up (nothing is **returned** to shareholders)
Pay off part of paid-up share capital out of surplus assets	Eg Company reduces nominal value of fully paid shares from $1 to 70c and repays this amount to shareholders	Assets of company are reduced by 30p in $
Cancel paid-up share capital which has been lost or which is no longer represented by available assets	Eg Company has $1 nominal fully paid shares but net assets only worth 50c per share. Difference is a debit balance on reserves. Company reduces nominal value to 50c, and applies amount to write off debit balance	Company can resume dividend payments out of future profits without having to make good past losses

2.3 Role of the court in reduction of share capital

When the court receives an application for reduction of capital its **first concern** is the effect of the reduction on the company's ability to pay its debts; that is, that the creditors are protected.

If the reduction is by extinguishing liability or paying off part of paid-up share capital, the court requires that **creditors** shall be **invited** by advertisement to state their objections (if any) to the reduction. Where paid-up share capital is cancelled, the court **may** require an invitation to creditors.

Normally the company persuades the court to dispense with **advertising for creditors' objections** (which can be commercially damaging to the company).

Two possible approaches are:

- To **pay off** all **creditors** before application is made to the court; or, if that is not practicable
- To produce to the court a **guarantee**, say from the company's bank, that its existing debts will be paid in full

The **second concern** of the court, where there is more than one class of share, is whether the reduction is fair in its effect on different classes of shareholder.

If the reduction is, **in the circumstances**, a **variation of class rights** the **consent** of the class must be obtained under the variation of class rights procedure.

Within each class of share it is usual to make a uniform reduction of every share by the same amount per share, though this is **not** obligatory.

The court may also be concerned that the **reduction should not confuse or mislead people who may deal with the company in future**. It may insist that the company add 'and reduced' to its name or publish explanations of the reduction.

2.3.1 Confirmation by the court

If the court is satisfied that the reduction is in order, it confirms the reduction by making an order to that effect. A **copy of the court order** and a **statement of capital**, approved by the court, to show the altered share capital is delivered to the Registrar, who issues a certificate of registration.

3 Distributing dividends

FAST FORWARD

Various rules have been created to ensure that dividends are only paid out of **available profits**.

Key term

A **dividend** is an amount payable to shareholders from profits or other distributable reserves.

3.1 Power to declare dividends

A company may only pay dividends out of **profits available for the purpose**. The power to declare a dividend is given by the articles, which often include the following rules.

Rules related to the power to declare a dividend
The **company** in **general meeting** may declare dividends.
No dividend may exceed the **amount recommended** by the directors, who have an implied power in their discretion to set aside profits as reserves.
The directors may declare such **interim dividends** as they consider justified.
Dividends are normally declared payable on the **paid up amount** of **share capital**. For example a $1 share which is fully paid will carry entitlement to twice as much dividend as a $1 share 50c paid.
A dividend may be paid **otherwise than in cash**.
Dividends may be paid by **cheque** or **warrant** sent through the post to the shareholder at their registered address. If shares are held jointly, payment of dividend is made to the first-named joint holder on the register.

Listed companies generally pay two dividends a year; an **interim dividend** based on interim profit figures, and a **final dividend** based on the annual accounts and approved at the AGM.

A **dividend becomes a debt** when it is **declared** and **due for payment**. A shareholder is not entitled to a dividend unless it is declared in accordance with the procedure prescribed by the articles and the declared date for payment has arrived. This is so even if the member holds **preference shares** carrying a priority entitlement to receive a specified amount of dividend on a specified date in the year. The directors may decide to withhold profits and cannot be compelled to recommend a dividend.

If the articles refer to 'payment' of dividends this means **payment in cash**. A power to pay dividends **in specie** (otherwise than in cash) is not implied but may be expressly created. Scrip dividends are dividends paid by the issue of additional shares. Any provision of the articles for the declaration and payment of dividends is subject to the overriding rule that **no dividend may be paid except out of profits distributable by law**.

3.2 Distributable profit

FAST FORWARD

Distributable profits may be defined as 'accumulated realised profits ... less accumulated realised losses'. **'Accumulated'** means that any losses of previous years must be included in reckoning the current distributable surplus. **'Realised'** profits are determined in accordance with generally accepted accounting principles.

ey term

Profits available for distribution are accumulated realised profits (which have not been distributed or capitalised) less accumulated realised losses (which have not been previously written off in a reduction or reorganisation of capital).

The word **'accumulated'** requires that any **losses** of **previous years** must be included in reckoning the current distributable surplus. A profit or loss is deemed to be **realised** if it is treated as realised in accordance with generally accepted accounting principles. Hence, financial reporting and accounting standards in issue, plus generally accepted accounting principles (GAAP), should be taken into account when determining realised profits and losses.

Depreciation must be treated as a **realised loss**, and debited against profit, in determining the amount of distributable profit remaining.

However, a **revalued asset** will have deprecation charged on its historical cost and the increase in the value in the asset. The Companies Act allows the depreciation provision on the valuation increase to be treated also as a realised profit. Effectively there is a cancelling out, and at the end **only depreciation that relates to historical cost will affect dividends**.

Illustration

Suppose that an asset purchased for $20,000 has a ten-year life. Provision is made for depreciation on a straight line basis. This means an annual depreciation charge of $2,000 ($20,000/10 years) must be deducted in reckoning the company's realised profit less realised loss.

After five years, the asset's written-down value is $10,000 ($20,000 less $2,000 × 5 years). Suppose that the asset is then revalued to $50,000. The increase in the value of the asset ($40,000) is credited to the revaluation reserve.

The consequences of this revaluation are that the annual depreciation charge is raised to $10,000 ($50,000/5 remaining years of the asset's life) and $8,000 ($40,000/5 years) is transferred from the revaluation reserve to realised profit each year for the remaining life of the asset.

The net effect is that each year realised profits are still reduced by $2,000 ($10,000 – $8,000) in respect of depreciation.

If, on a **general revaluation** of all fixed assets, it appears that there is a diminution in value of any one or more assets, then any related provision(s) need **not** be treated as a realised loss.

The Act states that if a company shows **development expenditure** as an asset in its accounts it must usually be treated as a realised loss in the year it occurs. However it can be carried forward in special circumstances (generally taken to mean in accordance with accounting standards).

3.3 Dividends of public companies

A public company may only make a distribution if its **net assets** are, at the time, **not less than the aggregate of its called-up share capital and undistributable reserves**. It may only pay a dividend which will leave its net assets at not less than that aggregate amount.

A public company may only make a distribution if its **net assets are**, at the time, **not less than the aggregate of its called-up share capital and undistributable reserves**. The dividend which it may pay is limited to such amount as will leave its net assets at not less than that aggregate amount.

Undistributable reserves are defined as:

(a)   **Share premium account**

(b)   **Capital redemption reserve**

(c)   Any **surplus** of **accumulated unrealised profits** over **accumulated unrealised losses** (known as a revaluation reserve). However, a deficit of accumulated unrealised profits compared with accumulated unrealised losses must be treated as a realised loss

(d)   Any **reserve** which the company is **prohibited** from **distributing** by **statute**, its **constitution** or **law**

 Illustration

Suppose that a public company has an issued share capital (fully paid) of $800,000 and $200,000 on share premium account (which is an undistributable reserve). If its assets less liabilities are less than $1 million it may not pay a dividend. If, however, its net assets are say $1,250,000, it may pay a dividend but only of such amount as will leave net assets of $1 million or more — so its maximum permissible dividend is $250,000.

The **dividend rules apply** to every form of **distribution of assets except** the following

- The **issue of bonus shares** whether fully or partly paid
- The **redemption** or **purchase** of the company's **shares** out of **capital** or **profits**
- A **reduction** of **share capital**
- A **distribution** of **assets** to members in a **winding up**

Exam focus point

You must appreciate how the rules relating to public companies in this area are more stringent than the rules for private companies.

3.4 Relevant accounts

The profits available for distribution are generally determined from the **last annual accounts** to be prepared.

Whether a company has profits from which to pay a dividend is determined by reference to its '**relevant accounts**', which are generally the last annual accounts to be prepared.

If the auditors have qualified their report on the accounts they must also state in writing whether, in their opinion, the subject matter of their qualification is **material** in determining whether the dividend may be paid. This statement must have been circulated to the members (for a private company) or considered at a general meeting (for a public company).

A company may produce **interim accounts** if the latest annual accounts do not disclose a sufficient distributable profit to cover the proposed dividend. It may also produce **initial accounts** if it proposes to pay a dividend during its first accounting reference period or before its first accounts are laid before the company in general meeting. These accounts may be unaudited, but they must suffice to permit a proper judgement to be made of amounts of any of the relevant items.

If a **public** company produces initial or interim accounts they must be full accounts such as the company is required to produce as final accounts at the end of the year. They need not be audited. However the auditors must, in the case of initial accounts, satisfy themselves that the accounts have been 'properly prepared' to comply with the Act. A copy of any such accounts of a public company (with any auditors' statement) must be delivered to the Registrar for filing.

3.5 Infringement of dividend rules

In certain situations the **directors** and **members** may be liable to make good to the company the amount of an **unlawful dividend**.

If a dividend is paid otherwise than out of distributable profits the company, the **directors and** the **shareholders** may be involved in making good the unlawful distribution.

The directors are held **responsible** since they either recommend to members in general meeting that a dividend should be declared or they declare interim dividends.

(a)   **The directors are liable if they declare a dividend which they know is paid out of capital.**

(b)   **The directors are liable if, without preparing any accounts, they declare or recommend a dividend which proves to be paid out of capital.** It is their duty to satisfy themselves that profits are available.

(c)   **The directors are liable if they make some mistake of law or interpretation of the constitution which leads them to recommend or declare an unlawful dividend.** However, in such cases the directors may well be entitled to relief as their acts were performed 'honestly and reasonably'.

The directors may, however, **honestly** rely on proper accounts which disclose an apparent distributable profit out of which the dividend can properly be paid. They are not liable if it later appears that the assumptions or estimates used in preparing the accounts, although reasonable at the time, were in fact unsound.

The **position of members** is as follows.

- A member may obtain an **injunction** to restrain a company from paying an unlawful dividend.

- Members voting in general meeting **cannot authorise** the payment of an unlawful dividend nor release the directors from their liability to pay it back.

- The company can **recover from members** an **unlawful dividend** if the **members knew** or had **reasonable grounds** to believe that it was unlawful.

- If the directors have to make good to the company an unlawful dividend they may claim **indemnity from members** who at the time of receipt knew of the irregularity.

- Members knowingly receiving an unlawful dividend may **not bring an action** against the directors.

If an unlawful dividend is paid by **reason of error** in the **accounts** the company may be unable to claim against either the directors or the members. The company might then have a claim against its **auditors** if the undiscovered mistake was due to negligence on their part.

Chapter Roundup

- The rules which dictate how a company is to manage and maintain its capital exist to maintain the delicate balance between the **members' enjoyment of limited liability** and the **creditors' requirements that the company shall remain able to pay its debts**.

- Reduction of capital can be achieved by: **extinguishing/reducing liability on partly-paid shares; cancelling paid-up share capital;** or **paying off part of paid-up share capital**. Court confirmation is required for public companies. The court considers the interests of creditors and different classes of shareholder. There must be power in the articles and a special resolution.

- Various rules have been created to ensure that dividends are only paid out of **available profits**.

- Distributable profits may be defined as 'accumulated realised profits ... less accumulated realised losses'. **'Accumulated'** means that any losses of previous years must be included in reckoning the current distributable surplus. **'Realised'** profits are determined in accordance with generally accepted accounting principles.

- A public company may only make a distribution if its **net assets** are, at the time, **not less than the aggregate of its called-up share capital and undistributable reserves**. It may only pay a dividend which will leave its net assets at not less than that aggregate amount.

- The profits available for distribution are generally determined from the **last annual accounts** to be prepared.

- In certain situations the **directors** and **members** may be liable to make good to the company the amount of an **unlawful dividend**.

1   Where application is made to the court for confirmation of a reduction in capital, the court may require that creditors should be invited by advertisement to state their objections. In which of the following ways can the need to advertise be avoided?

Select all that apply.

- Ⓐ   Paying off all creditors before application to the court
- B   Producing a document signed by the directors stating the company's ability to pay its debts
- Ⓒ   Producing a guarantee from the company's bank that its existing debts will be paid in full
- D   Renouncement by existing shareholders of their limited liability in relation to existing debts

2   **Fill in the blanks** in the statements below.

Distributable profits may be defined as ...*accumulated realised*... profits less ...*accumulated realised*... losses.

3   If a company makes an unlawful dividend, who may be involved in making good the distribution?

- A   The company only
- B   The directors only
- C   The shareholders only
- Ⓓ   The company, the directors and the shareholders

4   Give four examples of undistributable reserves.   *share premium account*
capital redemption reserve
revaluation reserve

5   **Fill in the blanks** in the statements below.

A private company does not need to apply to the court to reduce its share capital if it supports its ...*special resolution*... with a ...*solvency statement*...

Answers to Quick Quiz

1   A and C. The only guarantee that the courts will accept is from the company's bank.

2   Distributable profits may be defined as **accumulated realised** profits less **accumulated realised** losses.

3   D. All three may be liable.

4   Share premium account

    Capital redemption reserve

    A surplus of accumulated unrealised profits over accumulated unrealised losses (revaluation reserve)

    Any reserve which the company is prohibited from distributing by statute or by its constitution or any law.

5   A private company does not need to apply to the court to reduce its share capital if it supports its **special resolution** with a **solvency statement**.

Now try the questions below from the Practice Question Bank

Number
37, 38, 39

Management, administration and the regulation of companies

Company directors

15

Topic list	Syllabus reference
1 The role of directors	F1(a)
2 Appointment of directors	F1(b)
3 Remuneration of directors	F1(b)
4 Vacation of office	F1(b)
5 Disqualification of directors	F1(b)
6 Powers of directors	F1(c)
7 Powers of the Chief Executive Officer (Managing Director)	F1(c)
8 Powers of an individual director	F1(c)
9 Duties of directors	F1(d)

Introduction

In this chapter we turn our attention to the **appointment** and **removal**, and the **powers and duties, of company directors**.

The important principle to grasp is that the **extent of directors' powers is defined by the articles**.

If **shareholders** do not approve of the directors' acts they must either **remove them** or **alter the articles** to regulate their future conduct. However, they **cannot** simply **take over** the functions of the directors.

In essence, the directors act as **agents of the company**. This ties in with the **agency** part of your law studies. The different types of authority a director can have (implied and actual) are important in this area.

We also consider the **duties** of directors under statute and **remedies for the breach of such duties**.

Statute also imposes some duties on directors, specifically concerning openness when transacting with the company.

Finally we look at the duties and powers of the **company secretary** and **auditor**.

Study guide

		Intellectual level
F	**Management, administration and the regulation of companies**	
1	**Company directors**	
(a)	Explain the role of directors in the operation of a company, and the different types of directors, such as executive/ non-executive directors or de jure and de facto directors, shadow directors	2
(b)	Discuss the ways in which directors are appointed, can lose their office and the disqualification of directors	2
(c)	Distinguish between the powers of the board of directors, the managing director/chief executive and individual directors to bind their company	2
(d)	Explain the duties that directors owe to their companies, and the controls imposed by statute over dealings between directors and their companies, including loans	2

Exam guide

The relationship between members of a company and their directors could easily be examined. The detailed rules regarding directors and other company officers are all highly examinable.

1 The role of directors

FAST FORWARD

Any person who occupies the position of director is treated as such, the test being one of **function**.

Key term

A **director** is a person who is responsible for the overall direction of the company's affairs. In company law, director means any person occupying the position of director, by whatever name called.

Any person who occupies the position of director is treated as such. The test is one of **function**. The directors' function is to take part in **making decisions** by **attending meetings** of the board of directors. Anyone who does that is a director, whatever they may be called.

A person who is given the title of director, such as 'sales director' or 'director of research', to give them status in the company structure is not a director in company law. This is unless by virtue of their appointment they are a **member** of the **board** of **directors**, or they carry out functions that would be properly discharged only by a director.

1.1 De jure and de facto directors

Most directors are **expressly appointed** by a company and are known as **de jure** directors. A **de facto** director is **anyone** who is **held out by a company** as a director, **performs the functions** of a director and is **treated by the board** as a director, although they have **never been validly appointed**.

1.2 Shadow directors

A person might seek to **avoid the legal responsibilities of being a director** by avoiding appointment as such but using their power, say as a major shareholder, to manipulate the acknowledged board of directors. In other words they seek the **power** and **influence** that come with the position of director, but **without the legal obligations** it entails.

Company law seeks to prevent this abuse by extending several statutory rules to **shadow directors**. Shadow directors are directors for legal purposes if the board of directors is accustomed to act in accordance with **shadow directors' directions** and **instructions**. This **rule does not apply** to **professional advisers** merely **acting** in that **capacity**.

1.2.1 Shadow directors and de facto directors

Shadow directors differ from de facto directors because the **public** (and the **authorities**) are **rarely aware of their existence**. Whereas a **de facto director performs the everyday tasks that a director would** (dealing with suppliers and customers and being present at general meetings), shadow directors exerts their influence away from the day-to-day running of the business.

1.3 Alternate directors

A director may, if the articles permit, appoint an **alternate director** to attend and vote for them at board meetings which they are unable to attend. Such an alternate may be another director, in which case they have the vote of the absentee as well as their own. More usually they are an outsider. Company articles could make specific provisions for this situation.

1.4 Executive directors

> An **executive director** is a director who performs a specific role in a company under a **service contract** which requires a regular, possibly daily, involvement in management.

A director may also be an **employee** of their company. Since the company is also their **employer** there is a potential conflict of interest which, in principle, a director is required to avoid. To allow an individual to be **both a director and employee** the articles usually make express provision for it, but prohibit the director from voting at a board meeting on the terms of their own employment.

Directors who have additional management duties as employees may be distinguished by **special titles**, such as 'Finance Director'. However **any such title does not affect their personal legal position**. They have two distinct positions as:

- A member of the board of directors; and
- A manager with management responsibilities as an **employee**

1.5 Non-executive directors (NED)

> A **non-executive director** does not have a function to perform in a company's management but is involved in its governance.

In **listed companies**, the **UK Corporate Governance guidelines** state that boards of directors are more likely to be fully effective if they comprise both **executive directors** and strong, independent **non-executive directors**. The main tasks of the NEDs are as follows:

- **Contribute** an **independent view** to the board's deliberations
- **Help the board provide** the company with **effective leadership**
- **Ensure** the **continuing effectiveness** of the **executive directors** and management
- **Ensure high standards** of **financial probity** on the part of the company

Non-executive and **shadow** directors are subject to the **same duties** as **executive directors**.

1.6 The Chief Executive Officer (Managing Director)

> A **Chief Executive Officer** (also commonly known as a **Managing Director**) is one of the directors of the company appointed to carry out overall day-to-day management functions.

Boards of directors usually appoint one director to be **Chief Executive Officer** (this position is also commonly known as **Managing Director**) . A Chief Executive Officer (CEO) or Managing Director (MD) has a special position and has wider apparent powers than any director who is not appointed to that position.

1.7 Number of directors

Every company must have at least **one** director; for a **public** company the minimum is **two**. There is no statutory maximum in the UK, but the articles usually impose a limit. All directors must be a **natural person**, not a body corporate.

1.8 The board of directors

Companies are run by the directors collectively, in a **board of directors**.

> The **board of directors** is the elected representative of the shareholders, acting collectively in the management of a company's affairs.

One of the basic principles of company law is that the **powers** which are delegated to the directors, under the articles, are given to them as a **collective body**. The **board meeting** is the **proper place for the exercise of the powers,** unless they have been validly passed on, or 'sub-delegated', to committees or individual directors.

1.9 The Chair

According to the **UK Corporate Governance Code**, a company's Chair (or Chairman) is responsible for leading the board and ensuring its effectiveness. This is a very distinct role from that of the CEO/MD, who is responsible for leading the company's operations. The Chair's **power** may be contained within the company's **articles of association** and they should be **independent** of the company when they are appointed.

2 Appointment of directors

FAST FORWARD

> The method of appointing directors, along with their rotation and co-option is **controlled** by the **articles**.

As we saw earlier, a director may be **appointed expressly**, in which case they are known as a **de jure** director. Where a person acts as a director without actually being appointed as such (a **de facto** or **shadow director**) they incur the obligations and have some of the powers of a proper director. In addition, a shadow director is subject to many of the duties imposed on directors.

2.1 Appointment of first directors

The application for registration delivered to the Registrar to form a company **includes particulars of the first directors**, with their consents. On the formation of the company, those persons become the first directors.

2.2 Appointment of subsequent directors

Once a company has been formed further directors can be appointed, either to **replace** existing directors or as **additional** directors.

Appointment of further directors is carried out **as the articles provide**. Most company articles allow for the appointment of directors:

- By **ordinary resolution** of the shareholders, and
- By a **decision** of the directors.

However, the articles do not have to follow these provisions and may impose **different methods** on the company.

232 **15: Company directors** | Part F Management, administration and the regulation of companies

BPP
LEARNING MEDIA

When the appointment of directors is proposed at a general meeting of a public company, a **separate** resolution should be proposed for the election of **each director**. However the rule may be waived if a resolution to that effect is first carried without any vote being given against it.

2.3 Publicity

In addition to giving notice of the first directors, every company must, within **14 days**, give **notice** to the **Registrar** of any change among its directors. This includes any changes to the register of directors' residential addresses.

2.4 Age limit

The **minimum age** limit for a director is **16** and, unless the articles provide otherwise, there is no upper limit.

3 Remuneration of directors

Directors are entitled to **fees** and **expenses** as directors as per the articles, and **emoluments** (and compensation for loss of office) as per their service contracts (which can be inspected by members). Some details are published in the directors' remuneration report along with accounts.

Details of **directors' remuneration** is usually contained within their service **contract**. This is a contract where the director agrees to personally perform services for the company.

3.1 Directors' expenses

Most articles state that directors are entitled to **reimbursement** of **reasonable expenses** incurred whilst carrying out their duties or functions as directors.

In addition, most directors have **written service contracts** setting out their entitlement to emoluments and expenses. Where service contracts **guarantee employment** for longer than **two years** then an **ordinary resolution** must be passed by the members of the company that the contract is with.

3.2 Compensation for loss of office

Any director may receive **non-contractual** compensation for loss of office paid to them voluntarily. Any such compensation is lawful **only if** approved by members of the company in general meeting, after proper disclosure has been made to all members, whether voting or not.

This only applies to **uncovenanted payments**; approval is not required where the company is contractually bound to make the payment.

Compensation paid to directors for loss of office is distinguished from any payments made to directors **as employees** – to settle, for example, claims arising from the premature termination of the service agreements. These are contractual payments which do not require approval in general meeting.

3.3 Directors' remuneration report

Quoted companies are required to include a **directors' remuneration report** as part of their annual report, part of which is subject to audit. The report must cover:

- The details of each **individual director's remuneration package**
- The company's **remuneration policy**
- The **role** of the **board** and **remuneration committee** in deciding the **remuneration** of **directors**

It is the duty of the directors (including those who were a director in the preceding five years) to **provide any information about themselves** that is necessary to produce this report.

Quoted companies are required to allow a **vote by members on the directors' remuneration report**. The vote is purely advisory and does not mean the remuneration should change if the resolution is not passed. A negative vote would be a strong signal to the directors that the members are unhappy with remuneration levels.

Items not subject to audit

- Consideration by the directors (remuneration committee) of matters relating to directors' remuneration

- Statement of company's policy on directors' remuneration

- Performance graph (share performance)

- Directors' service contracts (dates, unexpired length, compensation payable for early termination)

Items subject to audit

- Salary/fees payable to each director
- Bonuses paid/to be paid
- Expenses
- Compensation for loss of office paid
- Any benefits received
- Share options and long-term incentive schemes – performance criteria and conditions
- Pensions
- Excessive retirement benefits
- Compensation to past directors
- Sums paid to third parties in respect of a director's services

3.4 Inspection of directors' service agreements

A company must make available for inspection by members a copy or particulars of **contracts of employment** between the company or a subsidiary with a director of the company. Such contracts must cover all services that a director may provide, including services outside the role of a director, and those made by a third party in respect of services that a director is contracted to perform.

Contracts must be **retained** for **one year** after expiry and must be available either at the **registered office**, or any other location permitted by the Secretary of State.

Prescribed particulars of **directors' emoluments** must be given in the accounts and also particulars of any **compensation for loss of office** and directors' **pensions**.

4 Vacation of office

FAST FORWARD

A director may vacate office as director due to: **resignation**; **not going** for **re-election**; **death**; **dissolution** of the company; **removal**; **disqualification**.

A **director may leave office** in the following ways.

- **Resignation**
- Not **offering themselves for re-election** when their term of office ends
- **Death**
- **Dissolution of the company**
- Being **removed** from office
- Being **disqualified**

A form should be filed with the **Registrar** whenever and however a director vacates office.

4.1 Retirement and re-election of directors

The **model articles** for **public companies** provide the following **rules** for the **retirement** and **re-election** of all directors ('rotation') at AGMs.

(a) At the **first AGM** of the company **all directors shall retire**.

(b) At every subsequent AGM any **directors appointed by the other directors** since the **last AGM** shall retire.

(c) Directors who were **not appointed** or **re-elected at one of the preceding two AGMs** shall retire.

Directors who are **retired by rotation** are eligible to offer themselves for **re-election**. This mandatory retirement of directors provides another **control over their performance**. Rather than having to go through the process of seeking a resolution to remove a director, members have the opportunity every three years to dispose of an underperforming director by **simply not electing** them.

4.2 Removal of directors

In addition to provisions in the articles for removal of directors, a director may be removed from office by **ordinary** resolution at a meeting of which **special notice** to the company has been given by the person proposing it.

On receipt of the special notice the company must send a copy to the director, who may require that a **memorandum of reasonable length** shall be issued to members. They also have the **right to address the meeting** at which the resolution is considered.

The articles and the service contract of the director **cannot override the statutory power**. However, the articles can **permit dismissal without the statutory formalities** being observed, for example dismissal by a resolution of the board of directors.

The power to remove a director is **limited** in its effect in four ways.

Restrictions on power to remove directors	
Shareholding qualification to call a meeting	In order to propose a resolution to remove a director, the shareholder(s) involved must call a general meeting. To do this they must hold either: • 10% of the paid up share capital, or • 10% of the voting rights, where the company does not have shares
Shareholding to request a resolution	Where a meeting is already convened, 100 members holding an average £100 of share capital each may request a resolution to remove a director.
Weighted voting rights	A director who is also a member may have weighted voting rights given to them under the constitution for such an eventuality, so that they can automatically defeat any motion to remove them as a director.
Class right agreement	It is possible to draft a shareholder agreement stating that a member holding each class of share must be present at a general meeting to constitute a quorum. If so, a member holding shares of a certain class could prevent a director being removed by not attending the meeting.

Exam focus point

The courts have stressed that the power of members to remove directors is an important right, but you should remember the ways in which members' intentions might be frustrated.

The dismissal of a director may also entail payment of a **substantial sum** to settle their claim for breach of contract, if they have a service contract. Under the Act no resolution may deprive a removed director of any compensation or damages related to their termination to which they are entitled to.

5 Disqualification of directors

FAST FORWARD

Directors may be required to vacate office because they have been disqualified on grounds dictated by the articles. Directors **may** be disqualified from a wider range of company involvements under the Company Directors Disqualification Act 1986 (CDDA).

A person cannot be appointed a director or continue in office if they are or become **disqualified** under the articles or statutory rules.

5.1 Disqualification under model articles

Model articles include a number of grounds for disqualification. These include where:

- A person **ceases to be a director** by virtue of any **provision of the Companies Act 2006**, or is prohibited from being a director by law;

- A **bankruptcy order** is made against that person;

- A composition is made with that **person's creditors** generally in satisfaction of that person's debts;

- A **registered medical practitioner** who is treating that person gives a written opinion to the company stating that that person has become physically or mentally incapable of acting as a director and may remain so for more than three months;

- Notification is received by the company from the director that the **director is resigning from office**, and such resignation has taken effect in accordance with its terms.

Unless the court approves it, an **undischarged bankrupt** cannot act as a director nor be concerned directly or indirectly in the management of a company. If they do continue to act, they become personally liable for the company's relevant debts.

In addition to the main grounds of disqualification, the articles may provide that **a director shall automatically vacate office** if they are **absent** from **board meetings** (without obtaining the leave of the board) for a **specified period** (say six months). The effect of this disqualification depends on the words used.

- If the articles refer merely to 'absence' this includes involuntary absence due to illness.
- The words 'if they shall absent himself' restrict the disqualification to periods of voluntary absence.

The **specified period** is reckoned to begin from the **last meeting** which the absent director did attend. The normal procedure is that a director who foresees a period of absence applies for leave of absence at the last board meeting which they attend; the leave granted is duly minuted. They are not then absent 'without leave' during the period.

If they fail to obtain leave but later offer a reasonable explanation the other directors may let the matter drop by simply not resolving that they shall vacate office. The general intention of the rule is to **impose a sanction against slackness**; a director has a duty to attend board meetings when they are able to do so.

5.2 Disqualification under statute

The **Company Directors Disqualification Act 1986** (CDDA 1986) provides that a **court may** formally **disqualify a person from being a director** or in any way directly or indirectly being concerned or taking part in the promotion, formation or management of a company.

Therefore, the terms of the disqualification order are very wide, and include acting as a consultant to a company. The Act, despite its title, is not limited to the disqualification of people who have been directors. **Any person** may be disqualified if they fall within the appropriate grounds.

5.3 Grounds for disqualification of directors

FAST FORWARD

Directors may be **disqualified** from acting as directors or being involved in the management of companies in a number of circumstances. They must be disqualified if the company is insolvent, and the director is found to be unfit to be concerned with management of a company.

Under the CDDA 1986 the court **may** make a disqualification order on any of the following grounds.

(a) **Where a person is convicted of an indictable offence (either in the UK or overseas) in connection with the promotion, formation, management or liquidation of a company or with the receivership or management of a company's property.**

An indictable offence is an offence which may be tried at a Crown Court; it is, therefore, a serious offence. It need not actually have been tried on indictment; if it was, the maximum period for which the court can disqualify is 15 years, compared with only 5 years if the offence was dealt with summarily (at a magistrate's court).

(b) **Where it appears that a person has been persistently in default in relation to provisions of company legislation.**

This legislation requires any return, account or other document to be filed with, delivered or sent, or notice of any matter to be given to the Registrar. Three defaults in five years are conclusive evidence of persistent default.

The maximum period of disqualification is five years.

(c) **Where it appears that a person has been guilty of fraudulent trading**. This means carrying on business with intent to defraud creditors, or for any fraudulent purpose – whether or not the company has been, or is in the course of being, wound up.

The person does not actually have to have been convicted of fraudulent trading. The legislation also applies to anyone who has otherwise been guilty of any fraud in relation to the company, or of any breach of their duty as an officer.

The maximum period of disqualification is 15 years.

(d) **Where the Secretary of State, acting on a report made by the inspectors or from information or documents obtained under the Companies Act, applies to the court for an order believing it to be expedient in the public interest.**

If the court is satisfied that the person's conduct in relation to the company makes that person unfit to be concerned in the management of a company, then it may make a disqualification order. Again the maximum is 15 years.

(e) **Where a director was involved in certain competition violations.** Maximum – 15 years.

(f) **Where a director of an insolvent company has participated in wrongful trading.** Maximum – 15 years.

The court **must** make an order where it is satisfied that the following apply:

(a) A person has been a director of a company which has at any time become **insolvent** (whether while they were a director or subsequently) and

(b) Their conduct as a director of that company makes them **unfit** to be **concerned** in the **management** of a company. The courts may also take into account their conduct as a director of other companies, whether or not these other companies are insolvent. Directors can be disqualified under this section even if they take no active part in the running of the business.

When determining **unfitness**, the following factors should be taken into account (the company concerned may be based in the UK or overseas):

- The extent to which the person was responsible for the company breaking the law

- The extent to which the person was responsible for causing the company to become insolvent

- The nature and extent of the loss or damage caused by the person's conduct

In such cases the **minimum** period of disqualification is two years.

Illustration

Offences for which directors have been disqualified include the following.

(a) **Insider dealing**

(b) **Failure** to **keep proper accounting records**

(c) **Failure to read the company's accounts**

(d) **Loans** to another company for the purposes of purchasing its own shares with **no grounds for believing the money would be repaid**

(e) **Loans** to associated companies on **uncommercial terms** to the detriment of creditors

5.4 Disqualification periods

In *Re Sevenoaks Stationers (Retail) Ltd 1991* the Court of Appeal laid down certain 'disqualification brackets'. The appropriate period of disqualification which should be imposed was a **minimum of two to five years** if the conduct was not very serious, **six to ten years** if the conduct was serious but did not merit the maximum penalty, and **over ten years** only in particularly serious cases.

Disqualification as a director need not mean disqualification from all involvement in management, so a disqualified director may continue to act as an **unpaid director** but only if the court gives leave to act.

5.4.1 Mitigation of disqualification

Examples of **circumstances** which have led the court to imposing a **lower period of disqualification** include the following.

- **Lack of dishonesty**
- **Loss of director's own money** in the company
- **Absence of personal gain**, for example excessive remuneration
- **Efforts to mitigate** the situation
- **Likelihood of reoffending**
- **Proceedings hanging over director** for a long time

5.5 Procedures for disqualification

Company **administrators**, **receivers** and **liquidators** all have a **statutory duty to report directors** to the government where they believe the conditions for a disqualification order have been satisfied.

The **Secretary of State** then decides whether to apply to the court for an order; if they do decide to apply, they must do so within two years of the date on which the company became insolvent.

5.6 Acting as a director whilst disqualified

Acting as a director whilst disqualified is a **serious offence**; where it is committed, **directors are personally liable for the debts of the company**.

5.7 Disqualification for commercial misjudgement

The courts' approach has been to view **'ordinary commercial misjudgement'** as insufficient to justify disqualification.

> *Re Uno, Secretary of State for Trade and Industry v Gill 2004*
>
> *The facts:* A group consisting of two furniture companies carried on trading while in serious financial difficulties, while the directors tried to find a way out of the situation. Uno continued to take deposits from customers for furniture to fund its working capital requirements.
>
> *Decision:* The directors were not disqualified for acting in this way as their behaviour was not dishonest or lacking in commercial probity and did not make them unfit to manage a company. They had been trying to explore realistic opportunities to save the businesses and were not to blame for the eventual collapse of the businesses and the subsequent loss to customers.

A **lack of commercial probity**, or gross negligence or total incompetence, however, might render disqualification appropriate.

> *Secretary of State for Trade and Industry v Thornbury 2008*
>
> *The facts:* A director failed to carry out any further investigation after receiving verbal assurances from other directors regarding the financial status of the company. The company was in breach of its statutory obligations to pay HMRC.
>
> *Decision:* Although the director had not been dishonest, it had not been reasonable for him to leave matters in the other directors' hands to such a degree. He was held to be unfit to be concerned in the management of a company and disqualified for two years.

xam focus oint

> An article on company director disqualification appeared in *Student Accountant* and is available on the ACCA website.

6 Powers of directors

FAST FORWARD

> The **powers** of the directors are **defined** by the **articles**.

The powers of the directors are **defined by the articles**. The directors are usually authorised 'to manage the company's business' and 'to exercise all the powers of the company for any purpose connected with the company's business'.

Therefore, they may take **any decision which is within the capacity** of the company **unless** either **the Act** or **the articles** themselves **require** that the **decision shall be taken by the members in general meeting**.

6.1 Restrictions on directors' powers

FAST FORWARD

> Directors' powers may be restricted by statute or by the articles. The directors have a duty to exercise their powers in what they honestly believe to be the **best interests** of the company and for the **purposes** for which the powers are given.

6.1.1 Statutory restrictions

Many transactions, such as an alteration of the articles or a reduction of capital, must by law be effected by passing a **special resolution**. If the directors propose such changes they must secure the passing of the appropriate resolution by shareholders in a general meeting.

6.1.2 Restrictions imposed by articles

As an example, the articles often set a maximum amount which the directors may borrow. If the directors wish to exceed that limit, they should **seek authority** from a **general meeting**.

When the directors clearly have the necessary power, their decision may be challenged if they exercise the power in the wrong way.

They must exercise their powers:

- In what they **honestly believe to be the interests of the company**
- For a **proper purpose**, being the purpose for which the power is given

6.1.3 Members' control of directors

There is a **division of power** between the board of directors (who manage the business) and the members (who, as owners, take the major policy decisions at general meetings). How, then, do the owners seek to 'control' the people in charge of their property?

- The members **appoint** the directors and may **remove** them from office.

- The members can, by **altering the articles** (special resolution needed), re-allocate powers between the board and the general meeting.

- Articles may allow the members to pass a **special resolution ordering** the **directors to act** (or **refrain from acting**) in a **particular way**. Such special resolutions cannot invalidate anything the directors have already done.

Remember that **directors are not agents of the members.** They cannot be instructed by the members in general meeting as to how they should exercise their powers. **The directors' powers are derived from the company as a whole** and are to be exercised by the directors as they think best in the **interests of the company**.

6.1.4 Control by the law

Certain powers must be exercised **'for the proper purpose'** and all powers must be exercised *bona fide* **for the benefit of the company**. Failure by the directors to comply with these rules will result in the **court setting aside their powers** unless the shareholders **ratify** the directors' actions by **ordinary resolution** (50% majority).

7 Powers of the Chief Executive Officer (Managing Director)

CEO

FAST FORWARD

The CEO or MD has **apparent authority** to make **business contracts** on behalf of the company. Their **actual authority** is whatever the **board gives** them.

In their dealings with outsiders the CEO or MD has **apparent authority** as agent of the company to **make business contracts**. No other director, even if they work full time, has that **apparent** authority as a director, though if they are employed as a manager they may have apparent authority at a slightly lower level. The CEO or MD's **actual authority** is whatever the board gives them.

Although appointment as CEO or MD has special status, it may be **terminated** just like that of any other director (or employee); they then revert to the position of an ordinary director. Alternatively, the company in general meeting may **remove them from their office of director** and they immediately cease to be CEO or MD since being a director is a necessary qualification for holding the post.

7.1 Agency and the CEO/MD

The directors are **agents of the company, not the members**. Where they have **actual or usual** authority they can **bind the company**. In addition a director may have **apparent authority** by virtue of **holding out**.

Holding out

Holding out is a basic rule of the law of agency. This means, if the principal (the company) holds out a person as its authorised agent they are estopped from denying that they are its **authorised agent**. They are bound by a contract they enter on the company's behalf.

apparent authority by virtue of holding out

Apparent authority is the authority which an agent appears to have to a third party. A contract made within the scope of such authority will bind the principal, even though the agent was not following their instructions.

Therefore if the board of directors **permits a director** to behave as if they are a **CEO** or **MD** duly appointed when, in fact, they are not, the company may be bound by their actions.

A CEO or MD has, by virtue of their position, **apparent authority** to make commercial contracts for the company. Moreover, if the board allows a director to enter into contracts, being aware of their dealings and taking no steps to disown them, the company will usually be bound.

Freeman & Lockyer v Buckhurst Park Properties (Mangal) Ltd 1964

The facts: A company carried on a business as property developers. The articles contained a power to appoint a Managing Director but this was never done. One of the directors of the company, to the knowledge but without the express authority of the remainder of the board, acted as if he were Managing Director. He found a purchaser for an estate and also engaged a firm of architects to make a planning application. The company later refused to pay the architect's fees on the grounds that the director had no actual or apparent authority.

Decision: The company was liable since by its acquiescence it had represented that the director was a Managing Director, with the authority to enter into contracts that were normal commercial arrangements, and which the board itself would have been able to enter.

Situations where the facts are similar to the *Freeman & Lockyer* case often occur in law exams, so be prepared to spot them.

In the *Freeman & Lockyer* case, the judge laid down **four conditions** which must be satisfied in claiming under the principle of **holding out**. The claimant must show that:

(a) A **representation** was made to them that the **agent had** the **authority** to enter, on behalf of the company, into the contract of the kind sought to be enforced.

(b) Such **representation** was **made by a person** who had **'actual'** authority to **manage** the **business** of the company.

   The board of directors would certainly have actual authority to manage the company. Some commentators have also argued that the CEO/MD has actual or apparent authority to make representations about the extent of the actual authority of other company agents. (However a third party cannot rely on the representations a CEO/MD makes about their own actual authority.)

(c) They were **induced** by the **representation** to enter into the contract; they had, in fact, relied on it.

(d) There must be **nothing** in the **articles** which would prevent the company from giving valid authority to its agent to enter into the contract.

8 Powers of an individual director

The position of any **other individual director** (not an MD) who is also an employee is that:

(a) They **do not have the apparent authority to make general contracts** which attaches to the position of MD, but they have **whatever apparent authority attaches** to their **management position**.

(b) **Removal** from the office of director may be a **breach** of their **service contract**, if that agreement stipulates that they are to have the status of director as part of the conditions of employment.

9 Duties of directors

FAST FORWARD

The Companies Act 2006 sets out the **seven principal duties** of **directors**.

The Company's Act 2006 sets out the **principal duties** that directors owe to their company. Many of these duties developed over time through the operation of **common law** and **equity,** or are **fiduciary duties** which have now been codified to make the law clearer and more accessible.

Point to note

When deciding whether a duty has been broken, the courts will consider the Companies Act primarily. All case law explained in this section applied before the 2006 Act, but is included here to help you understand the types of situation that arise and how the law will be interpreted and applied by the courts in the future.

In the text below on directors' statutory duties we have included references to sections of the Companies Act 2006. They have been provided purely for reference. Exam questions will focus on the content of the duties.

Key term

Fiduciary duty is a duty imposed upon certain persons because of the position of trust and confidence in which they stand, in relation to another. The duty is more onerous than generally arises under a contractual or tort relationship. It requires full disclosure of information held by the fiduciary, a strict duty to account for any profits received as a result of the relationship, and a duty to avoid conflict of interest.

Broadly speaking, directors must be **honest** and **not allow their personal interests to conflict with their duties as directors**. The directors are said to hold a **fiduciary position**, since they make contracts as **agents** of the company and have control of its property.

The duties included in the Companies Act 2006 form a **code of conduct** for directors. They do not tell them what to do but rather create a framework that sets out how they are expected to **behave** generally. This code is important, as it addresses situations where:

- A director may put their **own interests** ahead of the company's interests
- A director may be **negligent** and liable to an action in tort.

9.1 Who are the duties owed to?

Section 170 of the Companies Act makes it clear that directors owe their duties to the company, **not** the members. This means that **only the company itself can take action against a director** who breaches their duties. However, it is possible for a member to bring a derivative claim against the director, on behalf of the company.

The effect of the **duties are cumulative**; in other words, a director owes **every duty** to the company that could apply in any given situation. The Act provides guidance for this. Where a director is offered a bribe, for instance, they will be breaking the duty not to accept a benefit from a third party - and they will also not be promoting the company for the benefit of the members.

When deciding whether or not a director has breached a duty, the court should consider their actions in the context of **each individual duty** in turn.

9.2 Who are the duties owed by?

Every person who is **classed as a director** under the Act owes the company a number of duties. Certain aspects of the duties, regarding conflicts of interest and accepting benefits from third parties, also apply to **past directors**. This is to prevent directors from exploiting a situation for their own benefit by simply resigning. The courts are directed to apply duties to **shadow directors** where they are capable of applying.

Directors must, at all times, continue to **act in accordance with all other laws**; no authorisation is given by the duties for a director to breach any other law or regulation.

9.3 The duties and the articles

The **articles** may provide **more onerous regulations** than the Act, but they may not reduce the level of duty expected, unless it is in the following circumstances:

- If a director has **acted in accordance with the articles** they cannot be in breach of the duty to exercise independent judgement.

- Some **conflicts of interest by independent directors** are permissible by the articles.

- Directors will not be in breach of duty concerning **conflicts of interest** if they follow any **provisions in the articles for dealing with them**, as long as the provisions are lawful.

- The company may **authorise anything** that would otherwise be a breach of duty.

9.4 The duties of directors

FAST FORWARD

The **statutory duties** owed by directors are to:

- Act within their powers
- Promote the success of the company
- Exercise independent judgement
- Exercise reasonable skill, care and diligence
- Avoid conflicts of interest
- Not accept benefits from third parties
- Declare an interest in a proposed transaction or arrangement

7 statutory duties owed by directors

We shall now consider the duties placed on directors by the Act. Where cases are mentioned it is to **demonstrate** the previous common law or equitable principle that courts will follow when interpreting and applying the Act.

9.4.1 Duty to act within powers (s 171)

The directors owe a duty to act in accordance with the company's constitution, and only to exercise powers for the purposes for which they were conferred. They have a **fiduciary duty to the company to exercise their powers bona fide in what they honestly consider to be the interests of the company**. This honest belief is effective even if, in fact, the interests of the company were not served.

This duty is owed **to the company** and **not generally to individual shareholders**. The directors will not generally be liable to the members if, for instance, they purchase shares without disclosing information affecting the share price.

In exercising the powers given to them by the articles, the directors have a fiduciary duty not only to act *bona fide* **but also only to use their powers for a proper purpose.**

The powers are restricted to the **purposes** for **which they were given**. If the directors infringe this rule by exercising their powers for a collateral purpose the transaction will be invalid **unless** the **company** in **general meeting authorises it, or subsequently ratifies it**.

Most of the directors' powers are found in the **articles,** so this duty means that the directors must not act outside their power or the capacity of the company (in other words, *ultra vires*).

If the irregular use of directors' powers is in the **allotment of shares**, the votes attached to the new shares may not be used in reaching a decision in general meeting to sanction it.

> ### Howard Smith Ltd v Ampol Petroleum Ltd 1974
>
> *The facts:* Shareholders who held 55% of the issued shares intended to reject a takeover bid for the company. The directors honestly believed that it was in the company's interest that the bid should succeed. The directors allotted new shares to a prospective bidder so that the shareholders opposed to the bid would then have less than 50% of the enlarged capital and the bid would succeed.
>
> *Decision:* The allotment was invalid. 'It must be unconstitutional for directors to use their fiduciary powers over the shares in the company purely for the purpose of destroying an existing majority or creating a new majority which did not previously exist'.

Any **shareholder** may **apply to the court** to declare that a transaction in breach of s 171 should be set aside. However the practice of the courts is generally to **remit the issue** to the **members in general meeting** to see if the members wish to confirm the transaction. If the majority approve what has been done (or have authorised it in advance) that decision is treated as a proper case of **majority control**, to which the minority must normally submit.

> ### Hogg v Cramphorn 1966
>
> *The facts:* The directors of a company issued shares to trustees of a pension fund for employees, to prevent a takeover bid which they honestly thought would be bad for the company. The shares were paid for with money belonging to the company provided from an employees' benevolent and pension fund account. The shares carried ten votes each and, as a result, the trustees and directors together had control of the company. The directors had power to issue shares but not to attach more than one vote to each. A minority shareholder brought the action on behalf of all the other shareholders.
>
> *Decision:* If the directors act honestly in the best interests of the company, the company in general meeting can ratify the use of their powers for an improper purpose, so the allotment of the shares would be valid. But only one vote could be attached to each of the shares, because that is what the articles provided.

> ### Bamford v Bamford 1969
>
> *The facts:* The directors of Bamford Ltd allotted 500,000 unissued shares to a third party to thwart a takeover bid. A month after the allotment a general meeting was called, and an ordinary resolution was passed ratifying the allotment. The holders of the newly-issued shares did not vote. The claimants (minority shareholders) alleged that the allotment was not made for a proper purpose.
>
> *Decision:* The ratification was valid and the allotment was good. There had been a breach of fiduciary duty but the act had been validated by an ordinary resolution passed in general meeting.

These cases can be **distinguished** from the *Howard Smith* case (where the allotment was invalid) where the original majority would not have sanctioned the use of directors' powers. In the *Bamford* case the decision could have been sanctioned by a vote which excluded the new shareholders.

Ratification is not effective when it attempts to validate a transaction when

- It constitutes **fraud on a minority**.
- It involves **misappropriation of assets**.
- The transaction **prejudices creditors' interests** at a time when the company is insolvent.

Under the Companies Act, any resolution which proposes to **ratify the acts** of a director which are **negligent**, **in default** or in **breach of duty** or **trust** regarding the company must exclude the director or any members connected with them from the vote.

Much of the case law in this area concerns the **duty of directors** to exercise their power to allot shares.

This is only one of the powers given to directors that are subject to this **fiduciary duty**. Others include:

- Power to borrow
- Power to give security
- Power to refuse to register a transfer of shares
- Power to call general meetings
- Power to circulate information to shareholders

9.4.2 Duty to promote the success of the company (s 172)

An overriding theme of the Companies Act 2006 is the principle that the **purpose of the legal framework** surrounding companies should be **to help companies do business**. Their main purpose is to create wealth for the shareholders.

This theme is evident in the **duty of directors to promote the success of a company**. During the development of the Act, the independent Company Law Review recommended that company law should consider the interests of those for whom companies are run. It decided that the new Act should embrace the principle of **'enlightened shareholder value'**.

In essence, this principle means that the law should encourage **long-termism** and **regard for all stakeholders** by directors, and that **stakeholder interests** should be **pursued** in an **enlightened** and **inclusive** way.

To achieve this, a duty was created for directors to act in a way which, in **good faith**, promotes the success of the company for the benefit of the members as a whole.

The requirements of this duty are difficult to define and possibly problematic to apply, so the Act provides directors with a **non-exhaustive list** of issues to keep in mind.

When exercising this duty directors should consider:

- The **consequences of decisions** in the long term.
- The **interests of** their **employees**.
- The need to **develop good relationships** with **customers** and **suppliers**.
- The **impact of the company** on the **local community** and the **environment**.
- The desirability of **maintaining high standards of business conduct** and a **good reputation**.
- The need to **act fairly as between all members** of the company.

The list identifies areas of **particular importance** and **modern-day expectations** of **responsible business behaviour**, such as the interests of the company's employees and the impact of the company's operations on the community and the environment.

The **Act does not define** what should be regarded as the **success of a company**. This is down to a director's judgement in good faith. This is important as it ensures that business decisions are for the directors rather than the courts.

No guidance is given as to what the **correct course of action** would be where the various s 172 **duties** are in **conflict**. For example, a decision to shut down an office may be in the long-term best interests of the company - but it is certainly not in the interests of the employees affected, nor the local community in which they live. Conflicts such as this are inevitable and could potentially leave directors open to breach of duty claims by a wide range of stakeholders if they are not dealt with carefully.

9.4.3 Duty to exercise independent judgement (s 173)

This is a simple duty that states directors must **exercise independent judgement.** They should **not delegate** their powers of decision making or be **swayed by the influence of others**. Directors may delegate their functions to others, but they must continue to make independent decisions.

This duty is not infringed by acting in accordance with any agreement by the company that restricts the exercise of discretion by directors, or by acting in a way authorised by the company's constitution.

9.4.4 Duty to exercise reasonable skill, care and diligence (s 174)

Directors have a **duty of care** to show **reasonable skill, care and diligence**.

Section 174 provides that a director owes a duty to their company 'to exercise the same standard of care, **skill** and **diligence** that would be exercised by a reasonably diligent person' with:

(a) The general knowledge, skill and experience that may **reasonably be expected of a person carrying out the functions carried out by the director** in relation to the company; and

(b) The general knowledge, skill and experience that the **director has**.

There is, therefore, a **reasonableness test** consisting of two parts:

(a) An **objective test**

   Did the director act in a manner reasonably expected of a person performing the same role?

   A director, when carrying out their functions, must show such **care** as could **reasonably** be expected from a **competent person** in that role. If a 'reasonable' director could be expected to act in a certain way, it is no defence for a director to claim, for example, lack of expertise.

(b) A **subjective test**

   Did the director act in accordance with the skill, knowledge and experience that they actually have?

   In the case of *Re City Equitable Fire and Insurance Co Ltd 1925* it was held that a director is expected to show the **degree of skill** which may **reasonably be expected** from a person of their knowledge and experience. The standard set is personal to the person in each case. An accountant who is a director of a mining company is not required to have the expertise of a mining engineer, but they should show the expertise of an accountant.

The duty to be competent extends to **non-executive directors**, who may be liable if they fail in their duty.

Dorchester Finance Co Ltd v Stebbing 1977

The facts: Of all the company's three directors S, P and H, only S worked full-time. P and H signed blank cheques at S's request who used them to make loans which became irrecoverable. The company sued all three; P and H, who were experienced accountants, claimed that as non-executive directors they had no liability.

Decision: All three were liable; P's and H's acts in signing blank cheques were negligent and did not show the necessary objective or subjective skill and care.

In other words, the **standard of care** is an objective 'competent' standard, plus a higher 'personal' standard of application. If the director actually had particular expertise, that would lead to a higher standard of competence being reasonably expected.

The company may recover damages from its directors for loss caused by their negligence. However, something more than imprudence or want of care must be shown. It must be shown to be a case of **gross negligence**. This was defined in *Overend Gurney & Co v Gibb 1872* as conduct such that 'no men with any degree of prudence, acting on their own behalf, would have entered into such a transaction as they entered into'.

Therefore, in the absence of fraud it was difficult to control careless directors effectively. The statutory provisions on **disqualification** of directors of insolvent companies and on **liability** for wrongful trading therefore both set out how to judge a director's competence, and to provide more effective enforcement.

The company by decision of its members in general meeting decides whether to sue the directors for their negligence. Even if it is a case in which they could be liable, **the court has discretion under the Act to relieve directors of liability** if it appears to the court that:

*   The directors acted **honestly** and **reasonably**.
*   They **ought**, having regard to the circumstances of the case, **fairly to be excused**.

> **Re D' Jan of London Ltd 1993**
>
> *The facts:* D, a director of the company, signed an insurance proposal form without reading it. The form was filled in by D's broker. An answer given to one of the questions on the form was incorrect and the insurance company rightly repudiated liability for a fire at the company's premises in which stock worth some £174,000 was lost. The company became insolvent and the liquidator brought this action under s 212 of the Insolvency Act 1986, alleging D was negligent.
>
> *Decision:* In failing to read the form D was negligent. However, he had acted honestly and reasonably and ought, therefore, to be partly relieved from liability by the court.

The following is one of the **first cases on directors' statutory duties** and indicates how the law may be applied in the future.

> **Lexi Holdings plc (in administration) v Luqman 2009**
>
> The facts: Two sisters and their brother were directors of a company. The brother had convictions for offences of dishonesty in the past. The sisters knew this, but played no part in the company, demanded no explanations from their brother of his business dealings and did not advise the other directors, auditors and the bank of his convictions. The brother took nearly £60m in fictitious loans, false facility letters and by misappropriation of company funds.
>
> Decision: It was held that the sisters were, or ought to have been, aware of various matters in relation to the fraud perpetrated on the company by their brother. As a result, they were liable as they were in breach of their fiduciary and common law duties of care owed to the company.

9.4.5 Duty to avoid conflicts of interest (s 175)

Directors have a **duty to avoid circumstances** where their **personal interests conflict**, or may possibly conflict, **with the company's interests**. It may occur when a director makes personal use of information, property or opportunities belonging to the company, whether or not the company was able to take advantage of them at the time. Therefore directors must be careful not to breach this duty when they **enter into a contract** with their company or if they **make a profit in the course of being a director**.

This duty does not apply to a **conflict of interest** in relation to a **transaction** or **arrangement** with the company, **provided the director declared an interest**.

As **agents,** directors have a **duty to avoid a conflict of interest**. In particular:

- The directors must **retain their freedom of action** and **not fetter their discretion** by agreeing to vote as some other person may direct.

- The directors owe a fiduciary duty to **avoid a conflict of duty and personal interest**.

- The directors **must not obtain any personal advantage** from their position as directors **without the consent of the company** for whatever gain or profit they have obtained.

The following **cases** are important in the area of **conflict of interest**.

> *Regal (Hastings) Ltd v Gulliver 1942*
>
> *The facts:* The company owned a cinema. It had the opportunity of acquiring two more cinemas through a subsidiary to be formed with an issued capital of £5,000. However the company could not proceed with this scheme since it only had £2,000 available for investment in the subsidiary.
>
> The directors and their friends therefore subscribed £3,000 for shares of the new company to make up the required £5,000. The chairman acquired his shares not for himself but as nominee of other persons. The company's solicitor also subscribed for shares. The share capital of the two companies (which then owned three cinemas) was sold at a price which yielded a profit of £2.80 per share of the new company in which the directors had invested. The new controlling shareholder of the company caused it to sue the directors to recover the profit which they had made.
>
> *Decision:*
>
> (a) The directors were **accountable** to the company for their profit since they had obtained it from an opportunity which came to them as directors.
>
> (b) It was **immaterial** that the **company** had **lost nothing** since it had been unable to make the investment itself.
>
> (c) The directors might have kept their profit if the company had **agreed** by resolution passed in general meeting that they should do so. The directors might have used their votes to approve their action since it was not fraudulent (there was no misappropriation of the company's property).
>
> (d) The chairman was not accountable for the profit on his shares since he did not obtain it for himself. The solicitor was not accountable for his profit since he was **not a director** and so was not subject to the rule of accountability as a director for personal profits obtained in that capacity.

> *Industrial Development Consultants Ltd v Cooley 1972*
>
> *The facts:* C was Managing Director of the company which provided consultancy services to gas companies. A gas company was unlikely to award a particular contract to the company, but C realised that, acting personally, he might be able to obtain it. He told the board of his company that he was ill and persuaded them to release him from his service agreement. On ceasing to be a director of the company C obtained the contract on his own behalf. The company sued him to recover the profits of the contract.
>
> *Decision:* C was accountable to his old company for his profit.

Directors will **not be liable** for a breach of this duty if:

- The **members** of the company **authorised** their actions

- The **situation cannot reasonably be regarded** as likely to give rise to a conflict of interest

- The **actions have been authorised by the other directors**. This only applies if they are genuinely independent from the transaction and if:

  - The articles do not restrict such authorisation, in the case of a private company
  - The articles expressly permit it, in the case of a public company.

- The **company explicitly rejected the opportunity they took up**: *Peso Silver Mines v Cropper 1966*.

The following case was one of the first to apply the new statutory s 175 duty.

> **Towers v Premier Waste Management Ltd 2012**
>
> *The facts*: A company director accepted a personal loan of equipment from a customer without charge and without disclosing the transaction or seeking approval of it. The customer then invoiced the company, which sued the director for breach of duty.
>
> *Decision*: It was held that the director had gained an advantage from a potential conflict and had disloyally deprived the company of the opportunity to object to an opportunity being diverted from the company to the director personally. It was irrelevant that the company had suffered no loss or that the director had no corrupt motive.

> PO1 requires you to protect yourself against threats to your professional independence and this means avoiding conflicts of interest. Whilst you may not be a director, the rules in s 175 give you a good idea of what is expected by others who have the same duty.

9.4.6 Duty not to accept benefits from third parties (s 176)

This duty **prohibits the acceptance of benefits** (including bribes) from third parties conferred by reason of them being director, or doing (or omitting to do) something as a director. Where a director accepts a benefit that may also create or potentially create a conflict of interest, they will also be in breach of their s 175 duty.

Unlike s 175, an act which would potentially be in breach of this duty **cannot be authorised** by the **directors**, but **members do have the right to authorise it**.

Directors will not be in breach of this duty if the acceptance of the benefit **cannot reasonably** be regarded as likely to give rise to a conflict of interest.

9.4.7 Duty to declare interest in proposed transaction or arrangement (s 177)

Directors are required to disclose to the other directors the nature and extent of any interest, direct or indirect, that they have in relation to a **proposed transaction** or **arrangement** with the **company**. Even if the director is not a party to the transaction, the duty may apply if they are aware, or ought reasonably to be aware, of the interest. For example, the interest of another person in a contract with the company may require disclosure under this duty if that other person's interest is a direct or indirect interest on the part of the director.

Directors are required to disclose their interest in any transaction **before** the company enters into the transaction. Disclosure can be made by:

- Written notice
- General notice
- Verbally at a board meeting

Disclosure to the **members** is **not** sufficient to discharge the duty. Directors must declare the **nature** and **extent** of their interest to the **other directors** as well. If the declaration becomes **void** or **inaccurate**, a **further declaration** should be made. No declaration of interest is required if the director's interest in the transaction **cannot reasonably** be regarded as likely to give rise to a conflict of interest.

9.5 Consequences of breach of duty

Breach of duty comes under the **civil law** rather than criminal law and, as mentioned earlier, the company itself must take up the action. This usually means the other directors starting proceedings. **Consequences for breach** include:

- **Damages** payable to the company where it has suffered loss
- **Restoration** of company property
- **Repayment of any profits** made by the director
- **Rescission of contract** (where the director did not disclose an interest)

9.6 Declaration of an interest in an existing transaction or arrangement (s 182)

Directors have a **statutory obligation** to **declare any direct** or **indirect interest** in an **existing transaction** entered into by the company. This obligation is almost identical to the duty to disclose an interest in a proposed transaction or arrangement under s 177. However, this section is relevant to transactions or arrangements that have already occurred. A declaration under s 182 is **not** required if:

- It has **already been disclosed** as a proposed transaction under s 177

- The director is **not aware** of either
  - **The interest** they have in the transaction, or
  - **The transaction** itself

- The director's interest in the transaction **cannot reasonably** be regarded as likely to give rise to a conflict of interest

- The **other directors are aware** (or reasonably should be aware) of the situation

- It concerns the **director's service contract** and it has been considered by a board meeting or special board committee

Where a declaration is required it should be made as soon as **reasonably practicable** either by written notice, by general notice or verbally at a board meeting. If the declaration becomes **void** or **inaccurate**, a **further declaration** should be made.

9.7 Other controls over directors

The table below summarises other statutory controls over directors included in the Companies Act 2006.

CA06 Ref	Control
188	Directors' service contracts lasting more than two years must be approved by the members.
190	Directors or any person connected to them may not acquire a non-cash asset from the company without approval of the members. This does not apply where the asset's value is less than £5,000, or less than 10% of the company's asset value. All sales of assets with a value exceeding £100,000 must be approved.
197	Any loans given to directors, or guarantees provided as security for loans provided to directors, must be approved by members if over £10,000 in value.
198	Expands section 197 to prevent unapproved quasi-loans to directors of over £10,000 in value (PLCs only).
201	Expands section 197 to prevent unapproved credit transactions by the company for the benefit of a director of over £15,000 in value (PLCs only).
204	Directors must seek approval of the members where the company loans them over £50,000 to meet expenditure required in the course of business.
217	Non-contractual payments to directors for loss of office must be approved by the members.

9.8 Examples of remedies against directors

Remedies against directors for breach of duties include accounting to the company for a **personal gain**, **indemnifying the company**, and **rescission of contracts** made with the company.

The **type of remedy** varies with the breach of duty.

(a) The director may have to **account for a personal gain**.

(b) They may have to **indemnify the company** against loss caused by their negligence such as an unlawful transaction which they approved.

(c) If they contract with the company in a conflict of interest the **contract may be rescinded by the company**. However under common law rules the company cannot both affirm the contract and recover the director's profit.

(d) The court may declare that a transaction is *ultra vires* or unlawful.

A company may, either by its **articles** or by **passing a resolution** in general meeting, **authorise or ratify** the conduct of directors in breach of duty. There are some limits on the power of members in general meeting to **sanction a breach of duty** by directors or to release them from their strict obligations.

(a) If the directors **defraud** the company and vote in general meeting to approve their own fraud, their votes are invalid.

(b) If the directors **allot shares** to alter the balance of votes in a general meeting, the votes attached to those shares may not be cast to support a resolution approving the issue.

9.9 Directors' liability for acts of other directors

A director is **not liable** for acts of fellow directors. However, if they become aware of serious breaches of duty by other directors, they may have a duty to inform members of them or to take control of assets of the company without having proper delegated authority to do so.

In such cases the director is **liable for their own negligence** in what they allow to happen and not directly for the misconduct of the other directors.

9.10 Directors' personal liability

As a **general rule** a **director** has **no personal liability for the debts of the company**. But there are certain exceptions.

- Personal liability **may arise** by **lifting the veil** of incorporation.

- A **limited company** may by its articles or by **special resolution** provide that its directors shall have unlimited liability for its debts.

- A director may be **liable** to the **company's creditors** in certain circumstances.

- In cases of **fraudulent** or **wrongful trading** liquidators can apply to the court for an order that those responsible (usually the directors) are liable to repay all or some specified part of the company's debts.

Can a director be held personally liable for **negligent advice** given by their company? The case below shows that they can, but only when they assume responsibility in a personal capacity for advice given, rather than simply giving advice in their capacity as a director.

Williams and Another v Natural Life Health Foods Ltd 1998

The facts: The director was sued personally by claimants who claimed they were misled by the company's brochure. The director helped prepare the brochure, and the brochure described him as the source of the company's expertise. The claimants did not, however, deal with the director but with other employees.

Decision: The House of Lords overruled the Court of Appeal, and ruled that the director was not personally liable. In order to have been liable, there would have to have been evidence that the director had assumed personal responsibility. Merely acting as a director and advertising his earlier experience did not amount to assumption of personal liability.

Chapter Roundup

- Any person who occupies the position of director is treated as such, the test being one of **function**.

- The method of appointing directors, along with their rotation and co-option is **controlled** by the **articles**.

- Directors are entitled to **fees** and **expenses** as directors as per the articles, and **emoluments** (and compensation for loss of office) as per their service contracts (which can be inspected by members). Some details are published in the directors' remuneration report along with the accounts.

- A director may vacate office as director due to: **resignation**; **not going** for **re-election**; **death**; **dissolution** of the company; **removal**; **disqualification**.

- Directors may be required to vacate office because they have been disqualified on grounds dictated by the articles. Directors **may** be disqualified from a wider range of company involvements under the Company Directors Disqualification Act 1986 (CDDA).

- Directors may be **disqualified** from acting as directors, or being involved in the management of companies, in a number of circumstances. They must be disqualified if the company is insolvent, and the director is found to be unfit to be concerned with management of a company.

- The **powers** of the directors are **defined** by the **articles**.

- Directors' powers may be restricted by statute or by the articles. The directors have a duty to exercise their powers in what they honestly believe to be the **best interests** of the company and for the **purposes** for which the powers are given.

- The CEO or MD has **apparent authority** to make **business contracts** on behalf of the company. Their **actual authority** is whatever the **board gives** them.

- The Companies Act 2006 sets out the **seven principal duties** of **directors**.

- The **statutory duties** owed by directors are to:

    - Act within their powers
    - Promote the success of the company
    - Exercise independent judgement
    - Exercise reasonable skill, care and diligence
    - Avoid conflicts of interest
    - Not accept benefits from third parties
    - Declare an interest in a proposed transaction or arrangement

1   A person who is held out by a company as a director and performs the duties of a director without actually being validly appointed is a

   A   Shadow director
   B   De facto director
   C   Non-executive director
   D   Executive director

2   **Fill in the blanks** in the statements below.

   Under model articles directors are authorised to m.~~anage~~........ the b~~usiness~~........ of the company, and e.~~xercise~~........ the p.~~owers~~..........of the company.

3   Under which of the following grounds may a director be disqualified if they are guilty, and under which must a director be disqualified?

   may   A   Conviction of an indictable offence in connection with a company
   may   B   Persistent default with the provisions of company legislation
   may most   C   Wrongful trading
   D   Director of an insolvent company whose conduct makes them unfit to be concerned in the
   most   management of the company

4   What are the two principal ways by which members can control the activities of directors?

5   A public company must have two directors, a private company only needs one.

   True   ☒

   False   ☐

Answers to Quick Quiz

1   B. The description is of a de facto director.

2   Under model articles directors are authorised to **manage** the **business** of the company, and **exercise all** the **powers** of the company.

3   A to C are grounds under which a director may be disqualified; D is grounds under which a director must be disqualified.

4   Appointing and removing directors in general meeting

     Reallocating powers by altering the articles

5   True. Private companies only need one director.

Now try the questions below from the Practice Question Bank

Number
40, 41

16

Other company officers

Topic list	Syllabus reference
1 The company secretary	F2(a)
2 The company auditor	F2(b)

Introduction

In this short chapter we shall consider two other important company roles. That of **company secretary** and **auditor**. In each case we shall consider their appointment, duties and powers.

An important distinction to make is that a company secretary is a role performed by an individual **internal** to the company. An auditor is an **independent** third party.

Study guide

		Intellectual level
F	**Management, administration and the regulation of companies**	
2	**Other company officers**	
(a)	Discuss the appointment procedure relating to, and the duties and powers of, a company secretary	2
(b)	Discuss the appointment procedure relating to, and the duties and rights of, a company auditor and their subsequent removal or resignation	2

Exam guide

Exam questions on company secretaries may hinge on an application of agency law so it is important to revise this area if you are not certain about it. Questions on auditors may focus on their role and rights, duties and removal.

1 The company secretary

> Every public company must have a **company secretary**, who is one of the officers of a company and may be a director. Private companies are not required to have a secretary.

Every public company must have a **company secretary**, who is one of the officers of a company and may be a director. Private companies are not required to have a secretary. In this case the roles normally done by the company secretary may be done by one of the directors, or an approved person. The Secretary of State may require a public company to appoint a secretary where it has failed to do so.

1.1 Appointment of a company secretary

To be appointed as a **company secretary** to a plc, the directors must ensure that the candidate should be **qualified** by virtue of:

- **Employment** as a plc's secretary for **three out of the five years** preceding appointment

- **Membership** of one of a list of **qualifying bodies**: the ACCA, CIMA, ICAEW, ICAS, ICAI or CIPFA

- **Qualification** as a **solicitor**, **barrister** or **advocate** within the UK

- **Employment** in a position or **membership** of a professional body that, in the opinion of the directors, **appears to qualify that person** to act as company secretary

They should also have the 'necessary knowledge and experience' as deemed by the directors.

A **sole director** of a private company cannot also be the company secretary, but a company can have **two** or more joint secretaries. A **corporation** can fulfil the role of company secretary. A register of secretaries must be kept. Under **UK Corporate Governance guidelines** the appointment of the company secretary is a matter for the board as a whole.

1.2 Duties of a company secretary

The specific **duties** of each company secretary are **determined by the directors** of the company. As a company officer, the company secretary is responsible for ensuring that the company complies with its statutory obligations.

In particular, this means:

- **Establishing** and **maintaining** the company's **statutory registers**
- **Filing accurate returns** with the Registrar on time
- **Organising** and **minuting** company and **board meetings**
- **Ensuring** that **accounting records** meet **statutory requirements**
- **Ensuring** that **annual accounts** are **prepared** and **filed** in accordance with **statutory requirements**
- **Monitoring statutory requirements** of the company
- **Signing company documents** as may be required by law

Under **UK Corporate Governance guidelines** the company secretary should:

- **Ensure good information flows** within the board and its committees
- **Facilitate induction of board members** and assist with professional development
- **Advise** the **chairman** and the **board** on all **governance issues**

1.3 Powers and authority of a company secretary

The powers of the company secretary have historically been very limited. However, the common law increasingly recognises that they may be able to act as agents to exercise apparent or **ostensible authority**; they may, therefore, enter the company into contracts connected with the administrative side of the company.

> *Panorama Developments (Guildford) Ltd v Fidelis Furnishing Fabrics Ltd 1971*
>
> *The facts:* B, the secretary of a company, ordered cars from a car hire firm, representing that they were required to meet the company's customers at London Airport. Instead he used the cars for his own purposes. The bill was not paid, so the car hire firm claimed payment from B's company.
>
> *Decision:* B's company was liable, for he had apparent authority to make contracts such as the present one, which were concerned with the administrative side of its business. The decision recognises the general nature of a company secretary's duties.

2 The company auditor

FAST FORWARD

Every company (apart from certain small companies) must appoint appropriately qualified **auditors**. An audit is a check on the stewardship of the directors.

Every company (except a dormant private company and certain small companies) must **appoint auditors** for each financial year.

2.1 Appointment

The **first auditors** may be appointed by the directors, to hold office until the **first general meeting,** at which their appointment is considered. **Subsequent auditors** may not take office until the previous auditor has ceased to hold office. They will hold office until the end of the next financial period (private companies) or the next accounts meeting (public companies) unless re-appointed.

Appointment of auditors	
Members	• Usually appoint an auditor in general meeting by ordinary resolution
	• Auditors hold office from 28 days after the meeting in which the accounts are laid until the end of the corresponding period the next year. This is the case even if the auditors are appointed at the meeting where the accounts are laid.
	• May appoint in general meeting to fill a casual vacancy
Directors	• Appoint the first ever auditors. They hold office until the end of the first meeting at which the accounts are considered.
	• May appoint to fill a casual vacancy

Appointment of auditors	
Secretary of State	• May appoint auditors if members fail to
	• Company must notify Secretary of State within 28 days of the general meeting where the accounts were laid

2.1.1 Eligibility as auditor

Membership of a **recognised supervisory body** is the main prerequisite for eligibility as an auditor. An audit firm may be either a body corporate, a partnership or a sole practitioner.

The Act requires an auditor to hold an **'appropriate qualification'**. A person holds an 'appropriate qualification' if they:

- Have satisfied **existing criteria** for appointment as an auditor
- Hold a **recognised qualification** obtained in the UK
- Hold an **approved overseas qualification**

2.1.2 Ineligibility as auditor

Under the Companies Act 2006, a person may be ineligible on the grounds of **'lack of independence'**.

A person is **ineligible** for appointment as a **company auditor** if they are:

- An **officer** or **employee** of the company being audited

- A **partner** or **employee** of such a person

- A **partnership** in which such a person is a partner

- **Ineligible** by virtue of the above for appointment as auditor of any parent or subsidiary undertaking where there exists a **connection** of any description as may be specified in regulations laid down by the Secretary of State.

2.1.3 Effect of lack of independence or ineligibility

No person may act as auditor if they lack independence or become ineligible. If, during their term of office, an auditor loses their independence or eligibility they must **resign** with immediate effect, and **notify** their client of their resignation giving the reason.

A person continuing to act as auditor despite losing their independence or becoming ineligible is **liable to a fine**. However, it is a defence if they can prove they were not aware that they lost independence or became ineligible.

The legislation does **not** disqualify the following from being an auditor of a limited company:

- A shareholder of the company
- A debtor or creditor of the company
- A close relative of an officer or employee of the company

However, the **regulations** of the **accountancy bodies** applying to their own members are **stricter than statute in this respect**.

2.2 Reappointing an auditor of a private company

The rules on appointment make reference to a **meeting** where the accounts are laid. This is not always relevant for private companies as, under the Act, they are not required to hold an AGM or lay the accounts before the members.

Therefore **auditors of private companies are deemed automatically reappointed** unless one of the following circumstances apply.

- The auditor was **appointed by the directors** (most likely when the first auditor was appointed).
- The **articles require formal reappointment**.
- **Members holding 5% of the voting rights** serve notice that the auditor should not be reappointed.
- A **resolution** (written or otherwise) has been passed that prevents reappointment.
- The **directors have resolved that auditors should not be appointed** for the forthcoming year as the company is likely to be exempt from audit.

2.3 Auditor remuneration

Whoever appoints the auditors has power to **fix their remuneration** for the period of their appointment. It is usual when the auditors are appointed by the general meeting to leave it to the directors to fix their remuneration (by agreement at a later stage). The auditors' remuneration must be **disclosed** in a **note to the accounts**.

2.4 Exemption from audit

Certain **companies** are exempt from audit, provided the following conditions are fulfilled.

(a) A company is exempt from the annual audit requirement in a financial year if it meets the criteria for being a small company (two from, turnover being less than **£6.5 million**; **balance sheet total not more than £3.26 million**; having **50 or fewer employees**).

(b) The exemptions do not apply to **public companies**, **banking** or **insurance companies** or those subject to a **statute-based regulatory regime**.

(c) The company is a **non-commercial, non-profit making public sector body** which is subject to audit by a **public sector auditor**.

(d) **Members** holding **10%** or more of the capital of any company can veto the exemption.

(e) **Dormant companies** which qualify for exemption from an audit as a dormant company.

2.5 Duties of auditors

The **statutory duty** of auditors is to report to the members whether the accounts give a **true and fair view** and have been properly prepared in accordance with the Companies Act. They must also:

- **State** whether or not the **directors' report** is **consistent** with the **accounts**.
- For **quoted companies**, **report** to the members on the **auditable** part of the **directors' remuneration report**, including whether or not it has been properly prepared in accordance with the Act.
- Be **signed** by the **auditor**, stating their **name** and **date**. Where the auditor is a firm, the **senior auditor** must sign in their **own name** for, and on behalf of, the auditor.

To fulfil their statutory duties, the auditors **must carry out such investigations as are necessary** to form an opinion as to whether:

(a) **Proper accounting records** have been kept and proper returns adequate for the audit have been received from branches.

(b) The **accounts** are in **agreement** with the **accounting records**.

(c) The **information** in the **directors' remuneration report** is consistent with the **accounts**.

The auditors' report must be **read** before any general meeting at which the accounts are considered and must be open to inspection by members. Auditors have to make disclosure of other services rendered to the company and the remuneration received.

Where an auditor **knowingly** or **recklessly** causes their report to be **materially misleading**, **false** or **deceptive**, they commit a criminal offence and may be liable to a **fine**.

2.6 Rights of auditors

FAST FORWARD

The Companies Act provides **statutory rights** for auditors to enable them to carry out their duties.

The **principal rights** of auditors, excepting those dealing with resignation or removal, are set out in the table below, and the following are notes on more detailed points.

Access to records	A right of access at all times to the books, accounts and vouchers of the company.
Information and explanations	A right to require from the company's officers, employees or any other relevant person, such information and explanations as they think necessary for the performance of their duties as auditors.
Attendance at/notices of general meetings	A right to attend any general meetings of the company and to receive all notices of and communications relating to such meetings which any member of the company is entitled to receive.
Right to speak at general meetings	A right to be heard at general meetings which they attend on any part of the business that concerns them as auditors.
Rights in relation to written resolutions	A right to receive a copy of any written resolution proposed.

If auditors have **not received** all the information and explanations they consider necessary, they should state this fact in their audit report.

The Act makes it an **offence** for a company's officer knowingly or recklessly to make a statement in any form to an auditor which:

- Conveys, or purports to convey, any information or explanation required by the auditor, and
- Is materially misleading, false or deceptive

The **penalty** is a maximum of two years' imprisonment, a fine or both.

2.7 Auditors' liability

Under the Companies Act any **agreement** between an auditor and a company that seeks to **indemnify the auditor** for their own negligence, default or breach of duty or trust is **void**. However, an agreement can be made which **limits the auditor's liability** to the company.

Such **liability limitation agreements** can only stand for **one financial year** and must, therefore, be replaced annually.

Liability can only be **limited** to what is **fair and reasonable** having regard to the auditor's responsibilities, their contractual obligations and the professional standards expected of them.

Such agreements must be approved by the members and **publicly disclosed** in the **accounts** or **directors' report**.

2.8 Termination of auditors' appointment

FAST FORWARD

Auditors may leave office in the following ways: **resignation**; **removal from office** by an ordinary resolution with special notice passed before the end of their term; **failing** to **offer themselves** for re-election; and **not being re-elected** at the general meeting at which their term expires.

Departure of auditors from office can occur in the following ways.

(a)   Auditors may **resign** their appointment, by giving notice in writing to the company delivered to the registered office.

(b)   Auditors may **decline reappointment**.

(c)   Auditors may be **removed** from office, before the expiry of their appointment, by the passing of an ordinary resolution in general meeting. Special notice is required and members and auditors must be notified. **Private companies cannot remove an auditor by written resolution;** a meeting must be held.

(d)   Auditors **do not have to be reappointed** when their term of office expires, although in most cases they are. Special notice must be given of any resolution to appoint auditors who were not appointed on the last occasion of the resolution, and the members and auditor must be notified.

Where a private company resolves to **appoint** a replacement auditor by **written resolution**, copies of the resolution must be sent to the proposed and outgoing auditor. The outgoing auditor may circulate a **statement of reasonable length** to the members if they notify the company within 14 days of receiving the copy of the written resolution.

2.8.1 Resignation of auditors

However auditors leave office, they must either: state there are **no circumstances** which should be brought to **members' and creditors' attention**; or list **those circumstances**. Auditors who are resigning can also: **circulate a statement** about their resignation to members; **requisition a general meeting, or speak** at a general meeting.

Procedures for resignation of auditors	
Statement of circumstances	Auditors must deposit a statement at the registered office with their resignation, stating: • For quoted companies – the circumstances around their departure. • For non-quoted public companies and all private companies – that there are no circumstances that the auditor believes should be brought to the attention of the members or creditors. • If there are such circumstances, the statement should describe them. • Statements should also be submitted to the appropriate audit authority.
Company action	• The company must send notice of the resignation to the Registrar. • The company must **send** a copy of the statement of circumstances to **every person entitled to receive a copy of the accounts.**
Auditor rights	If the auditors have deposited a statement of circumstances, they may: • Circulate a statement of reasonable length to the members • Requisition a general meeting to explain their reasons • Attend and speak at any meeting where appointment of successors is to be discussed.

If the auditors decline to seek reappointment at an AGM, they must nevertheless fulfil the requirements of a **statement of the circumstances**, just as if they had resigned. The reason for this provision is to prevent auditors who are unhappy with the company's affairs keeping their suspicions secret. The statement must be deposited not less than **14 days** before the time allowed for next appointing auditors.

2.8.2 Removal of the auditor from office

Procedures for removal from office	
Auditor representations	If a resolution is proposed either to: • Remove the auditors before their term of office expires, or • Change the auditors when their term of office is complete, the auditors have the right to make representations of reasonable length to the company
Company action	The company must: • Notify members in the notice of the meeting of the representations • Send a copy of the representations in the notice • If it is not sent out, the auditors can require it is read at the meeting
Attendance at meeting	Auditors removed before expiry of their office may: • Attend the meeting at which their office would have expired • Attend any meeting at which the appointment of their successors is discussed
Statement of circumstances	If auditors are removed at a general meeting they must: • Make a statement of circumstances for members and creditors

Exam focus point

Remember: A statement of circumstances/no circumstances must be deposited **however** the auditors leave office.

BPP
LEARNING MEDIA

Chapter Roundup

- Every public company must have a **company secretary**, who is one of the officers of a company and may be a director. Private companies are not required to have a secretary.

- Every company (apart from certain small companies) must appoint appropriately qualified **auditors**. An audit is a check on the stewardship of the directors.

- The Companies Act provides **statutory rights** for auditors to enable them to carry out their duties.

- Auditors may leave office in the following ways: **resignation**; **removal from office** by an ordinary resolution with special notice passed before the end of their term; **failing** to **offer themselves** for **re-election**; and **not being re-elected** at the general meeting at which their term expires.

- However auditors leave office they must either: state there are **no circumstances** which should be brought to **members' and creditors' attention**; or list **those circumstances**. Auditors who are resigning can also: **circulate a statement** about their resignation to members; **requisition a general meeting**; or **speak** at a general meeting.

Quick Quiz

1   A private company with a sole director is not legally required to have a company secretary, but if it does, the sole director cannot also be the company secretary.

   True   ☒

   False ☐

2   State two reasons why a person would be ineligible to be an auditor under Companies Act 2006.

   (1)   ....

   (2)   ....

3   Which of the following is NOT a recognised qualification that allows an individual to act as a company secretary?

   A   ACCA
   B   Solicitor
   C   Business Studies degree
   D   Employment as a company secretary for three of the five preceding years

4   Zee plc is a retailer of sportswear. Last year its turnover was £3million and its balance sheet total was £1.5million.

   Zee plc is exempt from audit.   -plc !

   True   ☒

   False ☐ ✓

5   Which of the following resolutions is required to remove an auditor of a private company?

   A   Ordinary resolution with usual notice
   B   Ordinary resolution with special notice
   C   Special resolution with usual notice
   D   Special resolution with special notice

Answers to Quick Quiz

1   True. Sole directors cannot be company secretaries. Private companies are not legally required to have a company secretary.

2   Any of:

    (1)   Is an officer/employee of the company being audited
    (2)   A partner or employee of a person in (1)
    (3)   A partnership in which (1) is a partner
    (4)   Ineligible by (1), (2) and (3) to be auditor of any of the entity's subsidiaries

3   C. A degree is not a recognised qualification for acting as a company secretary.

4   False. Although its turnover and balance sheet total suggest the company is small and exempt from audit, the company is a plc and therefore the exemption does not apply. Zee plc must have an audit.

5   B. An ordinary resolution with special notice is required to remove an auditor of any company.

Now try the questions below from the Practice Question Bank

Number
42, 43

17

Company meetings and resolutions

Topic list	Syllabus reference
1 The importance of meetings	F3(a)
2 General meetings	F3(a)
3 Types of resolution	F3(b)
4 Calling a meeting	F3(c)
5 Proceedings at meetings	F3(c)
6 Class meetings	F3(a)
7 Single-member private companies	F3(a –c)

Introduction

In this chapter we consider the **procedures** by which companies are controlled by the shareholders, namely general meetings and resolutions. These afford members a measure of protection of their investment in the company. There are many transactions which, under the Act, cannot be entered into without a **resolution** of the company.

Moreover, a general meeting at which the annual accounts and the auditors' and directors' reports will be laid, must normally be held by public companies annually. This affords the members an opportunity of questioning the directors on their **stewardship**.

Study guide

		Intellectual level
F	**Management, administration and the regulation of companies**	
3	**Company meetings and resolutions**	
(a)	Distinguish between types of meetings: ordinary general meetings and annual general meetings	1
(b)	Distinguish between types of resolutions: ordinary, special and written	2
(c)	Explain the procedure for calling and conducting company meetings	2

Exam guide

For the exam you must be quite clear about the different types of resolution, when each type is used and the percentage vote needed for each type to be passed. This topic lends itself to multiple choice questions. However, resolutions in particular are important in many areas of the corporate part of the syllabus and meetings of members are an important control on the acts of the directors. Therefore, this topic could easily be incorporated into a scenario question.

1 The importance of meetings

FAST FORWARD Although the management of a company is in the hands of the directors, the **decisions which affect the existence of the company**, its structure and scope, are **reserved to the members** in general meeting.

The decision of a general meeting is only valid and binding if the meeting is **properly convened** by notice and if the **business** of the meeting is **fairly** and **properly conducted**. Most of the rules on company meetings are concerned with the issue of notices and the casting of votes at meetings to carry resolutions of specified types.

1.1 Control over directors

The members in general meeting can exercise control over the directors, though only to a limited extent.

(a) Under normal procedure **one-third** of the **directors retire** at each annual general meeting, though they may offer themselves for re-election.

(b) Member approval in general meeting is required, if the directors wish to:

    (i) **Exceed their delegated power** or to use it for other than its given purpose
    (ii) **Allot shares** (unless it is a private company with one class of shares)
    (iii) **Make a substantial contract** of sale or purchase with a director
    (iv) Grant a director a **long-service agreement**

(c) The **appointment and removal of auditors** is normally done in general meeting.

1.2 Resolution of differences

In addition, general meetings are the means by which **members resolve differences** between themselves by voting on resolutions.

2 General meetings

ST FORWARD

There are two kinds of general meeting of members of a company:

- **Annual general meeting (AGM)**
- **General meetings at other times**

2.1 Annual general meeting (AGM)

The **AGM** plays a major role in the life of a public company, although the business carried out often seems fairly routine. It is a statutorily protected way for members to have a regular assessment and discussion of their company and its management.

Private companies are **not required** to have an **AGM** each year, and therefore their business is usually conducted through **written resolutions**. However, members holding sufficient shares or votes can request a general meeting or written resolution.

Rules for directors calling an AGM
• Public companies must hold an AGM within **six months** of their year end
• Must be in **writing** and in **accordance** with the **articles**
• May be in **hard** or **electronic form** and may also be by means of a **website**
• At least **21 days' notice** should be given; a longer period may be specified in the articles
• **Shorter notice** is only valid if **all members** agree
• The notice must specify the **time**, **date** and **place** of the meeting and that the meeting is an AGM
• Where notice is given on a **website** it must be available from the **date of notification** until the **conclusion of the meeting**

The business of an annual general meeting usually includes:

- Considering the accounts
- Receiving the directors' report, the directors' remuneration report and the auditors' report
- Dividends
- Electing directors
- Appointing auditors

2.2 General meetings at other times

2.2.1 Directors

The **directors** may have power under the articles to convene a general meeting whenever they see fit.

2.2.2 Members

The directors of **public and private** companies may be required to convene a general meeting by **requisition of the members**.

Rules for members requisitioning a general meeting	
Shareholding	• The requisitioning members must hold at least **5%** of the **paid up share capital** holding **voting rights**.
Requisition	• They must deposit a **signed requisition** at the registered office, or make the request in electronic form. • This must state the 'objects of the meeting': the **resolutions proposed**.
Date	• A notice convening the meeting must be set out within **21 days** of the requisition. • It must be held within **28 days** of the notice calling to a meeting being sent out. • If the directors have not called the meeting within 21 days of the requisition, the **members may convene** the meeting for a date within three months of the deposit of the requisition.
Quorum	• If **no quorum** is present, the meeting is **adjourned**.

2.2.3 Court order

The court, on the application of a director or a member entitled to vote, may order that a meeting shall be held and may give instructions for that purpose, including fixing a quorum of one. This is a method of last resort to resolve a deadlock, such as the refusal of one member out of two to attend (and thus provide a quorum) at a general meeting.

2.2.4 Auditor requisition

An auditor who gives a statement of circumstances for their resignation or other loss of office in their written notice may also requisition a meeting to receive and consider their explanation.

2.2.5 Loss of capital by public company

The directors of a public company must convene a general meeting if the net assets fall to half or less of the amount of its called-up share capital.

3 Types of resolution

FAST FORWARD

A meeting can pass two types of resolution. **Ordinary resolutions** are carried by a simple majority (more than 50%) of votes cast and requiring 14 days' notice. **Special resolutions** require a 75% majority of votes cast and also 14 days' notice.

A meeting reaches a decision by passing a resolution (either by a show of hands or a poll). There are **two major kinds** of resolution, and an additional one for **private** companies.

Types of resolution	
Ordinary	For most business Requires simple (50%+) majority of the votes cast 14 days' notice
Special	For major changes Requires 75% majority of the votes cast 14 days' notice
Written (for private companies)	Can be used for all general meeting resolutions except for removing a director or auditor before their term of office expires. Either a simple (50%+) or 75% majority is required, depending on the business being passed.

3.1 Differences between ordinary and special resolutions

Apart from the required size of the majority and period of notice, the main differences between the types of resolution are as follows.

(a)   The **text** of **special resolutions** must be **set out** in **full** in the notice convening the meeting, and it must be described as a special resolution. This is not necessary for an ordinary resolution, if it is routine business.

(b)   A **signed copy** of every **special resolution** must be **delivered** to the **Registrar** for filing. **Some ordinary resolutions**, particularly those relating to share capital, have to be **delivered** for filing but many do not.

3.2 Special resolutions

A special resolution is required for **major changes** in the company such as the following.

- A change of name
- Restriction of the objects or other alteration of the articles
- Reduction of share capital
- Winding up the company
- Presenting a petition by the company for an order for a compulsory winding up

3.3 Written resolutions

FAST FORWARD

> A private company can pass any decision needed by a **written resolution**, except for removing a director or auditor before their term of office has expired.

As we saw earlier, a private company is **not** required to hold an **AGM**. Therefore the Act provides a mechanism for directors and members to conduct business solely by **written resolution**.

3.3.1 Written resolutions proposed by directors

Copies of the resolution proposed by directors must be sent to **each member** eligible to vote, by hard copy, electronically or by a website. Alternatively, the same copy may be sent to each member in turn.

The resolution should be accompanied by a statement informing the member:

- How to **signify their agreement** to the resolution
- The **date** the resolution must be passed by

3.3.2 Written resolutions proposed by members

Members holding 5% (or lower if authorised by the articles) of the **voting rights** may request a written resolution providing it:

- **Would be effective** (not prevented by the articles or law)
- Is **not defamatory, frivolous** or **vexatious**

A **statement** containing no more than **1,000 words** on the subject of the resolution may accompany it.

Copies of the resolution, and statements containing information on the subject matter, how to agree to it and the date of the resolution must be sent to each member within **21 days** of the request for resolution.

Expenses for circulating the resolution **should be met by the members** who requested it unless the company resolves otherwise.

The company may **appeal to the court** not to circulate the 1,000 word statement by the members, if the rights provided to the members are being abused by them.

3.3.3 Agreement

The members may indicate their agreement to the resolution in **hard copy** or **electronically**.

If no **period for agreement** is specified by the articles, then the default period is **28 days** from the date the resolution was circulated. Agreement after this period is ineffective. Once agreed, a member **may not revoke** their decision. Either a **simple** (50% plus one) or **75% majority** is required to pass a written resolution depending on the nature of the business being decided. Three further points should be noted concerning written resolutions.

(a) Written resolutions can be used **notwithstanding any provisions** in the company's **articles**.

(b) A written resolution **cannot** be **used to remove a director or auditor** from office, since such persons have a right to **speak** at a **meeting**.

(c) **Copies of written resolutions** should be **sent to auditors** at or before the time they are sent to shareholders. Auditors do not have the right to object to written resolutions. If the auditors are not sent a copy, the resolution remains valid; however the directors and secretary will be liable to a fine. The purpose of this provision is to ensure auditors are kept informed about what is happening in the company.

Exam focus point

> There are not too many ways resolutions can be tested. You are most likely to be asked to identify the rules concerning the three types.

4 Calling a meeting

FAST FORWARD

> A meeting cannot make valid and binding decisions until it has been properly convened. Notice of general meetings must be given **14 days** in advance of the meeting. The notice should contain **adequate information** about the meeting.
>
> Meetings must be called by a **competent person** or authority.

A meeting cannot make valid and binding decisions until it has been properly convened according to the company's articles, though there are also statutory rules.

(a) The meeting must generally be **called by** the **board of directors** or other competent person or authority.

(b) The notice must be issued to members in advance of the meeting, so as to give them **14 days'** clear notice of the meeting. The members may agree to waive this requirement.

(c) The **notice** must be sent to every member (or other person) entitled to receive the notice.

(d) The notice must include any information **reasonably necessary** to enable shareholders to know in advance what is to be done.

(e) As we saw earlier, members may require the directors to call a meeting if:

    (i) They hold at least **5% of the voting rights**

    (ii) They provide a **statement of the general business** to be conducted and the text of any proposed resolution

    The directors must, within **21 days, call a meeting** to be held no later than **28 days from the date of the notice** they send calling the meeting.

In most cases the notice need **not** be sent to a member whose shares do not give them a right to attend and vote (as is often the position of **preference shareholders**).

4.1 Electronic communication

We have already seen that **notice** may be given by means of a **website** and in **electronic form**. Also, where a company gives an **electronic address** in a notice calling a meeting, any information or document relating to the meeting may be sent to that address.

4.2 Timing of notices

AST FORWARD

Clear notice must be given to members. **Notice** must be **sent to all members** entitled to receive it.

Members may – and in small private companies often do – waive the required notice. For **short notice** to be effective:

(a) All **members** of a public company must consent in respect of an **AGM**.

(b) In respect of a **general meeting**, members holding 90% of the issued shares of a private company, and 95% of the issued shares of a public company, may agree to shorter notice.

The following specific rules by way of exception should be remembered.

- When **special notice** of a resolution is given to the company it must be given **28 days** in advance of the meeting.

- In a **creditors' voluntary winding up** there must be at least **seven days' notice** of the **creditors' meeting** (to protect the interests of creditors). The members may shorten the period of notice down to seven days, but that is all.

The **clear days rule** in the Act provides that the day of the meeting and the day the notice was given are **excluded** from the required notice period.

4.3 Special notice of a resolution

AST FORWARD

Special notice of 28 days' of intention to propose certain resolutions (removal of directors/auditors) must be given.

ey term

Special notice is notice of 28 days which must be given to a company of the intention to put certain types of resolution at a company meeting.

Special notice must be given **to the company** of the intention to propose a resolution for any of the following purposes.

- To **remove** an **auditor** or to **appoint** an **auditor other** than the **auditor** who was **appointed** at the **previous year's meeting**

- To **remove a director from office** or to appoint a substitute in their place after removal

A member may request a resolution to be passed at a particular meeting. In this case, the **member must give special notice** of their intention **to the company,** at **least 28 days** before the date of the meeting. If, however, the company calls the meeting for a date less than 28 days after receiving the special notice, that notice is deemed to have been **properly given**.

On receiving special notice a **public company may be obliged** to **include the resolution** in the **AGM notice** which it issues.

If the company gives notice to members of the resolution, it does so by a **21-day notice** to them that special notice has been received and what it contains. If it is not practicable to include the matter in the notice of meeting, the company may give notice to members by newspaper advertisement or any other means permitted by the articles.

Where special notice is received of intention to propose a resolution for the removal of a director or to change the auditor, the company must send a copy to the **director** or **auditor**. This is to allow them to exercise their statutory right to defend themselves by issuing a memorandum and/or addressing the meeting in person.

The essential point is that a **special notice is given to the company**; it is **not a notice from the company to members,** although it will be followed (usually) by such notice.

4.4 Members requisitioning a resolution

Members, rather than directors, may be able to requisition resolutions. This may be achieved by requesting the directors call a meeting, or proposing a resolution to be voted on at a meeting already arranged.

The directors normally have the **right to decide** what resolutions shall be included in the notice of a meeting. However, apart from the requisition to call a general meeting, members can also take the initiative to requisition certain resolutions be considered at the AGM.

Rules for members requisitioning a resolution at the AGM	
Qualifying holding	• The members must represent 5% of the voting rights, or
	• Be at least 100 members holding shares with an average paid up value of £100, per member.
Request	• Must be in hard copy or electronic form, identify the resolution and be delivered at least six weeks in advance of an AGM or other general meeting
Statement	• Members may request a statement (<1,000 words) be circulated to all members by delivering a **requisition**. Members with a qualifying holding may request a statement regarding their own resolution or any resolution proposed at the meeting.
	• The company must send the statement with the notice of the meeting, or as soon as practicable after.

In either instance, the **requisitionists** must bear the incidental costs unless the company resolves otherwise.

Exam focus point

The right of members to have resolutions included on the agenda of AGM or other meetings could easily be the subject of a question in your exam. It is an **important consideration if some of the members disagree with the directors**.

4.5 Content of notices

The **notice** convening the meeting must give certain details. The **date**, **time** and **place** of the meeting, and identification of AGM and special resolutions. Sufficient information about the business to be discussed at the meeting should be provided, to enable shareholders to know what is to be done.

The notice of a general meeting must contain adequate information on the following points.

(a) The **date**, **time** and **place** of the meeting must be given

(b) An **AGM** or a **special resolution** must be described as such

(c) Information must be given of the business of the meeting, **sufficient** to enable members (in deciding whether to attend or to appoint proxies) to **understand what will be done** at the meeting.

4.5.1 Routine business

In issuing the notice of an AGM it is standard practice merely to list the **items of ordinary or routine business** to be transacted, such as the following.

- Declaration of dividends (if any)
- Election of directors
- Appointment of auditors and fixing of their remuneration

The articles usually include a requirement that members shall be informed of any intention to **propose** the **election** of a director, other than an existing director who retires by rotation and merely stands for re-election.

5 Proceedings at meetings

5.1 How a meeting proceeds

FAST FORWARD Company meetings need to be properly run if they are to be **effective** and within the **law**.

A meeting can only reach binding decisions if:

- It has been properly **convened** by notice.
- A **quorum is present**.
- A **chairman presides**.
- The **business** is **properly transacted** and **resolutions** are **put to the vote**.

There is no obligation to allow a member to be present if their shares do not carry the right to attend and vote. However **full general meetings** and **class meetings** can be held when shareholders not entitled to vote are present.

Each **item of business** comprised in the notice should be taken separately, discussed and **put to the vote**.

Members may propose **amendments** to any resolutions proposed. The chairman should reject any amendment which is outside the limits set by the notice convening the meeting.

If the relevant business is an **ordinary resolution** it may be possible to amend the resolution's wording so as to **reduce its effect** to something less (provided that the change does not entirely alter its character). For example, an ordinary resolution authorising the directors to borrow $100,000 might be amended to substitute a limit of $50,000 (but not to increase it to $150,000 as $100,000 would have been stated in the notice).

5.2 The chair (chairman)

FAST FORWARD The meeting should usually be chaired by the **chairman** of the board of directors. They do not necessarily have a casting vote.

The articles usually provide that the **chair (chairman)** of the board of directors **is to preside** at general meetings; in their absence, another director chosen by the directors shall preside instead. As a last resort a member chosen by the members present can preside.

The chairman derives their authority from the articles and they have **no casting vote unless** the **articles give them one**. Their duties are to **maintain order** and to **deal** with the **agenda** in a methodical way, so that the business of the meeting may be properly transacted.

The chairman:

- **May dissolve** or **adjourn** the **meeting** if it has become disorderly or if the members present agree.
- Must **adjourn** if the meeting **instructs** them to do so.

5.3 Quorum

FAST FORWARD

> The **quorum** for meetings may be two or more (except for single-member private companies). **Proxies** can attend, speak and vote on behalf of members.

Key term

> A **quorum** is the minimum number of persons required to be present at a particular type of (company) meeting. In the case of shareholders' meetings, the figure is usually two, in person or by proxy, but the articles may make other provisions.

There is a legal principle that a 'meeting means a coming together of more than one person'. Hence it follows that, as a matter of law, **one person generally cannot be a meeting**.

The rule that at least two persons must be present to constitute a 'meeting' does not require that both persons must be members. Every member has a **statutory right to appoint a proxy** to attend as their representative.

5.3.1 Proxies

Key term

> A **proxy** is a person appointed by a shareholder to vote on behalf of that shareholder at company meetings.

Any member of a company which has a share capital, provided they are entitled to attend and vote at a general or class meeting of the company, has a statutory right to appoint an **agent**, called a **'proxy'**, to attend and vote for them.

Rules for appointing proxies	
Basic rule	• Any **member** may appoint a proxy • The proxy **does not** have to be a member • Proxies **may speak** at the meeting • A member may **appoint more than one proxy** provided each proxy is appointed in respect of a different class of share held by the member
Voting	• Proxies **may vote** on a **poll** and on a **show of hands** • Proxies may **demand a poll** at a meeting • Most companies provide **two-way proxy cards** that the member can use to instruct a proxy how to vote, either for or against a resolution
Notice	• Every notice of a meeting must **state** the member's right to a proxy • **Notice** of a proxy appointment should be given to the company at least 48 hours before the meeting (excluding weekends and bank holidays)

Hence one member and another member's proxy may, together, provide the quorum (if it is fixed, as is usual, at 'two members present in person or by proxy'). However, one member who is also the proxy appointed by another member cannot by themself be a meeting, since a **minimum of two individuals** present is required.

There may, however, be a meeting attended by one person only, if:

(a)   It is a **class meeting** and all the **shares** of that class are **held** by **one member**.

(b)   The **court**, in exercising a power to order a general meeting to be held, **fixes** the **quorum** at one. This means that in a two-member company, a meeting can be held with one person if the other deliberately absents themselves to frustrate business.

(c)   The company is a **single-member private company**.

The articles usually fix a **quorum** for general meetings which may be as low as two (the minimum for a meeting) but may be more – though this is unusual.

If the articles do fix a quorum of two or more persons present, the meeting lacks a quorum (it is said to be an 'inquorate' meeting) if either:

- The **required number** is **not present** within a **stipulated time** (usually half an hour) of the appointed time for commencing a meeting.

- The **meeting begins** with a **quorum** but the **number present dwindles** to less than the quorum – unless the articles provide for this possibility.

The articles usually provide for automatic and compulsory **adjournment of an inquorate meeting**.

The articles can provide that a meeting which begins with a quorum may continue despite a reduction in numbers present to less than the quorum level. However, there must still be **two or more persons present**.

5.4 Voting and polls

ST FORWARD Voting at general meetings may be on a **show of hands** or a **poll**.

The **rights of members** to **vote** and the **number of votes** to which they are entitled in respect of their shares are fixed by the **articles**.

One vote per share is normal but some shares, for instance preference shares, may carry no voting rights in normal circumstances. To shorten the proceedings at meetings the procedure is as follows.

5.4.1 Voting on a show of hands

y term

A **show of hands** is a method of voting for or against a resolution by raising hands. Under this method each member has one vote irrespective of the number of shares held, in contrast to a poll vote.

On putting a resolution to the vote the chairman calls for a show of hands. One vote may be given by each member present in person, including proxies.

Unless a poll is then demanded, the chairman's declaration of the result is **conclusive**. However, it is still possible to challenge the chairman's declaration on the grounds that it was fraudulent or manifestly wrong.

5.4.2 Voting on a poll

y term

A **poll** is a method of voting at company meetings which allows a member to use as many votes as their shareholding grants them.

If a **real test of voting strength** is required, a poll may be demanded. The result of the previous show of hands is then disregarded. On a poll every member, and also proxies representing absent members, may cast the full number of votes to which they are entitled. A poll need not be held at the time but may be postponed so that arrangements to hold it can be made.

A poll may be **demanded** by:

- Not **less than five members**
- Member(s) **representing** not less than **one-tenth** of the **total voting rights**
- Member(s) **holding shares** which **represent** not less than **one-tenth** of the **paid-up capital**

Any provision in the articles is **void** if it seeks to prevent such members demanding a poll or to exclude the right to demand a poll on any question other than the election of a chairman by the meeting or an adjournment.

When a poll is held it is usual to appoint **'scrutineers'** and to ask members and proxies to sign voting cards or lists. The votes cast are checked against the register of members and the chairman declares the result.

Members of a quoted company may require the directors to obtain an **independent report** in respect of a poll taken, or to be taken, at a general meeting if:

- They represent at least 5% of the voting rights, or
- They are at least 100 in number holding at least £100 of paid up capital

5.4.3 Result of a vote

In voting, either by show of hands or on a poll, the **number of votes cast determines the result**. Votes which are not cast, whether the member who does not use them is present or absent, are simply disregarded. Hence the majority vote may be much less than half (or three-quarters) of the total votes which could be cast.

Results of quoted company polls must be made available on a **website**. The following information should be made available as soon as **reasonably practicable**, and should remain on the website for at least **two years**.

- Meeting date
- Text of the resolution or description of the poll's subject matter
- Number of votes for and against the resolution

5.5 Minutes of company meetings

Minutes must be kept of all **general, directors'** and **management meetings**, and members can inspect those of general meetings.

Key term

Minutes are a record of the proceedings of meetings. Company law requires minutes to be kept of all company meetings including general, directors' and managers' meetings.

Every company is **required to keep minutes**, which are a formal written record of the proceedings of its general meetings, for ten years. These minutes are usually kept in **book form**. If a loose leaf book is used to facilitate typing there should be safeguards against falsification, such as sequential prenumbering.

The chairman **normally signs** the minutes. If they do so, the signed minutes are admissible evidence of the proceedings, though evidence may be given to contradict or supplement the minutes or to show that no meeting at all took place.

Members of the company have the **right to inspect** minutes of general meetings. The minutes of general meetings must be held at the registered office (or the single alternative inspection location (SAIL)) and be available for inspection by members, who are also entitled to demand copies.

5.6 The assent principle

A unanimous decision of the members is often treated as a substitute for a formal decision in general meeting properly convened and held, and is equally binding.

6 Class meetings

FAST FORWARD

Class meetings are held where the interests of different groups of shareholders may be affected in different ways.

6.1 Types of class meeting

Class meetings are of two kinds.

(a) If the company has more than one class of share, for example if it has 'preference' and 'ordinary' shares, it may be necessary to call a meeting of the holders of one class, to approve a proposed **variation** of the **rights** attached to their shares.

(b)   Under a **compromise** or **arrangement with creditors**, the holders of shares of the same class may nonetheless be divided into **separate** classes if the scheme proposed will affect each group differently.

When separate meetings of a class of members are held, the same procedural rules as for general meetings apply (but there is a different rule on quorum).

6.2 Quorum for a class meeting

The standard general meeting rules, on issuing notices and on voting, apply to a class meeting.

However the **quorum** for a class meeting is fixed at two persons who hold, or represent by proxy, at least **one-third** in nominal value of the issued shares of the class (unless the class only consists of a single member).

If no quorum is present, the meeting is **adjourned** (under the standard adjournment procedure for general meetings). When the meeting resumes, the quorum is **one** person (who must still hold at least one-third of the shares).

7 Single-member private companies

AST FORWARD   There are **special rules** for **private companies** with only **one shareholder**.

If the sole member takes any decision that could have been taken in general meeting, that member shall (unless it is a written resolution) provide the company with a **written record** of it. This allows the sole member to conduct members' business informally without notice or minutes.

Filing requirements still apply, for example, in the case of alteration of articles.

Written resolutions **cannot** be used to remove a director or auditor from office, as these resolutions require special notice.

Chapter Roundup

- Although the management of a company is in the hands of the directors, the **decisions which affect the existence of the company**, its structure and scope, are **reserved to the members** in general meeting.

- There are two kinds of general meeting of members of a company:
  - **Annual general meeting (AGM)**
  - **General meetings at other times**

- A meeting can pass two types of resolution. **Ordinary resolutions** are carried by a simple majority (more than 50%) of votes cast and requiring 14 days' notice. **Special resolutions** require a 75% majority of votes cast and also 14 days' notice.

- A private company can pass any decision needed by a **written resolution**, except for removing a director or auditor before their term of office has expired.

- A meeting cannot make valid and binding decisions until it has been properly convened. Notice of general meetings must be given **14 days** in advance of the meeting. The notice should contain **adequate information** about the meeting.

- Meetings must be called by a **competent person** or authority.

- **Clear notice** must be given to members. **Notice** must be **sent to all members** entitled to receive it.

- **Special notice of 28 days** of intention to propose certain resolutions (removal of directors/auditors) must be given.

- **Members**, rather than directors, may be able to requisition resolutions. This may be achieved by requesting the directors call a meeting, or proposing a resolution to be voted on at a meeting already arranged.

- The **notice** convening the meeting must give certain details. The **date**, **time** and **place** of the meeting, and identification of AGM and special resolutions. Sufficient information about the business to be discussed at the meeting should be provided, to enable shareholders to know what is to be done.

- Company meetings need to be properly run if they are to be **effective** and within the **law**.

- The meeting should usually be chaired by the **chairman** of the board of directors. They do not necessarily have a casting vote.

- The **quorum** for meetings may be two or more (except for single-member private companies). **Proxies** can attend, speak and vote on behalf of members.

- Voting at general meetings may be on a **show of hands** or a **poll**.

- **Minutes** must be kept of all **general, directors'** and **management meetings**, and members can inspect those of general meetings.

- **Class meetings** are held where the interests of different groups of shareholders may be affected in different ways.

- There are **special rules** for **private companies** with only **one shareholder**.

1   Which of the following decisions can only be taken by the members in general meeting?

Select all that apply.

A   Alteration of articles
B   Change of name
C   Reduction of capital
D   Appointment of a managing director

2   Before a private company can hold a general meeting on short notice, members holding a certain percentage of the company's shares must agree. Which one of the following percentages is correct?

51%	90%
75%	95%

3   A plc must hold its AGM within six months of its year end.

True   ☒

False   ☐

4   Minutes of company meetings must be kept for

A   One year
B   Five years
C   Ten years
D   Fifteen years

5   A member of a public company may only appoint one proxy, but the proxy has a statutory right to speak at the meeting.

True   ☐

False   ☒

Answers to Quick Quiz

1   A, B and C. The board can appoint someone to be managing director, so D is incorrect.

2   90%

3   True. A plc must hold its AGM within six months of its year end.

4   C. Under the Companies Act, minutes must be kept for ten years.

5   False. Public company members can appoint more than one proxy. They have a statutory right to speak.

Now try the questions below from the Practice Question Bank

Number
44, 45, 46

BPP
LEARNING MEDIA

Insolvency law

Insolvency and administration

Topic list	Syllabus reference
1 What is liquidation?	G1(a), G1(b)
2 Voluntary liquidation	G1(a)
3 Compulsory liquidation	G1(b), G1(c)
4 Differences between compulsory and voluntary liquidation	G1(a), G1(b)
5 Saving a company: administration	G1(d), G1(e)

Introduction

A **company in difficulty** or **in crisis** (an **insolvent** company) basically has a choice of two options:

(1) To carry on with the business, using statutory methods to help remedy the situation

(2) To stop

A company which is heading towards insolvency can often be **saved**, using a variety of **legal protections** from creditors until the problem is sorted out.

The first option does not have to mean carrying on as if everything is normal. It can mean **seeking help** from the **court** or a **qualified insolvency practitioner** to put a plan together to **save the company** and get it out of its poor financial position.

Unfortunately, many companies cannot be saved, and the members and directors are forced to take the second option, **to stop** operating the business through the company. Liquidation, sometimes called 'winding up', is **when a company is formally dissolved** and ceases to exist.

The Insolvency Act 1986 applies to this chapter unless otherwise stated.

Study guide

		Intellectual level
G	**Insolvency law**	
1	**Insolvency and administration**	
(a)	Explain the meaning of, and procedure involved in, voluntary liquidation, including members' and creditors' voluntary liquidation	2
(b)	Explain the meaning of, the grounds for, and the procedure involved in compulsory liquidation	2
(c)	Explain the order in which company debts will be paid off on liquidation	2
(d)	Explain administration as a general alternative to liquidation	2
(e)	Explain the way in which an administrator may be appointed, the effects of such appointment, and the powers and duties of an administrator	2

Exam guide

As well as being examined in questions in its own right, you may find that elements of insolvency creep into scenario questions on company finances and directors.

1 What is liquidation?

FAST FORWARD

Liquidation is the **dissolution** or **'winding up'** of a company.

Key terms

Liquidation means that the company must be dissolved and its affairs 'wound up', or brought to an end.

The assets are realised, debts are paid out of the proceeds, and any surplus amounts are returned to members. Liquidation leads on to **dissolution** of the company. It is sometimes referred to as **winding up**.

1.1 Who decides to liquidate?

FAST FORWARD

There are three different methods of **liquidation: compulsory, members' voluntary** and **creditors' voluntary**. Compulsory liquidation and creditors' voluntary liquidation are proceedings for insolvent companies, and members' voluntary liquidation is for solvent companies.

The **parties** most likely to be involved in the **decision to liquidate** are:

- The directors
- The creditors
- The members

The **directors** are best placed to know the financial position and difficulty that the company is in. The **creditors** may become aware that the company is in financial difficulty when their invoices do not get paid on a timely basis, or at all.

The **members** are likely to be the last people to know that the company is in financial difficulty, as they rely on the directors to tell them. In public companies, there is a rule that the directors must call a general meeting of members if the net assets of the company fall to half or less of the amount of its called-up share capital. There is no such rule for private companies.

As we shall see, there are three methods of winding up. They depend on **who has instigated the proceedings**. Directors cannot formally instigate proceedings for winding up; they can only make recommendations to the members.

However, if the **members refuse** to put the company in liquidation, and the directors feel that to continue to trade will prejudice creditors, they could resign their posts in order to avoid committing **fraudulent** or **wrongful trading**.

In any case, if the company was in such serious financial difficulty for this to be an issue, it is likely that a **creditor** would have commenced proceedings against it.

1.1.1 Creditors

If a creditor has sufficient grounds they may **apply to the court** for the **compulsory winding up** of the company.

Creditors may also be closely involved in a **voluntary winding up**, if the company is **insolvent** when the **members** decide to wind the company up.

1.1.2 Members

The members may decide to wind the company up (probably on the advice of the directors). If they do so, the company is **voluntarily wound up**. This can lead to two different types of members' winding up:

- Members' voluntary winding up (if the company is solvent)
- Creditors' voluntary winding up (if the company is insolvent)

1.2 Role of the liquidator

AST FORWARD

A **liquidator** must be an authorised, qualified insolvency practitioner.

Once the decision to liquidate has been taken, the company goes under the **control of a liquidator** who must be a **qualified** and **authorised** insolvency practitioner.

Although the liquidator's main role is to wind up the company, they also have a statutory duty to **report** to the Secretary of State where they feel that any **director** of the insolvent company is **unfit** to be involved in the management of a company.

1.3 Common features of liquidations

AST FORWARD

Once **insolvency procedures** have commenced, share trading must cease, the company documents must state that the company is in liquidation and the directors' power to manage ceases.

Regardless of what method of liquidation is used, similar **legal problems** may arise in each of them. In addition, the following factors are true at the start of any liquidation:

- **No share dealings** or **changes in members** are allowed
- All company documents (eg invoices, letters, emails) and the website must **state the company is in liquidation**
- The **directors' power to manage ceases**

2 Voluntary liquidation

AST FORWARD

A **winding up** is **voluntary** where the decision to wind up is taken by the company's members, although if the company is insolvent, the creditors will be heavily involved in the proceedings.

As we saw earlier there are two types of voluntary liquidation:

- A **members' voluntary winding up**, where the company is **solvent** and the members merely decide to 'kill it off'
- A **creditors' voluntary winding up**, where the company is **insolvent** and the members resolve to wind up in consultation with creditors

The **main differences** between a members' and a creditors' voluntary winding up are set out below.

| Function | Winding up | |
	Members' voluntary	Creditors' voluntary
(1) **Appointment of liquidator**	By members	Normally by creditors, though responsible to both members and creditors
(2) **Approval for liquidator's actions**	General meeting of members	Liquidation committee
(3) **Liquidation committee**	None	Up to five representatives of creditors

The effect of the voluntary winding up being a creditors' one is that the **creditors** have a **decisive influence** on the conduct of the liquidation.

Meetings in a creditors' voluntary winding up are held in the same sequence as in a members' voluntary winding up, but meetings of creditors are called at the same intervals as the meetings of members and for similar purposes.

In both kinds of voluntary winding up, the **court has the power to appoint a liquidator** (if, for some reason, there is none acting) or to remove one liquidator and appoint another.

2.1 Members' voluntary liquidation

FAST FORWARD

In order to be a members' winding up, the directors must make a **declaration of solvency**. It is a criminal offence to make a declaration of solvency without reasonable grounds.

Type of resolution to be passed	
Ordinary	This is **rare, but** if the **articles** specify liquidation at a certain point, only an ordinary resolution is required
Special	A company may resolve to be **wound up** by special resolution

The winding up **commences** on the passing of the resolution. A signed copy of the resolution must be delivered to the Registrar within 15 days. A **liquidator** is usually appointed by the same resolution (or a second resolution passed at the same time).

2.1.1 Declaration of solvency

A voluntary winding up is a members' voluntary winding up **only** if the directors make and deliver to the Registrar a **declaration of solvency**.

This is a **statutory declaration** that the directors have made full enquiry into the affairs of the company and are of the opinion that it will be able to pay its debts, within a specified period not exceeding 12 months.

(a)   The **declaration is made by all the directors** or, if there are more than two directors, by a **majority** of them.

(b)   The declaration includes a **statement of the company's assets and liabilities** as at the latest practicable date before the declaration is made.

(c)   The **declaration must** be:

(i)   Made not more than **five weeks** before the resolution to wind up is passed, and
(ii)   Delivered to the Registrar within **15 days** of the meeting.

If the liquidator later concludes that the company will be unable to pay its debts, they must call a meeting of creditors and lay before them a **statement of assets and liabilities**.

> It is a **criminal offence**, punishable by fine or imprisonment, for a director to make a declaration of solvency without having **reasonable grounds** for it. If the company proves to be insolvent they will have to justify their previous declaration or be punished.

In a members' voluntary winding up the **creditors play no part**, since the assumption is that their debts will be paid in full. The liquidator calls special and annual general meetings of contributories (members), to whom they report:

(a)   Within **three months** of each anniversary of the commencement of the winding up, the liquidator must call a meeting and lay before it an account of their transactions during the year.

(b)   When the liquidation is complete the liquidator calls a meeting to lay before it their **final accounts**.

After holding the final meeting the liquidator sends a **copy of their accounts** to the Registrar who dissolves the company three months later, by removing its name from the register.

2.2 Creditors' voluntary liquidation

ST FORWARD

> When there is no declaration of solvency there is a **creditors' voluntary winding** up.

If no declaration of solvency is made and delivered to the Registrar the liquidation proceeds as a creditors' voluntary winding up, **even if**, in the end, the company pays its debts in full.

To commence a creditors' voluntary winding up the directors convene a general meeting of members to pass a **special resolution** (private companies may pass a written resolution with a 75% majority). They must also convene a meeting of creditors, giving at least seven days' notice of this meeting. The notice must be advertised in the *London Gazette* and such other manner as the directors think fit. The notice must either:

•   Give the name and address of a **qualified insolvency practitioner**, to whom the creditors can apply before the meeting for information about the company, **or**

•   State a place in the locality of the company's principal place of business where, on the two business days before the meeting, a **list of creditors** can be inspected.

The **meeting of members** is held first and its business is as follows:

•   To resolve to wind up
•   To appoint a liquidator, and
•   To nominate up to five representatives to be members of the liquidation committee.

The **creditors' meeting** should preferably be convened on the same day, but at a later time, than the members' meeting; or on the next day; but in any event within 14 days of it.

One of the **directors** presides at the creditors' meeting and lays before it a full statement of the company's affairs and a list of creditors with the amounts owing to them. The meeting may nominate a liquidator and up to five representatives to be members of the liquidation committee.

If the creditors nominate a different person to be liquidator, **their choice prevails** over the nomination by the members.

Of course, the creditors may decide **not to appoint a liquidator** at all. They cannot be compelled to appoint a liquidator, and if they do fail to appoint one it will be the members' nominee who will take office.

However, even if creditors do appoint a liquidator, there is a period of up to two weeks before the creditors' meeting takes place at which they will actually make the **appointment**. In the interim it will be the members' nominee who takes office as liquidator.

In either case the presence of the members' nominee as liquidator has been exploited, in the past, for the purpose known as **'centrebinding'**.

> **Re Centrebind Ltd 1966**
>
> *The facts:* The directors convened a general meeting, without making a statutory declaration of solvency, but failed to call a creditors' meeting for the same or the next day. The penalty for this was merely a small default fine. The liquidator chosen by the members had disposed of the assets before the creditors could appoint a liquidator. The creditors' liquidator challenged the sale of the assets (at a low price) as invalid.
>
> *Decision:* The first liquidator had been in office when he made the sale and so it was a valid exercise of the normal power of sale.

In a 'centrebinding' transaction the assets are sold by an **obliging liquidator** to a new company formed by the members of the insolvent company. The purpose is to defeat the claims of the creditors at minimum cost and enable the same people to continue in business until the next insolvency supervenes.

The government has sought to limit the abuses during the period between the members' and creditors' meetings. The **powers of the members' nominee as liquidator are now restricted** to:

- Taking control of the company's property,
- Disposing of perishable or other goods which might diminish in value if not disposed of immediately, and
- Doing all other things necessary for the protection of the company's assets.

If the members' liquidator wishes to perform any act other than those listed above, they will have to **apply to the court for leave**.

3 Compulsory liquidation

FAST FORWARD

> There are **seven statutory reasons** for the compulsory liquidation of a company, which can all be found in Section 122 of the Insolvency Act 1986.

We shall consider the two most important here.

Statutory reasons for compulsory liquidation
Company is unable to pay its debts
It is just and equitable to wind up the company

The **parties** who can apply for the **compulsory liquidation** of a company will depend on the reason being cited.

In cases where the company is **unable to pay its debts**, it is a **creditor** who applies for the liquidation as a last resort when the company has not settled a debt.

In **'just and equitable'** cases, it is usually the **company itself**, the **members** or **directors** that decide the company should be wound up.

The **government** may petition for the compulsory winding up of a company:

- If a public company has not obtained a **trading certificate** within one year of incorporation
- Following a report by government inspectors that it is in the **public interest** and **just and equitable** for the company to be wound up

An **administrator** of a company may also apply for the company's compulsory liquidation, on behalf of the company, as a means of ending an **administration process**.

3.1 Company unable to pay its debts

FAST FORWARD

> A creditor may apply to the court to wind up the company if the company is **unable to pay its debts**. There are statutory tests to prove that a company is unable to pay its debts.

A creditor who petitions on the grounds of the company's insolvency must show that the company is **unable to pay its debts**. There are three permitted ways to do that.

(a) A **creditor owed more than £750 serves** the company, at its registered office, a **written demand** for payment and the **company fails** to **pay the debt** or to offer security for it within **21 days**.

   If the company denies it owes the amount demanded on apparently **reasonable grounds**, the court will dismiss the petition and leave the creditor to take legal proceedings for debt.

(b) A creditor obtains **judgement** against the company for debt, and attempts to enforce the judgement. However they are **unable to obtain payment** because no assets of the company have been found and seized.

(c) A creditor satisfies the court that, taking into account the contingent and prospective liabilities of the company, it is **unable to pay its debts**. The creditor may show this in one of two ways:

   (i) By proof that the company is not able to pay its debts as they fall due – the **commercial insolvency test**

   (ii) By proof that the company's assets are less than its liabilities – the **balance sheet test**

   This is a **residual category**. Any evidence of actual or prospective insolvency may be produced.

am focus
int

> A secured creditor might appoint a receiver to control the secured asset for the purpose of realising the creditors' loan. If the receiver cannot find an asset to realise, the creditor might file a petition for compulsory liquidation under (b).

3.2 The 'just and equitable' ground

ST FORWARD

A **dissatisfied member** may get the court to wind the company up on the '**just and equitable' ground**.

A member who is dissatisfied with the directors or controlling shareholders over the management of the company may petition the court for the company to be wound up on the '**just and equitable' ground**. For such a petition to be successful, the member must show that **no** other remedy is available. It is not enough for a member to be **dissatisfied** to make it just and equitable that the company should be wound up, since winding up what may be an otherwise healthy company is a **drastic step**.

3.2.1 Examples: When companies have been wound up

(a) **The substratum of the company has gone – the only or main object(s) of the company (its underlying basis or substratum) cannot be, or can no longer be, achieved.**

> *Re German Date Coffee Co 1882*
>
> *The facts:* The objects clause specified very pointedly that the sole object was to manufacture coffee from dates under a German patent. The German government refused to grant a patent. The company manufactured coffee under a Swedish patent for sale in Germany. A member petitioned for compulsory winding up.
>
> *Decision:* The company existed only to 'work a particular patent' and as it could not do so it should be wound up.

(b)   **The company was formed for an illegal or fraudulent purpose or there is a complete deadlock in the management of its affairs.**

> *Re Yenidje Tobacco Co Ltd 1916*
>
> *The facts:* Two sole traders merged their businesses in a company of which they were the only directors and shareholders. They quarrelled bitterly and one sued the other for fraud. Meanwhile they refused to speak to each other and conducted board meetings by passing notes through the hands of the secretary. The defendant in the fraud action petitioned for compulsory winding up.
>
> *Decision:* 'In substance these two people are really partners' and by analogy with the law of partnership (which permits dissolution if the partners are really unable to work together) it was just and equitable to order liquidation.

(c)   **The understandings between members or directors which were the basis of the association have been unfairly breached by lawful action.**

> *Ebrahimi v Westbourne Galleries Ltd 1973*
>
> *The facts:* E and N carried on business together for 25 years, originally as partners and, for the last 10 years, through a company in which each originally had 500 shares. E and N were the first directors and shared the profits as directors' remuneration; no dividends were paid. When N's son joined the business he became a third director and E and N each transferred 100 shares to N's son. Eventually there were disputes. N and his son used their voting control in general meeting (600 votes against 400) to remove E from his directorship.
>
> *Decision:* The company should be wound up. N and his son were within their legal rights in removing E from his directorship, but the past relationship made it 'unjust or inequitable' to insist on legal rights and the court could intervene on equitable principles to order liquidation.

> *Re A company 1983*
>
> *The facts:* The facts were similar in essentials to those in *Ebrahimi's case* but the majority offered, and the petitioner agreed, that they would settle the dispute by a sale of his shares to the majority. This settlement broke down, however, because they could not agree on the price. The petitioner then petitioned on the 'just and equitable' ground.
>
> *Decision:* An order for liquidation on this ground may only be made 'in the absence of any other remedy'. As the parties had agreed in principle that there was an alternative to liquidation the petition must be dismissed.

3.3 Other circumstances for compulsory liquidation

As mentioned previously, there are a **number of other circumstances** where compulsory liquidation may be commenced. These are:

- The **company passed a special resolution** that it should be wound up by the court

- The company registered as a **public limited company** more than a year previously but has not yet been issued with a **trading certificate**

- The company is an **'old' public company** (a PLC that existed on or before 22nd December 1980 and has remained as a PLC since)

- The company has **not begun trading within a year** of its incorporation or **has suspended its trading** for a whole year

- A **moratorium for a voluntary arrangement** for the company has passed and no voluntary arrangement is in place

3.4 Proceedings for compulsory liquidation

When a petition is presented to the **court** a copy is delivered to the **company** in case it objects. It is advertised so that other creditors may intervene if they wish.

The petition **may** be presented by a member. If the petition is presented by **a member** they **must show** that:

(a)   The company is **insolvent** or, alternatively, refuses to supply information of its financial position, and

(b)   They have been a **registered shareholder** for at least six of the 18 months up to the date of their petition. However, this rule is not applied if the petitioner acquired their shares by allotment direct from the company or by inheritance from a deceased member or if the petition is based on the number of members having fallen below two.

tention!

> The court will not order compulsory liquidation on a member's petition if they have nothing to gain from it. If the company is insolvent they would receive nothing since the creditors will take all the assets.

Once the court has been petitioned, a **provisional liquidator** may be appointed by the **court**. The **official receiver** is usually appointed, and their powers are conferred by the court. These usually extend to taking control of the company's property and applying for a special manager to be appointed.

ey term

> The **official receiver** is an officer of the court. They are appointed as liquidator of any company ordered to be wound up by the court, although an insolvency practitioner may replace them.

3.5 Effects of an order for compulsory liquidation

The effects of an **order** for compulsory liquidation are:

(a)   The **official receiver becomes liquidator**.

(b)   The liquidation is **deemed to have commenced at the time when the petition was first presented**.

(c)   Any **disposition** of the **company's property** and any transfer of its shares subsequent to the commencement of liquidation is **void**, unless the court orders otherwise.

(d)   Any **legal proceedings** in progress against the company are halted (and none may thereafter begin) unless the court gives leave. Any seizure of the company's assets after commencement of liquidation is void.

(e)   The **employees** of the company are **automatically dismissed**. The liquidator assumes the powers of management previously held by the directors.

(f)   Any **floating charge crystallises**.

The assets of the company may remain the company's legal property but **under the liquidator's control** unless the court by order **vests** the assets in the liquidator. The business of the company may continue, but it is the liquidator's duty to continue it with a view only to realisation, for instance by sale as a going concern.

Within 21 days of the making of the order for winding up, a **statement of affairs** must be delivered to the liquidator verified by one or more directors and by the secretary (and possibly by other persons). The statement shows the assets and liabilities of the company and includes a list of creditors with particulars of any security.

The liquidator may require that any **officers or employees** concerned in the recent management of the company shall join in submitting the statement of affairs.

3.5.1 Investigations by the official receiver

The official receiver **must investigate**:

- The **causes of the failure** of the company, and
- Generally the **promotion**, **formation**, **business dealings** and **affairs** of the company.

The official receiver **may report** to the court on the results.

(a) The official receiver may require the **public examination** in open court of those believed to be implicated (a much-feared sanction).

(b) The official receiver may apply to the court for public examination where half the **creditors** or three-quarters of the **shareholders** (in value in either case) so request. Failure to attend, or reasonable suspicion that the examinees will abscond, may lead to arrest and detention in custody for contempt of court.

3.5.2 Meetings of contributories and creditors

Key term

> **Contributories** are **members** of a company.
>
> At winding up, members may have to make payments to the company in respect of any unpaid share capital or guarantees.

The official receiver has 12 weeks to decide whether or not to convene **separate meetings** of creditors and contributories. The meetings provide the creditors and contributories with the opportunity to appoint their own nominee as permanent liquidator to replace the official receiver, and a **liquidation committee** to work with the liquidator.

If the official receiver believes there is little interest and that the creditors will be unlikely to appoint a liquidator, they can **dispense with a meeting**, informing the court, the creditors and the contributories of the decision. They can always be required to call a meeting if at least 25% in value of the creditors require them to do so.

If no meeting is held, or one is held but no liquidator is appointed, the official receiver continues to act as liquidator. If the creditors do hold a meeting and **appoint their own nominee**, this person automatically becomes liquidator, subject to a right of objection to the court. Any person appointed to act as liquidator must be a qualified insolvency practitioner.

At any time after a winding up order is made, **the official receiver may ask the Secretary of State to appoint a liquidator**. Similarly, they may request an appointment if the creditors and members fail to appoint a liquidator.

If separate meetings of creditors and contributories are held and different persons are nominated as liquidators, it is the **creditors' nominee** who **takes precedence**. Notice of the order for compulsory liquidation and of the appointment of a liquidator is given to the Registrar and in the *London Gazette*.

If, while the liquidation is in progress, the liquidator decides to call meetings of contributories or creditors, they may arrange to do so under powers vested in the court.

3.6 Order of payments on liquidation

In a compulsory liquidation (and often in a voluntary one) the liquidator follows a **prescribed order** for distributing the company's assets:

	Order	Explanation
1	Costs	These include the costs of selling the assets, the liquidator's remuneration and all costs incidental to the liquidation procedure.
2	Preferential debts	• Employees' wages (subject to a statutory maximum) • Accrued holiday pay • Contributions to an occupational pension fund
3	Debts secured by floating charges	Subject to the 'prescribed part' (see below)
4	Debts owed to unsecured ordinary creditors	A proportion of assets (known as the 'prescribed part') is 'ring-fenced' for unsecured creditors. This proportion (which is subject to a statutory maximum) is calculated as 50% of the first £10,000 of realisations of debts secured by floating charge and 20% of the floating charge realisations thereafter (subject to a prescribed maximum).
5	Deferred debts	These include dividends declared but not paid, and interest accrued on debts since liquidation.
6	Members	Any surplus (unlikely in compulsory and creditors' voluntary liquidations) is distributed to members according to their rights under the articles or the terms of issue of their shares.

It is important to remember that **creditors with fixed and floating charges may appoint a receiver** to sell the charged asset – any surplus is passed onto to the liquidator. In the event of a shortfall they become unsecured creditors for the balance.

3.7 Completion of compulsory liquidation

When the liquidator completes their task they report to the government, which **examines their accounts**. They may apply to the court for an order for dissolution of the company.

An official receiver may also apply to the Registrar for an **early dissolution** of the company if its realisable assets will not cover their expenses and further investigation is not required.

4 Differences between compulsory and voluntary liquidation

AST FORWARD >>

The differences between compulsory and voluntary liquidation are associated with **timing**, the **role** of the **official receiver, stay of legal proceedings** and the **dismissal of employees**.

The main differences in **legal consequences** between a compulsory and a voluntary liquidation are as follows.

	Differences
Control	Under a members' voluntary liquidation the members control the liquidation process. Under a creditors' voluntary liquidation the creditors control the process. The court controls the process under a compulsory liquidation.
Timing	A voluntary winding up commences on the day when the **resolution to wind up is passed**. It is not retrospective. A compulsory winding up, once agreed to by the court, commences on the day the **petition was presented**.
Liquidator	The **official receiver** plays **no role** in a **voluntary winding up**. The members or creditors select and appoint the liquidator, who is not an officer of the court.
Legal proceedings	In a voluntary winding up there is no automatic **stay of legal proceedings** against the company, nor are previous dispositions or seizure of its assets void. However, the liquidator has a general right to apply to the court to make any order which the court can make in a compulsory liquidation. They would do so, for instance, to prevent any creditor obtaining an unfair advantage over the other creditors.
Management and staff	In any **liquidation the liquidator replaces the directors** in the management of the company (unless they decide to retain them). However, the employees are **not automatically dismissed by commencement of voluntary liquidation**. Insolvent liquidation may amount to repudiation of their employment contracts (provisions of the statutory employment protection code apply).

5 Saving a company: administration

Administration is a method of **'saving' a company from liquidation**, under the Enterprise Act 2002.

5.1 What is administration?

An **administrator** is appointed primarily to try to rescue the company as a going concern. A company may go into administration to carry out an established plan to save the company.

Key term

Administration puts an **insolvency practitioner** in **control** of the company, with a defined programme for **rescuing the company** from insolvency as a going concern.

Its purpose is to **insulate** the company **from its creditors while it seeks**:

- To save itself as a going concern, or failing that
- To achieve a better result for creditors than an immediate winding up would secure, or failing that
- To realise property so as to make a distribution to creditors

Administration orders and liquidations are **mutually exclusive**. Once an administration order has been passed by the court, it is **no longer possible to petition the court** for a **winding up** order against the company. Similarly, however, once an order for winding up has been made, an administration order cannot be granted (except when appointed by a floating chargeholder).

Administration can be initiated **with** or **without a court order**.

5.2 Appointment without a court order

Some parties – **secured creditors** and **directors** and the **members** by resolution – can appoint an administrator without a court order.

It is possible to appoint an administrator **without reference to the court**. There are three sets of people who might be able to do this:

- Floating chargeholders
- Directors
- Company

5.2.1 Floating chargeholders

Floating chargeholders have the right to appoint an administrator without reference to the court, even if there is no actual or impending insolvency. They may also **appoint an administrator, even if the company is in compulsory liquidation**. This enables steps to be taken to save the company before its financial situation becomes irreversible.

In order to qualify for this right, the **floating charge must entitle the holder to appoint an administrator**. This would be in the terms of the charge. It must also be over all, or substantially all, of the company's property.

Point to note

> In practice, such a floating chargeholder with a charge over all or substantially all of the company's property is likely to be a **bank**.

However, the **floating chargeholder may only appoint an administrator** if:

- They have given **two days'** written notice to the holder of any prior floating charge, where that person has the right to appoint an administrator.
- Their floating charge is **enforceable**.

After any relevant two-day notice period, the floating chargeholder will file the following **documents** at court:

- A **notice of appointment** in the prescribed form, identifying the administrator
- A **statement by the administrator** that they **consent to the appointment**
- A **statement by the administrator** that, in their **opinion**, the **purpose of the administration** is likely to be **achieved**
- A **statutory declaration** that they **qualify** to make the appointment

Once these documents have been filed, the **appointment is valid**. The appointer must notify the administrator, and other people prescribed by regulations, of the appointment as soon as is reasonably practicable.

5.2.2 Company and directors

The process by which a company commences appointing an administrator will depend upon its **articles of association**. A company or its directors may appoint an administrator if:

- The company has not done so in the last 12 months or been subject to a **moratorium** as a result of a voluntary arrangement with its creditors in the last 12 months

- The company is, or is likely to be, **unable to pay its debts**

- **No petition for winding up** nor any **administration order** in respect of the company has been presented to the court and is outstanding

- The company is **not in liquidation**

- **No administrator** or **receiver** is already in office

The company or its directors must give notice to any floating chargeholders entitled to appoint an administrator. This means that the **floating chargeholders may** appoint their own administrator within this time period, and so **block the company's choice of administrator**.

5.3 Appointment with a court order

FAST FORWARD Various parties can apply for **administration** through the court.

There are **four sets of parties** that may **apply to the court** for an administration order:

- The **company** (that is, a majority of the members by (ordinary) resolution)
- The **directors** of the company
- One or more **creditors** of the company
- The **Justice** and **Chief Executive of the magistrates' court** following non-payment of a fine imposed on the company

The court will grant the **administration order** if it is satisfied that the company is, or is likely to be, **unable to pay its debts**, and the administration order is reasonably likely to **achieve the purpose of administration**. The application will name the person whom the applicants want to be the **administrator**. Unless certain interested parties object, this person is appointed as administrator.

5.4 The effects of appointing an administrator

FAST FORWARD The **effects** of administration depend on whether it is effected by the **court** or by a **floating chargeholder**, to some degree.

Effects of an administrator appointment
A **moratorium** over the company's debts commences (that is, no creditor can enforce their debt during the administration period without the court's permission). This is the advantageous aspect of being 'in administration'.
The court must give its permission for: • **Security** over company property to be **enforced** • Goods held under hire purchase to be **repossessed** • A landlord to conduct **forfeiture** by peaceable entry • Commencement/continuation of any **legal process** against the company
The **powers of management** are subjugated to the authority of the administrator and managers can only act with their consent.
All outstanding **petitions for winding-up** of the company are **dismissed**.
Any **administrative receiver** in place must **vacate office**. No appointments to this position can be made.

5.5 Duties of the administrator

FAST FORWARD The administrator has **fiduciary duties** to the company as its agent, plus some legal duties.

The administrator is an **agent of the company** and the **creditors as a whole**. They therefore owe fiduciary duties to them and have the following legal duties.

Legal duties of the administrator
As soon as **reasonably practicable** after appointment they must:
• **Send notice** of appointment to the company
• **Publish notice** of appointment
• Obtain a list of **company creditors** and send notice of appointment to each
• Within seven days of appointment, send notice of appointment to **Registrar**
• Require certain relevant people to provide a **statement of affairs** of the company
• Ensure that every **business document** of the company **bears the identity** of the administrator and a statement that the affairs, business and property of the company are being managed by him
• Consider the **statements of affairs** submitted to them and set out their **proposals** for achieving the aim of administration. The proposals must be **sent to the Registrar** and the company's **creditors,** and be made available to **every member of the company** as soon as is reasonably practicable, and **within eight weeks**
• Whilst preparing their proposals, the administrator must **manage the affairs** of the company

The **statement of affairs** must be provided by the people from whom it is requested, within 11 days of it being requested. It is in a prescribed form, and contains:

- Details of the **company's property**
- The company's **debts** and **liabilities**
- The **names** and **addresses** of the **company's creditors**
- Details of any **security** held by any **creditor**

Failing to provide a statement of affairs, or providing a statement in which the writer has no reasonable belief of truth, is a **criminal offence** punishable by fine.

5.6 Administrator's proposals

AST FORWARD

The administrator must either **propose a rescue plan**, or state that the **company cannot be rescued**.

Having considered all information the administrator must, within **eight weeks**, (subject to possible extension):

- Set out their proposals for achieving the aim of the administration; or

- Set out why it is not reasonable and practicable that the company be rescued. In this case they will also set out why the creditors as a whole would benefit from winding up.

The **proposal** must **be sent to all members** and **creditors** they are aware of. It must not

- Affect the right of a **secured creditor** to enforce their security
- Result in a non-preferential debt being paid in priority to a preferential debt
- Result in one preferential creditor being paid a smaller proportion of their debt than another.

5.6.1 Creditors' meeting

The administrator must call a **meeting of creditors**, within ten **weeks** of their appointment, to approve the proposals. The creditors may either accept or reject them. Once the proposals have been agreed, the administrator cannot make any substantial amendment without first gaining the creditors' consents.

5.7 Administrator's powers

AST FORWARD

The administrator takes on the **powers** of the directors.

An **administrator** of a company may do **anything necessarily expedient** for the management of the affairs, business and property of the company.

Administrators have **the same powers as those granted to directors** and the following **specific powers** to:

- Remove or appoint a **director**
- Call a **meeting of members or creditors**
- **Apply to court for directions** regarding the carrying out of their functions
- Make payments to **secured or preferential creditors**
- With the permission of the court, **make payments to unsecured creditors**

The administrator usually requires the permission of the court to make payments to unsecured creditors. However, this is not the case if the administrator feels that paying the unsecured creditor will assist the **achievement of the administration**. For example, paying a major supplier to enable trading to continue.

5.8 End of administration

FAST FORWARD Administration can last up to **12 months**.

The **administration period ends** when:

- The administration has been successful
- Twelve months have elapsed from the date of the appointment of administrator
- The administrator or a creditor applies to the court to end the appointment
- An improper motive of the applicant for applying for the administration is discovered.

The administrator automatically vacates office after **12 months of their appointment**. This time period can be extended by court order, or by consent from the appropriate creditors.

Alternatively, the administrator may **apply to the court** when they think:

- The purpose of administration cannot be achieved
- The company should not have entered into administration
- The administration has been successful (if appointed by the court)

They must also apply to the court if required to by the **creditors' meeting**. Where the administrator was appointed by a chargeholder or the company/its directors, and they feel that the purposes of administration have been achieved, they must file a **notice** with the court and the Registrar.

5.9 Advantages of administration

FAST FORWARD Administration has many advantages for the **company**, the **members** and the **creditors**.

Advantages of administration	
To the company	The company does not necessarily cease to exist at the end of the process, whereas liquidation will always result in the company being wound up.
	It provides a temporary breathing space from creditors to formulate rescue plans.
	It prevents any creditor applying for compulsory liquidation.
	It provides for past transactions to be challenged.
To the members	They will continue to have shares in the company which has not been wound up. If the administration is successful, regenerating the business should enhance share value and will restore any income from the business.
To the creditors	Creditors should obtain a return in relation to their past debts, from an administration.
	Unsecured creditors will benefit from asset realisations.
	Any creditor may apply to the court for an administration order, while only certain creditors may apply for other forms of relief from debt. For example, the use of receivers or an application for winding up.
	Floating chargeholders may appoint an administrator without reference to the court.
	It may also be in the interests of the creditors to have a continued business relationship with the company once the business has been turned around.

Chapter Roundup

- **Liquidation** is the **dissolution** or 'winding up' of a company.

- There are three different methods of **liquidation: compulsory, members' voluntary** and **creditors' voluntary**. Compulsory liquidation and creditors' voluntary liquidation are proceedings for insolvent companies, and members' voluntary liquidation is for solvent companies.

- A **liquidator** must be an authorised, qualified insolvency practitioner.

- Once **insolvency procedures** have commenced, share trading must cease, the company documents must state that the company is in liquidation and the directors' power to manage ceases.

- A **winding up** is **voluntary** where the decision to wind up is taken by the company members, although if the company is insolvent, the creditors will be heavily involved in the proceedings.

- In order to be a members' winding up, the directors must make a **declaration of solvency**. It is a criminal offence to make a declaration of solvency without reasonable grounds.

- When there is no declaration of solvency there is a **creditors' voluntary winding** up.

- There are **seven statutory reasons** for the compulsory liquidation of a company, which can all be found in Section 122 of the Insolvency Act 1986.

- A creditor may apply to the court to wind up the company if the company is **unable to pay its debts**. There are statutory tests to prove that a company is unable to pay its debts.

- A **dissatisfied member** may get the court to wind the company up on the 'just and equitable' ground.

- The differences between compulsory and voluntary liquidation are associated with **timing**, the **role** of the **official receiver, stay of legal proceedings** and the **dismissal of employees**.

- An **administrator** is appointed primarily to try to rescue the company as a going concern. A company may go into administration to carry out an established plan to save the company.

- Some parties – **secured creditors** and **directors** and the **members** by resolution – can appoint an administrator without a court order.

- Various parties can apply for **administration** through the court.

- The **effects** of administration depend on whether it is effected by the **court** or by a **floating chargeholder**, to some degree.

- The administrator has **fiduciary duties** to the company as its agent, plus some legal duties.

- The administrator must either **propose a rescue plan**, or state that the **company cannot be rescued**.

- The administrator takes on the **powers** of the directors.

- Administration can last up to **12 months**.

- Administration has many advantages for the **company**, the **members** and the **creditors**.

1   Complete the following definition

Liquidation means that a company must be ………*dissolved*………… and its affairs wound up.

2   Name three common effects of liquidations.

(1) …*no further changes in membership*…………………

(2) *all documents must state it*……………………

(3) …*directors' power to manage ceases*……………………

3   What are the two most important grounds for compulsory liquidation?

(1) …*Insolvency*……………………

(2) …*it is just & equitable*……………………

4   A members' voluntary winding up is where the members decide to dissolve a healthy company.

True   ☒

False   ☒

5   Name two advantages of administration.

(1) …*relief from creditors*……………………

(2) …………………………………

Answers to Quick Quiz

1   Dissolved

2   (1) No further changes in membership permitted
     (2) All documents must state prominently that company is in liquidation
     (3) Directors' power to manage ceases

3   (1) Company is unable to pay its debts
     (2) It is just and equitable to wind up the company

4   True. Members can decide to wind up a healthy company.

5   (1) It does not necessarily result in the dissolution of the company
     (2) It prevents creditors applying for compulsory liquidation

     Subsidiary advantages are

     (3) All creditors can apply for an administration order
     (4) The administrator may challenge past transactions of the company

Now try the questions below from the Practice Question Bank

Number
47, 48

P
A
R
T

H

Corporate fraudulent and criminal behaviour

301

19

Fraudulent and criminal behaviour

Topic list	Syllabus reference
1 Financial crime	H1 (a-f)
2 Insider dealing	H1(a)
3 Market abuse	H1(b)
4 Money laundering	H1(c)
5 Bribery	H1(d)
6 Criminal activity relating to companies	H1(e), H1(f)

Introduction

In this chapter, we shall look specifically at some **financial crimes** and the **measures** that have been put into place to combat them.

Insider dealing is a statutory offence relating to the trading of shares or other securities. It has proved difficult to convict people of the crime of insider dealing, hence the introduction of the civil wrong of market abuse.

The issue of **money laundering** is a highly topical issue. Money laundering is the process of 'legalising' funds raised through crime. Money laundering crosses national boundaries and it can be difficult to enforce the related laws.

Finally we shall look at some **other offences** in relation to companies.

Study guide

		Intellectual level
H	**Corporate fraudulent and criminal behaviour**	
1	**Fraudulent and criminal behaviour**	
(a)	Recognise the nature and legal control over insider dealing	2
(b)	Recognise the nature and legal control over market abuse	2
(c)	Recognise the nature and legal control over money laundering	2
(d)	Recognise the nature and legal control over bribery	2
(e)	Discuss potential criminal activity in the operation, management and liquidation of companies	2
(f)	Recognise the nature and legal control over fraudulent and wrongful trading	2

Exam guide

Financial crime is highly examinable, in both types of question. Expect to be asked to identify whether or not a crime has been committed, or explain the opportunities that exist for perpetrating such crimes.

1 Financial crime

> **FAST FORWARD**
>
> Crime is **conduct prohibited by the law**. Financial crime can be international in nature, and there is a need for international co-operation to prevent it.

Law tends to be organised on a **national basis**. However, as we shall see later, some crime, particularly money laundering, is perpetrated **across national borders**. Indeed the international element of the crime contributes to its success.

Particularly with regard to money laundering, international bodies are having to **co-operate** with one another in order to control financial crimes which spreads across national boundaries.

1.1 Example: international financial crime

Money laundering is a crime in Country A but not in Country B. Money laundering can be effected legally in Country B and the proceeds returned to Country A. Hence Country A cannot prosecute for the crime of money laundering, which has not been committed within its national boundaries.

 PO1 requires you to apply professional ethics, values and judgement. Prevention of financial crime is an important part of this.

2 Insider dealing

> **FAST FORWARD**
>
> Insider dealing is the statutory offence of **dealing** in securities while in **possession** of **inside information** as an insider, the securities being price-affected by the information.

The **Criminal Justice Act 1993** (CJA) contains the rules on **insider dealing**. It was regarded and treated as a crime since a few people are enriched at the expense of the reputation of the stock market and the interests of all involved in it.

2.1 What is insider dealing?

y term

> **Insider dealing** is dealing in securities while in possession of inside information as an insider, the securities being **price-affected** by the information.

To prove **insider dealing**, the prosecution must prove that the possessor of inside information:

- **Dealt** in **price-affected securities** on a regulated market, or

- **Encouraged another** to **deal** in them on a regulated market, or

- **Disclosed** the **information** other than in the proper performance of their employment, office or profession

2.1.1 Dealing

Dealing is **acquiring or disposing** of, or **agreeing** to **acquire** or **dispose** of, relevant securities, whether **directly** or **through an agent** or nominee or a person acting according to direction.

2.1.2 Encouraging another to deal

An offence is also committed if an individual, having information as an insider, **encourages another person** to deal in price-affected securities in relation to that information. They must **know** or have reasonable cause to believe that **dealing** would **take place**.

It is irrelevant whether:

- The person encouraged realises that the securities are **price-affected** securities

- The **inside information is given** to that person. For example, a simple recommendation to the effect that 'I cannot tell you why, but now would be a good time to buy shares in Bloggs plc' would infringe the law

- **Any dealing takes place**, the offence being committed at the time of encouragement

2.2 Securities covered by the Act

Securities include **shares** and **associated derivatives**, **debt securities** and **warranties**.

2.3 Inside information

ey term

> **Inside information** is **'price-sensitive information'** relating to a **particular issuer** of **securities** that are price-affected and not to securities generally.

Inside information must, if made public, be likely to have a **significant effect on price** and it must be **specific or precise**. 'Specific' would, for example, mean information that a takeover bid would be made for a specific company; 'precise' information would be details of how much would be offered for shares.

2.4 Insiders

Under the CJA a person has information as an **insider** if it is (**and** they **know** it is) inside information, and if they have it (**and know** they have) from an inside source:

- Through being a **director**, **employee** or **shareholder** of an issuer of securities
- Through access because of **employment**, **office** or **profession**

A person does not have to actually be one of the above to be an insider. They will also be an insider if they are given the **inside information** by someone who is an **inside source** – for example, a friend or family member.

2.5 General defences

An individual has a **defence** regarding **dealing and encouraging others to deal** if they prove that:

- They did **not expect** there to be a **profit** or avoidance of loss
- They had **reasonable grounds** to **believe** that the information had been **disclosed widely** enough to ensure that those taking part in the dealing would be prejudiced by having the information
- They would have **done** what they did **even** if they did not have the **information**, for example, where securities are sold to pay a pressing debt

Defences to **disclosure of information** by an individual are that:

- They **did not expect** any person to deal
- Although dealing was expected, **profit** or **avoidance of loss** was **not expected**

2.6 'Made public'

Information is made public if:

- It is **published** under the rules of the regulated market, such as the Stock Exchange
- It is in **public records**, for example, notices in the *London Gazette*
- It can **readily be acquired** by those likely to deal
- It is **derived** from **public information**

Information **may** be treated as made public even though:

- It can **only** be **acquired** by **exercising diligence** or expertise (helping analysts to avoid liability).
- It is **communicated only** to a **section** of the **public** (thus protecting the 'brokers' lunch' where a company informs only selected City sources of important information).
- It can be **acquired** only by **observation**.
- It is **communicated** only on a **payment of a fee** or is published outside the UK.

2.7 Penalties

Maximum penalties given by the statute are **seven years' imprisonment** and/or an **unlimited fine**. Contracts remain valid and enforceable at civil law.

2.8 Territorial scope

The offender or any professional intermediary must be **in the UK** at the time of the offence, or the market must be a UK-regulated market.

2.9 Problems with the laws on insider dealing

FAST FORWARD

The law on insider dealing has had some **limitations**, and new offences, such as market abuse, have been brought in to reduce security-related crime.

The courts may have problems deciding whether information is **specific** or **precise**. The statute states that information shall be treated as relating to an issuer of securities not only when it is **about the company** but also where it may **affect the business prospects** of the company.

The requirement that price-sensitive information has a **significant effect on price** limits the application of the legislation to fundamental matters. These include an impending takeover, or profit or dividend levels which would be out of line with market expectations. As a result, the concept of **'market abuse'** was introduced in the UK in 2000. This was partly in response to the perceived ineffectiveness of the insider dealing provisions in the Criminal Justice Act 1993.

Exam focus point

Exam questions may be set on insider dealing and market abuse. If this is the case, remember that insider dealing is a criminal offence, market abuse is a civil matter.

3 Market abuse

ST FORWARD

Market abuse relates to behaviour which amounts to abuse of a person's position regarding the stock market.

y term

Market abuse is behaviour which satisfies one or more of the prescribed conditions likely to be regarded as a failure on the part of the person or persons concerned to **observe the standard of behaviour reasonably expected of a person in their position in relation to the market**.

The offence of **market abuse** under the Financial Services and Markets Act 2000 complements legislation covering insider dealing by providing a civil law alternative. The FCA has issued a **Code of Market Conduct,** which applies to any person dealing in certain investments on recognised exchanges and which does not require proof of intent to abuse a market.

The FCA has statutory civil powers to impose unlimited fines for the offence of **market abuse. It also has statutory** powers to require information, and requires anyone to co-operate with investigations into market abuse.

Market abuse is often connected with activities such as **recklessly making a statement** or **forecast** that is **misleading, false or deceptive**, or engaging in a **misleading course of conduct** for the purpose of inducing another person to exercise, or refrain from exercising, rights in relation to investments.

3.1 Examples of market abuse

The following are other examples of behaviour that would constitute **market abuse**.

3.1.1 Misuse of information

This is any behaviour by an individual that is based on information that is **not publically available**, but if it was, it would **influence an investor's decision**. For example, a person who buys shares in a company that they know is a takeover target of their employer, before a general disclosure of the proposed takeover is made.

3.1.2 Manipulating transactions

This behaviour involves **interfering with the normal process of share prices** moving up and down in accordance with supply and demand for the shares. For example, an individual who trades, or places orders to trade, that create a misleading impression of the supply or demand of securities and that has the effect of raising the price of the investment to an abnormal or artificial level.

3.1.3 Manipulating devices

This behaviour is the same as manipulating transactions except that the trading is followed by the **creation of false statements**, so that other investors make incorrect trading decisions. For example, an individual buys a large number of shares to artificially raise the share price and then makes false statements to the market that encourage other investors to buy the shares, driving the price up further.

3.1.4 Market distortion

This is any behaviour that **interferes with the normal process of market prices** moving up and down in accordance with supply and demand, such as a Chief Executive Officer who increases the activities of their business in order to make the company appear busier than it actually is. This improves the image and prospects of the business and suggests that a share price increase is imminent, encouraging investors to buy shares.

3.1.5 Dissemination of information

This behaviour involves the creation of **false or misleading information** about supply and demand or prices and values of investments and then leaking it into the public domain. For example, a person who posts an inaccurate story about a company's future plans on an internet bulletin board.

Remarks made by the judge when sentencing in *R v Bailey 2005* suggested that **directors will be held personally responsible for public announcements** in order to ensure the integrity of the market is preserved and the public protected.

4 Money laundering

4.1 What is money laundering?

> **FAST FORWARD**
>
> Money laundering is the attempt to **make money from criminal activity appear legitimate**, by disguising its original source.

Key term

> **Money laundering** is the term given to attempts to make the proceeds of crime appear respectable.
>
> It covers any activity by which the apparent source and ownership of money representing the proceeds of income are changed, so that the money appears to have been obtained legitimately.

Money laundering is a **crime** that is **against the interests of the state**, and it is associated with drug and people trafficking in particular, and with organised crime in general.

Money laundering legislation has been influenced by a number of different Acts of Parliament:

- Drug Trafficking Offences Act 1986
- Criminal Justice Act 1993
- Terrorism Act 2000
- Anti-terrorism Crime and Security Act 2001
- Proceeds of Crime Act 2002
- Money Laundering Regulations 2007

4.2 Categories of criminal offence

> **FAST FORWARD**
>
> In the UK, there are various offences relating to **money laundering**, including tipping off a money launderer (or suspected money launderer) and failing to report reasonable suspicions.

There are **three categories of criminal offences** in the Proceeds of Crime Act.

- **Laundering**: acquisition, possession or use of the proceeds of criminal conduct, or assisting another to retain the proceeds of criminal conduct and concealing, disguising, converting, transferring or removing criminal property. This relates to its nature, source, location, disposition, movement or ownership of the property. Money laundering includes possession of the proceeds of one's own crime, and facilitating any handling or possession of criminal property, which may take any form, including in money or money's worth, securities, tangible property and intangible property. There is no *de minimis* limit, so an offence may be committed in respect of only $1.

- **Failure to report** by an individual: failure to disclose knowledge or suspicion of money laundering (suspicion is more than mere speculation, but falls short of proof or knowledge).

- **Tipping off**: disclosing information to any person if disclosure may prejudice an investigation into drug trafficking, drug money laundering, terrorist-related activities, or laundering the proceeds of criminal conduct.

For the purposes of laundering, '**criminal property**' is defined by the CJA as property which the alleged offender knows (or suspects) constitutes or represents being related to any criminal conduct.

This is any conduct that constitutes or would constitute an offence in the UK. In relation to **laundering**, a person may have a **defence** if they make disclosure to the authorities:

- As soon as possible after the transaction
- Before the transaction takes place

Alternatively, they may have a defence if they can show there was a **reasonable excuse** for not making a disclosure.

In relation to **failure to report**, the person who suspects money laundering must disclose this to a nominated **Money Laundering Reporting Officer** (MLRO) within their organisation if it has one, or alternatively directly to the **National Crime Agency** (NCA) in the form of a Suspicious Activity Report (SAR). The NCA has responsibility in the UK for collecting and disseminating information related to money laundering and related activities. The nominated MLRO in an organisation acts as a filter and notifies NCA too.

In relation to **tipping off**, this covers the situation when a person making a disclosure to the NCA also tells the person at the centre of their suspicions about the disclosure. There is a **defence** to the effect that the person did not know that tipping off would prejudice an investigation.

4.3 Penalties

The law sets out the following penalties in relation to money laundering:

(a) 14 years' imprisonment and/or a fine, for **knowingly assisting** in the **laundering** of criminal funds

(b) 5 years' imprisonment and/or a fine, for **failure to report knowledge** or the **suspicion** of money laundering

(c) 5 years' imprisonment and/or a fine for **tipping off** a suspected launderer.

The **money laundering process** usually involves three phases:

- **Placement** – this is the initial disposal of the proceeds of the initial illegal activity into apparently legitimate business activity or property

- **Layering** – this involves the transfer of monies from business to business, or place to place, to conceal the original source

- **Integration** – having been layered, the money has the appearance of legitimate funds

For accountants, the most worrying aspect of the law on money laundering relates to the offence of '**failing to disclose**'. It is relatively straightforward to identify actual 'knowledge' of money laundering, and therefore the need to disclose it, but the term 'suspicion' of money laundering is not defined. The nearest there is to a definition is that suspicion is more than mere speculation but falls short of proof or knowledge. It is a question of judgement.

To fulfill PO4 you should comply with all money laundering regulations and contact the relevant person in your organisation if you have any suspicions that it may be occuring.

4.4 The Money Laundering Regulations 2007

The **Money Laundering Regulations 2007** require **organisations** to **establish internal systems** and **procedures** which are designed to deter criminals from using the organisation to launder money or finance terrorism. Such systems also assist in detecting the crime and prosecuting the perpetrators.

These regulations apply to all '**relevant persons**', a term which covers a wide range of organisations, including banking and investment businesses, accountants and auditors, tax advisers, lawyers, estate agents and casinos.

As each organisation is different, **systems** should be designed which are **appropriate and tailored to each business**.

These include:

(a) **Internal reporting procedures**

These should include appointing a Money Laundering Reporting Officer (MLRO) to receive internal reports of suspected money laundering and, where appropriate, to report them to the NCA.

(b) **Customer due diligence measures**

These should include identifying and verifying customers and monitoring the business relationship according to the level of risk of money laundering.

(c) **Record-keeping procedures**

Such procedures may include, for example, retaining copies of customer identity details such as passports. These procedures are important in proving compliance with the regulations.

(d) **Ensuring that employees are educated**

Employees should receive appropriate training concerning the law relating to money laundering and the business's policies and procedures in dealing with it.

Should a business fail to implement these measures a criminal offence, punishable with a maximum sentence of **two years' imprisonment and/or an unlimited fine**, is committed irrespective of whether money laundering has taken place. Civil penalties may also be imposed.

<table>
<tr><td>

Exam focus point

</td><td>

You must be clear as to how these rules seek to prevent or minimise money laundering.

</td></tr>
</table>

5 Bribery

FAST FORWARD

Bribery is a serious offence which often relates to the **offering** and **receiving** of **gifts** or **hospitality**.

The **Bribery Act 2010** came into effect in July 2011. The Act brought together, and is intended to simplify, the previous law on bribery and corruption, which was contained in both common law and statute.

5.1 Bribery offences

The **Bribery Act** created **four main offences,** the first three of which are committed by **individuals,** while the fourth is a **corporate** offence. The offences are:

- Bribing another person
- Being bribed
- Bribing a foreign public official
- Corporate failure to prevent bribery

5.1.1 Bribing another person

This offence is committed where a person **offers, promises or gives financial** or **other advantages** to another person with the intention of inducing that person to **perform improperly** a **relevant function** or **activity**, or to **reward** them for such **improper performance**.

It does not matter whether or not the person being bribed is the **same person** as the one who would **usually perform** the function or whether the offer is made **directly** or via a **third party**. This offence can also be committed where **acceptance of an advantage** itself **constitutes improper performance** of a function or activity.

5.1.2 Being bribed

This offence committed where a person **requests** or **accepts** a **financial** or **other advantage improperly**, or as a **reward** for **improper performance** of a **relevant function** or **activity**, or intending **that improper performance should result**. It does not matter whether the advantage is received **direct** or through a **third party**. The offence also applies if a person **receives** a benefit on **behalf of another person**.

5.1.3 Relevant function or activity

Both of the above offences make reference to a **'relevant function or activity'** and it is important to be aware of what this means. In terms of the Act, a relevant function or activity includes any function of **a public nature** or any **activity connected with business** or **carried out in the course of employment**. It applies to individuals who perform that function or activity from a **position of trust** or are otherwise expected to perform it in **good faith** or **impartially**.

It is irrelevant whether the **function** or **activity** has a **connection with the UK** – for example if it is performed outside the UK. 'Improper' performance means performance which does not meet the **standard** that a **reasonable person** in the UK would expect.

5.1.4 Bribing a foreign public official

This offence is similar to that of **bribing another person**, but is committed where the bribe is offered to a **foreign public official** (FPO). It is committed where a person offers financial or other advantages to an **FPO** or a **third party** with the intention of influencing the FPO in that capacity and to obtain or retain business or an advantage in the conduct of business, where that official is not permitted or required by the written law applicable to them to be so influenced.

An **FPO** is any individual who holds a **legislative**, **administrative** or **judicial position** of any kind outside the UK, or who exercises a **public function** outside the UK, or who is an **official** or **agent** of a **public international organisation**.

5.1.5 Defences and penalties for individual offences

It is a **defence** for an individual charged with a bribery offence if they can prove that their **conduct was necessary for the proper exercise of any function of an intelligence service** or the **proper exercise of any function of the armed forces when engaged on active service**.

The maximum **penalty** for bribery under the Act is **ten years' imprisonment** and/or an **unlimited fine**.

5.1.6 Corporate failure to prevent bribery

The offence of corporate failure to prevent bribery is **committed by an organisation** that **fails to prevent** a **bribery offence** being committed by a **person who performs services** for it in any capacity – such as an agent, employee or subsidiary. Under the Act, an **organisation** includes **companies** and **partnerships** based in the UK or doing business in the UK.

5.1.7 Defence and penalties for corporate offences

An organisation has a **defence** to this offence if it can prove that it had in place **'adequate procedures'** designed to prevent persons associated with it from committing bribery.

'Adequate procedures' are not defined by the Act, but the Secretary of State's non-prescriptive published guidance on adequate procedures is based around six principles:

(a) **Proportionate procedures** – organisations should have procedures in place aimed at preventing bribery. The scale and complexity of the procedures should be proportionate to the size of the organisation. The procedures expected of a small organisation will differ from that of a large one.

(b) **Top-level commitment** – an organisation's senior management should be committed to preventing bribery and should foster a culture in the organisation that sees bribery as unacceptable.

(c) **Risk assessment** – organisations should assess the nature and extent of their exposure to bribery from both inside and outside the organisation. Some industries and some overseas markets are seen, by their nature, as more susceptible to bribery and therefore risk assessments in these areas should be even more stringent.

(d) **Due diligence** – organisations should perform due diligence procedures in respect of those who perform services for the organisation or on its behalf, to mitigate the risk of bribery.

(e) **Communication** – anti-bribery policies and procedures should be embedded in the fabric of the organisation and communicated both internally and externally. This is likely to include relevant training, if proportionate to the risk.

(f) **Monitoring and review** – the anti-bribery policies and procedures should be regularly monitored and reviewed. Amendments and improvements must be made as appropriate. This is because the risks an organisation faces will change, so adaptation is necessary.

Whether an organisation had **adequate procedures is a matter for the courts** who will look at the particular circumstances an organisation is faced with. However, the onus is on the organisation to prove that its procedures were adequate. **Reasonable** and **proportionate hospitality** is **not prohibited,** although what is reasonable and proportionate will be determined in future cases.

The **maximum penalty** that may be imposed on a guilty organisation is an **unlimited fine.** However, it is likely that its **business will suffer,** too, as a consequence of **loss of reputation** and **compensation payable** for civil claims against the directors for failure to maintain adequate procedures.

Bribery cases are mainly heard in magistrates' and Crown Courts and go largely unreported. Examples of cases that have resulted in convictions include a court clerk who accepted £500 for not adding motoring offences to the court record; a person taking a driving test to become a taxi driver, who offered £300 to their examiner to turn a failure into a pass; and a university student who offered his tutors £5,000 for remarking an essay from a 37% fail to a pass at 40%.

Exam focus point

> The Bribery Act was the subject of a technical article in *Student Accountant* and is available on the ACCA website.

6 Criminal activity relating to companies

We have already seen a number of potential **crimes** in relation to the operation and management of companies, and the way in which these can be investigated.

With regard to the **operation and management of companies**, a company as a legal person may be prosecuted for many different types of crime. However, this is nearly always in conjunction with the directors and/or managers of the company. Companies have been prosecuted for manslaughter (unsuccessfully), fraud and breaches of numerous laws for which fines are stated as being punishment, such as health and safety laws.

Where there is evidence that a company or partnership has committed certain offences, such as fraud, money laundering, bribery or forgery, it is possible for the prosecution and the organisation to make a **deferred prosecution agreement** (DPA) under the **Crime and Courts Act 2013**.

Such agreements mean that the **organisation admits wrongdoing** but stops short of pleading guilty to the offence. In return, a judge awards a fine against the business, but **no criminal prosecution takes place**. This saves the prosecution time and money in bringing the case to court and, in return, the organisation is saved the reputational damage that a court case would bring.

It is up to the **prosecution** to determine whether a DPA should be offered. Offering it should be in the interests of justice and its terms must be fair, reasonable and proportionate. No individual should benefit from the offer of a DPA, which is why they are only offered to business organisations.

6.1 Criminal offences in relation to winding up

ST FORWARD

> **Criminal offences** in relation to **winding up** include: making a declaration of solvency without reasonable grounds and fraudulent trading.

Prosecutions are often brought against directors of **insolvent** companies for **fraudulent** trading and **wrongful trading**.

The law seeks to **protect creditors** who may be disadvantaged by the company being liquidated. **Directors** can be found guilty of various criminal offences if they try to **deceive** creditors and, in some cases, even if they do not attempt to deceive creditors, but the effect is the same as if they had.

6.2 Declaration of solvency

A winding up can only be a members' voluntary winding up if the company is solvent. If the company is not solvent, the creditors are far more involved in the winding-up process. In order to carry out a members' voluntary winding up, the directors have to file a **declaration of solvency**.

It is a **criminal offence** punishable by fine or imprisonment for a director to make a **declaration of solvency without** having **reasonable grounds** for it. If the company proves to be insolvent, they will have to justify their previous decision, or be punished.

6.3 Fraudulent trading

This **criminal offence** occurs under the **Companies Act 2006**, where a company has traded with **intent to defraud creditors** or for any fraudulent purpose. For example, a director obtaining credit when there is no good reason to expect that the company will be able to repay the debt; *R v Grantham 1984*. Offenders are liable to imprisonment for up to ten years or a fine.

There is also a **civil offence** of the same name under section 213 of the Insolvency Act 1986 that applies to companies which are in liquidation or administration. Under this offence courts may declare that **any persons** who were knowingly parties to carrying on the business in this fashion shall be liable for the debts of the company.

Various rules have been established to determine **what is fraudulent trading**:

(a) Only persons who **take the decision** to carry on the company's business in this way, or play some active part, are liable.

(b) **'Carrying on business'** can include a single transaction and also the mere payment of debts as distinct from making trading contracts.

(c) It relates not only to **defrauding creditors**, but also to carrying on a business for the purpose of any kind of fraud.

Under the civil offence, if the liquidator considers that there has been fraudulent trading they should apply to the court for an order that those responsible are liable to make good to the company all, or some specified part of, the **company's debts**.

6.4 Wrongful trading

The problem which faced the creditors of an insolvent company before the introduction of **'wrongful trading'** was that it was exceptionally difficult to prove the necessary fraud. Therefore a further civil liability for 'wrongful trading' was introduced, which means that the director will have to make such contribution to the company's assets as the court sees fit.

Directors will be liable if the liquidator or administrator proves the following.

(a) The director(s) of the insolvent company **knew**, or **should have known**, that there was **no reasonable prospect** that the **company** could **have avoided insolvency**. This means that directors cannot claim they lacked knowledge, if their lack of knowledge was a result of failing to comply with Companies Act requirements, such as preparation of accounts.

(b) The director(s) did not take **sufficient steps** to minimise the potential loss to the creditors.

Directors will be deemed to know that the company could not avoid insolvency if that would have been the conclusion of a **reasonably diligent person** with the **general knowledge**, **skill and experience** that might reasonably be expected of a person carrying out that particular director's duties. If the director has greater than usual skill, then they will be judged with reference to their own capacity.

6.5 Other offences in relation to winding up

Other **offences** which may be committed just before or during a liquidation include the following.

6.5.1 Acting as a director whilst disqualified

The **Company Directors Disqualification Act 1986** makes a person who **acts as a director whilst disqualified** personally liable for the company's debts. Directors of insolvent companies may be disqualified under the Act if the court deems they are unfit to be involved in the management of a company.

6.5.2 Phoenix companies

Phoenix companies are created by directors of insolvent companies as a **method of continuing their business**. Very often they have similar names as (or similar enough to suggest an association with) the insolvent company. The Insolvency Act 1986 makes it a **criminal offence** where a director **creates such a company within five years of the original company being liquidated**. The person is liable for a fine or imprisonment.

6.5.3 Fraud and deception

The Insolvency Act 1986 makes it a criminal offence to **conceal** or **fraudulently remove company assets** or **debt** – including falsifying records. It is also an offence to **dispose of property** that was **acquired on credit** that has **not been paid** for.

6.5.4 Defrauding creditors

Once a winding up commences, the Insolvency Act 1986 makes it an offence to make a **gift** of, or **transfer company property**, unless it can be proved there was no intent to defraud creditors.

6.5.5 Misconduct during a liquidation

A **company officer** may be **liable** for a number of offences due to their **misconduct**. These include:

- Not identifying company property to the liquidator
- Not delivering requested books and papers to the liquidator
- Not informing the liquidator if identified debts do not turn out to be debts

6.5.6 Falsification of company books

The **destruction**, **mutilation**, **alteration** or **falsification of company books** is an offence under the Insolvency Act 1986.

6.5.7 Omissions

It is an offence under the Insolvency Act 1986 to **omit material information** when making statements concerning a company's affairs.

6.6 Examples: offences in relation to winding up

The standard expected of a listed company director would be **higher** than for the director of a small owner-managed private company.

Halls v David and Another 1989

The facts: The directors sought to obtain relief from liability for wrongful trading by the application of the Companies Act 2006. This stated that in proceedings for negligence, default, breach of duty or breach of trust against a director, if it appears that he has acted honestly and reasonably the court may relieve him wholly or partly from liability on such terms as it sees fit.

Decision: The Companies Act 2006 is not available to excuse a director from liability.

Re Produce Marketing Consortium Ltd 1989

The facts: Two months after the case above, the same liquidator sought an order against the same directors - this time, that they should contribute to the company assets (which were in the hands of the liquidator) since they had been found liable for wrongful trading.

Decision: The directors were jointly and severally liable for the sum of £75,000 plus interest, along with the costs of the case. The judge stated that the fact that wrongful trading was not based on fraud was not a reason for giving a nominal or low figure of contribution. The figure should, however, be assessed in the light of all the circumstances of the case.

This case was significant for creditors, since the assets available for distribution in a winding up will (potentially) be much increased by a **large directors' contribution**. It serves as a warning to directors to take professional advice sooner rather than later.

6.7 Companies Act 2006 offences

The Companies Act 2006 includes provision for a **number of offences** in relation to the **management** and **operation** of a company.

6.7.1 Company records

Company records and **registers**, such as the register of members and record of resolutions, **must be kept adequately for future reference**. Officers in default are liable to a fine. **Falsification** of **information**, **hiding falsification,** or **failing to prevent falsification** are also offences and the wrongdoer is liable to a fine.

6.7.2 Accounting records

Where a company fails to **keep adequate accounting records**, every officer who defaults is subject to a fine. However, they have a **defence** if they **acted honestly** and the **circumstances** surrounding the company's business makes the default **excusable**.

6.7.3 Trading disclosures

Companies are required to disclose **certain information** (such as its name) in **specific locations**. If these disclosures are not made then defaulting officers are criminally liable for a fine and may also be liable for losses under the civil law.

6.7.4 Filing accounts

If a company fails to **file its accounts within the time limit following its year end** then any defaulting officer is liable to a fine. However they will have a **defence** if they took **reasonable steps** to **ensure the requirements** were **complied with.**

6.7.5 False information

Company officers are liable for making **false disclosures** in relation to the **directors' report**, **directors' remuneration report** and **summary financial statements** based on those reports. An officer is also liable for **providing false** or **misleading information to an auditor**. Punishment is either imprisonment or a fine.

6.8 The Fraud Act 2006

The **Fraud Act 2006,** to which directors and secretaries are subject, created a **single offence of fraud,** which a person can commit in three different ways by:

- **False representation**: dishonestly making a false representation of fact or law, intending thereby to make a gain for themselves or another, or to cause another party loss, or to expose that party to the risk of making loss

- **Failure to disclose information when there is a legal duty to do so**: dishonestly failing to disclose to another person information which they are under a legal duty to disclose, thereby intending to make a gain for themselves or another, or to cause another party loss or expose that party to the risk of making loss

- **Abuse of position**: occupying a position in which they are expected to safeguard, or not to act against, the financial interest of another person, and dishonestly abusing that position, thereby intending to make a gain for themselves or another, or to cause another party loss or expose that party to the risk of suffering loss

Chapter Roundup

- Crime is **conduct prohibited by the law**. Financial crime can be international in nature, and there is a need for international co-operation to prevent it.

- Insider dealing is the statutory offence of **dealing** in securities while in **possession** of **inside information** as an insider, the securities being price-affected by the information.

- The law on insider dealing has had some **limitations**, and new offences, such as market abuse, have been brought in to reduce security-related crime.

- **Market abuse** relates to behaviour which amounts to abuse of a person's position regarding the stock market.

- Money laundering is the attempt to **make money from criminal activity appear legitimate** by disguising its original source.

- In the UK, there are various offences relating to **money laundering**, including tipping off a money launderer (or suspected money launderer) and failing to report reasonable suspicions.

- **Bribery** is a serious offence which often relates to the **offering** and **receiving** of **gifts** or **hospitality**.

- **Criminal offences** in relation to **winding up** include: making a declaration of solvency without reasonable grounds and fraudulent trading.

Quick Quiz

1   Insider dealing is a criminal offence.

   True   ☒

   False   ☐

2   **Fill in the blanks.**

   Inside information is 'Price-sensitive information' relating to a particular issuer of **securities** that
   are price-affected and not to securities generally.

3   Define money laundering.

4   Which one of the following is **not** a UK offence relating to money laundering?

   A   Concealing the proceeds of criminal activity
   B   Tipping off
   C   Dealing in price-affected securities
   D   Failing to report suspicion of money laundering

5   What is placement?

Answers to Quick Quiz

1   True. Insider dealing is a criminal offence.

2   **Inside information** is **'price-sensitive information'** relating to a **particular issuer** of **securities** that are
   price-affected and not to securities generally.

3   **Money laundering** is the term given to attempts to make the proceeds of crime appear respectable.

   It covers any activity by which the apparent source and ownership of money representing the proceeds of
   income are changed so that the money appears to have been obtained legitimately.

4   C. This could be insider dealing, if the person dealing was an insider and was using inside information.

5   Placement is the disposal of the initial proceeds of the illegal activity.

Now try the questions below from the Practice Question Bank

Number
49, 50, 51

Practice question and
answer bank

Question 1

Which of the following describes the role of judges in a civil law legal system?

- A   To draft the law only
- B   To apply the law only
- C   To draft and apply the law   (1 mark)

Question 2

In Sharia law, what is the name given to the concept of unlawful gain, which is usually translated as meaning interest?

- A   Riba
- B   Ijma
- C   Sunnah
- D   Qiyas   (2 marks)

Question 3

In the English civil law system, which TWO of the following are the parties involved in a case?

- (1)   Prosecution
- (2)   Accused
- (3)   Defendant
- (4)   Claimant

- A   1 and 4
- B   1 and 2
- C   2 and 3
- D   3 and 4   (2 marks)

Question 4

In the English legal system, one role of a judge is to interpret statute law.

Which rule of statutory interpretation considers what the legislation is trying to achieve?

- A   Golden rule
- B   Purposive approach
- C   Literal rule
- D   Contextual rule   (2 marks)

Question 5

Which of the following statements describes conflict of laws?

- A   Disagreements between nations concerning protectionist trade policies

- B   Disagreements between nations concerning differences between human rights legislation

- C   Disagreements between business organisations in different nations caused by different national laws   (1 mark)

Question 6

The International Court of Arbitration was set up by which of the following organisations?

A   OECD
B   WTO
C   EU
D   ICC

(2 marks)

Question 7

To act as a forum to discuss, develop and refine economic and social policies is the purpose of which international organisation?

A   WTO
B   UNCITRAL
C   ICC
D   OECD

(2 marks)

Question 8

Which of the following statements, regarding the validity of arbitration agreements under the UNCITRAL Model Law on International Commercial Arbitration, is correct?

A   Arbitration agreements must be in writing
B   Arbitration agreements must be filed with the International Court of Arbitration
C   Arbitration agreements must specify the arbitrators that should be appointed

(1 mark)

Question 9

Under the UNCITRAL Model Law on International Commercial Arbitration, in which form should arbitral awards be made?

A   Newspaper announcement
B   Verbal
C   Web page
D   In writing to the parties

(2 marks)

Question 10

In the English criminal law system, in which court do all cases begin?

A   Divisional Court of Queen's Bench
B   Magistrates' court
C   Crown Court

(1 mark)

Question 11

At which point is a contract formed under the UN Convention on Contracts for the International Sale of Goods?

A   When both the offeror and offeree have performed their obligations under a validly accepted offer
B   When an offer has been made and validly accepted
C   When an offer has been made
D   When the offeror has performed their obligations under a validly accepted offer

(2 marks)

Question 12

At which point does acceptance become effective under the UN Convention on Contracts for the International Sale of Goods?

A   When it is written
B   When it is posted
C   When it is delivered to the offeror   **(1 mark)**

Question 13

Which of the following ICC Incoterms applies only to contracts involving marine transport?

A   FAS
B   DAP
C   DDP
D   FCA   **(2 marks)**

Question 14

Which of the following correctly states the conformity requirements for goods sold under the UN Convention on Contracts for the International Sale of Goods?

A   Fit for any purpose the buyer may put them to
B   Fit for the purpose that the goods could reasonably be put to
C   Fit for the purpose that goods of the same description would ordinarily be used   **(1 mark)**

Question 15

Under the UN Convention on Contracts for the International Sale of Goods, where a buyer is late in paying for the goods, which of the following remedies is the seller entitled to?

A   Damages only
B   Interest only
C   Interest and damages   **(1 mark)**

Question 16

Under the UN Convention on Contracts for the International Sale of Goods, where a contract includes carriage but does not state where risk passes, at which point does the risk to the goods pass from seller to buyer?

A   When the buyer receives the goods
B   When the goods are passed to the first carrier for delivery to the buyer
C   When the goods leave the seller's country of export
D   When the goods enter the buyer's country of import   **(2 marks)**

Question 17

Lise, a wholesaler from Snodland, entered into a contract with Pascal, a manufacturer from Pipland to supply her with machinery that was to be built according to her specific design. Several months into Pascal's build process, Lise decided that she did not require the machines after all, and notified Pascal of her intention not to pay for the machines.

You should assume that the UN Convention on Contracts for the International Sale of Goods applies.

Required

(a)   State the type of breach of contract that Lise committed.   **(2 marks)**

(b)   Explain the most appropriate remedy for Pascal for Lise's breach of contract.   **(4 marks)**

(Total = 6 marks)

Question 18

What is the name given to a letter, issued by a parent company to a potential creditor of one of its subsidiaries, that acknowledges the parent company's approval of the subsidiary's attempt to raise finance?

A   Letter of support

B   Letter of comfort

C   Letter of endorsement

D   Letter of credit   **(2 marks)**

Question 19

What is the name of the process that allows an International Bill of Exchange to be presented for payment by a different party than the one originally intended?

A   Transfer

B   Negotiation

C   Endorsement   **(1 mark)**

Question 20

Under the UN Convention on International Bills of Exchange and International Promissory Notes, what is the person who receives the payment known as?

A   Drawee

B   Payee

C   Acceptor

D   Drawer   **(2 marks)**

Question 21

BCD Co ordered a consignment of commercial widgets from XYZ Co, which is based in another country. Payment for the widgets was to be made by bank transfer. The transfer process would be begun by BCD Co instructing its bank, F-bank, to transfer funds to G-bank based in the same country as XYZ Co. G-bank would then handle the transfer to XYZ Co's bank, H-bank. H-bank would then make the funds available to XYZ Co.

During the transfer, G-bank delayed the transfer to H-bank by several days and XYZ Co is seeking compensation.

You should assume that the UNCITRAL Model Law on International Credit Transfer applies.

Required

(a)	State the TWO parties that are defined as the 'originator'.	**(2 marks)**
(b)	State the party that is the receiving bank.	**(2 marks)**
(c)	State whether XYZ Co is entitled to a remedy for the delay caused by G-bank.	**(2 marks)**

(Total = 6 marks)

Question 22

'Holding out' is a key element of which form of agency?

A   Agency by estoppel
B   Agency by necessity
C   Agency by implied agreement   **(1 mark)**

Question 23

What is the extent of an agent's ostensible authority?

A   What is usual in the circumstances only
B   What is implied from the agency relationship only
C   What the principal gives the agent expressly only
D   What is usual in the circumstances and what the principal gives them expressly or impliedly

(2 marks)

Question 24

In the context of partnership law, a partner's actual authority to bind the partnership in a contract is determined by which of the following?

A   What is agreed between the partners
B   The perception third parties have of the purpose of the partnership
C   The actual purpose of the partnership   **(1 mark)**

Question 25

To wind up a Limited Liability Partnership (LLP), which of the following is required?

A   An order from the Registrar of Companies
B   It must be formally wound up
C   A deed signed by the partners
D   A court order   **(2 marks)**

Question 26

Which of the following companies does not have share capital?

A   A public company
B   A company limited by guarantee
C   An unlimited liability company   (1 mark)

Question 27

Which of the following is a company that has its shares traded on a public stock exchange?

A   Unlimited company
B   Listed company
C   Public company
D   Private company   (2 marks)

Question 28

Before it can trade, which of the following criteria must a public company meet?

A   Its shares must be listed on a stock exchange
B   It must have appointed an auditor
C   It must obtain a trading certificate from the Registrar of Companies   (1 mark)

Question 29

Which of the following statements concerning promoters is correct?

A   A promoter may not make a profit as a result of their position

B   An accountant who acts in a professional capacity in the formation of a company is a promoter

C   A promoter may not own shares in the company that they are forming

D   A promoter that acts as an agent for others must not put themselves into a position where their own interests clash with that of the company they are forming   (2 marks)

Question 30

In regards to a company changing its articles of association, which of the following statements is correct?

A   A company must send copies of the amended articles to the Registrar of Companies within 28 days of the amendment taking place

B   A company may only change its articles once in a financial year

C   A company requires a special or written resolution with a 75% majority to change its articles   (1 mark)

Question 31

Under the Companies Act 2006, which of the following parties is contractually bound by a company's constitution?

A   Members in a capacity other than as a member
B   The company
C   Third parties with a business relationship with the company
D   Company directors   (2 marks)

Question 32

National Hair Brushes plc was incorporated in June 20X6. The directors have received a letter from another company, Lancashire Hair Brushes plc, stating that it was incorporated in 20X5, that its business is being adversely affected by the use of the new company name and demanding that National Hair Brushes plc changes the company name.

Required

(a) State the nature of a 'passing-off' action. **(2 marks)**

(b) State what Lancashire Hair Brushes would need to prove in order to establish that it is a victim of 'passing-off'. **(2 marks)**

(c) State an alternative course of action that Lancashire Hair Brushes could take to force National Hair Brushes to change its name. **(2 marks)**

(Total = 6 marks)

Question 33

Which of the following statements correctly describes a rights issue?

A   An offer to debentureholders to purchase shares in the company
B   An offer to existing shareholders to purchase further shares in the company
C   The allotment of additional shares to existing shareholders in proportion to their holdings **(1 mark)**

Question 34

Which of the following statements correctly describes a company's called up share capital?

A   The type, class, number and amount of shares issued and allotted to shareholders
B   The maximum amount of share capital that a company can have in issue
C   The amount the company has required shareholders to pay on existing shares
D   The amount shareholders have paid on existing shares **(2 marks)**

Question 35

A floating charge will crystallise on the occurrence of which of the following events?

A   Sale of the assets subject to the charge
B   Resignation of the finance director
C   The chargee appointing a receiver **(1 mark)**

Question 36

In the context of debentures, which of the following MUST be created using a debenture trust deed?

A   Debenture stock
B   A single debenture
C   Register of debentureholders
D   Series debentures **(2 marks)**

Question 37

Which type of dividend is paid by the issue of additional shares?

A   Scrip dividends
B   Equity dividends
C   Capital dividends   **(1 mark)**

Question 38

Dividends that are paid part of the way through a company's financial year are known by which of the following names?

A   Interim dividends
B   Semi-dividends
C   Dividends paid in specie
D   Preference dividends   **(2 marks)**

Question 39

Reginald owns 100 shares of Linsey Ltd. Each share has a nominal value of $2.50 and Reginald paid $1.00 per share on issue.

Linsey Ltd also issued some debentures which are secured as follows. A fixed charge over a property in favour of Margaret on 1 May 20X7. It then created a floating charge in favour of Chris over the same property on 13 May 20X7. The company has Chris's charge registered on 25 May 20X7, and Margaret's charge on 29 May 20X7.

Required

(a)   State the extent of Reginald's liability in the event of Linsey Ltd's liquidation.   **(2 marks)**
(b)   Explain the priority of the charges issued to Margaret and Chris.   **(4 marks)**

                                       (Total = 6 marks)

Question 40

Which of the following statements correctly describes a Chief Executive Officer's (Managing Director's) actual authority?

A   The authority that the Chief Executive Officer says to others they have
B   The authority that the board expressly gives to them
C   The authority that is usual for a Chief Executive Officer   **(1 mark)**

Question 41

Which of the following is a director who has not been validly appointed, but is held out by the company to be a director?

A   De facto director
B   De jure director
C   Alternate director
D   Shadow director   **(2 marks)**

Question 42

A company secretary is a company officer that MUST be appointed by which of the following companies?

A   Public limited company
B   Private limited company
C   Unlimited liability company   **(1 mark)**

Question 43

A company auditor has which of the following rights?

A   To vote in the company's general meetings
B   To attend board meetings
C   To appoint non-executive directors
D   To access, at all times, the books, accounts and vouchers of the company   **(2 marks)**

Question 44

What is the notice period for a meeting at which a special resolution is to be voted on?

A   14 days
B   21 days
C   28 days   **(1 mark)**

Question 45

The ordinary business of an annual general meeting includes which of the following?

A   Reducing the company's share capital
B   Changing the company's name
C   Appointing an administrator
D   Approving the payment of dividends   **(2 marks)**

Question 46

The Chief Executive Officer of KL Ltd is Jeremy. Jeremy also runs his own business, FD Ltd, in his spare time. KL Ltd recently contracted to buy a significant amount of commercial goods from FD Ltd. Jeremy attended the KL Ltd board meeting that approved the contract and voted in favour of it, without revealing his association with FD Ltd.

Required

(a)   State what is meant by a director's fiduciary duties.   **(2 marks)**
(b)   Explain which of a director's statutory duties Jeremy may have breached.   **(4 marks)**

(Total = 6 marks)

Question 47

There are various grounds for the compulsory winding-up of a company. In which of the following situations will a court order the winding up of a company on the 'just and equitable' ground?

A   Where 50% of the members disagree with the actions of the directors
B   Where the company has failed to pay its creditors for three months
C   When the main object of the company cannot be achieved   **(1 mark)**

Question 48

What is the name given to the person in charge of a voluntary winding up of a company?

A   Administrator
B   Receiver
C   Chargee
D   Liquidator   **(2 marks)**

Question 49

In the offence of money laundering, what is the name given to the initial disposal of the proceeds of criminal activity?

A   Placement
B   Layering
C   Integration   **(1 mark)**

Question 50

Which of the following is a defence to a charge of insider dealing?

A   The individual had reasonable grounds to believe that the information was about to be published
B   The individual had no expectation of profit
C   The individual was not seeking to profit from the transaction personally
D   The individual had reasonable grounds to believe their action was in the public interest   **(2 marks)**

Question 51

Vlad generates a substantial income from illegal tax evasion and sought advice from Gloria (his personal accountant) on how to dispose of his illegal earnings. Gloria suggested that to disguise the source of the funds, Vlad should purchase a chain of restaurants and pass his gains from the illegal operation through the restaurants' accounts. Vlad agreed with Gloria's proposal and appointed her as the restaurant chain's finance director and together they passed the illegal money through the operation.

Required

(a)   State the offence of money laundering.   **(2 marks)**
(b)   State whether Gloria has any liability for money laundering.   **(2 marks)**
(c)   State whether Vlad has any liability for money laundering.   **(2 marks)**

(Total = 6 marks)

Answer 1

B   In a civil law legal system, the role of judges is to apply the law. They do not create law.

Syllabus area A1(dii)

Answer 2

A   Riba is the concept of unlawful gain. Ijma is a consensus of opinion. Qiyas is an analogical deduction. Sunnah is a source of Shaira law.

Syllabus area A1(diii)

Answer 3

D   A civil law case is between the claimant and defendant. A criminal law case is between the prosecution and accused.

Syllabus area A1(a)

Answer 4

B   Under the purposive approach to statutory interpretation, the purpose (or what the legislation is trying to achieve) is considered.

Syllabus area A2(c)

Answer 5

C   Conflict of laws are disputes between parties in different nations – not between national governments. The disputes are caused by each country having different laws on a particular issue.

Syllabus area A2(a)

Answer 6

D   The ICC (International Chamber of Commerce) set up the International Court of Arbitration in 1923. The European Union (EU), WTO (World Trade Organisation) and OECD (Organisation for Economic Co-operation and Development) are all international organisations, but they did not set up the ICA.

Syllabus area A2(c)

Answer 7

D   The purpose of the Organisation for Economic Co-operation and Development (OECD) is to be a forum to discuss, develop and refine economic and social policies.

Syllabus area A2(c)

Answer 8

A   To be valid, arbitration agreements must be in writing. There is no need to specify arbitrators in the agreement and the agreement does not have to be filed with the ICA.

Syllabus area A3(c)

Answer 9

D The model law states that arbitral awards should be made in writing.

Syllabus area A3(d)

Answer 10

B In the English criminal law system, all cases begin in a magistrates' court.

Syllabus area A3(a)

Answer 11

B Under UNCISG, a contract is formed when a offer is validly accepted.

Syllabus area B1(b)

Answer 12

C Under UNCISG an acceptance becomes effective when it reaches the offeror.

Syllabus area B1(b)

Answer 13

A FAS means 'free alongside ship'. The seller discharges their obligations when the goods have been placed alongside the ship in the country of export.

Syllabus area B1(c)

Answer 14

C Under the UN Convention on Contracts for the International Sale of Goods, goods must be fit for the purpose for which goods of the same description would ordinarily be used.

Syllabus area B2(aii)

Answer 15

C Where a buyer is late in paying for the goods under a contract, the seller may claim interest on the overdue amount at the statutory rate. This does not prejudice any extra claim for damages.

Syllabus area B2(ciii)

Answer 16

B In these circumstances, risk passes when the goods are handed over to the first carrier for transmission to the buyer.

Syllabus area B2(d)

Answer 17

(a) Lise's notification that she does not intend to pay for the machines is an anticipatory breach. As it substantially deprives Pascal of what he is entitled to expect under the contract, this is a fundamental breach of contract.

(b) Pascal should first declare the contract avoided. There seems little point in him waiting to see if Lise changes her mind, because she has been very clear about her intentions. He will want to claim damages for the loss he has suffered as a result of Lise's fundamental breach, but he is under a duty to mitigate this loss.

Pascal has commenced work on the machines. Depending on the nature of the specification (that is, whether there is an open market for such machines), he might be best served finishing the machines and trying to sell them to another party. However, if the specification was unique for Lise and there is not likely to be an open market for the machinery, he would be better served by not incurring any further costs of production and, if possible, using the materials from the machines in other production.

Answer 18

B Such a letter is known as a letter of comfort. It usually offers the potential creditor no protection if the subsidiary becomes insolvent.

Syllabus area C1(e)

Answer 19

C Endorsement allows a bill of exchange to be presented for payment by a party other than the original payee.

Syllabus area C1(d)

Answer 20

B Under the model law, the party who receives the payment is the payee. The party making the payment is known as the drawer. The drawee is the party (usually a bank) on whom the bill is drawn and who has not accepted it. The acceptor is a party who takes liability for the bill above the drawer.

Syllabus area C1(d)

Answer 21

(a) The 'originator' is defined as the sender and the sender's bank. Therefore BCD Co and F-bank are the originator.

(b) The receiving bank is the bank in the beneficiary's state that receives the funds from the sender's state. In this case it is G-bank.

(c) Under the UNCITRAL Model Law on International Credit Transfer, the beneficiary is entitled to a payment of interest for any delay in the transfer process. Therefore XYZ Co is entitled to an interest payment from G-bank that is appropriate to the number of days of delay.

Answer 22

A   Agency by estoppel occurs where one party 'holds out' to another that a person is acting as their agent.

Syllabus area D1(b)

Answer 23

D   Ostensible authority is wide ranging and includes whatever is usual in the circumstances plus whatever the principal gives the agent, either expressly or impliedly.

Syllabus area D1(c)

Answer 24

A   Partnership authority is based on agency law. Actual authority is determined by what the partners agree.

Syllabus area D2(c)

Answer 25

B   To dissolve an LLP, it needs to be wound up, in a similar way to a company.

Syllabus area D2(e)

Answer 26

B   Companies limited by guarantee do not have share capital.

Syllabus area D3(c)

Answer 27

B   A public company does not have to have its shares traded on a public stock exchange. If it does so, then it becomes known as a listed (or quoted) company.

Syllabus area D3(c)

Answer 28

C   Before it can trade, a public company must be issued with a trading certificate from the Registrar of Companies. None of the other options are criteria for obtaining a trading certificate.

Syllabus area D4(c)

Answer 29

D   Where a promoter acts as an agent for others, they must not put themselves into a position where their own interests clash with those of the company. Accountants acting in a professional capacity are not promoters. A promoter may make a legitimate profit as a result of their position. There is nothing to stop a promoter from owning shares in the company that they form.

Syllabus area D4(a)

Answer 30

C   A special or written resolution with a 75% majority is sufficient to change a company's articles. There is no restriction on the number of times a year the articles may be changed. Copies of the amended articles must be submitted to the Registrar within 15 days of the amendment taking effect.

Syllabus area D4(g)

Answer 31

B   A company's constitution contractually binds the company and members in their capacity as members.

Syllabus area D4(e)

Answer 32

(a)   A 'passing-off action', is a common law action which applies when one company believes that another's conduct (here the use of a company name) is causing confusion in the minds of the public over the goods which each company sells.

(b)   In order to be successful, Lancashire Hair Brushes plc will need to satisfy the court that confusion has arisen because of National Hair Brushes' use of its registered name and that it lays claim to something exclusive and distinctive and not something in general use.

(c)   Lancashire Hair Brushes plc could object to the Company Names Adjudicator that the name National Hair Brushes is too like its own name and is causing confusion. They would be appealing for the Adjudicator to exercise their power under the Companies Act to compel a change of name.

Answer 33

B   A rights issue is an offer to existing shareholders to buy further shares in the company. A bonus issue is the allotment of additional shares to shareholders in proportion to their holdings.

Syllabus area E1(c)

Answer 34

C   Called-up share capital is the amount the company has required shareholders to pay on existing shares. A company's issued share capital is the type, class, number and amount of shares issued to shareholders. The amount which existing shareholders have paid on existing shares is the paid-up share capital.

Syllabus area E1(a)

Answer 35

C   Active intervention by the chargee, such as appointing a receiver, will cause the charge to crystallise. The other options will not cause the charge to crystallise.

Syllabus area E2(d)

Answer 36

A   Out of the options, only debenture stock must be created using a debenture trust deed. Single and series debentures may use a debenture trust deed, but this is not compulsory.

Syllabus area E2(b)

Answer 37

A   Scrip dividends are paid by issuing additional shares.

Syllabus area E3(b)

Answer 38

A   Dividends paid part of the way through a company's financial year are known as interim dividends. Dividends paid in specie are paid using a method other than cash.

Syllabus area E3(b)

Answer 39

(a)   Reginald is liable to pay the unpaid capital on his shares. This is $150 (100 × $1.50).

(b)   Margaret's charge would have taken precedence because it was created first and because it is a fixed charge, had it been registered within the allowed period of 21 days, up to 22 May. However it was not registered until 29 May, and Chris's charge was legitimately registered in the period between 22 and 29 May when Margaret's charge was void. The court would probably have allowed late registration of Margaret's charge, but not at the expense of Chris's rights.

Answer 40

B   A CEO's actual authority is whatever the board gives to them.

Syllabus area F1(c)

Answer 41

A   A de jure director is expressly appointed. A de facto director is held out by the company to be a director. A shadow director is neither; they are a person whose instructions the actual directors are accustomed to follow. An alternate director is appointed by a director of a company to attend and vote for them at board meetings they are unable to attend.

Syllabus area F1(a)

Answer 42

A   Only a public limited company must have a company secretary.

Syllabus area F2(a)

Answer 43

D   A company auditor has the right, at all times, to access the books, accounts and vouchers of the company.

Syllabus area F2(b)

Answer 44

A   14 days' notice is required for a special resolution.

Syllabus area F3(b)

Answer 45

D   Approving dividends is included in the ordinary business of an AGM.

Syllabus area F3(a)

Answer 46

(a)   Since they make contracts as agents of the company and have control of its property, directors are said to be akin to trustees and therefore owe fiduciary duties to the company. A fiduciary duty is one based on common law principles of trust and honesty. Therefore a director must act bona fide and honestly and not seek any personal advantage when dealing with the company.

(b)   Jeremy has disclosed neither his interest in FD Ltd nor his interest in this particular contract. Under s 177 of the Companies Act the interest should have been stated at the board meeting that Jeremy attended which approved the contract. It was not. It should also have been declared under s 182 of the Companies Act once it had occurred – but it was not, either. He will therefore have to account to KL Ltd for any profit that he makes on the transaction and he may also be subject to a fine. Had he dealt honestly with KL Ltd by declaring his interest and obtaining company approval, he would have been permitted to retain any profit which is made.

Answer 47

C   The 'just and equitable' ground will be applied where the object of the company cannot be achieved. For example, where the company only existed to 'work a particular patent' *Re German Date Coffee Co 1882*. The other options are not grounds for the just and equitable winding up of a company.

Syllabus area G1(b)

Answer 48

D   A liquidator is in charge of a voluntary winding up. The official receiver is in charge of a compulsory winding up. An administrator is in charge of an administration.

Syllabus area G1(a)

Answer 49

A   The initial disposal of the proceeds of a crime is known as placement.

Syllabus area H1(c)

Answer 50

B   No expectation of profit is a valid defence to a charge of insider dealing. The other options are not valid defences.

Syllabus area H1(a)

Answer 51

(a) Money laundering is the term given to attempts to make the proceeds of crime appear respectable. It covers any activity by which the apparent source and ownership of money representing the proceeds of crime are changed, so that the money appears to have been obtained legitimately.

(b) Gloria has assisted in Vlad's money laundering, so may be convicted of money laundering under the Proceeds of Crime Act. She may also be found guilty of failure to report under the Proceeds of Crime Act.

(c) Vlad is guilty of the main offence of money laundering, under the Proceeds of Crime Act.

List of cases and index

BPP
LEARNING MEDIA

Review Form – Paper F4 Corporate and Business Law (GLO) (02/16)

Please help us to ensure that the ACCA learning materials we produce remain as accurate and user-friendly as possible. We cannot promise to answer every submission we receive, but we do promise that it will be read and taken into account when we update this Study Text.

Name: _____   Address: _____

_____

_____

How have you used this Study Text?
(Tick one box only)

☐ On its own (book only)

☐ On a BPP in-centre course _____

☐ On a BPP online course

☐ On a course with another college

☐ Other _____

Why did you decide to purchase this Study Text? *(Tick one box only)*

☐ Have used BPP Study Texts in the past

☐ Recommendation by friend/colleague

☐ Recommendation by a lecturer at college

☐ Saw information on BPP website

☐ Saw advertising

☐ Other _____

During the past six months do you recall seeing/receiving any of the following?
(Tick as many boxes as are relevant)

☐ Our advertisement in *ACCA Student Accountant*

☐ Our advertisement in *Pass*

☐ Our advertisement in *PQ*

☐ Our brochure with a letter through the post

☐ Our website www.bpp.com

Which (if any) aspects of our advertising do you find useful?
(Tick as many boxes as are relevant)

☐ Prices and publication dates of new editions

☐ Information on Study Text content

☐ Facility to order books

☐ None of the above

Which BPP products have you used?

| Study Text | ☑ | Passcards | ☐ | Other | ☐ |
| Kit | ☐ | i-Pass | ☐ | | |

Your ratings, comments and suggestions would be appreciated on the following areas.

	Very useful	Useful	Not useful
Introductory section	☐	☐	☐
Chapter introductions	☐	☐	☐
Key terms	☐	☐	☐
Quality of explanations	☐	☐	☐
Case studies and other examples	☐	☐	☐
Exam focus points	☐	☐	☐
Questions and answers in each chapter	☐	☐	☐
Fast forwards and chapter roundups	☐	☐	☐
Quick quizzes	☐	☐	☐
Question Bank	☐	☐	☐
Answer Bank	☐	☐	☐
Index	☐	☐	☐

| Overall opinion of this Study Text | Excellent ☐ | Good ☐ | Adeqate ☐ | Poor ☐ |

Do you intend to continue using BPP products?   Yes ☐   No ☐

On the reverse of this page is space for you to write your comments about our Study Text. We welcome your feedback.

The author of this edition can be emailed at: accaqueries@bpp.com

Please return this form to: Head of ACCA & FIA Programmes, BPP Learning Media Ltd, FREEPOST, London, W12 8AA

TELL US WHAT YOU THINK

Please note any further comments and suggestions/errors below. For example, was the text accurate, readable, concise, user-friendly and comprehensive?